PUBLIC INTERNATIONAL LAW

A Guide to Information Sources

Elizabeth Beyerly

MANSELL
LONDON AND NEW YORK

First published in 1991 by Mansell Publishing Limited
A Cassell Imprint
Villiers House, 41/47 Strand, London WC2N 5JE, England
387 Park Avenue South, New York, NY 10016-8810, USA

©Elizabeth Beyerly 1991

All rights reserved. No part of this publication may be reproduced or transmitted in any form or by any means, electronic or mechanical including photocopying, recording or any information storage or retrieval system, without prior permission in writing from the publishers or their appointed agents.

British Library Cataloguing in Publication Data

Beyerly, Elizabeth
   Public international law: a guide to information sources.
   1. International public law
   I. Title
   341

ISBN 0-7201-2082-9

Library of Congress Cataloging-in-Publication Data

Beyerly, Elizabeth.
  Public international law: a guide to information sources/ Elizabeth Beyerly.
      p.   cm.
  Includes index.
  ISBN 0-7201-2082-9
  1. International law—Bibliography. I. Title.
Z6461.B49 1991
[JX3091]   90-47238
016.341—dc20   CIP

Printed and bound in Great Britain by
Biddles Ltd, Guildford and King's Lynn

To my parents

Contents

Preface		xi
Acknowledgements		xiii
List of abbreviations		xv
Introduction		1

Part I Evidentiary status of PIL material

A Typology of PIL information sources and resources   9
    i Normative sources: primary evidence   11
    ii Analytical resources: secondary evidence   26
    iii Auxiliary resources: reference aids   35

B A bibliography of selected PIL information sources:
form approach   46
    i Primary sources   46
        a Treaties   46
        b International customary law   57
        c Judicial decisions   62
        d Official publications   66
    ii Secondary resources   70
        a Treatises, manuals, textbooks   70
        b Commemorative essays   85
        c Dissertations   93
        d Periodicals, yearbooks   94
        e Encyclopaedias, dictionaries   107

		f	Conferences, colloquia	111
	iii	Reference aids		113
		a	Guides to research	113
		b	Bibliographies, indexing journals	115
		c	Abbreviations, reviews, series	126
		d	Directories (biographical, institutional)	128
		e	Librarianship, publishers	141

Part II Substantive aspects of PIL materials. A selected subject bibliography: topical approach

A	Interdisciplinarity			149
	i	PIL and municipal law		149
	ii	Private and public international law		150
	iii	PIL and comparative law		151
	iv	PIL and international relations		154
B	Intradisciplinary aspects			162
	i	History of PIL		162
	ii	Evolution of PIL		164
	iii	Historiography, doctrinal schools		166
	iv	Ideological, regional perceptions		171
	v	Methodology of PIL		176
C	Public international law in general			185
	i	Theories		185
	ii	Sources		188
	iii	Subjects		195
	iv	Jurisdiction, competence		199
		a	Law of the sea	201
		b	Air, space law	210
	v	Representation, diplomatic practice		212
	vi	Settlement of disputes		214
	vii	Peace, war		216
		a	Peace	216
		b	Disarmament	218
		c	Neutrality	221
		d	Use of force, war	221
		e	Humanitarian law	223
D	Specialized aspects of PIL			231
	i	Law of international organization		231
		a	General	231
		b	United Nations	243
		c	Selected Specialized Agencies	257
	ii	Human rights		262

iii	International criminal law	264
iv	International law of the environment	267
v	International development	269
	a International law of economic development	271
	b New International Economic Order	272
vi	International trade law	274
vii	International transport law	277
viii	International law of communication, information	278
ix	PIL and science/technology	279

Index-Thesaurus   281

Preface

The proper assessment of the theory and practice of any steadily evolving discipline must take into account a number of substantive or qualitative, as well as documentary and/or quantitative, elements. This is notably the case for international law, the specificity and effectiveness of which have often been questioned. The continued debate about the essence of public international law has generated a vast body of incessantly growing literature. Is public international law only literature, albeit none the worse for it?[1] Or is it mainly the manifestation of international, predominantly inter-state, relations? What constitutes the substantive evidence of international legal practice? To what extent do doctrinal perceptions reflect the *lex ferenda* (ought) aspect of public international law?[2] Which extra-legal considerations are relevant to public international law in terms of its *lex lata* (is) aspect? These and similar other questions have elicited and continue to elicit divergent answers.

In order to gain a certain perspective of both the real and the 'fictional'[3] state of the art of public international law it seems appropriate, from time to time, selectively to examine its relevant and available primary, secondary and auxiliary materials. This *Guide* is an attempt to provide partial inventory assistance through the maze of proliferating evidentiary, interpretative and auxiliary sources that constitute the broadly defined discipline of public international law; as such, the *Guide* is but a link in the chain of similar guides beginning with Ompteda [347], subsequently refined by Robinson [334] and variously updated by Delupis [342], Merrills [341] and Kleckner [330], to mention only the most outstanding examples.

The *Guide* inevitably reflects the assumptions underlying the materials included in it. The focus of the *Guide*, especially in its subject bibliography (Part II), is on public international law materials published mainly in the late twentieth century; as a result, an impression of the predominantly 'dynamic' nature of public international law emerges, in particular with reference to secondary publications, many of which are in a 'revisionist'[4] vein. The problem of how to convey qualitative conceptual divergencies without falling prey to quantitative perceptual redundancies made for difficult choices in drawing up the selection criteria of the *Guide*. The intent of providing elusive information certainty in the face of fluctuating substantive knowledge may have led to the *Guide*'s contents at times striking a controversial note. The resultant documentary uncertainty tends to be compounded by the blurred borderline between the substance and the form of a given public international law source, as well as by the often insufficient distinction between the international law-creating agency and the sources it creates.

The *Guide*, which is often bibliographic in content and sometimes historiographic in emphasis, illustrates the motto '*qui embrasse trop, étrenne mal*'. Be that as it may, I nevertheless hope that the pleasure in learning I had in the course of compiling the *Guide* may, in turn, benefit its users. I acknowledge many inevitable errors of substance and form attendant upon the *Guide*'s overall conception, selection criteria and documentary information, and invite comments for improving these.

NOTES

1 Carty, A. p. 128, in [461b]
2 Virally, M. p. 519, in [204]
3 Riphagen, W. p. 565, in [201]
4 Hoof, G.J.H. van p. 58, in [547a]

Acknowledgements

Needless to say, without the generous and sustained assistance of the publishers and my many friends and colleagues, this *Guide* might never have materialized.

In the preparation of the *Guide* I greatly benefited from the advice of Mr Colin Hutchens; to him and the publishers I owe much gratitude for the encouragement and patience shown to me. Likewise, I wish to express my profound appreciation for the unstinting help extended to me by the staff of the United Nations Office at Geneva, in particular its Library; the Dag Hammarskjöld Library, New York; the Graduate Institute of International Studies, Geneva and its Library; the Henry-Dunant Institute, Geneva and its Library; the Peace Palace Library, The Hague; the Library of the International Court of Justice, The Hague; The Hague Academy of International Law; the Institut de hautes études internationales, Paris; UNESCO, especially its Division of Information Services, and its Publications Unit; the Institute of Advanced Legal Studies Library, London; the Squire Law Library, Cambridge; the Max-Planck Institute of Foreign and Public International Law, Heidelberg and its Library; the Institut für Völkerrecht und ausländisches öffentliches Recht, Salzburg; the Institut für internationales Recht and Völkerrecht, Universität München; the Leo Goodman Library, Institut für internationales Recht, Abt. Rechtsvergleichung, Universität München; the Institut für Ostrecht, Köln; and the Documentation Office for Eastern European Law, Leiden.

In particular, I should like to record my very special thanks to: Mrs M. Anderson, London; Mr J. Bennett, Paris; Prof. W. E. Butler, London; Mr F. C. Chapman, Lausanne; Ms M. Croese, The Hague; Mlle C. Cros, Paris; Mlle S. Dryfus, Paris; Mr A. C. G. Eyffinger, The Hague; Prof. F. J. M. Feldbrugge,

Leiden; Dr D. Frenzke, Köln; Mr S. Friedman, Paris; Mr C. García-Godoy, Washington, DC; Dr M. Geistlinger, Salzburg; Dr L. O. Grasern, Salzburg; Mr P. Hajnal, Toronto; Mr M. Jarvinen, Paris; Mr T. Kearley, Baton Rouge, LA; Mr M. Meitzel, Bonn; Mrs S. Meitzel, Geneva; Prof. J. Miranda, Lisboa; Mr E. S. Newman, New York; Dr A. Obradović, Beograd; Mlle M. Prétot, Paris; Mr R. Schaaf, Washington, DC; Mr J. Schalekamp, The Hague; Mr J. Schwietzke, Heidelberg; Mr A. Sprudzs, Chicago; Dr T. Stein, Heidelberg; Mr W. A. Steiner, Cambridge; Mrs K. Tegner, Stockholm; Dr J. Toman, Geneva; Mr A. T. Witteveen, The Hague; and Mrs J. Yackle, Cambridge, MA.

I derived much benefit from the counsel and information of the aforementioned; however, the responsibility for any errors of omission or commission is entirely my own.

List of Abbreviations

AAA	Association of Attenders and Alumni of [The Hague] Academy
AALL	American Association of Law Libraries
AALS	Association of American Law Schools
ACCIS	Advisory Committee for the Co-ordination of Information Systems
ACUNS	Academic Council on the United Nations System
AFDI	*Annuaire français de droit international*
AIL	Association of International Libraries
AJBD	Arbeitsgemeinschaft für juristisches Bibliotheks-, Dokumentationswesen
AJIL	*American journal of international law*
ALA	American Library Association
ALB	*Annual legal bibliography*
ASDI	*Annuaire suisse de droit international*
ASIL	American Society of International Law
ASILS	Association of Student International Law Societies
BFSP	*British and Foreign State Papers*
BGL	*Bibliographic guide to law*
BYIL	*British yearbook of international law*
CAEM	*See* CMEA
CBI	*Current bibliographic information*
CICR	Comité international de la Croix Rouge
CLB	*Current legal bibliography*

LIST OF ABBREVIATIONS

CLI	*Current law index*
CMEA	Council for Mutual Economic Assistance
CNRS	Centre national de la recherche scientifique
CTS	*Consolidated treaty series*
Clunet	*Journal du droit international*
COMECON	see CMEA
CYIL	*Canadian yearbook of international law*
DHL	Dag Hammarskjöld Library
DUNDIS	*Directory of United Nations databases and information systems*
DUSPIL	*Digest of United States practice in international law*
ECDC	Economic Co-operation among Developing Countries
ENCD	Eighteen-Nation Conference on Disarmament
Enc. PIL	*Encyclopedia of public international law*
FID	Fédération internationale de la documentation
GIPRI	Geneva International Peace Research Institute
GODORT	Government Documents Round Table (ALA)
GYIL	*German yearbook of international law*
HOLLIS	Harvard On-Line Library Information System
IAEA	International Atomic Energy Agency
IALL	International Association of Law Libraries
IALS	Institute of Advanced Legal Studies
IAPSUN	International Association of Political Scientists for the United Nations
IBID	*International bibliography, information, documentation*
IBRD	International Bank for Reconstruction and Development
ICJ	International Court of Justice
ICLQ	*International and comparative law quarterly*
ICRC	International Committee of the Red Cross
ICSID	International Centre for Settlement of International Disputes
IDI	Institut de droit international
IFLA	International Federation of Library Associations and Institutions
IFLP	*Index to foreign legal periodicals*
IGO	Inter-governmental organization
IJLI	*International journal of legal information*
IJLL	*International journal of law libraries*
IHEI	Institut de hautes études internationales
ILA	International Law Association
ILC	International Law Commission
ILM	*International legal materials*
ILP	*Index to legal periodicals*
ILR	*International law reports*
IMT	*Index to multilateral treaties*

LIST OF ABBREVIATIONS xvii

INTELSAT	International Telecommunications Satellite Organization
INMARSAT	International Maritime Satellite System
IOB	Inter-Organization Board for Information Systems
IPSA	International Political Science Association
IUHEI	Institut universitaire de hautes études internationales
IUS '81	*The spirit of Uppsala*
JILE	*Journal of international law and economics*
LC	US Library of Congress
LDC	Least Developed Countries
LGDL	Librairie générale de droit et jurisprudence
LIWA	London Institute of World Affairs
LoN	League of Nations
MB I–II	*Monthly bibliography, I–II*
MT	*Multilateral treaties*
NCL	Normative concept of law
NGO	Non-governmental organization
NIEO	New International Economic Order
NLB	*National legal bibliography*
NILR	*Netherlands international law review*
NYIL	*Netherlands yearbook of international law*
OAS	Organization of American States
PCIJ	Permanent Court of International Justice
PGI	General Information Programme (UNESCO)
PIL	Public international law
PPL	Peace Palace Library
RCADI	*Recueil des cours de l'Académie de droit international*
RGDIP	*Revue générale de droit international public*
RIO	[Foundation for the] Reshaping the International Order
RMIL	Recognized manifestation of international law
RML	Recognized manifestation of law
SA	Specialized agency
SCORPIO	Subject-content-oriented retriever for processing information on-line (LC)
Sdn	Société des Nations
SEMP	*Sovetskiĭ ezhegodnik mezhdunarodnogo prava*
S–G	Secretary-General (UN)
SIONUT	Système informatisé de l'ONU pour les traités
SIPRI	Stockholm International Peace Research Institute
ST	*Statement of treaties*
TIAS	*Treaties and other international act series*
UIA	Union of International Associations
UN	United Nations
UNBIS	United Nations Bibliographic Information System
UNCITRAL	United Nations Commission on International Trade Law

UNCLOS III	Third United Nations Conference on the Law of the Sea
UNCTAD	United Nations Conference on Trade and Development
UNDOC	*United Nations documents: current index*
UNESCO	United Nations Educational, Scientific and Cultural Organization
UNIDROIT	International Institute for the Unification of Private Law
UNIDIR	United Nations Institute for Disarmament Research
UNISIST	World Science Information System (UNESCO)
UNITAR	United Nations Institute for Training and Research
UNOG	United Nations Organization at Geneva
UNTIS	United Nations Treaty Information System
UNTS	*United Nations treaty series*
UP	University Press
UST	*United States treaties and other international agreements*
WTI	*World treaty index*
WOMP	World order models project
ZaöRV	*Zeitschrift für ausländisches öffentliches Recht und Völkerrecht*

Introduction

International law as a discipline has a venerable history even though at times the tendency to confuse the field of study with the coherent body of law has loomed large.[1] But whereas 'it is clear that there are professors of international law', 'it is not at all that clear that there is such a thing as international law'.[2] This sceptical assertion has been echoed by many contemporary critics of the discipline. Yet if the sheer number of works (*see* p. 9) dealing with general and specialized, public and private international law would appear to defy the discipline's detractors, the essence of international law continues to be divergently defined. The question of what constitutes the narrow confines of international law, specifically public international law (PIL), is perhaps best approached by keeping several substantive and methodological distinctions in mind.

To begin with, it is vital to distinguish between the extant body of international legal principles, norms and rules, on the one hand, and the legal practice of constituent members of the international community PIL is meant to govern, on the other. Awareness of such a distinction helps to bridge unavoidable gaps between PIL theoretical constructs and the actual PIL practice and effectiveness.

The conceptual framework of PIL should not be examined in a vacuum, but should be viewed as firmly anchored in the historical context within which PIL precepts arise, tend to be modified and at times appear to perish. History's temporal and spatial perspectives provide the necessary continuum along which the origin and development of a given international legal principle, norm, rule and its practical application may be traced.

Cutting across the conceptual and historical contexts there are often inextricable doctrinal considerations. Doctrinal perceptions of PIL theory and practice are rarely static, derived as they are from scholarly activities and corresponding analytical tools, all of which are exposed to constantly, if imperceptibly, changing ideas and ideologies. Moreover, doctrinal assumptions influence, albeit intangibly, the practical development of PIL. Therefore account must be taken of inevitable dialectics underlying PIL as it 'is', as opposed to the proposition of PIL as it 'ought' to be. The perils of 'legal fiction'[3] sometimes attributed to PIL may in part be traced to the (often doctrinal) confusion between PIL's substance and the perception or interpretation thereof.

It is rarely easy to draw clear demarcation lines between PIL and certain legal and non-legal disciplines (say, the nexus between PIL and municipal law, or between PIL and international relations), or between general and specialized aspects of PIL itself (e.g. the appropriate substantive slot within PIL of the law of international organization, or that of the law of the sea, environment, etc.). However, imperfect as they may be, inter- and intra-disciplinary delimitations are useful means for circumscribing the broad and narrow confines of PIL.

In addition to the aforementioned theoretical, practical, historical and ideological aspects of PIL a methodological concern with the 'transitional' phase of PIL, midway between its classical and modern[4] conceptions, should be mentioned. Accessory to this contemporary (post-1945) perception of PIL in transition are, on the one hand, uncertainty as to what constitutes an acceptable PIL 'sources test'[5] and, on the other hand, the postulate of a dynamic PIL alternating between continuity and change.

The objectives of this *Guide* may be summed up as follows. With a view to circumscribing the evidentiary status of PIL, a typology of PIL information sources according to their normative, analytical and auxiliary roles is advanced in Part I/A; to illustrate this typology, Part I/B contains a bibliography of selected published primary, secondary and reference sources and resources of PIL. Underlying the selected subject bibliography in Part II/A-D is the assumption that the ever growing quantity of PIL materials (especially secondary resources) requires, from time to time, a close look at a limited number of PIL publications, even though their substantive, temporal or regional significance may not always elicit consensus.

With a few exceptions, the *Guide* includes PIL information sources published worldwide since the mid-twentieth century, and the emphasis in Part II is on late twentieth century imprints. The *Guide* only incidentally helps the user to find the appropriate sequence of documentary searches to be undertaken to arrive at the required substantive or procedural answers contained in the selected PIL information sources and resources cited. Last but not least, the number and diversity of materials chosen permitted, at best, indicative annotations; critical and comparative evaluation of these materials' substantive, contextual essence was understandably beyond the scope of the *Guide*.

Part I/A-B follows the hierarchy of PIL sources referred to in article 38 of the Statute of the International Court of Justice; Part II/A-D follows, in the main, a broad classification combining PIL concepts, topics, aspects and branches. Needless to say, neither classificatory presentation is exempt of inconsistencies, of which the following examples are among the most flagrant.

Part I/B.i (treaties) includes bibliographies of and indexes to treaty collections, despite the auxiliary nature of these resources, while Part II/C.ii (sources) includes secondary resources dealing with treaties; in other words, references to normative, interpretative and auxiliary aspects of the 'law of treaties' are scattered between the two bibliographic parts of the *Guide*. Despite the growing specialization, notably of the law of the sea and the law of war, references to these areas are assigned to general (Part II/C.iv, vii) rather than specialized PIL. However, despite the continued methodological uncertainty as to the proper classificatory slot for the law of international organization, references to this area are assigned to specialized PIL (Part II/D.i); yet, references to the development by the UN of the law of the sea, law of treaties, international trade, etc. are assigned to other relevant topical subsections of Part II. Finally, overlaps between PIL theory and methodology, history and historiography, the Third World and the international law of development, etc. account for the scattering of relevant references among the different sections in Part II. The detailed index-thesaurus at the end of the *Guide* should enable the user to overcome these classificatory inconsistencies.

Just as one may cavil at the classificatory presentation, so the representativeness[6] of the PIL materials included in the *Guide* may be questioned. The subjective element of choice inevitably circumscribes the substantive, temporal, spatial and formal limits of materials selected, especially because of the sheer limitless quantity of secondary PIL materials published worldwide in countless languages. The *Guide* is no exception to the dictates of selectivity that is undeniably subjective but in part traceable to selection criteria adopted by previous compilers of similar guides.[7]

The scope of the *Guide* is to some extent defined by its criteria of exclusion. Thus it was assumed that students and researchers alike might benefit from a restrictive approach, i.e. the emphasis is on information sources specific to public international law or its closest interdisciplinary links. In this sense only a very limited number of references to municipal, comparative and private international law are included in the *Guide*. The complexities of the various national legal systems and the multitude of states to which such, often combined, systems apply made for the general exclusion from the *Guide* of references to PIL within the context of municipal law materials. On the other hand the *Guide* includes national and international 'official' materials (or bibliographic guides thereto), given the importance of such materials for locating evidence of international customary law. Similarly, although the ratio of politics to law may appear higher in the international than in the national legal domain, the *Guide* excludes references to predominantly political, in particular bilateral inter-state relations, as well as to individual country, case-studies.

Altogether, Part II/D of the *Guide* falls short of adequately encompassing the many and increasingly specialized aspects of PIL. The *Guide* excludes reference to highly technical elements of international air, space, telecommunications, etc., law and to the many interdisciplinary implications of the international economic law or the various extra-legal ramifications of the law of human rights. It confines its (often scant) bibliographic coverage to the following specialized aspects of PIL: (1) the law of international organization, with focus on the United Nations (the law of the European Community is excluded altogether); (2) human rights (but only marginally complementing the references contained in the 1987 *Keyguide* [693a]); (3) international criminal law; (4) international law of the environment; (5) international law of development; (6) international trade law; (7) international transport law; (8) international law of communication; and (9) PIL and science and technology. An exhaustive bibliographic coverage of these and many more, increasingly specialized, aspects of PIL remains a task for the future.

In addition to the aforementioned topical limitations upon the scope of the *Guide*, a number of form-based exclusion criteria should be mentioned. Thus the *Guide* on the whole contains PIL monographs rather than periodical articles, but does list relevant indexes to the latter; a number of articles in PIL yearbooks, commemorative essays and The Hague Academy's Collected courses [220a] are included.[8] To compensate for the scarcity of certain information sources relative to given aspects of PIL, the *Guide* includes a limited number of appropriate legal and general information sources and resources, notably auxiliary aids such as directories, citators, review journals and the like.

While an effort was made to list representative PIL materials published throughout the world, in practice certain linguistic (and relevant script) limitations were inevitable. The preponderance in the *Guide* of English-, French-, German- and Russian-language items reflects the overall publication output in these languages.[9] Despite the undisputed importance of PIL publications in non-Indo-European languages (often in non-Roman script), regrettably the *Guide* could include only a very limited number of references to Arabic, Chinese, Japanese and other language works on PIL, usually available in translated form. The *Guide* follows the US Library of Congress transliteration of Cyrillic script for Slavic, especially Russian-language works.

Mention should also be made of a certain linguistic and geographical overlap, especially with reference to English-language[10] PIL materials published in countries where English is not the official language, whether in Europe (e.g. the tradition in the Netherlands for publishing works written in English, or English translation projects in the USSR), in Asia (e.g. the widespread use of English in Indian publications) or in Africa (e.g. English-language publications in Ghana, Kenya, Nigeria or the Republic of South Africa). A similar linguistic and geographical overlap exists for Romance-language materials published in Europe and Central and South America. Notwithstanding the considerable general and legal PIL publication output in these languages, the *Guide* falls short of a representative coverage of PIL materials, especially in Portuguese and Spanish. Limited physical availability of and insufficient bibliographic access to such materials account for the *Guide*'s shortcomings in this field. Partly as a result of the aforementioned overlaps, but also geographically to illustrate recent PIL publication trends, the arrangement in Part I/B.ii (secondary resources) is broadly geographical (by continents and countries). This should at a glance disclose extant available PIL treatises or periodicals in given countries, as well as permitting the subsequent completion or updating of the present information.

The items in the *Guide* are consecutively numbered; the alpha-numerical subdivisions of certain items are meant to reflect certain chronological, linguistic or geographic aspects of related substantive information, all the while attesting to the inevitable subjective criteria of the compiler. The full citation (main entry) of an item is indicated only once in the *Guide*; cross-references are used to link segments of an item to its main entry and also related items scattered across the *Guide*. Occasionally *see also* cross-references refer, at the end of a given section, to further general or legal materials.

As far as possible,[11] the contents of the information sources included in the *Guide* were examined; items with an asterisk (*) could not be examined. Where pertinent, brief indicative (rather than evaluative) annotations are provided under the main entry; the annotations usually summarize the contents and/or list book reviews, various editions and translations (but time and space constraints often precluded the citation of titles known to exist in other than the original language, especially materials issued by international organizations).

The bibliographic description of the items cited in the *Guide* generally follows the Anglo-American Cataloguing Rules (AACR 2) in conjunction with the relevant International Standard Bibliographic Description (ISBD). The names of countries, and adjectives thereof, in the main reflect the terminology practice of the United Nations [374b].

A detailed author (individual, corporate), subject (topical, conceptual) and (selective) title index, in one alphabetical sequence, concludes the *Guide*.

NOTES

1 Barkun, M., 1972, International norms as facts and ideals. In *ASIL proceedings*, p. 41. This work considers 'all manner of confusion' to underlie the approach to PIL as a 'coherent body of law'. Schachter, O., in [378a] p. 412, views PIL as a self-contained discipline not least because of its category of concepts, vocabulary and the 'questions it seeks to answer and the modes of inquiry considered appropriate.'
2 Dinstein, Y., p. 200, in [460], refers to the view of Holland, T. E., 1933, *Lectures on international law*, London.
3 Riphagen, W., p. 565 in [201], is mainly concerned with the 'fiction' of the state as an entity and sovereignty as its conceptual attribute.
4 Whereas McWhinney, E. [462e] stresses the topical aspects ('buzz-words', *Stichworte*), temporal aspects (periodization) are at the core of Grewe, W., in [202], while Tunkin, G., in [203], illustrates the Soviet point of view on the matter.
5 Jennings, R., p. 281, in [169].
6 On the analogy with the 'substantive' representativeness (however questionable) of PIL, referred to by O. Schachter, p. 419, in [378a].

7 Notably Robinson, J. [334] and Delupis, I. [342]. This *Guide*'s selection criteria include: the reputation of the author, and/or of the publication; the number of editions and/or translations (mainly into English); the quantity and quality of bibliographic notes or indices. On the whole, a middle course was adhered to, balancing the importance or novelty of a given publication against seemingly insignificant works potentially useful in relevant linguistic or regional contexts.

8 The inclusion of such articles or analytics was partly conditioned by delays in the publication of cumulative indexes of the *Collected courses* [220a], and the insufficient bibliographic access, specifically to PIL commemorative essays, from 1980 onward.

9 The *UNESCO statistical yearbook* (1987 edition lists mainly 1984 imprints) provides a geographical breakdown by 97 countries and therein by subject areas. For example, the number of legal publications including PIL in France was 4,400, in the Federal Republic of Germany 2,403 (compared to 100 titles published in the area in the German Democratic Republic, or 176 titles published in Austria) and in the USSR 1,156. Tracking down specifically PIL publication figures in a given language is at best hazardous, given the multilingual publishing that occurs in certain countries (e.g. non-Russian imprints in the USSR) and the use of some languages (e.g. Spanish or Arabic) in several countries. *See also* note 10 below.

10 *International books in print. English language titles published outside the US and UK*, 7th edn. München: Saur, 1988. 4 volumes in 2 parts. The work lists some 180,000 titles in English issued by over 6,000 publishers worldwide; class 340/law, including PIL, contains some 5,000 titles published in 1985.

11 Keeping in mind the distinction between bibliographic access to and physical availability of PIL materials, it should also be mentioned that the *Guide* reflects resources available to the compiler mainly in European (especially Swiss and Dutch) libraries.

PART I

Evidentiary Status of PIL Material

I/A. Typology of PIL Information Sources and Resources

The substantive evidence of 'what is law' in general is rarely unequivocal. What constitutes public international law in particular is not only conditioned by its often overlapping theoretical, ideological interdisciplinary contexts, but also by the seemingly inextricable overlap between PIL facts and (doctrinal) perceptions thereof. Moreover, the quantity and variety of PIL materials, broadly defined, not only tend to obscure at times their substantive and qualitative merits, but also account for an 'infinite paper chase'[1] with respect to their physical accessibility.

Leaving aside the question of whether PIL as a discipline should be classified with the social sciences or humanities,[2] it might be noted that compared to the relatively quick obsolescence of the literature of the natural sciences, PIL materials tend to retain research and reference value over decades and even centuries.[3] Taking into account mainly secondary resources of international (public and private) law, at the end of the eighteenth century Ompteda [347] discussed some 2,000 seventeenth and eighteenth century imprints, whereas by the mid-twentieth century the *Catalog of international law and relations* [338a] contained an accumulation of over 80,000 imprints from the early nineteenth century onward. On the basis of current bibliographies and indexing journals of law and PIL, an annual growth of some 700–800 PIL monographs proper may be hazarded,[4] a tentative figure to which annually several thousand articles in periodicals[5] and countless (often elusive) official (national and international) documents must be added.

Under the circumstances, substantive PIL may be usefully approached by attempting a typology of PIL materials, which is in turn to some extent aimed at reducing the 'category blindness'[6] of overspecialization. To this end the *Guide* makes an admittedly tenuous distinction between substantive (what is PIL) and documentary (where or how is PIL found) evidence. Without entering into the types of and criteria for establishing substantive PIL evidence,[7] the *Guide* essentially centres on a documentary typology exclusively of published[8] PIL materials with an evidentiary hierarchy that reflects a broad[9] interpretation of article 38 of the Statute of ICJ. Taking into account the substantive difficulties in dissociating the PIL substance from its form,[10] in documentary terms this requires an additional distinction between the contents or form of a given PIL rule or principle and the documentary aspect of the rule or principle; thus, by analogy with general historical research, one might examine PIL evidence from its substantive, internal or documentary, external perspective. In other words, a digest of state practice represents the documentary form of selected international customary principles, the substance of which is only marginally at issue in the digest. Keeping in mind the evidentiary hierarchy of the PIL materials it presumes to order, the *Guide*'s documentary typology is concerned with a number of 'external' elements such as the provenance (national or international; official or unofficial), the author (corporate or personal), the date (of publication versus the temporal span of the materials examined), the form (full text or summary), etc.

If R. Jennings, Justice of the ICJ, is understandably concerned with the 'reasonable certainty'[11] of the (primary) PIL sources test, a documentary typology of PIL materials of needs must go beyond the inclusion of only the 'raw materials'[12] of the discipline. Moreover, the *Guide*'s broad classificatory scheme not only deals with PIL primary and secondary sources, as well as auxiliary resources,[13] but also contains within these categories certain types of materials whose evidentiary status continues to be variously interpreted.

In terms of article 38 of the Statute of ICJ treaty, custom and general principles of law form the 'main' categories of (primary) PIL sources. However, the *Guide* includes among (normative) primary PIL materials decisions of intergovernmental organizations (chiefly UN resolutions and declarations) and of international adjudicatory bodies. Article 38 refers to 'judicial decisions' as 'subsidiary means' and is not explicit as regards decisions of international bodies. The *Guide* follows the assignment by article 38 of the 'teachings of the most highly qualified publicists' among (analytical) subsidiary PIL resources, but extends these to cover scholarly treatises, commemorative essays, periodicals and so on, all of which to varying degrees illustrate doctrinal positions (generally broader than '*la doctrine*' in the French legal/PIL concept). Finally, the *Guide* includes relevant auxiliary[14] resources, which by means of their 'interposed' (bibliographic, reference) functions complement 'direct' information contained in substantive (primary, main) sources and (secondary, subsidiary) resources. It might be added that the bibliographic section Part I/B.iii (Reference aids) lists auxiliary materials of a general nature, but that certain auxiliary aids are discussed alongside relevant primary or secondary PIL materials in Part I/B and Part II/A-D.

NOTES

1. Sprudzs, A., 1983, International legal research: an infinite paper chase. *Vanderbilt journal of transnational law*, **16**, 521-536; Briggs, H. W. 1948, Finding international law. *AJIL*, **42**, 101-103.
2. Gould, W., 1965, Inventory and retrieval of literature as aids to interdisciplinary approaches to international law. *ASIL proceedings*, **59**, 98-104; *see also* [343].
3. The continued reference in contemporary PIL literature to the 'classics' of PIL and certain 'classical' PIL cases implies that age does not detract from the relevance of a large body of PIL materials; this in turn partly explains the concern of law librarians over the cumulative effect of such materials, e.g. Grimm, D., 1985 Juristische Literatur: zu viel, zu teuer? *AJBD Mitteilungen*, **15** (1), 1-4.
4. This estimate is in part based on that kindly supplied by the Peace Palace Library, The Hague. It might be noted that in 1985 the US Library of Congress's law collection (including PIL works) contained some 500,000 titles published worldwide since the eighteenth century. Class K (law) of the LC classification shows an annual growth of some 23,000 legal (including PIL imprints) (courtesy of Mr R. Schaaf, Senior Specialist in UN and SA materials, LC, in letter of 29 April 1989).
5. The indexing service *Public international law* [361] annually lists some 4,000 periodical articles relative to international (private and public) law. This selective global coverage of needs excludes numerous materials, often exhaustively covered in certain national PIL bibliographies, e.g. [348] lists 9,000 imprints published in 1984 in Canada.
6. Reference to Brownlie by Cheng, B., p. 109, in [499b].
7. How such evidence is established and classified largely depends on the analytical tools applied to given sources considered 'normative'; for a comparative approach *see* Butler, W. E., p. 38, in [428b], or for a conceptual analysis *see* Bleckmann, A., p. 283, in [492].
8. The *Guide* is not concerned with the so-called 'prenatal' unpublished (often archival) materials, reference to which is made by W. Rozkuszka, The art and acquisition of foreign official publications, pp. 1-11, in [69e]. The undisputed quality of the (accessible) national, international archival materials in terms of their relevance to PIL merits a separate study.
9. Higgins, R., p. 28, in [499b].
10. Lachs, M., pp. 99-112, in [194].
11. Jennings, R. Y., *passim* [509c].
12. Green, L. C., 1980, The raw materials of international law. *ICLQ*, **29**, 187-205. This is concerned mainly with treaties and custom.
13. If 'sources' concern mainly normative materials with primary evidence, 'resources' tend to include analytical and auxiliary materials with varying degrees of secondary evidence; *see also* [328].
14. In documentary terms 'auxiliary' almost exclusively refers to reference aids; in substantive terms 'auxiliary' may be but a variant of 'subsidiary'; *see* Starzhina, J., in [523b].

i. NORMATIVE SOURCES: PRIMARY EVIDENCE

a. Treaties

In the wake of the Congress of Vienna (1815), the Treaty of Versailles (1918) and especially the Second World War, but most notably after the 1960s, the number of sovereign states and of inter-governmental organizations has steadily increased. The resultant proliferation of bi- and multilateral conventions, agreements, peace treaties and other formal legal instruments spelling out the rights and obligations of the contracting parties governed by PIL has stepped up the concern with treaties in all their complex aspects. The importance of treaties as the 'most readily identifiable'[1] primary PIL source has in part been ideologically[2] conditioned; however, the ascendancy of treaties over custom in the hierarchy of primary PIL sources as yet remains in doubt, not least because of the doctrinal divergence as to the nature and extent of obligation or binding force attributed to either of these sources.[3]

The *Vienna Convention on the Law of Treaties* [1], a primary PIL source in its own right, and in substance and form a multilateral treaty, represents a codified approach under the aegis of the UN to the complexities inherent in the 'law of treaties' as a whole. In documentary terms, if the original or translated text, in full or excerpt form, of this or any other treaty or convention is needed, a number of global and national, current and retrospective treaty collections can be consulted, always keeping in mind a certain complementarity of the various collections. The law of treaties [512a,b,c] in general deals with types of law-making and contractual treaties or their procedural aspects (conclusion, ratification, interpretation, etc.), but locating the text of a treaty remains among the most important documentary tasks of treaty research. To this end the collections of treaty texts must be considered above all.

The concerted individual endeavour of the Göttingen scholar G. F. Martens gave rise in the nineteenth century to the remarkable *Recueil des traités* [7], which continued to be published by Martens's successors until 1943. There are over 130 volumes of the *Recueil*, containing the text of treaties concluded by European powers between 1761 and 1940. In the twentieth century, the British scholar C. Parry compiled the *Consolidated treaty series* [6]. Published between 1969 and 1986, *CTI* is a collection of photo-reproduced texts of treaties concluded between 1648 and 1918, including the bulk of treaties in the Martens *Recueil*. The Martens and Parry collections of treaty texts (individually compiled, commercially published, complete with chronological, alphabetical indexes) are of a retrospective nature and encompass treaty texts from the mid-seventeenth century to the early twentieth century.

For the period 1648–1985 it has been variously estimated that extant collections of treaties contain up to 30,000; from the mid-twentieth century onward an annual growth of 400–500 treaties may be estimated.[5] Under the circumstances, it has become virtually impossible for any one individual to undertake a comprehensive collection of treaties.[6] Instead, individual endeavours have been geared to providing selections of treaty texts [8a–e] adjudged most representative or important in a given substantive, chronological or regional context; often commercially published such selections complement given PIL textbooks used in teaching. Because comprehensive collections of treaty texts require the kind of resources that are usually only available at the international or at certain exceptional national levels, the task of officially, systematically and extensively registering bi- and multilateral treaties, conventions and agreements, and of publishing their texts after the treaties entered into force, was entrusted in 1920 to the League of Nations (in accordance with article 18 of its Covenant) and in 1946 to the United Nations (in accordance with article 102 of its Charter).

While most countries maintain a register (published or otherwise) of treaties concluded, the very large number of treaties concluded by, say, the USA, the UK, the USSR or France makes the treaty collections compiled in and published (officially or commercially) by these countries equally relevant to countries that are parties to treaties in these national collections. On the other hand, the frequently difficult access to national treaty collections (especially outside the given country) has made the globally available *United Nations Treaty Series* [2] one of the most important documentary sources for tracking down texts (in the original, with English and/or French translations where required) of post-1946 bi- and multilateral treaties concluded worldwide. However, *UNTS* provides texts only of treaties already in force. Among the deficiencies ascribed to *UNTS* is its nearly 7 year publication lag, i.e. the lapse of time between the conclusion of a given treaty, its entering into force and its being made available in published form.[7] This means that texts of treaties within this *UNTS* backlog (aggravated by the lack of cumulative indexes) must be tracked down either through the quarterly *International legal materials* [219a] or through a variety of nationally published official gazettes, collections of statutes, etc.

In addition to these collections of treaty texts, mention should be made of the *List of treaty collections* [25a]. Although this was published over thirty years ago under the auspices of the UN Office of Legal Affairs, it remains, in the absence of any similar current auxiliary resource, the most useful comprehensive bibliography of treaty collections. The *List* contains annotated references to some 700 treaty collections in some 70 countries.

Treaty texts are complex legal instruments whose substantive contents may be variously approached through appropriate chronological topical/systematic indexes. The extant manual [28] and, of late, computer-produced indexes to treaty collections, although invaluable, reflect the limits of the collections indexed.

Treaties that are concluded are generally subject to ratifications before they enter into force. Determining the status of a given treaty (list of signatories, accessions to, ratifications) remains a constant, if thorny, problem. *Multilateral treaties deposited with the Secretary-General* [3], issued by the UN Office of Legal Affairs, and *Treaties in force* [10], issued by the US Department of State, are two of the most important documentary tools facilitating the often 'esoteric'[8] research into the status of, especially, multilateral treaties of recent vintage.

The nexus between PIL and municipal law relative to the basis and manner by which treaties become part of the 'law of the land,'[9] the methodological aspects of treaty interpretation, or 'discerning, anticipating and accommodating "cultural" patterns in international treaties'[10] are but some of the research problems dealt with in secondary PIL resources, notably doctrinal works [512a-c]. Complementing these substantive research works are various documentary guides to treaty research [24a-c] which focus on treaty texts, status information, etc.

In uncovering the documentary evidence relative to general and specialized treaties account should be taken of: the material and linguistic availability of a treaty text, singly[11] or in a collection; national versus international treaty collections[12]; comprehensive versus selective; current[13] versus retrospective coverage of texts in treaty collections; and indexes to the contents of treaty collections. Fortunately, various documentary studies, notably by Sprudzs [24a], have helped to reduce the pitfalls inherent in the 'world treaty jungle', although 'matters will have to get worse before they get better'.[14] Such caution seems particularly pertinent with reference to collections of regional [9] and specialized or topical [680a, 713a] treaties. Whether the benefits of computerized retrieval of treaty information (bibliographic, full text) will outweigh inevitable problems (user priority, costs, etc.) of such retrieval also remains to be seen.

NOTES

1 Jennings, R., p. 61, in [509c].
2 Scholars of, or concerned with, the Third World have tended to accord greater importance to treaties than to international customary law, simultaneously contesting the validity of treaties that are perceived as 'unequal' [516a], dating from colonial times. The socialist doctrinal approach to treaties has until recently stressed the importance of treaties because of the explicit 'voluntarist' consent of the parties to given treaties [514a,b].
3 Adede, A.O., pp. 57-58, in [470a], speaks of the 'rules of the game in multilateral treaty-making' and distinguishes between declaratory and constitutive effects of treaties.
4 In treaty terms 'collection' (*recueil* in French) generally denotes that full treaty texts (in the original language and/or translation) are comprehensively or selectively included in the collection. Treaty collections may be published officially or commercially, at international or national level. A computerized multilateral treaty information bank has so far only been partly achieved [29, 30].
5 If *LoNTS* [4] grew at the rate of roughly 180 treaties annually, *UNTS* [2] appears to be annually accruing at the rate of some 400 treaties.
6 While there have been several outstanding individual compilations, 'the task is perhaps one which is insufficiently attractive . . . to permit the expectation that it will be undertaken privately within any reasonable time without encouragement and support from some central source such as either the [UN] Secretariat or national committees or institutions', p. 113, in [31]. With the proliferation of treaties, this statement, made over forty years ago, still seems pertinent.
7 Tabory, M., p. 362, in [2], notes that the Vienna Convention on the Law of Treaties concluded in 1969 entered into force only in 1980; the text of the Convention was included in *UNTS* only in 1987 (but was included in the *UN juridical yearbook* in 1969). The need for English and French translations of treaty texts also partly accounts for the *UNTS* publication lag.

8 Jennings, R., in [509c]; an opinion confirmed by Sprudzs, note 1, p. 11.
9 Butler, W. E., p. 82, in [428b], advocates the comparative study of municipal law and institutions with a view to anticipating national legal obstacles to international treaties, thereby facilitating the task of those drafting the treaties.
10 Butler, W. E., p. 44, in [428b].
11 The text of a recent bilateral treaty is usually first published in the relevant national official gazettes, or may be issued as a separate fascicule in an official or commercial series. The text of a multilateral treaty (if convened under the UN auspices) is usually included in the *Official records* relating to the Conference giving rise to the treaty, or may be issued as a separate UN sales publication; the text is often reproduced (in the original or translation) in relevant national PIL periodicals.
12 Sprudzs, A., *passim*, in [24a: *Treaty sources*], pointed to the widening gap between *UNTS* and certain national treaty collections, as a result of the selective coverage in the latter. Yet according to Schwietzke, J., p. 45, in [329], national treaty collections 'will remain probably more up-to-date than the *UNTS*', in part because of the better indexing of the national collections.
13 Most collections of treaties in fact represent a retrospective coverage of treaties concluded or ratified one, ten or more years ago. For truly current treaties (concluded in the course of a given 'current' week, month or year and as a result rarely in force, more often than not the texts (sometimes in preliminary form) are available in print at best within one week after the conclusion of the treaty. However, the latest international official records or national official gazettes containing such treaty texts may take one month or more to become (materially) available.
14 Sprudzs, A., p. 536, note 1, p. 11.

b. International customary law

Compared with the relative substantive clarity of and documentary access to the primary evidence of treaties, the international customary law-creating quality of national (and increasingly international) practice continues to be assessed with a measure of doctrinal ambiguity.[1] Questions such as 'when does customary law become an authoritative treaty text?' and 'when does a treaty provision give rise to a customary rule?' attest to a continued concern with the hierarchy of treaty and custom.[2] For international customary law proper, the proof of its constitutive elements tends to yield various answers. Material, factual (international legal) practice as one of the constitutive elements of custom is rarely questioned; but whether international customary law is evidence of international legal practice, or whether such practice is evidence of custom,[3] may be of more than academic interest. The subjective, psychological *opinio juris sive necessitatis* as the other constitutive element of custom elicits doctrinal divergence.[4]

These substantive divergencies necessarily influence the documentary approach to the primary evidence of various aspects of international customary law and legal practice. Moreover, in both substantive and documentary terms several issues should be taken into account. (1) The traditional, narrow, definition of international legal practice comprised practice exclusively generated by states, while the contemporary, broad,[5] conception of such practice also includes the practice of inter-governmental organizations. (2) Although in terms of article 38 of the ICJ Statute judicial decisions are considered 'subsidiary' means for determining the rule of international law (treaty and custom being the 'main' sources), international legal practice often, if implicitly, includes judicial decisions, much as negotiating draft treaties and conducting international affairs tend to be considered sub-categories within such practice.[6] (3) As a constitutive component of international customary law, *opinio juris* falls within the category of 'main' sources; however, the divergent doctrinal assessment of this component to some extent relegates it to 'subsidiary' sources.

In substantive terms it is often difficult to determine which international legal practice, in conjunction with which kind of *opinio juris*, gives rise to which international customary rules. In turn, the variety and quantity of (nationally and internationally generated) international legal practice make for a complex documentary approach to the primary evidence of international customary law.

The absence of a continuous, exhaustive and worldwide survey of international legal practice engaged in by states was as early as 1922 deplored by V. Bruns in the introduction to his *Fontes juris gentium*, series B/I [49a], and again underscored in 1949 by the Committee on the Progressive Development of International Law [31]. The model proposed under the aegis of the Council of Europe for the classification of state practice manifestations [32] only partly remedies the persistent lack of relevant documentary tools.

The dearth of collections of full texts of given states' international legal practices has to some extent been offset by increasingly available digests and summaries of such practices. Digests of state practice 'convey to the reader an approximate general impression of the meaning of the passage reproduced and the manner and context in which the statement was made in order that [the reader] may be spared superfluous research of all appropriate record'.[7] Implied in this definition is the selective approach, often restricting the coverage of the digest to a given country, topic (e.g. diplomacy, adjudication) or chronological coverage (mostly retrospective). Cutting across these geographical, topical and temporal aspects are different forms grouping the practice according to diplomatic correspondence, judicial awards, legislative and administrative records, the judicious selection and presentation of which contribute to the substantive and documentary strength of a given state practice digest.

Generally speaking, digests of state practice (broadly conceived) tend to be traced to a specifically American initiative. The nearly one-hundred-year-old tradition of publishing (until the mid-twentieth century commercially, thereafter officially) digests of international legal practice engaged in by the United States [34] bears the mark of individual compilers, notably M. M. Whiteman. Since 1945 a number of European and a few Asian countries have patterned their respective digests of state practice [35, 36, 44, 45] on the successive American models. However, it remains a matter of doctrinal perception whether recently published digests reflect the 'existence and reality'[8] of PIL in general and of international customary law in particular, or merely attest to the 'westernization'[9] thereof. Be that as it may, from a documentary point of view the number of known, available digests of state practice is disproportionately small compared to the number of sovereign states in the contemporary world community, and especially lacking in the states of the Third World.[10] Under the circumstances, and because over forty years ago the compilation of digests of international legal practice was already 'beyond the powers or resources of any one individual', the belief that 'governments alone are fitted to undertake the task of comprehensive digests of international law'[11] may be gaining currency.

Diplomacy as part of a state's conduct of international affairs occupies an important substantive and documentary place in the analysis of international legal practice. The *Digest of diplomatic correspondence of European States* [569] summarizes diplomatic state practice engaged in by the European Powers in the third quarter of the nineteenth century. Published in the 1930s, the *Digest* attests to the trend for diplomatic records to become publicly available. The idea that 'publication of internation [diplomatic] correspondence may be used against [states] as a precedent and that, in consequence, it ought to be kept secret as far as possible'[12] began to become obsolete after the First World War. On the one hand, diplomatic, and other, archives have gradually become accessible[13] for historical research, and countries have increasingly undertaken (often officially) to publish records, mostly retrospective, of their foreign and diplomatic relations as part of international state practice, legal and otherwise. The continuous, even if only selective, publication of diplomatic correspondence remains, however, a worldwide desideratum.[14]

As far as could be ascertained only about a dozen countries issue digests of their international state practice. Consequently, to locate evidence, especially of current legal state practice in general, and for countries without known digests of such practice in particular, recourse to so-called 'official', 'government' publications or documents becomes almost inevitable. For a long time national governments in the course of their various activities at the federal and component levels have been generating official publications (often in ephemeral document or pamphlet form). The growing quantities and complexity of such official materials [67a,b] have given rise to various national and international attempts[15] to define, standardize and classify such materials. Increasingly attention has centred on the not inconsiderable amount of evidence within such material that reflects not only the legal system of a given country, but also the international legal practice in keeping with the country's common, civil, legal tradition.

The important legal content of national legislative and judicial materials (including constitutions, laws, statutes, decrees, regulations, etc.) and the large number of states generating such official legal publications led UNESCO in 1953 to publish the *Register of legal documentation in the world* [62a]. Although it is out of date, the *Register* still serves as a reliable guide to official legal publications throughout the world. Patterned on, and complementing, this *Register* is the *Catalogue des sources de documentation juridique des pays socialistes* [62b], which deals with official legal materials in European socialist countries. Government gazettes represent a special category of serially issued national legal materials. Often published at daily or weekly intervals, gazettes are important primary legal (including PIL) sources, containing the most current records of national, judicial and administrative decisions. Correspondingly, the *Guide to official gazettes and their contents* [66] is an important documentary tool, based as it is on the vast holdings of official gazettes in the US Library of Congress.

It is beyond the scope of the *Guide* to provide even a cursory analysis of the legal content of the numerous and diverse nationally issued official publications; instead reference is made to several (often individually compiled and commercially published) guides to such publications,[16] notably in the UK by Pergamon Press [68] and Mansell [69a]. Given the often considerable holdings of official publications in national and special libraries, it is useful to consult the 1983 UNESCO/PGI document on the *Availability and use of official publications in libraries* [67c].

The preceding comments have dealt, albeit summarily, with the substantive aspect of international practice engaged in by states and the corresponding documentary form (digests, official materials) of such practice. It bears repeating that the more doctrinal perception stresses the conflictual interests of states, the more likely it is that 'there will be controversy until new [customary] law emerges from the cauldron of claim and counterclaim'.[17] Given that article 38 of the ICJ Statute refrains from deriving international custom as explicit evidence of either state or international organization practice, it is not surprising that doctrinal divergence persists, in particular with reference to the international customary law creation of inter-governmental organizations (IGO). This divergence may be caused in part by the elusive distinction between IGOs as subjects of PIL (i.e. governed by PIL tenets), and the legal practice of IGOs giving rise to primary (treaty and customary) international rules (i.e. generating PIL tenets). As a corollary to this distinction might be mentioned the internal, mainly administrative legal, aspects of IGO activities, and their external, politico-legal components, which are more conducive to the development of PIL tenets.

In substantive terms codificatory activities of IGOs, especially the UN, are most likely to lead to the development of PIL in general, and international customary rules in particular. The decisions arrived at in the course of such activities (often taking the form of international conferences convened under the auspices of the UN) may represent codified restatements of given segments of international customary law, or exemplify resolutions, declarations or guidelines adopted by relevant forums. Special mention must be made of the codificatory activities of the International Law Commission [662a]. In accordance with article 18 of its Statute, the ILC selects segments of international customary law and prepares draft restatements thereof for submission to the UN General Assembly, thereby providing opportunity to states to comment on and revise the proposed restatements. The international customary law topics selected and the progress of their codification are contained in the *Yearbook* of the ILC [662b]. Following the publication of the preparatory texts of codified customary law segments in the UN *Legislative series* [645], the *Yearbook* of the ILC generally carries the definitive texts which, often with commentaries, tend to be published in relevant legal or PIL periodicals.

International conferences (especially those convened by the UN) usually provide the preparatory work (in some ways the 'legislative history') of resulting multilateral conventions. The proceedings and final act (generally comprising the text of the convention) of the conference are issued as part of the UN official records,[18] of other relevant (legislative) document series[19] or as a separate sales publication. Once the convention has entered into force its text is published in *UNTS* [2].

The substantive evidence of international customary law is largely developed through the research and codificatory activities of the ILC or the resolutions, declarations, etc. taken in the UN General Assembly and the Security Council. The documentary approach to such and similar other evidence requires a sometimes tenuous distinction between the (often contested) customary law-creating status of a given inter-governmental body and the extent of primary PIL and customary evidence contained (in full text or summary form) in the publications of, or relative to, that body.

Given the importance attributed to international conferences [537a, 584c], multilateral conventions [537b, 566a] and resolutions [643a,b, 682b] their (full) texts or summaries of proceedings are relatively easily located. For summaries of the general, including legal, practice of IGOs, mention should be made of the commercially published *Digest of legal activities of international organizations and other institutions* [619a], which summarizes the (often more operational than legal) activities of selected inter-governmental and non-governmental international organizations. The *Repertory of practice of the United Nations organs* [641a] and the *Répertoire of the practice of the Security Council* [644a], while more and more out of date, provide digests of (selected) politico-legal activities engaged in and published by the United Nations.

In view of the more than 300 IGOs and over 3,000 NGOs (*see* [630a]), it is quite beyond the scope of the *Guide* to attempt even a cursory outline of the presumed legal evidence contained in the vast publishing output of the IGOs, especially given the estimated 125,000 documents produced annually by the UN alone.[20] Instead attention should be paid to Kleckner's specific study on *Major publications of the [UN] Office of Legal Affairs* [659a] and the increasing concern of the International Association of Law Libraries [415a] with the relevance to international legal research of official materials produced by IGOs and NGOs. It might be added that if IGOs have not been overly successful in reducing their publishing output, bibliographic access to this output has been increasingly facilitated through indexes issued by given IGOs and guides [660d, 679d, 681d] that are often individually compiled and commercially published.

In conclusion, the divergence over the type of international legal practice (states and IGOs), and the kind of primary evidence of customary law (diplomatic, judicial or codificatory) to be derived thereof, needs to be underscored. In turn, this divergence on the substance of international customary law inevitably affects the documentary approach to the proper primary sources (digests, official materials) containing (undisputed) evidence of international custom.

NOTES

1 Dinstein, Y., p. 203, in [460], believes international law to be 'much more dependent than the modern national system on customary law'. D'Amato, A. A., *passim*, in [519f], considers the ambiguities inherent in the concept of 'custom in international law' a methodological obstacle to a proper approach to PIL (primary) sources in general.
2 Jennings, R., pp. 59–61, in [509c].
3 Butler, W. E., p. 33, in [428b], asks: 'How far back in the history of international relations may a modern international lawyer reach for evidence of State practice?' Bleckmann, A., p. 19, in [509b], conceives of the creation of customary law as largely a methodological problem, although he does not wholly dispel the positivist concern with the (elusive) binding force of international custom.
4 Jennings, R., p. 69, in [509c], asks: 'How is one to distill an *"opinio juris"* from a welter of ostensibly authoritative but mutually incompatible opinions?' Rosas, A., p. 224, in [460], points to the traditional concept of *opinio juris* as part of *lex lata*, rather than (as in some contemporary doctrinal concepts) as part of *lex ferenda*. Feliciano, F. P. and Solidum, E. D., p. 219, in [460], juxtapose the 'ought' of *opinio juris* with the 'is' of state practice. *See also* [458a].
5 Rosas, A., p. 223, in [460], includes in such a broad conception not only the commissions and omissions of state actions, but also statements in the form of resolutions and declarations, especially through the UN General Assembly. *See also* Higgins, R., p. 33, in [499b], concerning the 'evidence of repeated breaches of international law' and Reisman, W. M., p. 36, in [460], on 'indicators' of international practice in terms of protest actions, condemnations, etc. The emerging 'new' law of the sea implicitly projects a broad conception of PIL in that continental shelf boundaries, deep-sea mining, etc. do not lend themselves 'usefully to the traditional customary law kind of inquiry ', as per Jennings, R., p. 69, in [509c].
6 Lillich, R. B., p. 420, in [460], considers international practice to encompass 'a whole substructure of rules and principles . . . building up . . . in the various regional organizations, in the domestic laws of various States, in State practice emanating from bi-lateral treaties [and] in numerous international human rights instruments'.
7 V. Bruns' definition is cited on p. 25, in [31]. Another definition of a digest refers to 'ready means of reference to conclusions which have . . . been reached on the same kindred questions' according to Cadwallader, J. L., in his Preface to the *Digest of the published opinions of the Attorneys General and the leading decisions of the Federal Courts with reference to international law, treaties and kindred questions*, cited by Williams, J. W., p. 160, in [328].
8 Jennings, R., p. 278, in [169].
9 Ferrari-Bravo, L., p. 301, in [519a], speaks of 'l'occidentalisation du droit international'.
10 In 1990 there were 159 Member States of the UN; with notable exceptions the few extant digests of state practice are either incomplete or outdated, and are rarely available outside the country concerned (or of publication). At the Consultation informelle sur l'enseignement et la recherche en droit international public [499a], attention was drawn to the need for compiling 'des répertoires de la pratique en vigueur' in Third World countries.
11 Stated on p. 112, in [31].

12 Lauterpacht, H., in *BYIL*, 1945, **22**, p. 310.
13 The customary median period of 50 years (preceding a given 'current' year) during which diplomatic and other archives tended to be closed for research, began to be reduced (to 20 to 30 years); moreover, various national 'right to information' acts have improved research access to various, formerly closed government or other official files.
14 Edwards, R.W., 1967, Electronic data processing of international law. *AJIL*, **61**, p. 88. This refers to a memorandum prepared by the Historical Office of the US Department of State reporting that of 77 countries surveyed only three-quarters made provision for the separate serial publication of diplomatic correspondence, even on a selective basis.
15 The Official Publications Section of IFLA in August 1983 proposed the definition of an official publication as 'any item produced by reprographic or any other method, issued by an organisation that is an official body, and available to an audience wider than that body'. This definition does not address the standardized aspects of substance, form, frequency and so on of an official 'document', confirmed by various national assessments thereof (Dorokhov, I.A., 1982, Poniatie dokumenta v sovetskom prave. *Pravovedenie*, **2**, 53–60 versus the definition of a public document as 'any publication in book, serial or non-book form published by or for a government agency, e.g. the publications of Federal, State, Local and Foreign governments and of intergovernmental organizations'. In *Documents to the people*, 1977, **5** (5), p. 187). *See also* note 20 below.
16 Understandably, such guides tend to deal with official publications issued by federal and subsidiary government bodies in countries such as the USA, the USSR and the FRG, to mention but a few countries generating vast amounts of such materials, the substance of which often transcends national delimitations.
17 Merrills, J.G., p. 9, in [575a].
18 *Official records* (*OR*) represent authoritative accounts or records of decisions arrived at in meetings of the principal policy-making UN organs and the main committees thereof. *OR* is not a UN document symbol but a methodological device for organizing the 'primary' source aspects of UN documents in accordance with their provenance (i.e. issuing body).
19 *Official records* (see note 18 above) to some extent illustrate legislative aspects in general, but should not be confused with the UN *Legislative series* [645] proper. The legislative history of a given IGO decision may be traced by examining the texts of such decisions through their drafting stages and in accordance with procedural rules of relevant standing committees and advisory bodies. Such a documentary approach must take into account the doctrinal divergence concerning the legislative substance. Verzijl, J.H.W., p. 391, in [157, vol. 1], speaks of 'pseudo-legislative activities of the collective organs of the international community'. *See also* Szasz, P., 1979, Improving the international legislative process. *Georgia journal of international and comparative law*, **9**, p. 519.
20 The UN headquarters in New York annually produces some 100,000 documents (whose exact linguistic breakdown is difficult to determine, some documents being issued only in English, others in two to six official languages of the UN), while the UN Office at Geneva produces some 25,000 documents annually; in 1987 UN sales publications comprised some 250 titles. It might be noted that UN documents and publications are defined on p. 213, in [660b] as follows: 'A document is an official paper issued under the authority of a United Nations organ and bearing an official United Nations symbol, regardless of size or form of issuance.' 'A publication is a text issued under the authority of the [UN] Publications Board, usually in printed or near-printed form, as part of the publication programme of the United Nations. A "publication" may also be a "document".'

c. Judicial decisions

The substantive analysis of national and international adjudication is directed, among other things, to the elucidation and systematization of representative legal or PIL tenets and rules contained in relevant judicial decisions and cases. 'In a law where there is fluidity and change, and where there is accordingly a need for identification and elaboration of new kinds of customary law, judicial decisions must play an important and frequently decisive role.'[1] In this statement, R. Jennings, Justice of the ICJ, was above all concerned with PIL and the importance in it of decisions by international adjudicatory bodies.

Before turning to the documentary survey of PIL evidence contained in judicial decisions, attention should be drawn to doctrinal divergence concerning (1) the kind of 'recognized manifestation of international law' (RMIL)[2] implicit in (international) judicial decisions and opinions,[3] (2) the normative extent or 'objective' binding force of such decisions[4] and (3) the possible relevance of precedent[5] carried by certain decisions. The 'subsidiary' status assigned by article 38 of the ICJ Statute to judicial decisions may in part reflect doctrinal uncertainty surrounding the 'judge-made'[6] rules and principles of PIL.

Leaving aside the matter of the methodological slot for judicial decisions (as part or not of the larger international legal practice), in documentary terms it is useful to distinguish between information reflecting the judicial process and the formal decisions resulting therefrom. Accordingly, the *Guide* deals with formal decisions (judgements, opinions, awards) mainly of international adjudicatory bodies in Part I (such decisions are considered separately from international legal practice), and refers to the substantive or procedural practice of selected international tribunals under relevant sections in Part II.

The documentary approach to locating primary PIL evidence contained in judicial decisions (regardless of their 'main' or 'subsidiary' PIL source status) of international and selected national tribunals generally means locating relevant case or law reports.[7] The purpose of municipal[8] and international law reporting is the exposition of fundamental legal or PIL principles (issues of law rather than fact) upon which the judicial decisions were based, as well as the summary of essential facts and the nature of pleadings relative to the cases heard by relevant courts. A documentary analogy between 'digests' of international legal practice, which may or may not include relevant judicial decisions, and 'law reports', which are restricted to legal or PIL rules, principles and relevant facts, might be drawn, in the sense that both digests and law reports provide cogent summaries (rather than full texts) by recognized legal scholars or practitioners of appropriate (diplomatic, judicial, etc.) primary PIL sources.

Judicial decisions emanating from the Permanent Court of International Justice (PCIJ) and its successor, the International Court of Justice (ICJ), represent an unbroken continuity (except between 1940 and 1945) from 1919 to the present day of what tends to come closest to a coherent body of PIL case law.[9] The official publications [48a,b] issued respectively by the PCIJ and the

ICJ provide substantive/documentary access to the full texts of the judgements, advisory opinions and pleadings of the two tribunals. The commercially published *International law reports* [50] and *Fontes juris gentium* [49a] represent law reports and as such summarize not only decisions of the aforementioned two international tribunals but also those of selected municipal courts that are relevant to PIL. The *Répertoire des décisions . . . de la CPJI et de la CIJ* [49b], initiated by P. Guggenheim, and *International law as applied by international courts and tribunals* [49c], undertaken by G. Schwarzenberger, provide in-depth analyses (in French and English respectively) of selected PIL principles or issues underlying the judicial activities and decisions of the PCIJ and ICJ.

In addition to general international adjudication, mention should be made of specialized topical decisions, such as those of the International Military Tribunal [710a] or of the UN Administrative Tribunal [619b] and of arbitral awards in general, e.g. *Reports of international arbitral awards* [48c] or in particular the UNCITRAL arbitration [732b]. In regional terms, apart from the extensive substantive analysis of and documentary access to the judicial process and decisions of the European Courts of Justice (omitted from the *Guide*), as far as could be ascertained no regional African or Asian general international tribunals exist. For (mainly Latin) America, the Inter-American Court of Human Rights of the OAS [696a] should be mentioned, even though documentary evidence of the Court's decisions is fairly scant and scattered.

If in substantive terms the 'limitations imposed by international law on the jurisdiction of municipal courts'[10] or the evidence of customary international law as derived from given decisions of certain municipal tribunals[11] are matters of dispute, in documentary terms tracking down municipal court decisions relative to PIL is time-consuming and rarely fully satisfactory.[8] That is to say, whereas the inclusion in the *International law reports* [50] of municipal decisions concerned with PIL principles is of necessity selective, the relatively few law reports reflecting national court 'cases' of relevance to PIL tend to provide a retrospective rather than current coverage of such decisions.

Two outstanding examples of national retrospective law reports of international law cases need to be mentioned, i.e. *American international law cases* [53], spanning the period 1783-1985, and *Fontes juris gentium* Series A. Section II [58], representing a collection of German jurisprudence relative to PIL for the period 1879-1985. The extensive historico-legal research cost attendant upon such national retrospective PIL-oriented law reports may explain the dearth of such publications; as far as could be ascertained, apart from the USA and FRG, only Great Britain, Italy and the Netherlands [59, 60, 61] have published such retrospective collections. Increasingly, however, a trend is pointing to the inclusion of recent[12] national PIL-oriented decisions in given national yearbooks of PIL and in relevant periodicals.

All in all, the documentary evidence of international and national or municipal adjudication (general, specialized) relative to PIL continues to be impeded by (1) the considerable time lag between the date of a judgement, advisory opinion, award, etc. rendered, and the publication (in the original or translation) of the full text or summaries thereof; and by (2) the general lack of cumulative detailed subject indexes without which it is time-consuming to approach the varied topical aspects within such cases or decisions.

NOTES

1 Jennings, R., p. 287, in [169].
2 Bos, M., p. 79, in [490], states that 'as compared to the other RMIL, [judicial decisions] . . . are an intermittent and uneven rather than regular manifestation, and eminently temporary'.
3 The ICJ Justice F. Amoun, p. 287, in *ICJ Reports 1970/3* (Barcelona traction/Second phase) distinguishes between the opinion of the ICJ as a whole, and the separate (or dissenting) opinion of an individual ICJ justice, concerning the legal issues of a case before the ICJ.
4 Article 59 of the ICJ Statute states that the 'decision of the Court has no binding force except between parties and in respect of that particular case'. Mensah-Brown, A. K., *passim*, in [457c], raises the question of judicial decisions within the context of African international practice and with reference to the binding force or recognition of such decisions and practice upon (sometimes adversely affected) non-African countries.
5 Jennings, R., p. 74, in [509c], sees 'no binding precedent in international law' because of the absence of a hierarchy of courts as in municipal law, but he believes that 'there is room for more discipline in the extraction from decided cases'.
6 Combacau, J., 1982, Les réactions de la doctrine à la création du droit par les juges en droit international public. Association H. Capitant. *Travaux*, **31**, pp. 392-405.
7 Breem, W. W. S., Primary sources: law reports, pp. 125-188, in [411a, 2nd edn], distinguishes between two categories of law reports, i.e. primary, enunciating a general principle, and secondary, commenting on the application of authoritative evidence. *See also* Kavass, I. I., 1977, Law reporting: comparison between Western Europe and Common Law countries. *IJLL*, **5**, pp. 104-120.
8 Between the two World Wars the Institut juridique international in The Hague reported in its *Bulletin* judicial decisions relative to PIL by a number of (mostly European) municipal courts. But on the whole 'the great need for an authoritative repository of the decisions of municipal courts of the various countries' remains as acute today as it was forty years ago (as per ASIL cited in [31]).
9 Marek, K., p. xviii, in [49b, vol. 1] considers the ICJ to represent a 'permanent element of international life and organization' but cautions against the misconception of the Court as a 'scientific academy' abstractly developing PIL; the very case law of the ICJ shows it to be an instrument for settling international disputes.
10 Akehurst, M., p. 129, in [170].
11 Cited on p. 99, in [31]. *See also* Lauterpacht, H., 1929, Decisions of municipal courts as a source of international law. *BYIL*, **10**, pp. 65-95.
12 'Recent' generally denotes that texts and summaries of judicial decisions are made available in published form within 12-15 months from the time the decisions were made.

d. General principles of law

In terms of article 38 of the ICJ Statute, treaties, custom and general principles of law as the (implicitly) main categories of PIL sources are followed by the (explicitly) subsidiary categories of judicial decisions and the teachings of most qualified publicists. Despite, or perhaps because of, this hierarchy, the 'primary', 'main' PIL evidence in the general principles of law continues to fuel doctrinal debates. It has been argued that these principles are based on custom so universal and well established 'that the judge or arbitrator relying upon them does not think it necessary to adduce precedence for their proof'.[1] None the less, the ambiguity implicit in the very 'general', 'universal' meaning of these principles has given rise to various conflicting views of the exact substance and applicability of such principles. Exception has been taken to the limitation in article 38 of the ICJ Statute of general principles of law to those 'recognized by civilized nations'. This anachronistic wording[2] has given way to views that 'all states are now "civilized" '[3] or that such principles apply within all systems of law 'that have achieved a comparable state of development'.[4]

In substantive terms general principles of law tend to be circumscribed mainly according to their relevance to municipal and international law,[5] or according to their procedural implications and methodological aspects; most often such principles are equated with good faith and, increasingly, human rights.[6] In elucidating (mostly) international customary rules, generally with reference to minimum standards of procedural fairness and equitable interpretation of rules, it is quite usual to invoke general principles of law. The assumption that such principles represent not so much a source of municipal or international law, but rather a methodological yardstick[7] for analysing various sources of law, has pointed up the need for studying the impact of such principles within the comparative legal context.[8]

Altogether, notwithstanding the status assigned to them by article 38 of the ICJ Statute, general principles of law tend to be considered more as guidelines for certain judicial application[9] of PIL in general than as specific PIL sources in particular. This substantive disparity necessarily affects the documentary evidence of such principles, chiefly resting on conflicting doctrinal assertions often dispersed as chapters in PIL treatises or analysed in periodical articles. As a result, the *Guide* includes selected references (besides the outstanding if outdated monograph by B. Cheng [521f]) to general principles of law among secondary resources in Part II/C.ii.

NOTES

1 Virally, M., p. 144, in [76].
2 Jennings, R., p. 71, in [509c], considers this wording to reflect the position of the Committee of Jurists (of the LoN) in 1920, in turn traceable to 'the polities

then contemplated as subjects of international law'.
3 Jennings, R., p. 72, in [509c].
4 Virally, M., p. 144, in [76].
5 Akehurst, M., p. 79, in [170], views general principles as representing 'something more than the mathematically common factor of technical rules common to all [legal] systems', yet they remain principles rather than rules of PIL. Parry, C., p. 83, in [509e], considers such principles as 'maxims' rather than rules of law.
6 Van Boven, T., p. 118, in Vasak, K., *The international dimensions of human rights*. Paris: Unesco, 1987 (French edn). Van Boven considers human rights as general principles of law and as such 'constituent des normes impératives du droit international général'.
7 Bos, M., Chapter 9, in [490], deals with the methodology of the content and reception of such principles into general PIL. Bleckmann, A., p. 26, in [492], examines such principles in terms of analytical reasoning and as tools of analogous arguments.
8 Butler, W. E., p. 40, in [428b], considers that 'references in [international] judicial and arbitral opinions to national legislation conceal intellectual and evidentiary concerns of great moment', and as such are in need of comparative study.
9 Jennings, R., p. 72, in [509c], considers that 'article 38(c) is truly an historical remnant of the 1920s and should be regarded today as having little more than academic interest', construing the intention of the article to have been 'to limit the discretion of Judges . . . lest they be tempted to impose subjective notions of justice'.

ii. ANALYTICAL RESOURCES: SECONDARY EVIDENCE

The preceding section outlined the categories of primary PIL sources generally considered to contain normative evidence of PIL. The following survey deals with secondary PIL resources (*see* note 13, p. 11) in which 'interposed' primary PIL evidence is often of an analytical, interpretative nature.

It has been said that 'the role of the scholar in expounding the law is of much greater significance in international law than in other branches of legal scholarship'[1]. Determining the impact of PIL doctrinal works upon the dynamic development of PIL in general,[2] and upon the decisions of courts[3] and codificatory bodies in particular, is at best a difficult task. While certain doctrinal positions incontestably represent authoritative (re)statements on given PIL issues, the scholarly doctrine of PIL is also criticized,[4] not least because of inadvertent confusion of doctrinal tenets with those of PIL proper.[5] Be that as it may, scholarly or doctrinal 'ascertainment of the positive law . . . guidance for its development and as a means of filling its deficiencies'[6] remains an indispensable research factor in elucidating legal and PIL principles and rules.

Keeping in mind the occasionally ideological divergence of substantive doctrinal approaches to PIL, in documentary terms doctrinal works tend to take the form of (1) treatises, manuals, textbooks, (2) dissertations, (3) commemorative essays and (4) periodicals, yearbooks. Cutting across these documentary categories are analytical and reference aspects, with varying further temporal connotations. In this sense, PIL treatises, essays, dissertations and contributions to encyclopaedias or periodicals may be said to represent analytical[7] resources in that they variously reflect expository scholarly syntheses of research findings.

Many of the monographs among such analytical resources may be published as part of academic or publishers' series. In temporal[8] terms such analytical secondary PIL resources are to some extent 'historical' in that they provide state-of-the-art overviews of general and specialized PIL research findings, whether presented as lengthy syntheses as in treatises and manuals or geared for teaching as in didactically streamlined textbooks and casebooks.

To the extent that encyclopaedias, and also many scholarly manuals and treatises, are primarily meant for consultations rather than sustained reading, the aforementioned PIL analytical resources may also be said to comprise a 'reference' aspect,[9] such as definitions, classification of concepts, glossaries, bibliographic notes, references, etc. However, the distinction between analytical and reference resources, and between the various sub-categories therein, would seem to be one of degree, depending on the purpose (research or teaching) and contents (comprehensive or expository) of the given secondary PIL resource. Correspondingly, the *Guide* illustrates a subjective, pragmatic rather than didactic, formal approach to the selected PIL secondary resources.

NOTES

1 Merrills, J. G., p. 29, in [575a]; echoed by Jennings, R., p. 78, in [509c].
2 Schwarzenberger, G., p. 31, in [495a], states that 'the foremost task of doctrine must remain that of testing the accuracy of any claim that the dynamics of international law have led to any asserted change of existing international law'. *See also* Chapter 2 on the matter in [495b].
3 Robinson, J., p. 37, in [334], stresses the influence of the 'professor' in law, but especially PIL: while the teachings of PIL publicists have not been referred to in the majority of ICJ decisions, doctrinal positions are 'fairly well represented in dissenting opinions [of ICJ justices]'.
4 Parry, C., p. 104, in [509e], considers PIL [doctrinal] literature 'unduly theoretical, insufficiently practical, and prone to oversimplification' and echoes Schwarzenberger's position in [171, 3rd edn] that 'courts and writers do not make law: they only say what it is'. Leurquin de Visscher, L., in [501b], distinguishes between 'la doctrine' in municipal law (after législation, jurisprudence) and in international law (after traité, coûtume). Salmon, J. J. A., in [501a], scoffs at PIL doctrine as vast and inexact, and as a source hierarchically subordinate to treaty and custom.
5 Butler, W. E., pp. 79-80, in [428a], cautions against confusing the history of international legal doctrine with the history of international law itself, yet believes that 'the role of doctrinal writings of a country' should be examined (comparatively) in the national, international context.
6 Virally, M., p. 153, in [76].
7 Williams, J. W., p. 16, in [328], defines analytical tools as those helping 'the researcher grapple with the information obtained' regardless of its source; Williams lists among analytical resources textbooks, classics dictionaries and encyclopaedias.
8 Williams, J. W., p. 10, in [328], classifies 'temporal' categories according to a 'time frame' ranging from instant, present, current, recent to historical. Thus evidence of customary international law as found in official gazettes would qualify as 'current'. Whether a PIL treatise should be termed 'historical' or 'recent' depends on the

historiographical, methodological and other criteria applied; the continued relevance of L. Oppenheim's 'semi-classic' manual [173a] is a case in point.
9 Williams, J.W., p. 15, in [328], distinguishes between reference and research problems. The former mainly concern the locating of a specific document or citation, while the latter analyse the content or meaning of a fact or event as contained in the document or citation.

a. Treatises, manuals, textbooks

The expository or descriptive writings of the 'most qualified publicists' 'analyse, distil, explain, clarify and describe'[1] PIL as it is embodied in PIL treatises, manuals, textbooks, etc. PIL treatises are often influenced by 'elements of national style'[2] and characterized by conceptual speculations[3] and terminological variants, and are legion.[4] In documentary terms this raises the problem of 'appropriate' selection criteria, in turn reflecting qualitative (substantive or evaluative) and quantitative (linguistic or geographic) elements. What characterizes the 'most qualified publicists'? Who among these fit the sometimes tenuous labels 'traditional', 'modern', revisionist', 'Eurocentrist', etc.? Moreover, the historiographical 'rise and fall' in the evaluation of doctrinal thought in general, but especially of PIL secondary works, makes at best for arguable documentary selection criteria (*see* Introduction, note 7). An example in point is the reappraisal of the 'classics' of PIL [463, 464] from 'founders' or 'fathers' of PIL to 'largely speculative thinkers and rationalizers of the naturalist period of the doctrine of international law'.[5] Correspondingly, the *Guide* assigns 'classical' treatises to historiography (Part II/B.iii) rather than to treatises in general (Part I/B.ii.a). Finally, it should be noted that it may take up to ten years for relevant evidence in primary PIL sources to be incorporated in given PIL treatises and manuals. In this sense most treatises have a certain 'historical' aspect reflecting the 'state of the art' up to a given (research) period in time. The frequently revised PIL textbooks are teaching adjuncts to the scholarly syntheses often contained in the more extensive, if less 'current', treatises.

The numerous PIL treatises, manuals and textbooks published throughout the world increasingly require assessment of their scholarly or cultural importance within and outside the countries of their origin. Such assessment may take the form of a comprehensive, comparative historiographical evaluation or of selective, descriptive bibliographic citation. In either case two methodological considerations should not be lost from view: the place of publication of a given treatise should not *ipso facto* be considered synonymous with the nationality or ethnic origin of the author, given the mobility of scholars and transnational publishing trends [420c]; and the extent of the physical versus linguistic accessibility of a work, e.g. the availability in the original Russian or Japanese of a treatise as opposed to the sometimes selective and deficient English or German translations of a given treatise.

Historiographical studies generally trace the historical and substantive development of a given discipline, in terms of the contributions to it by either a single scholar or a doctrinal school. In PIL terms the few expressly historiographical analyses [463-473] in existence give rise in part to the question of whether such analyses are feasible or even desirable.[6] Midway between historiographies and bibliographies are the reviews by J.W. Williams of mainly Anglo-American twentieth-century PIL treatises and textbooks [74] and the reviews of such works from the USSR by W.E. Butler [354] and B. Meissner [355]. D.H.L. Ompteda [347] and K. Strupp [344] are mainly concerned with the in-depth analyses of outstanding eighteenth- and nineteenth-century PIL doctrinal works. Altogether, the ever-growing quantity of PIL secondary resources in general, and of treatises, etc., in particular, may explain the concern with bibliographic control (*see* p. 36) rather than historiographic analysis of such works, many of which are midway between treatises and textbooks or casebooks.[7]

NOTES

1 Jennings, R., p. 77, in [509c], adds that 'it is in a way natural that the place of text writers should decline as the importance of case law increases'.
2 Butler, W.E., p. 80, in [428a], views this national style as an 'aggregate of extra-legal, quasi-legal and legal factors' and on pp. 43-44 that it is to be 'understood in the larger context of doctrinal style in the society concerned.'
3 McDougal, M.S., p. 194, in [428b], refers to 'technical doctrines of the highest level of ambiguity' inherent in doctrinal description of past decisions, but especially in prescriptions for future decisions. Doctrinal speculation is at times indistinguishable from the 'ought' of PIL; however, according to Eisenmann, C., p. 38, in [499g], in pure legal dogmatics a legal rule interpreted as 'it should be' applied, represents a valid feature of the (doctrinal) theory of law, even though it is inapplicable in legal practice.
4 Simpson, A.W.B., 1981, The rise and fall of the legal treatise: legal principles and the forms of legal literature. *University of Chicago law review*, 48, pp. 632-679. The continued (qualitative) relevance of a given treatise might also be (quantitatively) traced by way of repeated references to that work in the *Social sciences citation index* (Philadelphia, PA, 1973-, one to three times yearly).
5 Schwarzenberger, G., p. 228, in [428b], adds that the continued relevance of classics well into the twentieth century 'hardly establishes a legal continuity between systems of international law applied in ancient and our days'.
6 Verzijl, J.H.W., p. 401, in [157, vol. 1], advocated an 'inventory' of such analyses as a way of avoiding the duplication of scholarly effort.
7 The *Collected courses* [220a] of The Hague Academy of International law [380a] illustrate such a midway approach, as do the numerous Anglo-American textbooks and casebooks. Way, D.J., in [411a, 2nd edn], traces the casebook teaching method to the USA and Great Britain. Williams, J.W., p. 187, in [328], distinguishes between the casebook and case-study approaches; the former centres on selected legal cases to present specific or narrow points of law, while the latter presents a factual and legal, problem-oriented analysis of a complex international situation. Bishop, W., *International law: cases and materials* [83] represents a casebook approach; Henkin, L., *How nations behave* (2nd edn, 1979) illustrates an interdisciplinary (PIL and international relations) case-study approach. Williams, J.W., pp. 183-185, in [328], dwells at length on 'hornbooks' as the 'basic and comprehensive treatise on a specific subject, consisting entirely

of the author's prose, little if any quotations, and sufficient footnotes to lead the reader to the law itself'. For Williams treatises are 'more an author's interpretation of the law rather than a repetition of the current state of law'. Accordingly Williams considers the work by Brierly [172] as a treatise and that of Akehurst [170] as a hornbook.

b. Commemorative essays

Commemorative essays generally honour an outstanding scholar, or less frequently an academic or professional institution [379a]. As opposed to the gathering of an author's essays and articles in an edition specifically reprinted for the purpose [192], they contain contributions by colleagues or pupils of the scholar so honoured, and include bio-bibliographic information concerning the scholar. The tradition of commemorative tributes in the form of Festschriften, mélanges, essays, etc. dedicated to scholars having distinguished themselves in various fields of scholarship goes back to the nineteenth century. The steady growth in the twentieth century of such commemorative essays has given rise to bibliographies of essays in general (with important sections on law and PIL) [176] and of law and PIL commemorative essays in particular [175]. The *Guide* complements the aforementioned bibliographies in that it lists commemorative essays specific to PIL scholars [177-212] and published mainly between 1975 and 1985. Apart from occasional references to relevant individual contributions, it was clearly beyond the scope of the *Guide* to provide a complete list of all contributions in the essays selected.

c. Dissertations

Broadly defined, dissertations or theses represent original research findings generally based on primary source materials; specific study tends to be undertaken by graduate or post-graduate researchers aspiring to an advanced academic degree or a specialized academic or professional achievement. Academic requirements governing the contents and submission of dissertations for obtaining advanced degrees in law vary not only according to country but also from one academic institution to another in the same country.

The fact that international law has not always and everywhere been an independent discipline [499b, 500b] in part accounts for problems in tracing and evaluating dissertations specific to PIL.[1] It could not be ascertained whether the series *Bibliotheca Visseriana* [214], which is entirely devoted to the publication of outstanding (if mainly Dutch) PIL dissertations, has ceased or has been replaced by a similar outlet for the publication (on a worldwide basis) of research findings gathered by scholars who are as yet not widely known.

Since the Second World War the trend worldwide has been away from costly publishing of dissertations towards microform reproduction of such research. The computer-produced bibliographic services, such as *Dissertation abstracts* or

Comprehensive dissertation index [215], while exceedingly useful, only marginally encompass PIL dissertations (which are particularly inaccessible from outside a given country or university). Keeping track of PIL dissertations is made all the more difficult since PIL scholarship transcends national frontiers, i.e. nationals of one country may acquire advanced degrees in other countries and their dissertations (in partial fulfilment of their degrees) may be published in yet other countries.

NOTE

1 It is extremely difficult to arrive at a reliable number of dissertations specific to PIL. Way, D.J., p. 210, in [411a], mentions that between 35 and 50 legal dissertations are annually accepted for higher degrees at the universities of Great Britain and Ireland, and that these dissertations 'contain a bias toward international law'.

d. Periodicals, yearbooks

Compared to the rather retrospective research character of most monographic sub-categories of secondary PIL resources (treatises, essays, dissertations), PIL periodicals and yearbooks are generally geared to making known current or recent[1] PIL research findings. With the exception of the primary evidence contained in the quarterly *International legal materials* [219] and certain periodically published national digests of international legal practice [e.g. 34, 47], PIL periodicals and yearbooks reflect mainly secondary evidence. On the whole, the view[2] that a history and content analysis of periodicals of international law has not been written still holds true in the late 1980s. This omission may be partly traced to the imperfect state of the history of PIL in general, and to the mainly post-1945 origin of periodicals specifically devoted to PIL matters.

According to the latest edition of *Ulrich's international periodicals directory* [216], in 1989 some 1,000 periodical titles relating to law were published worldwide; of these about 200 titles concern public and private international[3] and comparative law. Of the 100 'core' PIL periodicals published worldwide, more than 40 are entirely or partly in English, even though English may not be the 'official' language in the country publishing the periodicals (e.g. India, Nigeria, etc.); there are some 30 titles in Slavic languages, about ten titles each in French, German and Spanish, and one title in Arabic [222]. In terms of periodicity, some twenty are yearbooks reflecting PIL theory and practice in given countries; the rest are issued semi-annually, quarterly, bimonthly or monthly. Official gazettes [66], often issued weekly or even daily, while periodicals in form, represent primary evidence in content and as such are assigned within the context of the *Guide* to the category of official publications (Part I/B.i.d).

NOTES

1 In the sense that such research findings are the latest known and available. It might be noted that the lag between the submission of an article and its publication in a relevant periodical (PIL or other) often exceeds one year.
2 Robinson, J., p. 365, in [334].
3 In the field of international public and private law Robinson [334] lists 91 titles compared to 71 titles listed by Williams [328]. Allowing for the overlap in substance (public versus private international law) and form (periodicals versus yearbooks), a core of about 100 PIL periodicals published worldwide (but excluding student-edited PIL journals in the USA [228]) might be advanced.

e. Encyclopaedias, dictionaries

Encyclopaedias contain authoritative scholarly syntheses, complete with conceptual and methodological (bibliographic, etc.) information, on a given field of knowledge. From the eighteenth century onwards, the broad, all-encompassing surveys of knowledge began to yield to encyclopaedias that focused more narrowly on increasingly specialized knowledge. After the First World War, when international law began to evolve into a separate legal discipline, projects[1] for an encyclopaedic overview also began to be advanced.

Patterned on the German encyclopaedia, *Wörterbuch des Völkerrechts* [303], a comprehensive multi-volume English *Encyclopedia of public international law* [297] saw its inception in 1981 under the auspices of the Max-Planck Institute for Comparative Public Law and International Law [402]. Complementing this comprehensive encyclopaedia are the one-volume *Encyclopedic dictionary of international law* [298], the one-volume *Encyclopedia of the United Nations and international agreements* [658] and, to some extent, the *International encyclopedia of comparative law* [431].

As compared with the numerous mono- and multilingual legal dictionaries, there are few explanatory or interpretative[2] terminological dictionaries specific to PIL. Notable are the bilingual *Harrap's German and English glossary of terms in international law* [311] and the multilingual *Manual of the terminology of public international law* (English, French, Spanish, Russian) [310].

The semantics[3] of international law represent a vast, often interdisciplinary and, as yet, insufficiently explored field. Among the questions requiring further study are: (1) the cross-cultural assimilation or rejection[4] of given PIL concepts and terms; (2) linguistic status or paramountcy[5] in international law and diplomacy; (3) translation problems inherent in the multilingual publications (including PIL matters) issued by inter-governmental organizations [636a,b] on the one hand, and relative to the (transnational) doctrinal impact of treatises selected for translation[6] on the other; (4) the authentication of texts, especially of treaties concurrently produced in several languages, and the effect thereof upon the interpretation of such texts. So far, the world terminological activities coordinated by the International Information Centre for Terminology in Vienna [636f] appear to be only indirectly concerned with the compilation, evaluation and standardization of PIL concepts and terms.

NOTES

1 Verzijl, J.H.W., *Un projet d'encyclopédie de droit international public et privé* (*Bibliotheca Visseriana*, **23**, 1931). Submitted to the Académie Royale, Amsterdam, this project went unheeded, much as did that earlier proposed to the American Society of International Law (*ASIL proceedings*, 1918, **12**, p. 9).
2 Moys, E., p. 399, in [411a], distinguishes, with reference to law in general, between explanatory and interpreting terminologies: the former defines the (current) meaning of legal terms, based on authoritative statutes and cases, whereas the latter refers to legislative, judicial contexts from which the (interpretative) terms evolved.
3 By analogy with White, J.B., *When words lose their meaning: constitutions and reconstitutions of language, character and community*. Chicago: Chicago UP, 1984, 377 pp. Critically reviewed in *Michigan law review* 1985, **83**(4), pp. 848–893.
4 Butler, W.E., p. 59, in [428a], in correlating terminology with the reception of international law, defines reception as 'the transfer of international legal terms and concepts from one society to another' rather than as the traditional 'transmission of international legal rules into municipal legal systems'.
5 Butler, W.E. *ibid. See also* Introduction, notes 9 and 10, concerning linguistic aspects of law and PIL publications.
6 The need for translations (from and into English) of leading PIL treatises was voiced by Professor C.G. Fenwick (referred to in [31, note 237 on p. 87]). Note that *Index translationum* (Paris: UNESCO) vol. 36 (published in 1988 and covering translations dating from 1981–3), class 3: law, social sciences, education, indicates for the USA, 141 translations of legal works (out of a total of 1,086 in class 3) and for Switzerland, 72 translations of legal works (out of a total of 897 in class 3). The figures include some PIL works without disclosing the criteria underlying the selection of these works for translation.

f. Conferences, colloquia

International and regional conferences, congresses, symposia, colloquia and seminars are geared mainly to sharing advances in a given field of knowledge and/or (thereby) solving perceived common political, humanitarian or scientific problems. In substantive PIL terms, the often codificatory deliberations of international conferences, especially those convened by or under the auspices of intergovernmental organizations,[1] are generally intended to contribute to the 'progressive development of international law'.

International conferences have been convened for centuries, for different purposes and on numerous topics. The substantive, organizational and temporal aspects of such gatherings, but above all of their published outcome[2] (usually with a time lag of several years between the date of the conference and the date of the published records), remain difficult to assess, notwithstanding the concerted efforts by the Union of International Associations [315] to achieve bibliographic control of conference records. In general documentary terms, conference records tend to contain information that may be primary or secondary material in a given field.

For international legal and PIL conferences, documentary control of the number, periodicity or date, place and records of such conferences is problematic, and this is compounded by a lack of consensus on the type of PIL evidence such records reflect.[3] In addition to international conferences convened by or for inter-governmental organizations, there are conferences, colloquia, workshops, etc., directly or indirectly relevant to PIL, that are sponsored by non-governmental organizations, national institutions or research bodies. Outstanding among this type of conference are : (1) the annual conferences convened at the international (and occasionally at the national) level by the International Law Association [379]; (2) the annual conferences of the Société française de droit international [403] and of the American Society of International Law [387a]; (3) the workshops sponsored annually by The Hague Academy of International Law [380a]; (4) the symposia held under the auspices of the Universities of London [428a] and Uppsala [460]. Scholarly, expert contributions to these and many other, less regularly held, conferences across the globe describe the latest (often theoretical) developments of international public and private law.

Bibliographic control of and physical access to many of the aforementioned PIL-oriented conference records remain erratic at best. While a number of PIL periodicals and indexing services fairly regularly contain references to relevant conferences, tracking down the actual, preliminary or final, records[4] of such conferences (not to mention of seminars, workshops, etc.) is time-consuming or impossible. The timeliness of the potentially primary PIL evidence contained in the records of many conferences may be adversely affected by the frequent inaccessibility of such records.

NOTES

1 Franck, T.M., p. 203, in [460], refers to the procedural innovations (use of rapporteurs, professional conference services which include the translation, distribution and storage of conference records, etc.) of many IGOs, but especially of the UN, in the conduct of international conferences, which in turn generate 'negotiating momentum'.
2 Not all contributions presented at conferences find their way into print. The texts of papers submitted to conferences may undergo title or content modifications once published.
3 Working papers, preliminary drafts, addenda and corrigenda are some of the stages records, especially of international conferences convened by the UN, pass through before a final (selective or comprehensive) version of such records is published; the records of UNCLOS III [538a,b] illustrate the point. Schermers, H.G., p. 538, in [620b, vol. 2], holds that because the dynamism of international organizations influences the status of their records, these could never be 'final' sources for interpreting the decisions of these organizations. *See also* note 19, p. 21.
4 The 'International law symposium' (1983) sponsored by the AALL [415b], while exclusively concerned with the documentary evidence of international law, did not deal with the bibliographic control and citation of records containing such evidence.

See also Hanson, C.W. and James, M., 1961, Coverage by abstracting journals of conference papers. *Journal of documentation (London)*, **17**, pp. 134-149.

iii. AUXILIARY RESOURCES: REFERENCE AIDS

Within the context of the *Guide*, auxiliary PIL resources encompass bibliographic guides to and surveys of PIL and related literature (monographs, periodical articles, etc.) on the one hand, and various reference aids (biographical and institutional directories, citators, series, etc.) that are rarely specific to PIL alone on the other. Leaving aside the research versus reference aspects of auxiliary resources (*see* note 9, p. 28), the interposed, indicative nature of auxiliary resources should be underlined. In the substantive, documentary hierarchy of evidence and records, the primary evidence contained in the full text of a treaty ranks above the evidence contained in an excerpt from the treaty text, while a bibliographic reference to the title of the treaty (or the official record thereof) has indicative rather than evidentiary value. Similarly, biographical information about a scholar represents an auxiliary complement to the substantive information which that scholar provides in, say, a commentary or treatise. However, it should be noted that in the absence of certain primary PIL sources, such as collections of treaty texts or relevant documents of international state practice, certain auxiliary resources, such as indexes to treaties or digests of international practice, take on the status of interposed primary PIL sources.

Without entering into the general theory or methodology of bibliographic compilations,[1] it is worth stressing that the essential function of such compilations is to provide a key to the accumulated literature concerning a given discipline. Substantively complex, geographically dispersed and, over time, steadily increasing secondary PIL resources[2] are particularly in need of bibliographic control, which, incidentally, provides a quantitative clue to the growth rate of such materials (*see also* note 4, p. 11).

If 'a comprehensive and classified bibliography of the literature of international law' was deemed desirable in 1948,[3] different bibliographic compilations have since tended to contradict the need for a global bibliographic approach to PIL materials.[4] Whatever the approach (selective or comprehensive, general or specialized, etc.), in order to gauge the kind of coverage to be found in PIL bibliographies, both past and present, their substantive, temporal, geographic and form elements should be examined. This is generally one of the objectives of guides to PIL research.

NOTES

1 Li, T., *Social science reference sources; a practical guide*. Westport, CT: Greenwood Press, 1980, p. 288. 'Bibliographic services deal with the organizational control of information.

In theory, any device used for the purpose of locating specific information is a bibliographic service.' Walter, R. E. and Heidtmann, F., *Wie finde ich juristische Literatur*, 2nd edn. Berlin: Berlin Verlag/A. Spitz, 1984, pp. 177-183. These authors distinguish between direct subject information, '*Sachauskunft*', and indirect information concerning the literature of the subject, '*Literaturauskunft*'.

2 This is not to say that primary PIL sources are satisfactorily under bibliographic control. Rather, apart from bibliographies of and indexes to treaty collections and various bibliographic guides to national and international official materials, the lack of (substantive or documentary) consensus on what constitutes primary PIL sources compounds their bibliographic inaccessibility.

3 Referred to on p. 86, in [31].

4 Robinson, J., p. 147, in [334], considered that 'in the conditions of the 1960s the publication of such a [comprehensive] bibliography would be a vast undertaking of dubious value, involving personnel, funds, and time in such quantities as to make it prohibitive and practically unrealizable'. *See also* Cohen, M., 1960, Some bibliographic problems of public international law. *McGill law journal*, **6**, pp. 277-291. It might be noted that social scientists in general, and legal scholars in particular, tend to prefer a narrow bibliographic approach to specific subject aspects over a comprehensive canvassing of the literature of a discipline.

a. Guides to research

Bibliographic guides to PIL materials (mainly published) tend to transcend PIL bibliographic compilations in that guides often follow a typology of the materials according to their form (e.g. primary or secondary evidence, official or commercial publications, monographs or periodical articles, mono- or multilingual) and generally provide research tips for the use of the selected materials. Illustrating this approach are the guides by Williams [328], Kleckner [330] and Robinson [334].

b. Bibliographies, indexing journals

The bibliographic control of PIL materials is necessarily conditioned by their relentless growth and incessant specialization. The more and more specific and restricted PIL areas require an in-depth subject approach, and hence there are bibliographies of the law of the sea [559], space law [565], humanitarian law [614], etc. Conversely, the growing amount of general PIL materials requires broad temporal (retrospective, current), geographical and linguistic (national, regional) bibliographic approaches.

While in substance PIL materials tend to become less quickly superannuated than other legal materials, in documentary terms it is useful to distinguish between retrospective and current[1] bibliographic coverage of general PIL materials. Retrospective PIL bibliographies range from catalogues[2] such as those of the libraries of the Harvard Law School [338a], Cambridge University [340] and the Peace Palace [339a], to individual bibliographic compilations, such as Merrills [341] and Delupis [342], or to the so-called end-bibliographies.[3] Complementing these retrospective PIL bibliographies (with a worldwide coverage and an almost unbroken temporal span from the mid-nineteenth century to the 1970s) are selected bibliographies covering the 'national' output of PIL materials, which in countries such as the USA, USSR or France tend to be considerable. For geographically weighted retrospective bibliographies it may be in order to distinguish between the origin or country of publication of the bibliography and the national imprints such a bibliography records. Thus the bibliography of Soviet PIL materials [353a], published in the USSR, is to some degree complemented by and duplicated by similar bibliographies published in Great Britain [354] and the Federal Republic of Germany [355].

Many retrospective PIL bibliographies emphasize monographic publications, but the focus of current legal and PIL bibliographies (frequently referred to as indexing, less often as abstracting, journals) tends to be mainly on articles in relevant PIL periodicals and contributions to commemorative essays, conference papers, etc. The general legal indexing services *Index to legal periodicals* [364a], *Index to foreign legal periodicals* [364b] and the *Karlsruher juristische Bibliographie* [367] have since 1920, 1960 and 1963, respectively, provided current bibliographic access to the contents of legal (including PIL) periodicals and other relevant serial publications worldwide. Since 1975 the semi-annual *Public international law* [361], which covers PIL information scattered in periodicals, has been complementing, and in part duplicating,[4] the aforementioned general legal indexing services. Singly or combined, the aforementioned current bibliographies and indexing journals analyse and report the contents of nearly 1,000 legal (including the core PIL) periodicals published worldwide. However, especially in the case of some Asian and African countries, additional searches through available general national[5] and legal bibliographies may be useful.

In documentary terms, legal and PIL retrospective bibliographies and current indexing services represent inventories of relevant concepts and facts, recording titles, and sometimes contents, of selected monographic and periodical PIL materials, predominantly of the secondary resource category. The indicative value of auxiliary resources, especially of indexing journals, increases with the timely provision of information, which is itself enhanced by the physical availability of the records containing the information. At present, the 'current' awareness of substantive PIL developments is conditioned by a time lag of from 6 to 18 months between the publication of an article in a legal or PIL periodical and the reference to this article in the relevant indexing journal. Despite this time lag the continued need for bibliographic access to primary and secondary PIL materials is underscored by the fact that the rocketing publication, subscription and storage costs of such materials increasingly restrict their physical availability to a few specialized institutions and libraries.

With the advent of automated information retrieval, specialized (including law) libraries have gradually been shifting from manual to computerized operations increasingly geared to the retrieval or reference use of acquired materials. Because of the cost of publications the need for resource-sharing has come to the fore, leading to the creation and electronic searching of full text and bibliographical databases. With increasing use of general and legal (if only marginally PIL[6]) databanks [412a], there must be cooperative[7] solutions to attendant legal, documentary and technological problems.[8] The distinction between legal information and legal aspects of the computerized retrieval thereof,[9] and the right to access such information, are areas in need of exploration.

These all too cursory comments point to the growing computerized retrieval of legal and PIL information contained chiefly in secondary resources. Alongside non-official and commercial automated retrieval of information, mostly from legal and PIL periodicals and yearbooks, increased attention, often at the government or official level, has been directed to the automated retrieval of information contained in primary legal and PIL sources. At the national level (especially in common law countries) the focus has been on the automated retrieval from available, increasingly full-text, legal databases of municipal law records (legislative, statutory acts, judicial decisions, etc.) and more and more on computerized treaty information (especially indexes to treaty collections). At the international level mention should be made of the computer-assisted indexing services undertaken since the 1950s within the United Nations system. Listed in *DUNDIS* [632a], these general auxiliary resources have progressively facilitated intermediate bibliographic access to the 'main series' of the UN and SA generated international official materials. Although only a fraction of such materials is relevant to PIL, the United Nations Treaty Information System [29] represents a computerized auxiliary resource intended to facilitate access to treaties, the primary PIL source *par excellence*.

NOTES

1 Upon publication any bibliography, however 'current' at the time of compilation, assumes a 'retrospective' character. Methodologically, the distinction between a 'current' bibliography (especially if issued only once a year) and an indexing or abstracting journal issued at regular intervals is but one of degree.

2 Generally issued in book form or microform, such library catalogues not only represent specialized subject bibliographies based on extensive library holdings, but also usually permit the location of individual items in the given library.

3 The very wealth of such end-bibliographies and bibliographic notes often confers 'research' status to given treatises or encyclopaedias.

4 As far as could be ascertained no detailed analysis of the substantive and geographical complementarity or duplication of these indexing services has as yet been made. If duplicate indexing of the core PIL periodicals seems inevitable, it would be useful for us to know the type and extent of complementary indexing of legal and PIL periodicals.

5 Beaudiquez, M., *Bibliographical services throughout the world*. Paris: UNESCO, 1955-. Latest supplement 1983-4 (published in 1987). Alphabetically arranged by countries, the guide lists general national (retrospective and current) bibliographies, as well as special official materials published in a given country.

6 Collier, M., 1986, The future of information technology in law libraries. *The law librarian*, **17**(1), pp. 34-36; *see also* note 14, p. 21.

7 Establishing a 'Center for the computerization of law internationally' was among the

proposals advanced in 1967 by the World Peace through Law Center [388], but it has so far failed to materialize.
8 Mihram, D., mentions data structuring, thesaurus building, search techniques; these and related problems were discussed at the Third International Conference on Data-Bases in Humanities and Social Sciences, Rutgers University, New Jersey, USA, June 1983, summarized in *Reference services review*, 1984, **12**(1), pp. 27–34.
9 Leurquin de Visscher, L., p. 67, in [501b], distinguishes between legal information, '*information juridique*', and the legal aspects of computerized information, '*droit de l'informatique*'. The former includes the complexities, dispersal, etc. of legal documentary resources, whereas the latter concerns computer errors and ownership of computer programs.

c. Abbreviations, reviews, series

Most of the reference aids in this category only marginally concern PIL, but they should nevertheless be kept in mind for possible auxiliary information. Thus the general legal *Uniform system of citation* [369] contains a section on international law citation; similarly *Law books in print*[1] [372] and *Law books in review* [371a] on occasion refer to PIL publications.

The linguistic aspects of PIL in connection with dictionaries and terminological research have been alluded to (*see* p. 32); mention should also be made of the relevance of geographical information to international law. The geographical aspects of most PIL issues in general, and the problems of changing and contested frontiers within the interdisciplinary context of international relations and PIL in particular, require the choice of chronologically and topographically appropriate atlases and maps. However, apart from the outdated *Atlas de direito internacional* [374a], there is only a wealth of general maps and atlases. Bearing in mind the frequent modifications of country and place names, it is useful to consult the frequently updated lists of *Names of countries and adjectives of nationality* [374b] issued by the United Nations. *See also* [297, vol. 12].

In addition to the various legal series mostly issued by commercial publishers, several series issued or sponsored by law faculties, intitutes and international bodies contain publications specific to PIL issues. Among such series mention should be made of the International Law Studies [373a], Bibliothèque de droit international [373h], Grotius Classic Reprint series [410] and UNESCO's New Challenges to International Law [679b]. While sooner or later individual, monographic, titles in the various legal and PIL series tend to be referred to in relevant bibliographies, apart from a bibliography listing and analysing titles of publications issued exclusively in German-language legal and PIL series [373j], no bibliographies of legal series (and titles of publications therein) appear to exist.

NOTE

1 *Law books in print* provides bibliographic access to legal publications available in print. For full-text *re*prints, especially of PIL classics, *see* the works in the pre-1945 series of the Carnegie Endowment for International Peace [463, 464] and works in the post-1970s Grotius Classic Reprint series [410].

d. Directories (biographical, institutional)

Apart from the intrinsic substantive and evidentiary aspect of PIL materials their authors or institutional provenance also need to be considered. Biographical information about a given author of or requisite data on an institution sponsoring or publishing such materials are generally contained in that category of auxiliary resources known as directories.[1]

The 'who's who' type of directories tend to provide biographical information about practitioners (often only the most prominent) in given disciplines, worldwide or at the national or regional level. Because complex legal, diplomatic and political aspects permeate the vast domain of international law, biographical information about its protagonists is often scattered, except in the *Biographical directory of internationalists* [375]. However, since the latter includes only a restricted number of the most prominent international legal scholars, the annually issued *International who's who*, along with available national, general and specialized biographical dictionaries, should also be consulted.[2] The *Dictionnaire diplomatique* [573c] and *Who's who in the UN and related agencies* [635] contain extensive biographical notices ranging from the nineteenth to the mid-twentieth centuries.

Altogether it is easier to find biographical information concerning prominent scholars, often deceased, than data on authors with reputations in the making. Commemorative essays usually include biographies and lists of publications by the scholar honoured. Similar bio-bibliographic information generally precedes the individual scholarly contributions to the *Collected courses* [220a] of The Hague Academy of International Law.[3] In his *Teacher of international law* [499c], ICJ Justice M. Lachs provides extensive bio-bibliographical information on outstanding twentieth-century PIL scholars, many from Eastern Europe. Bio-bibliographies of the justices of the International Court of Justice are included in its *Yearbook* [662b]. Finally, it should be noted that available published proceedings of relevant national and international PIL conferences, symposia, etc. [460, 507b, 647c] generally include lists of participants complete with academic titles and institutions affiliated with.

Among the many directories providing structural and functional information relative to general and specialized, national and international academic and professional institutions, few exclusively or comprehensively cover institutional aspects of PIL. The *Directory of teaching and research institutions in international law* [377a], published by UNESCO, provides profiles of such institutions in some 50 countries (mainly in Europe and the Americas). This information is complemented by that contained globally in the *World of learning* [377]. Institutional information on over 3,000 international IGOs and NGOs, some partly or wholly relevant to PIL, is contained in the *Yearbook of international organizations* [630a].

NOTES

1 Lengenfelder, H., *International bibliography of directories/Internationale Bibliographie der Fachadressbücher*, 7th edn. München: K. G. Saur, 1983. 474 pp. Includes directories in different subjects and disciplines.
2 Farrell, M., *Who's who: an international guide to sources of current biographical information.* New York: New York Public Library/METRO, 1979. 102 pp. (METRO Miscellaneous Publications, 21); Slocum, R. B., *Biographical dictionaries and related works: an international bibliography*. Detroit, MI: Gale, 1967, 1057 pp.
3 *Livre jubilaire* [380a] is a commemorative essay honouring The Hague Academy of International Law and simultaneously providing information on its academic and institutional activities. Another example of institutional (bio-bibliographic) information is Ökrös, E., *A tudományegyetemnek jogtörténeti kutatóinak és oktatóinak publikácios tevékenysége az egyetemi és kari kiadványok tükrében, 1945-1983.* Budapest: ELTE sokszoritás, 1983. 39 pp. (Allami és jogtudomány bibliográfiák, 8). This work concerns the academic, teaching and publishing activities of the staff of Budapest University law faculty.

e. Librarianship, publishing

The survey of auxiliary resources would not be complete without a few remarks on the role of specialized law libraries in the ordering and use of the abundant and varied legal and PIL materials. Manuals on law librarianship generally deal with policies and techniques underlying the acquisition, processing, storage and information retrieval of different categories of relevant materials. Moys's manual [411a] is particularly useful as it also contains a typology and analysis of PIL materials [327]. The increasing quantity and cost of legal publications (especially periodicals) have at times given rise to calls for the pooling of legal resources at the national level,[1] but in particular for expanding the traditional scope of law libraries to that of legal information centres[2] with a focus on databases, computerized retrieval, etc. Mention should also be made of the roles the International Association of Law Libraries [415a] and the American Association of Law Libraries [415b] play in furthering cooperative, standardized law library practices in general, and in facilitating the use of national and international 'official' materials for legal and PIL research in particular.

In 1948 the need was expressed for an inventory of existing library collections specifically containing materials documenting the evidence of international customary law, as well as 'the establishment and maintenance of standard libraries of international law in different parts of the world'.[3] Until such a specific directory becomes available, guides to library subject collections (including PIL) [416] should be used in conjunction with extant national directories of law libraries and *World of learning* [377].

42 EVIDENTIARY STATUS OF MATERIALS

In addition to the very extensive law and PIL materials in the US Library of Congress [417a] and the Harvard Law School Library [417b], special mention should be made of the important collections of the Peace Palace Library in The Hague [418], the libraries of the Institute of Advanced Legal Studies in London [409] and the Max-Planck Institute for Comparative Law and International Law in Heidelberg [402a], and, last but not least, the law collections in Geneva libraries, notably the libraries of the United Nations Office [419a], and the Graduate Institute of International Studies [407a]. Complementing the aforementioned general law collections are various, often highly specialized, collections in the libraries of inter-governmental organizations.[4] Besides maintaining library collections primarily in support of a given IGO's general and functional activities, the library of a given organization is usually also the custodian of the sum total[5] of documents generated by that organization,[6] and frequently a depository[7] of relevant materials issued by other IGOs. The *Directory of United Nations databases and information systems* [632a] allows the number and kind of special collections (including international official materials) maintained and serviced (increasingly by computerized means) by libraries in the UN system to be gauged.

By virtue of their outstanding collections and specialized staff,[8] many of the aforementioned national and international libraries actively further the bibliographic control of relevant legal and PIL materials. Thus, libraries have published catalogues of their law and PIL collections [338a, 339a, 340], or issued selected topical bibliographies [530, 539a]. Apart from such retrospective bibliographies, many libraries provide current awareness services, mainly in the form of accession lists that list newly acquired monographs and draw attention to relevant articles in periodicals currently subscribed to. The *Monthly bibliography I-II* [368a] is an example of a current awareness service offering selected legal, socio-economic materials published worldwide, provided for internal and external use by the UNOG Library [419a]. The *National legal bibliography* [366a], a commercial computerized service, permits bibliographic access to the holdings (with worldwide imprints) of selected law libraries in the United States.

Among predominantly English-language periodicals regularly reporting on developments in law librarianship as well as on substantive legal and PIL issues (mainly in the form of book reviews) the pride of place belongs to the *International journal of legal information* [414a], closely followed by the *Law library journal* [414b]. Mention should also be made of the *Legal reference services quarterly* [414c], *International bibliography* [632c] and *Government publications review* [68c], which report on rather specialized aspects of library services and materials.

The need for bibliographic control in general and PIL materials in particular is partly in response to the growth in the publishing of such materials.[9] It is beyond the scope of the *Guide* to analyse the innovations[10] in publishing procedures in general, or the implications for law libraries[11] of the cost and quantity of the legal publishing output. Leaving aside the important, if complex, 'official' publishing by IGOs (*see* note 6, p. 43) or that of multiple national government bodies, suffice it to say that the bulk of commercial[12] publishing of legal and PIL works (including some dissertations) is confined to some dozen publishers, mainly in the USA, UK, France and the Netherlands [420].

NOTES

1. Mersky, R.M., 1984/5, National law library. *Law library journal*, **77**(2), p. 367, examines the possibilities of extending the scope of the US Library of Congress with a view to providing national law library services to the legal profession. Anderson, M., Bloomfield, B. and Hamilton, G., 1986, Future co-operation in library provision for law. *Law librarian*, **17**(3), pp. 91–93, show that 'the permanent constraints on the British Library precluded the possibility of setting up a national open access library on the lines of the Law Library of the [US] Library of Congress'.
2. Marke, J.J., *Planning the law library as a legal information center*. Dobbs Ferry, NY: Oceana/Glanville, 1987. (Law Library Information Reports.)
3. Referred to on p. 114, in [31]. It might be noted that the AALL-sponsored survey of foreign, comparative and international law collections in the United States (in press) should go a considerable way towards constituting a worldwide inventory of such collections.
4. International institutional libraries are not only repositories of requisite administrative and subject-oriented materials, but also provide information retrieval thereof to their staff and accredited external readers. Thus the library of the Interparliamentary Union in Geneva has built up an important collection of national parliamentary, legislative materials issued worldwide, which are much in demand by researchers.
5. The totality of a given IGO's 'documentary' output includes publications, documents (*see also* note 20, p. 21) and archival materials, often unpublished. The latter are records that permit the tracing (on the principle of the 'provenance' of the records) of the structural or functional evolution of an organization. The *Guide to the archives of the UN system* [633b] outlines the different archival collections reflecting the development of the UN and SAs. An IGO library may through its archives section be custodian of the 'historical' archival collections of the given organization, while a Records Management section (separate from the library) generally administers the 'current' archival records, notably correspondence.
6. 'Official records' (*see also* notes 18 and 19, p. 21) are only a part of the multitude of materials issued under the 'official' imprint of IGOs, especially the UN. An IGO library may through its 'documents' section be the custodian of all official (excepting archival) materials issued by the given organization. A limited number of UN and UNESCO sales publications co-produced by certain commercial publishers (e.g. Pedone, de Gruyter or Pergamon) may or may not be considered 'official' publications. The physical availability and bibliographic citation of such publications are still problematic.
7. A distinction should be made in the depository function between (1) selected international official materials generated by IGOs and stored in designated depository libraries worldwide and (2) selected materials generated by a given IGO and stored in the requisite documents section of the library of another IGO.
8. Baade, H.W., 1983, The civilizing (and civilianizing) functions of international law librarians. *Law library journal*, **76**(3), pp. 565–570.
9. Robinson, J., p. 12, in [334], considered book reviews as a 'remedy of the publication explosion', an opinion still valid today, even if book reviews cover but a fraction of titles published.
10. Aveney, B., 1983, Electronic publishing and the information transfer. *Special libraries*,

74(4), pp. 338-344. Aveney surmises that as the full texts of certain journals become available online, the number of published bibliographies and indexing services will correspondingly decline.
11 Marke, J., 1970, The gentle art of making enemies or law publishing revisited. *Law library journal*, **63**(3), p. 4. Marke contended that in the USA in the 1960s practising attorneys rather than law libraries made up the predominant market for law book publishers. With the advent of (admittedly costly) information retrieval of increasingly shared resources, the institutional and library acquisition of legal and PIL publications may have supplanted, even in the USA, the individual acquisition of such materials.
12 This category includes university presses, especially in the USA; in socialist countries the distinction would be between institutional (academic, university) and specialized (legal, technological, etc.) publishing.

CONCLUSION

To conclude the typology of PIL information sources and resources outlined in this part the following remarks might be stressed. The often tenuous distinction between the substantive and documentary aspects of published PIL materials allows us to envisage the type of substantive evidence in its normative or primary and analytical or secondary quality as it were separately from the type of documentary records (collections of treaties, law reports, treatises, etc.) containing the relevant evidence. The continued doctrinal divergence as to what constitutes PIL sources especially primary sources (e.g. the evidentiary value of IGO decisions), and their hierarchy (e.g. the subsidiary aspect of judicial decisions), as well as the frequently overlapping contents and form of documentary records (e.g. digests of state practice including judicial decisions, or the reference aspect of treatises) makes the typology of the *Guide* at best tentative.[1]

The contested evidentiary quality of primary PIL sources makes it difficult to point to relevant uncontestable documentary records. Conversely, the worldwide multilingual quantity of secondary PIL resources of needs makes for contestable selection criteria underlying the choice of the 'most representative' (in substantive, linguistic, geographic and methodological terms) among such resources. The geographic representativeness may be justly challenged given the lack in the *Guide* of general PIL treatises, textbooks and periodicals issued in African, Asian and Latin American countries. On the other hand, the abundance of secondary PIL resources in the countries of Europe and North America has at times led to the inclusion in the *Guide* of the most 'recent' rather than the most 'outstanding'[2] works in the relevant categories.

Finally, the altogether scant overview in the *Guide* of auxiliary resources points to a disparity between the relatively numerous bibliographic surveys of PIL materials proper (mainly secondary) and the comparatively few biographical, geographical and linguistic reference aids of only marginal PIL relevance.

NOTES

1 McWhinney, E., p. 351, in [462e], states that 'only a neo-positivist seeking refuge in his own pessimistic legal abstractions, is likely to strain too much . . . in worrying whether the legal principles involved can be fitted into one or other *a priori* categories of formal legal "sources" ordained by "classical" international law teachings'.
2 What makes for an outstanding doctrinal work in part depends on its context of combined legal tradition (common, civil law) and linguistic or geographic elements. Breem, W.W.S., p. 248, in [411a, 2nd edn], notes that the base of evidence has been broadened in English municipal law, i.e. whereas once only works of dead authors could be cited in English courts, increasingly treatises of (outstanding) living authors are admitted as secondary evidence. Steiner, W.A., p. 326, in [411a, 1st edn] shows the German-speaking countries to emphasize doctrinal works in the form of commentaries, whereas in countries of 'French inspiration' doctrinal works tend to be systematic expositions. Are commentaries 'more' outstanding than systematic expositions, and of the latter, are the treatises of living scholars 'less' outstanding that those of deceased authors?

The preceding typology of PIL information sources and resources is illustrated by the bibliography in Part I/B, which lists selected PIL materials according to the form of evidentiary information (primary, secondary, auxiliary) contained in such materials. Completing this bibliographic form approach is the topical approach used in Part II to draw attention to various substantive concerns with PIL in general (Part II/A-C) and a few specialized PIL areas in particular (Part II/D). Neither bibliographic approach is free of inconsistencies. Thus in Part I/B several items, despite their auxiliary 'form', have been assigned to relevant primary sources (e.g. bibliographies of treaties [25a,b]) and secondary resources (e.g. bibliographies of essays [175a-c]); similarly, some intradisciplinary items [458a, 459] in Part II/B could have equally well been assigned to general PIL in Part II/C.

Because the topical bibliography in Part II is meant to illustrate the contemporary (mostly late twentieth-century) general and specialized evolution of PIL, the items included in the bibliography appear to underscore a shift from the classical, often Eurocentric, to the modern pluralist doctrinal appraisals of PIL developments. The often ideological, revisionist aspects of the latter assessments tend to come to the fore in re-evaluations of the theoretical foundations of PIL in general [504a, 507b, 531d] or with reference to complex interdisciplinary issues of the law of the sea [540a, 544], the international law of development [723a,e], and, last but not least, the law of international organization [621a-d, 627a]. In view of the continually shifting PIL practice and theory (tenets of which are fairly inextricable from conflicting doctrinal assertions), the topical bibliography in Part II/A-D is but a signpost in the vast PIL landscape.

I/B. A Bibliography of Selected PIL Information Sources: Form Approach

i. PRIMARY SOURCES

a. Treaties

1. *Vienna Convention on the Law of Treaties*, 1969. Text of Convention in *UNITS*, vol. 1,155 (1987), pp. 331-512 and as separate UN document, A/CONF.39.27.

The Convention is the outcome of the United Nations Conference on the Law of Treaties, Vienna, 1968-9. The documents of the Conference are contained in *Official Records*. New York: UN, 1971. 303 pp. (also UN sales publication 70.V.5; UN document A/CONF.39.11). Apart from reports, proposals, the Final Act, etc. of the Conference, the *Official Records* include the text of the Convention and the comparative table of the numbering of the articles of the Convention. Part I of the Convention contains definitions relative to the law of treaties (a separate *Glossary on the law of treaties* was issued in 1969 by the UN Conference Services); Parts 2-4 refer to the conclusion, entry into force, interpretation, invalidity, etc. of treaties; part 7 concerns depositories and their registration functions; Part 8 contains final provisions relative to the signature and ratification of the Convention. The Convention aims at the codification and progressive development of the law of treaties in accordance with the UN Charter; rules of international customary law continue to apply to matters not regulated by the provisions of the Convention. For commentaries and critical evaluations (especially of the *jus cogens* principle) *see* [512a, 516a].

Collections of treaties: international

2. *United Nations Treaty Series: treaties and international agreements registered or filed and recorded with the Secretariat of the United Nations/Recueil des traités. Traités et accords internationaux enregistrés ou classés et au répertoire au Secrétariat de l' Organisation des Nations Unies.* New York: UN, 1946-, vol. 1-. Indexes. Vols 1-600 out of print but available in microfiche edition.

UNTS carries out the provision of article 102 of the UN Charter requiring that all treaties entered into by any of the UN Member States be registered with the UN Secretariat and published. Superseding *LoNTS* [4], *UNTS* contains the full treaty texts (in the original language followed by English and French translation where necessary) of bi- and multilateral treaties concluded since 1944 by states (and until 1979 also by selected inter-governmental organizations). For the period 1946-85 *UNTS* contains the texts of some 16,000 treaties. *UNTS* publishes the text in the order of the registration with the UN Secretariat of a given treaty rather than the date of the signature and conclusion thereof, and only after the treaty's entry into force. The growing number and variety of agreements concluded and filed, compounded by a number of technical difficulties, in part account for the nearly eight-year time lag between a treaty being filed or registered and its text being published in *UNTS*. Thus, volume 1,240, published in 1989, contains treaty texts 'registered or filed and recorded' to 1981, making for a retrospective rather than current coverage by *UNTS*. The computerized UN Treaty Information System [29] is intended to provide treaty information on a current basis; *see also* Tabory, M., 1982, Recent developments in UN treaty registration and publication practices. *AJIL*, **76**, pp. 350-363. There are indexes in individual *UNTS* volumes, as well as cumulative (country, subject, chronological) indexes in English and French published up to volume 400 for every 100 volumes, and thereafter for every 50 volumes; index volumes 1-14 (published 1950-1986) cover *UNTS* volumes 1-900 (i.e. treaties of 1972-3). Vambery, J. and Vambery, V., *Cumulative list and index to treaties and international agreements registered or filed and recorded with the Secretariat of the United Nations.* Dobbs Ferry, NY: Oceana, 1977, 2 vols. This is a cumulative index (according to subjects and parties) to *UNTS* treaties (nos 10,043-13,731) for the period December 1969 to December 1974; *see also* [26, 27].

3a. *Multilateral treaties deposited with the Secretary-General; status as at [year]/Traités multilatéraux déposés auprès du Secrétaire-Général; état [année].* New York: UN Office of Legal Affairs, 1949-, 1-, annual bound volume + loose-leaf annex (UN sales publication. [English; French] date. V; UN document ST/LEG [English; French]/1 + Annex).

Title varies: during 1968-80 titled *Multilateral treaties in respect of which the Secretary-General performs depository functions* (UN document ST/LEG/SER.D/1 + Annex); during 1949-67 titled *Status of multilateral conventions in respect of which the Secretary-General performs depository functions* (UN document ST/LEG/3). The annual bound volume of *MT* (arranged in topical and chronological order) provides status information (i.e. accessions, reservations, ratifications, etc.) proper; the irregular loose-leaf annex reproduces the final clauses (i.e. how a state may become party to a treaty) to most treaties listed in the bound volume. *MT* cumulates the status information listed in the monthly *ST* [3b].

—b. *Statement of treaties and international agreements registered or filed and recorded with the Secretariat of the United Nations/Relevé des traités et accords internationaux enregistrés ou classés et inscrits au répertoire au Secrétariat de l'Organisation des Nations Unies.* New York: UN Office of Legal Affairs, 1947-, 1-, monthly (since 1950 issued as UN document ST/LEG/SER.A).

Part 1 details *ex officio* agreements (i.e. before the text is published in *UNTS*); Part 2 lists the (state) filed and (UN) recorded agreements; the Annex indicates the status of treaties. Numerical (treaty) and alphabetical (subject) indexes facilitate the use of *ST*, the information in which is annually cumulated in *MT* [3a].

4. *League of Nations Treaty Series/Recueil des traités de la Société des Nations.* Geneva: LoN, 1920-46, 205 vols + General Index, 9 vols.

Preceding *UNTS* [2], *LoNTS* contains the texts (in the original language followed by English and French translations where necessary) of over 4,800 treaties concluded by members and non-members of the LoN during 1920-44. *The Chronology of international treaties and legislative measures.* Geneva: LoN, 1930-40, 11 vols, gives both a chronological index to and status information of the treaties in the *LoNTS*.

5. Hudson, M.O., *International legislation: a collection of the texts of multipartite international instruments of general interest, beginning with the Covenant of the League of Nations.* Washington, DC: Carnegie Endowment for International Peace, 1931-50, 9 vols. Reprinted by Oceana, Dobbs Ferry, NY, 1970-2.

Contains a selection of some 670 multilateral treaties for the period 1919-45, texts of which are generally omitted from *LoNTS* [4] and/or *BFST* [23]. Texts, in English and often in French, are preceded by 'editor's notes' (including bibliographic references). Each volume includes a chronological list of treaties and a subject index.

6. Parry, C., *Consolidated treaty series, 1648-1918.* Dobbs Ferry, NY: Oceana, 1969-86. 231 vols + 12 vols of Index-guides, i.e. Special chronological list, 1984, 2 vols; General chronological list, 1979-85, 5 vols; Party index, 1986, 5 vols.

Contains photoreproduced treaty texts (in the original, as well as English or French translations). The retrospective coverage of *CTS* includes Martens's *Recueil* [7] and ends where *LoNTS* [4] begins. *See also* [25c].

7. Martens, G.F., *Recueil des principaux traités d'alliances, de paix, de trêve, de neutralité, de commerce, de limites d'échanges, etc., conclus par les Puissances de*

l'Europe tant entre elles qu'avec les Puissances et états d'autres parties du monde, depuis 1761. Göttingen: Dietrich, 1791–1801. 7 vols, being the 1st edn of the 1st series.

Martens's comprehensive treaty collection was the first of its kind. It was continued, supplemented and updated (as *Nouveau recueil*) by various editors, for which *see* Martitz, F., *Der Recueil Martens: ein Beitrag zur Literaturgeschichte des Völkerrechts*. Tübingen: Mohr, 1919, pp. 22–72 (reprinted from *Archiv des öffentlichen Rechts* Band 40, Heft 1, 1921). The over 130 volumes (in five series with supplements), complete with indexes, contain texts of treaties concluded by European Powers during an almost unbroken period between the eighteenth century and the Second World War. Despite the complex numbering of the series, volumes and indexes, the *Recueil* remains an outstanding, if historical, primary PIL source.

8a. Grenville, J. A. S. and Wasserstein, B., *The major international treaties since 1945: a history and guide with texts*. London: Methuen, 1987, 528 pp. 1st edn 1974.

The collection includes texts illustrating the foundations of post-Second World War diplomacy, i.e. wartime conferences and peace treaties, as well as examples of treaties concluded by the USA, USSR and countries of South-East Asia, Middle East and Latin America. The geographical approach in this collection is complemented by the topical (security, space, environment, etc.) approach in [8b,c].

—b. Münch, I. and Buske, A., *International law: the essential treaties and other relevant documents*. Berlin: W. de Gruyter, 1985, 702 pp.

—c. Millar, T. B. and Ward, R., *Current international treaties*. London: Croom Helm, 1984, 557 pp.

—d. Reuter, P. and Gros, A., *Traités et documents diplomatiques*, 5th edn. Paris: Presses universitaires de France, 1982, 558 pp.

—e. Randelzhofer, A., *Völkerrechtliche Verträge: UNO, Beistandspakte, Menschenrechte, See-, Luft- und Weltraumrecht*, 4th edn. Nördlingen: Beck, 1987, 549 pp. 3rd edn 1983 (edited by Berber, W. and Randelzhofer, A.).

See also [130, 154, 174].

Collections of treaties: regional, national

The Americas

9. Organization of American States. *Inter-American treaties and conventions: signatures, ratifications and deposits with explanatory notes*. Washington: OAS, General Legal Division, 1948–, 1–, irregular (OAS Treaty Series, 9).

Superseding the *Pan-American Union Treaty Series* (1934–45), the *OAS Treaty Series* contains English and Spanish texts of multilateral treaties concluded among countries of the Western Hemisphere. The last volume in the *Series* was published in 1988 and covered treaties concluded in 1985. Complementing this collection of treaty texts is the *Status of Inter-American treaties and conventions/Estado de los tratados*, published annually as *OAS Treaty Series, 5*. *See also* Calvo, C., *Colección histórica completa de los tratados, convenciones de todos los Estados de la América Latina . . . desde el año de 1493 hasta nuestros dias*. A facsimile edition issued in Paris and Madrid in 1862-9, 5 vols; reprinted by Topos Verlag, Vaduz, Liechtenstein, 1978.

10a. *United States treaties and other international agreements (UST)*. Washington, DC: Government Printing Office, 1949-, 1-, annual, indexes.

Contains texts (including reservations) of treaties to which the United States has been party since 1950. The treaty texts are arranged in numerical order in which the treaties are issued by the US Department of State in slip or pamphlet form within the *Treaties and other international act series (TIAS)*. Cumulative indexes cover retrospective periods: 1776-1959, 4 vols; 1950-70, 5 vols; 1971-5, 1 vol.; 1976-9, 1 vol.; current coverage since 1982. Compiled by Kavass, I.I. and Sprudzs, A., the cumulative indexes have been published by W.S. Hein, Buffalo, NY, since 1973. *See also* Kavass, I.I. and Sprudzs, A., *Unpublished and unnumbered treaties index, 1986: a cumulative index to the US treaties and agreements not published in TIAS, through December 1986*. Buffalo, NY: W.S. Hein, 1987-, annually updated.

—b. Bevans, C.I., *Treaties and other international agreements of the United States, 1776-1949*. Washington, DC: Government Printing Office, 1968-76, 13 vols.

Contains texts of US unnumbered treaties and agreements prior to 1950; for indexes *see* [10a].

—c. *Catalog of [US] treaties (1814-1918)*. Washington, DC: Government Printing Office, 1919. Reprinted by Oceana, Dobbs Ferry, NY, 1964

Includes references to selected important treaties to which the United States was not party.

—d. *Treaties in force*. Washington, DC: Government Printing Office, 1929-, annual.

Between annual volumes the status information contained in *TIF* is updated in the US *Department of State Bulletin* and/or the *Congressional record*. *See also* Kavass, I.I. and Sprudzs, A. *Guide to United States treaties in force*. Buffalo, NY: W.S. Hein (Part I, bilateral treaties, 1982-; Part II, multilateral treaties, 1984-). This provides numerical and topical bibliographic access to treaties in force (as listed in *TIAS* or earlier treaty numbering systems). Because the USA is party to a very large number of international treaties, the texts of which have been regularly published over nearly two centuries, the retrospective and current collections of US treaties, along with their indexes and status information, also represent important information sources for relevant countries without, or with incomplete, national treaty collections. Given the complexities of US treaties, *see also* Kavass, I. I., 1983, United States treaties and international agreements: sources of publications and 'legislative history' documents. *Law library journal*, **76**(3), pp. 442-457; Sprudzs, A., 1977, Basic US sources for current research in international law: an elementary vade-mecum. *IJLL*, 5(3), pp. 347-358.

11. Wiktor, C. L., *Canadian treaty calendar, 1928-1978*. Dobbs Ferry, NY: Oceana, 1982, 2 vols.

Contains references to titles of nearly 1,500 treaties whose texts are contained in the *Canadian Treaty Series* (1928-). Arranged numerically with chronological and subject indexes; does not indicate which treaties are no longer in force.

Asia

12a. Chiu, H., *Agreements of the People's Republic of China, 1966-1980: a calendar of events*. New York: Praeger, 1981, 329 pp. (Praeger Special Studies).

Continues Johnston, D. M. and Chiu, H., *Agreements of the People's Republic of China, 1949-1967: a calendar of events*. Cambridge, MA: Harvard UP, 1968, 286 pp. Complementing the aforementioned analyses is Rhode, G. F. and Whitlock, R. E., *Treaties of the People's Republic of China, 1949-1978: an annotated compilation*. Boulder, CO: Westview Press, 1980. 207 pp.

—b. Scott, G. L., *Chinese treaties: the post-revolutionary restoration of international law and order*. Alphen a/R: Sijthoff & Noordhoff, 1975, 312 pp.

Contains a quantitative and qualitative analysis of the practice underlying over 1,600 bilateral Chinese treaties (some 950 with socialist, some 600 with Third World, and some 100 with other countries). *See also* Chiu, H., *The People's Republic of China and the law of treaties*. Cambridge, MA: Harvard UP, 1972. For references to treaty collections, mostly retrospective, of several Asian countries *see* [329].

Europe, Eastern

13. Organizatsiiā Varshavskogo Dogovora. *Dokumenty i materialy*. Editor: V. F. Mal'tsev. Moskva: Izd. Polit. Lit., 1975-; vol. 1, 1955-75, published in 1975; vol. 2, 1955-80, published in 1980; vol. 3, 1955-85, published in 1986.

Contains texts of documents concerning the Warsaw Pact. Issued in Russian by the Ministry of Foreign Affairs of the USSR, the texts have also been translated into the languages of the Pact's member countries, e.g. vol. 2: Polish edition (Warsaw, 1986); German edition (East Berlin, 1980), etc.

14. *Sbornik na mezhdunarodni dogovori deistvuvavshti mezhdu NR Bŭlgariiā i drugi dŭrzhavi; vlezli v sila prez . . . g. 1965/1966-*. Sofiiā: Nauka i Izkustvo, 1967-.

Collection of international treaties in force concluded by Bulgaria since 1965; last known volume published in 1970.

15. Halmosy, D., *Nemzetközi szerzödések, 1945-1982*. Budapest: Közgazdasági és Jogi Könyvkiadó, 1985, 674 pp.

Collection of international treaties concluded by Hungary between 1945 and 1982.

16. *Zbiór umów międzynarodowych Polskiej RL, 1954-*. Warszawa: Polski Inst. Spraw Międzynarod., 1960-.

Collection of international treaties concluded by Poland since 1954; last known volume published in 1973. For a retrospective collection see Makowski, J., *Umowy międzynarodowe Polski, 1919-1934*. Warszawa: Łazarski, 1935, 368 pp.

17. Ionascu, I., Barbulescu, P. and Gheorghe, G., *Tratalele internationale ale României; texte rezumate, adnotari, bibliografie*. Bucureşti: Ed. Stiint. si Enciclop., 1975-, 1-.

Summaries, with bibliographic notes, of international treaties concluded by Romania. Vol. 1, 1354-1920 (1975); vol. 2, 1921-39 (1980); vol. 3, 1939-65 (1983); vol. 4, 1965-75 (1986).

18a. Olkçuen, A. G. and Ökçün, A. R., *Türk antlaşmalari rehberi, 1920-1973*. Ankara, 1974, 558 pp.

Contains references to Turkish treaties concluded in the twentieth century.

—b. *Novadounghian, G., *Recueil d'actes internationaux de l'Empire Ottoman: traités, conventions, arrangements . . . relatifs au droit public extérieur de la Turquie*. Paris: Librairie Cotillon, 1897-1903, 4 vols.

Contains texts of treaties concluded by the Ottoman Empire between the fourteenth and nineteenth centuries.

19a. *Sbornik deĭstvuĭushchikh dogovorov, soglashenii i konventsii, zakliuchennykh SSSR s inostrannymi gosudarstvami, vyp. 10-35, 1954-1981*. Moskva: Izd. Polit. Lit., 1956-81. Superseded by *Sbornik mezhdunarodnykh dogovorov SSSR, vyp. 36-*. Moskva: Mezhdunarodnye Otnosheniia, 1982-, annual.

Contains the texts of treaties, agreements, etc. concluded by the USSR since 1945; until vyp. 35, 1981, it included only treaties in force.

—b. Martens, F., *Sobranie traktov i konventsii zakliuchennykh Rossieiu s inostrannymi derzhavami po porucheniiu Ministerstva Inostrannykh Del/Recueil des traités et conventions conclus par la Russie avec les puissances étrangères publié d'ordre du Ministère des Affaires Etrangères*. Sankt Peterburg: A. Böhnke, 1874-1909, 15 vols.

Contains Russian and French texts of treaties concluded by Russia between 1648 and 1906 with Austria, England, France and Germany. *See also Sbornik dogovorov Rossii s drugimi gosudarstvami, 1856-1917*. Moskva: Izd. Polit. Lit., 1952, 462 pp.

Among works (mainly analyses and indexes) in English related to Soviet treaties note: Slusser, R.M. and Triska, J.F., *A calendar of Soviet treaties, 1917-1957*. Stanford, CA: Stanford UP, 1959, 530 pp.; continued by Ginsburgs, G. and Slusser, R.M., *A calendar of Soviet treaties, 1958-1973*. Alphen a/R: Sijthoff & Noordhoff, 1981, 908 pp. The two works represent chronological lists of references to Soviet treaties concluded between 1917 and 1973, and as such in part serve as an index to [19a]. *See also* Shapiro, L., *Soviet treaty series*. Washington, DC: Georgetown UP, 1950-5, 2 vols. Based on his doctoral dissertation (1952), Shapiro analyses multilateral treaties concluded by the USSR during the period 1917-39.

20. *Međunarodni ugovori FNR Jugoslavije*. Beograd: Ministarstvo Inostranih Poslova, 1947-. Some 100 fascicules per year, last known fascicule published in 1960.

For information on current treaties concluded by Yugoslavia *see* [272]. *See also* Tchirkovich, S., Liste des traités et des engagements internationaux du Royaume de Yougoslavie, 1919-1935. In *Annuaire de l'Association yougoslave de droit international*. Beograd, vol. 2, 1934.

Europe, Western

21. *Verträge der Bundesrepublik Deutschland. Serie A. Multilaterale Verträge*, hrsg. vom Auswärtigen Amt. Bonn: Heymann, 1955-, 1-.

Contains texts of multilateral treaties concluded by the FRG since 1955. For current information *see Verzeichnis und Stand der Verträge* (1960-, 1-, loose-leaf) as well as *Fundstellennachweis. B. Völkerrechtliche Vereinbarungen und Verträge mit der DDR*, hrsg. vom Bundesministerium für Justiz. Bonn: Bundesanzeiger Verlag, 1968-, 1-, annual (supplement to *Bundesgesetzblatt*, Teil 2). *Fundstellennachweis* includes, in addition to the status of German treaties, status information on international treaties in general.

22. Pinto, R. and Rollet, H., *Recueil des traités et conventions en vigueur auxquels la France est partie*. Paris: Imprimerie nationale, 1973-5, 7 vols.

Contains the texts (formerly scattered in numerous official and other publications) of some 3,600 bilateral treaties concluded by France since 1945; to be complemented by *Recueil des traités et accords de la France*. Paris: Ministère des Affaires étrangères, 1959-, containing only agreements since 1958 published in the *Journal officiel*. Current, mainly status, information is provided by the *Liste des traités et accords de la France en vigueur au [date]*. Paris: Imprimerie nationale (subsequently Direction des Journaux officiels) 1973-, initially edited by H. Rollet, since 1982 by M.F. Surbiguet *et al*.

—a. *Censo de tratados internacionales suscritos por España*. Madrid, 1976.

Essentially an index to bilateral treaties concluded by Spain from the thirteenth century to 1975. For a retrospective collection of texts *see* Olivart, R. de Dalman, [345].

23. *British and foreign state papers*. Compiled by the librarian and keeper of the papers, Foreign Office. London: J. Ridgeway (after 1887, HMSO), 1941-77, 170 vols.

Contains the texts of the principal political and commercial documents, including texts of treaties for the period 1814-1968, as well as of treaties concluded before 1814 and still in force. Each volume contains a subject index; for a cumulative (chronological, subject) index *see* Parry, C. and Hopkins, C., *An index of British treaties, 1101-1968*. London: HMSO, 1970, 4 parts in 3 vols. *Treaty series*. Prepared by the Foreign Office. London: HMSO, 1973-, 1-. A sub-series of the 'Command Papers', *TS* contains texts of treaties, only after ratification, concluded by the UK since 1970. Annual indexes have been cumulated every three years; the last cumulation, 1977-9, was published in 1983.

Guides to treaty research

24a. Sprudzs, A., 1983, Fundamentals of foreign treaty research. *Law library journal*, **76**(3), pp. 458-463.

Emphasizes current national and international treaty developments. *See also* Sprudzs, A., 1981, Problems with sources of information in international law and relations: the case of the world-wide treaty jungle. *IJLL*, 9(5), pp. 195-202 (mainly relative to *LoNTS* and *UNTS*); Sprudzs, A., *Treaty sources in legal and political research: tools, techniques and problems, the convention and the new*. Tucson, AZ: University of Arizona Press, 1971, 63 pp. (originally presented as 'Information on recent treaties' to the Eighth International Congress of Comparative Law, Pescara, Italy, 1970); Sprudzs, A. in [10d].

—b. Parry, C., 1980, Where to look for your treaties. *IJLL*, **8**(1), pp. 8-18.

Analyses the coverage by and omissions from the *CTS*, *LoNTS* and *UNTS* and refers to some outstanding national (mainly retrospective) treaty collections and chronologies.

—c. Roberts, A. D., 1949, Searching for the text of treaties. *Journal of documentation (London)*, 5(1), pp. 136-163.

Discusses outstanding national and international treaty collections; although out of date, the survey is still useful for its concise comparative comments.

Bibliographies of treaty collections

25a. *List of treaty collections/Liste de recueils de traités/Lista de colecciones de tratados*. New York: United Nations, 1956, 174 pp. (UN document ST/LEG 5, 1955; UN sales publication 1956, V. 2). Reprinted by W.W. Gaunt/Symposia Press, Holmes Beach, FL, 1981.

Jointly prepared by the Dag Hammarskjöld Library of the UN and several law libraries in the USA, the list was intended to supersede Myers' *Manual* [25b]. The *List* contains in chronological arrangement nearly 700 general, subject and national treaty collections pertaining to 70 countries; an author, subject and title index concludes the *List*. Although out of date, the *List* remains the most 'recent' bibliography of treaty text collections.

—b. Myers, D. P., *Manual of collections of treaties and of collections relating to treaties*. Cambridge, MA: Harvard UP, 1922, 685 pp. Reprinted by Burt Franklin, New York, 1966.

Contains references to some 2,000 treaty collections estimated to total around 30,000 treaties concluded between the sixteenth century and 1914. Arranged by countries and subjects.

—c. Martens, G. F., Discours préliminaire sur les differents recueils de traités publiés à ce jour, *In* his *Recueil* [7], tome 1/supplément. Reprinted in [6], vol. 1, pp. viii–lviii.

Indexes to treaty collections

26. Bowman, M.J. and Harris, D.J., *Multilateral treaties: index and current status*. London: Butterworth, 1984, 516 pp. 2nd cumulative supplement 1985, 70 pp.; 3rd cumulative supplement 1986, 101 pp.

Computer-produced at the University of Nottingham [30c], the index provides alphabetical subject access to the chronologically arranged selection of some 800 multilateral treaties concluded between 1856 and 1986. The index entries refer to the numbers of the full texts in *UNTS* [2] and *LoNTS* [4], the treaty's title, date of conclusion, entry into force, signatories and reservations.

27. Rohn, P., *World treaty index*. Santa Barbara, CA: ABC-Clio Press, 2nd edn 1983, 5 vols. 1st edn 1974.

Computer-produced at the University of Washington [30a], the *WTI* provides bibliographic access to *UNTS* [2], *LoNTS* [4] and some 40 national treaty collections, or an estimated total of over 40,000 treaties concluded in the twentieth century (the 1st edn indexes treaties of the period 1920–70; the 2nd edn indexes those of the period 1970–80). Vol. 1 contains various reference data, including a thesaurus, statistical tables, an analysis of *UNTS* and *LoNTS*, and a survey of treaty patterns (of which an earlier separate edition was published as *Treaty profiles*, 1976, 256 pp.); vols 2 and 3 represent the main entries (chronologically 1900–59, 1960–80); vol. 4 is the party index and vol. 5 is the keyword (subject) index.

28a. Mostecky, V., *Index to multilateral treaties: a chronological list of multiparty international agreements from the 16th century through 1963, with citations to their texts*. Cambridge, MA: Harvard UP, 1965, 301 pp. Supplements 1966–8.

IMT provides bibliographic (subject and country) access to some 3,800 treaties concluded between 1596 and the mid-1960s. The index entries include reference to the source of the treaty's full text, date and place of conclusion, and signatories, but exclude status information.

—b. *Konferenzen und Verträge. Vertrags-Plötz, ein Handbuch geschichtlich bedeutsamer Zusammenkünfte, Vereinbarungen, Manifeste und Memoranden.* Bielefeld, Würzburg: A. G. Plötz, 1953-, Teil II/1-. Edited by Rönnefarth, H. *et al.*

Essentially an index, the work provides brief notes about (mostly) multilateral treaties, conference acts, declarations, etc. from the fifteenth century on. The annotations include the place, date, objective and participants of the treaties, with references to primary and secondary treaty sources. In chronological arrangement, the five volumes so far published (vol. 5, 1963-70, was published in 1975) cover treaties from 1492 to 1970.

Computerized treaty information

29. United Nations Treaty Information System (UNTIS)/Système informatisé de l'ONU pour les traités (SIONUT) Treaty Section. Office of Legal Affairs, United Nations, New York, NY 10017, USA.

Created in 1975, UNTIS is a computerized system for registering and retrieving treaty information (including ratifications, accessions, signatures). This information is available to the UN Secretariat and Member States; as yet UNTIS cannot be accessed from any other source, but should eventually be linked to UNBIS [419b].

30a. Treaty Research Center, University of Washington, Seattle, WA 98195, USA.

Directed by P. Rohn, the Center has maintained since the 1970s a bibliographical database of international and national treaty collections, the contents of which are made bibliographically accessible through the computer-produced *World treaty index* [27]. The Center provides statistical and other custom searches of its treaty database.

—b. Treaty Project, Queen's University, Kingston, Ontario, Canada.

Since the 1960s concerned with storage and retrieval of bibliographic information contained in treaties of Canada and the UK.

—c. Treaty Centre, University of Nottingham, Nottingham, UK.

Created in the 1980s, the Centre's database of multinational treaties has served to produce the treaty index [26].

b. International customary law

General

31. *Ways and means of making the evidence of customary international law more readily available.* Lake Success, NY: United Nations, 1949, 107 pp. (UN sales publication 1949.V.6; UN General Assembly. *Official records*, 4th session, 1949, supplement 10).

The 1949 publication is the outcome of the memorandum concerning 'Methods for encouraging the progressive development of international law and its eventual codification' (UN document A/AC.10/7, 6 May 1947) submitted on the basis of a preparatory study by L. Gross [192]) by the UN Secretariat to the Committee on the Progressive Development of International Law and its Codification, convened at Lake Success between 12 May and 17 June 1947. At the Committee's second meeting on 13 May 1947 the US delegate advocated an active role by the United Nations in stimulating the publication, by government or private initiative, 'of digests or other compilations . . . revealing the customary practice of States', while the Yugoslav delegate stressed the need for 'municipal instruments connected with international law' in addition to the *UNTS* [2]. *Ways and means* surveys collections, mostly pre-1945, of official and unofficial materials in terms of digests of state practice in general; reports of decisions by international adjudicatory bodies; reports of decisions on questions of international law by municipal courts; national legislation relative to international law issues; decisions by international organizations concerning the development of international law. The survey revealed a substantial if varyingly incomplete or overlapping body of primary evidence of international customary law available for some 50 countries. The Committee's recommendations for remedying the substantive and documentary shortcomings revealed by the survey to this date remain methodological yardsticks, if rarely applied. In part followed up by [32].

32. Council of Europe. Committee of Ministers. *Model plan for the classification of documents concerning State practice in the field of public international law.* Strasbourg: Council of Europe, 1968, pp. 32–43.

The *Model plan* is the outcome of Resolution (68)17 adopted by the Council of Europe on 28 June 1968, recommending the publication of digests of documents relating to the international practice of Member States in the Council, thereby implementing UN Resolution 2099(XX) of 1965 with reference to the teaching, study, dissemination and wider understanding of PIL [672a]. The *Model plan* represents a 15-part PIL classification scheme, encompassing the entire PIL (i.e. sources, subjects, jurisdiction, dispute settlement, etc.) and implicitly meant to facilitate the ordering, *inter alia*, of the evidence of state practice across the PIL spectrum.

State practice: regional, national
Africa

As far as could be ascertained, retrospective and current digests of international legal practice by African states seem largely non-existent or unavailable. Compensating in part for this is [301b].

The Americas

33a. Macdonald, R. St John (ed.), *Canadian perspectives on international law and organization*. Toronto: University of Toronto Press, 1974, 972 pp. Reviewed in *CYIL*, 1974, **12**, pp. 366-369.

An overview (rather than properly a digest) of post-1945 Canadian international practice concerning treaty-making, participation in international organizations, maritime claims settlements, etc. The chapter on 'Canadian approaches to international law' (pp. 940-954) refers to the main trends, uses and teachings of PIL in Canada, without qualifying these approaches as a specific 'national style' (p. 944).

—b. Green, L. C., *International law: a Canadian perspective* (title 81 from vol. 17 of the *Canadian encyclopedic digest*, 3rd edn). Toronto: Carswell, 1984, 352 pp.

Arranged broadly by PIL topics, the work provides a selection of Canadian doctrinal positions relative to Canadian state practice, mainly in terms of Canadian judicial decisions. Complements and updates the same author's *International law through the cases* (4th edn 1978), which is based largely on non-Canadian materials. *See also* [386].

34a. *Digest of United States practice in international law*. Washington, DC: Government Printing Office, 1973-, 1-, annual. Editor A. W. Rovine.

Continuously published (with slight title changes) since the 1880s, *DUSPIL* represents the oldest national digest of international legal practice. *DUSPIL* provides (according to a detailed classification system) summaries on treaties, executive agreements, diplomatic memoranda, legislation and federal court decisions relative to US practice in international law in a given year. The time lag between the date of publication of the annual *DUSPIL* volume and the period of the international practice covered is 2-4 years: the volume covering the 1979 practice was published in 1983. *DUSPIL* is in part complemented and updated by [236] and the quarterly section 'Contemporary practice of the United States relating to international law', in [227]. *DUSPIL* continues [34b].

—b. Whiteman, M. M., *Digest of international law*. Washington, DC: Department of State. Office of the Legal Adviser, 1963-73, 15 vols, index.

Superseding the digests of G. H. Hackworth (1940-44, 8 vols), J. B. Moore (1906, 9 vols) and F. Wharton (1887, 3 vols), the Whiteman digest covers different aspects of United States, as well as selected other national, practices of international law, spanning the period 1940-60. The index (in vol. 15) contains a list of cases, alphabetical subject headings and abbreviations. The Whiteman digest served as a model for a number of national digests, notably the French [43] and Swiss [46].

—c. *United States contributions to international organizations*. Washington, DC: Government Printing Office, 1951/1952-, 1-, annual.

The 'Report to the Congress' by the Department of State Bureau of International Organization Affairs. Arranged according to IGOs and NGOs, the Report indicates the US (financial) contributions to the UN, SAs etc.

—d. Oliver, C.T., 1977, The USA and international public law, 1900-1976. *St Mary's Law Journal* (San Antonio, TX), **9**(1), pp. 1-29; Nadelmann, K.H., 1976. International law at America's centennial. . . . *AJIL*, **70**(3), pp. 519-529; Wigmore, J., *A guide to American international law practice*. Albany, NY: Bender, 1943.

The last is a bibliographic analysis, compared to the substantive analyses of the preceding two articles.

35. Trindade, A.A.C., *Repertório da prática Brasileira do direito internacional público*. Brasilia: Fundaçao A. de Gusmão. Período 1919-40, 1941-60, 1961-81, 3 vols; Período 1899-1918 (518 pp., published in 1986). Indice general analítico (235 pp., published in 1987).

The retrospective digest of Brazilian international legal practice for the period 1899-1981.

Asia and Australasia

36a. Wang, D.T.C., *Les sources du droit de la République populaire de Chine*. Genève: Droz, 1982, 223 pp. (Comparativa, 22).

Contains extensive commentaries on constitutional, administrative and judicial state practice of modern China. Part 2 is a bibliographic survey of monographs and periodical articles published worldwide relating to law and PIL in China.

—b. Cohen, J.A. and Chiu, H., *People's China and international law: a documentary study*. Princeton, NJ: Princeton UP, 1974, 2 vols. Reviewed in *Virginia journal of international law*, 1975, **15**(1), pp. 237-241; *Journal of Asian studies*, 1975, **34**, pp. 528-531.

Contains examples of China's international legal practice, with an indication of mostly pre-1970 original Chinese sources. Vol. 2 includes a bibliography (of many Asian legal imprints) and an English-Chinese glossary of PIL terms (complementing Chiu, H., The development of Chinese international terms and the problem of their translation into English. In Cohen, J.A., *Contemporary Chinese law: research problems and perspectives*. Cambridge, MA: Harvard UP, 1970;

Bilancia, P. R., *Dictionary of Chinese law and government*. Stanford, CA: Stanford UP, 1981, 822 pp. See also Cohen, J. A., *China's practice of international law: some case studies*. Cambridge, MA: Harvard UP, 1972, 417 pp. (Harvard Studies in East Asian Law, 6).

—c. Jaschek, S., 1978, Die chinesische Völkerrechtstheorie im Lichte der Drei-Welten Theorie. *GYIL*, **21**, pp. 363-386; Kaminski, G., *Chinesische Positionen zum Völkerrecht*. Berlin: Duncker & Humblot, 1973, 369 pp. (Schriften zum Völkerrecht, 31).

37. *Singh, N., *Indian and international law*. New Delhi: Chand, 1973, Vol. 1, *Ancient and medieval* (State practice of India series).

38. Oda, S. and Owada, H., *The practice of Japan in international law, 1961-1970*. Tokyo: University of Tokyo Press, 1982, 471 pp.

See also Cohen, J. A., 1977, Japan's emerging views of international law. *ASIL* proceedings, **71**, pp. 148-169.

39. Pae, C., Chai, N. Y. and Park, C., *Korean international law*. Berkeley, CA: Institute of East Asian Studies, 1981, 53 pp.

40. Ryan, K. W., *International law in Australia*, 2nd edn. Sydney: The Law Book Co., 1984, 523 pp.

Europe, Eastern

41. Sipkov, I., 1982, The public international law of Bulgaria: development and status. *IJLI*, **10**(6), pp. 326-343.

42a. *Mironov, N. V., *Sovetskoe zakonodatel'stvo i mezhdunarodnoe pravo*. Moskva, 1968.

—b. Ginsburgs, G., 1978, Primary sources on the Soviet practice of international law: a breviary. *IJLL*, **6**(1), pp. 1-14.

See also Butler, W. E., Maggs P. B. and Hazard, J. N., *The Soviet legal system: fundamental principles and historical commentary*, 3rd edn. Dobbs Ferry, NY: Oceana, 1977, 598 pp., and [73b].

Europe, Western

43. Kiss, A. C., *Répertoire de la pratique française en matière de droit international public*. Paris: CNRS, 1962-72, 6 vols.

Based on published official legislative and judicial materials, this retrospective digest covers French international legal practice from 1789 to the 1950s. For current coverage see [282].

44. Ago, R., *La prassi italiana di diritto internazionale, 1861-1945*. Under the auspices of the Società italiana per l'Organizzazione Internazionale. First and Second Series. Reprinted by Oceana, Dobbs Ferry, NY, 1970-.

The First Series covers the period 1861-86 in 2 vols; the Second Series covers 1887-1918 in 4 vols. An index in English, French, Italian and Spanish facilitates access to this retrospective digest of parliamentary, legislative and diplomatic materials (excluding judicial decisions, for which *see* [59]).

45. Van Panhuys, H. F., *International law in the Netherlands*. Under the auspices of the T.M.C. Asser Institute, Alphen a/R: Sijthoff & Noordhoff, 1978-80, 3 vols.

A retrospective digest of Dutch international legal practice from 1813, with the focus on the post-1945 period.

46. *Répertoire suisse de droit international public: documentation concernant la pratique de la Confédération en matière de droit international public, 1914-1934*, présenté par P. Guggenheim, avec le concours de L. Caflisch, C. Dominicé, B. Dutoit et J.-P. Ritter. Basel: Helbing & Lichtenhahn, 6 vols.

A retrospective digest of Swiss international legal practice derived from numerous previously unpublished diplomatic documents, federal and cantonal circulars and decisions of the federal court. For the post-1945 practice *see* [292]; *see also* [166].

47a. Parry, C. and Fitzmaurice, G., *A British digest of international law, compiled principally from the archives of the Foreign Office*. London: Stevens, 1965-, 1-.

Projected to cover British international legal practice for the period 1860-1960, this retrospective digest is derived from published and unpublished materials of the Foreign Office and the Home Office on parliamentary debates, judicial decisions and doctrinal writings. The digest is 'something more than a collection of documents, since it has been sought to reproduce every document selected for annotating in its context' (general preface to vol. 5). The individual volumes concern specific PIL topics (e.g. vol. 2b, *Territory*; vol. 7, *Organs of state*). Each volume has a table of cases, a table of statutes and an index.

—b. Shaw, M. and Lowe, V., *British practice in international law, 1946-1980*. Cambridge: Research Centre for International law, 1983; Lauterpacht, E., *The contemporary practice of the United Kingdom in the field of international law*. London: British Institute of International and Comparative Law, 1964-71, 8 fascicules in 1 vol. (covers the period 1963-7).

—c. McNair, A.D., *International law opinions: selected and annotated*. Cambridge: Cambridge UP, 1956, 3 vols.

Traces the development of PIL through the opinions offered to the Crown by its law officers and other legal advisers during 1782-1902; while these are not law, McNair considers such opinions as 'another source of international law' (p. xviii).

See also the international legal practice by IGOs [640a, 641a].

c. Judicial decisions

International adjudicatory decisions

48a. International Court of Justice/Cour internationale de la justice, *Reports of judgements, advisory opinions and orders/Recueil des arrêts, avis consultatifs et ordonnances.* Leiden: Sijthoff, 1947/1948-, 1-.

The *ICJ Reports* contain the English and French texts of the Court's decisions, including dissenting opinions. The analytical index (in English only) published in January of each year refers to the Court's decisions of the previous year. No indexes exist for 1965, 1967-8, 1977, 1979 and 1983. The *ICJ Reports* combine and supersede the Series A Collection of judgements, Series B Collection of advisory opinions and Series A/B (1931-) Judgements, orders, advisory opinions, which were issued under the auspices of the Permanent Court of International Justice, The Hague, 1922-46. The PCIJ series are also available from the Kraus Reprint Co., New York. *See also* [49a].

—b. International Court of Justice/Cour internationale de la justice, *Pleadings, oral arguments and documents/Mémoires, plaidoiries et documents.* Leiden: Sijthoff, 1948-, 1-.

The ICJ *Pleadings* are irregularly published after the relevant decisions have been given by the Court and contain, in English and French, information concerning the given case, i.e. the text instituting proceedings, the written pleadings, the verbatim records of the oral proceedings, and documents or correspondence submitted to the Court; one or more volumes may be issued per case. The *ICJ Pleadings* supersede the Series C (1931-) *Pleadings, oral statements and documents* issued under the auspices of the PCIJ [48a].

—c. Permanent Court of Arbitration, *Reports of international arbitral awards/Recueil des sentences arbitrales.* New York: United Nations, 1948-, 1-. Vols 1-17 on microfiche; vol. 18, published in 1980, contains texts of 1966-78 awards.

Continues the *Reports of the PCA/Recueil d'actes.* The Hague, 1902-31, 18 fascicules in 3 vols. The Registry of the ICJ prepared for publication the text of the awards for the period 1920-41. Note that a digest of the PCA awards made during 1902-28 is contained in *Fontes juris gentium* [49a], Series AI, vol. 2 (published in 1931, now out of print).

—d. *The Hague Court reports. Second series, comprising the awards accompanied by syllabi, the agreements for arbitration, and other documents in each case submitted to the Permanent Court of Arbitration and to the Commissions of Inquiry under the provisions of the Conventions of 1899 and 1907 for the pacific settlement of disputes*, edited with an introduction by J.B. Scott. New York: Oxford UP, 1932, 2 vols. First series: in English, 1916; in French, 1921 (Carnegie Endowment for International Peace).

—e. La Pradelle, A. and Politis, N., *Recueil des arbitrages internationaux*. Paris: Pédone, 1905-54, 3 vols.

Vol. 1, 1798-1855 (1905); vol. 2, 1856-72 (1923); vol. 3, 1872-5 (1954). Contains (French) texts and lengthy commentaries on arbitration awards made during 1798-1875.

—f. Stuyt, A.M., *Survey of international arbitrations, 1794-1970*. Leiden: Sijthoff, 1972, 572 pp., 1st edn 1939 (covers 1794-1938).

Continues in English the work originally published in French by La Fontaine, H., *Pasicrisie internationale: histoire documentaire des arbitrages internationaux, 1794-1900*. Berne: Stämpfli, 1902, 670 pp. (microfiche edition, Zug, Switzerland: Inter-Documentation Co., 1971).

49a. *Fontes juris gentium*. Berlin: Heymann, 1931-8, edited by V. Bruns; Berlin: Springer, 1948-, edited by H. Mosler and R. Bernhardt.

Since 1948 published for the Max-Planck Institute [402a], *Fontes* represent retrospective and current digests of international (PCIJ, ICJ, PCA) and national (German) court decisions, as well as of nineteenth-century European diplomatic correspondence. *Fontes* consist of several series (complete with indexes) as follows:

Series AI. Vols 1, 3 and 4 are the *Digest of the Permanent Court of International Justice/Répertoire des décisions de la Cour permanente de justice internationale/Handbuch der Entscheidungen des Ständigen Internationalen Gerichtshofs*, i.e. decisions for the periods: vol. 1, 1922-30 (published 1931, reprinted 1964); vol. 3, 1931-4 (published 1935, reprinted 1964); vol. 4, 1934-40 (published 1963). For vol. 2 in series AI *see* [48c]. Vols 5-7 are the *Digest of the Decisions of the International Court of Justice/Répertoire des décisions de la Cour internationale de justice/Handbuch der Entscheidungen des Internationalen Gerichtshofs*, i.e. decisions for the periods: vol. 5, 1947-58 (1961, 1,256 pp.); vol. 6, 1959-75 (1978, 1,600 pp.); vol. 7, 1976-85 (in preparation). Series AI of the *Fontes* thus presents a retrospective digest in English or French of all PCIJ decisions for the period 1920-40, and a current digest of all ICJ decisions from 1947 onward. In part complementing and duplicating the *Fontes* are [49d,e].

Series AII of the *Fontes* is the *Decisions of German Courts relating to public international law* [58].

Series BI of the *Fontes* is the *Diplomatic correspondence of the European States* [569].

—b. *Répertoire des décisions et des documents de la procédure écrite et orale de la Cour Permanente de justice internationale et de la Cour internationale de justice*. Genève: Droz, 1961-.

Published (under the direction of P. Guggenheim and since 1970 of L. Caflisch) for the Graduate Institute of International Studies [407a], the *Répertoire* aims to provide an in-depth analysis in French of PIL topics and problems underlying the judicial activities and decisions of the PCIJ and ICJ. The emphasis is on the proceedings leading up to court decisions. So far, the volumes published as part of the *Répertoire* (and as the Institute's *Publications* 38, 47, 51, 53 and 54) concern the decisions of the PCIJ in the latter's formal and final, or contextual and preparatory materials, e.g. vol. 1, Marek, K., *Droit international et droit interne*, 1961, 1,017 pp.; vol. 2, Marek, K. *et al.*, *Les sources du droit international*, 1967, 1,290 pp.; vol. 3, Caflisch, L. *et al.*, *Les sujets du droit international*, 1973, 792 pp.; vol. 4, Haggenmacher, P. and Perruchoud, R., *Les compétences de l'Etat*, 1984, 1,768 pp.; vol. 5, Haggenmacher, P. *et al.*, *La responsabilité internationale: la guerre et la neutralité*, 1989, 1,639 pp.

—c. Schwarzenberger, G., *International law as applied by international courts and tribunals*. London: Stevens, 1957-86, 4 vols. Vol. 1, *General principles*, 1st edn 1945, 3rd edn 1957; vol. 2, *Law of armed conflicts*, 1968; vol. 3: *International constitutional law*, 1976; vol. 4: *International judicial law*, 1986. The essays in this collection examine the perceived seven principles of PIL (*see also* [171, 456a]) as these are manifest in the decisions of the PCIJ and ICJ. Using the inductive approach (*see* [495b]) Schwarzenberger critically evaluates the working of the international courts with reference to sovereignty, responsibility and good faith in general, and the constitutional rather than institutional instruments (UN Charter, ICJ Statute, etc.) of organizations in the UN system in particular. To some extent, Schwarzenberger's work, which is in English, complements the *Répertoire des décisions* [49a] in French (so far confined to the decisions of the PCIJ).

—d. Hambro, E. *et al.*, *The case law of the International Court/La jurisprudence de la Cour internationale*. Leiden: Sijthoff, 1952, 6 vols in 8 parts: supplements to 1973.

A digest of PCIJ and ICJ decisions for the period 1918-70.

—e. Hudson, M.O., *World Court reports: a collection of the judgements, orders and opinions of the Permanent Court of Justice*. Washington, DC: Carnegie Endowment for International Peace, 1934-43, 4 vols. Reprinted by Oceana, Dobbs Ferry, NY, 1969.

A digest of PCIJ decisions for the period 1922-42. *See also* his *Cases* [83].

—f. Moore, J.B., *International adjudication, ancient and modern: history and documents*. New York: Oxford UP, 1929-33, 6 vols (Publications of the Carnegie Endowment for International Peace, Modern Series, 1-6).

A selection of (mostly common law) court decisions relative to PIL, based on materials not readily available in other law reports.

50. *International law reports*. London: Butterworth, 1950-86, vols 17-72; Cambridge: Grotius Publications, 1987-, vols 73-. Editor E. Lauterpacht. Cumulative indexes for vols 1-35 and 35-45.

ILR superseded the *Annual digest [and reports] of public international law cases*. London: Longmans & Green, 1929-47, 11 vols. Editor H. Lauterpacht, until 1942. This covered the period 1919-42. *ILR* provides authoritative reports and summaries of decisions by international, regional and selected national courts relating to international law; the reports comprise the (abridged) court decision and relevant contextual facts (including the legal contentions of the parties, principles upon which decisions were based, etc.) The extensive coverage by *ILR* has been questioned by G. Schwarzenberger (preferring selected cases embodying new or important principles) and C. Parry (against the inclusion of national court decisions).

Regional or national adjudicatory decisions

51. Parry, C. and Hopkins, J. A., *Commonwealth international law cases*. Dobbs Ferry, NY: Oceana, 1974-85, 11 vols.

Includes relevant PIL decisions of tribunals in Commonwealth countries and the jurisprudence of all overseas British courts. *See also* McGowan, Y. H., *A guide to Commonwealth law reports, legislation and journals in the Lincoln's Inn Library*, 2nd edn. London: The Library, 1967, 79 pp.

The Americas

52. Mackenzie, N. and Laing, L. H., *Canada and the law of nations: a selection of cases in international law, affecting Canada or Canadians*. New York: Kraus Reprints, 1972.

53. *American international law cases*. Dobbs Ferry, NY: Oceana, 1971-, 1-, index.

Reports decisions of US courts relative to international law from 1783 on. Edited by F. Deak, vols 1-20 report decisions during 1783-1968; edited by F. S. Ruddy, vols 21-31 report decisions during 1969-78; edited by B. D. Reams (the 2nd series), vols 32- report decisions from 1979 on. A loose-leaf index, published in 1989, provides contents, subjects and cases up to 1986.

54a. Ruiz Moreno, I., *El derecho internacional público ante la Corte Suprema*, 2nd edn. Buenos Aires: EUDEBA, 1970, 280 pp.

—b. *El derecho internacional interpretado por la Corte Suprema de la Nación, 1863-1956*, Introducción R. Rodriguez Araya. Rosario: Universidad Nacional del Litoral, 1958, 284 pp.

Asia

55. *Tandon, M. P. and Tandon, R., *Cases on international law*, 3rd edn. Allahabad: Allahabad Law Agency, 1982.

See also *International Law Reporter*. New Delhi, 1970-, 1-.

56. *Oda, S. and Sogawa, T., *Judicial decisions of the Japanese courts involving international law*. Tokyo, 1978.

57. *Jayakumar, S., *Public international law cases from Malaysia and Singapore*. Singapore: Singapore UP, 1974, 458 pp.

Europe, Western

58. *Deutsche Rechtsprechung in völkerrechtlichen Fragen/Decisions of German courts relating to public international law/Décisions des cours allemandes en matière de droit international public*. Berlin: Springer, 1956-, 1-, every five years. Editor H. Mosler.

Series AII of *Fontes juris gentium* [49a]. Reports decisions by the courts of (East and West) Germany relative to PIL since 1879; chapter 17 concerns the international legal status of post-1945 German states. The first two volumes of the work were titled *Die Entscheidungen des deutschen Reichsgerichts in völkerrechtlichen Fragen* and covered decisions for 1879–1929 (published in 1931, reprinted in 1969) and for 1929–45 (published in 1960). *Deutsche Rechtsprechung* covers decisions from 1945 onward, i.e. [AII] vol. 3, 1945–49 (published in 1956), etc.; [AII] vol. 9, 1981–5 (published in 1989).

59. Lamberti-Zanardi, P. et al., *La giurisprudenza di diritto internazionale*. Napoli: Jovene, 1973, 2 vols.

Vol. 1 reports decisions of Italian courts for 1861–75, vol. 2 for 1876–90.

60. *Repertorium op de nederlandse volkenrechtelijke rechtspraak, 1839–1978*. The Hague: T.M.C. Asser Instituut. Afdeling Volkenrecht, 1980, 134 pp. Supplements 1–3, 1981–3.

61. Parry, C., *British international law cases: a collection of decisions of courts in the British Isles on points of international law*. Under the auspices of the British Institute of International and Comparative Law. London: Stevens; Dobbs Ferry, NY: Oceana, 1964–73, 9 vols.

Contains decisions of courts in the British Isles from the Middle Ages to 1970, as well as decisions of the Judicial Committee of the Privy Council and the Court of Appeal for British overseas territories.

d. Official publications

62a. *Catalogue des sources de documentation juridique dans le monde*, établi par le Comité international de droit comparé avec le concours du Comité international pour la documentation des sciences sociales/*A register of legal documentation in the world*, prepared by the International Committee of Comparative Law with the support of the International Committee for Social Science Documentation, 2nd rev. enlarged edn. Paris: UNESCO, 1957, 423 pp. 1st edn 1953, 362 pp.

Although it is out of date, with its worldwide coverage the *Register* represents 'an inventory of the most universally and commonly used sources of' law, notably constitutions, codes and/or collections of law, official gazettes, law reports, etc. Arranged alphabetically by the French names of countries or regional entities, the *Register* lists, in addition to principal national legal sources, institutions engaged in legal research, as well as periodicals and bibliographies in the field of law; as such the *Register* in part complements the section on national official materials contained in [31]. Reviewed in [371b].

—b. *Katalog iuridicheskikh dokumentatsionnykh istochnikov sotsialisticheskikh stran/ Catalogue des sources de documentation juridique des pays socialistes/Verzeichnis der juristischen Dokumentationsquellen der sozialistischen Länder* [edited by L. Nagy]. Potsdam-Babelsberg: Akademie für Staats- und Rechtswissenschaft der DDR. Informationszentrum Staat und Recht, 1976-8, 5 vols (Spezialbibliographien zu Fragen des Staates und des Rechts, 16).

Vol. 1, USSR, German Democratic Republic; vol. 2, Hungary, Poland; vol. 3, Yugoslavia, Romania; vol. 4, Bulgaria, Czechoslovakia; vol. 5, supplementary information relative to these countries. Each volume lists references to primary and secondary legal sources, as well as institutions engaged in legal research; as such the *Katalog* complements and updates the information contained in [62a].

63a. Blaustein, A.P. and Flanz, G.H. (eds), *Constitutions of the countries of the world: a series of updated texts, constitutional chronologies, and annotated bibliographies.* Dobbs Ferry, NY: Oceana, 1971-, in 1988 17 vols + supplemental binder.

This loose-leaf collection provides periodically updated English-language texts of some 160 national constitutions. The inconsistent citation of original sources complicates the checking of the accuracy of the translated texts (especially of amendments). Complemented by Blaustein, A.P. (ed.), *Constitutions of dependencies and special sovereignties.* 1975-, 7 binders in 1988.

—b. Peaslee, A.J. (ed.), *Constitutions of nations*, 4th rev. edn. The Hague: Nijhoff, 1968-74, 4 vols, 3rd edn 1964.

Contains texts in English with references to original primary and secondary sources.

—c. *Corpus constitutionnel: recueil universel des constitutions en vigueur.* Leiden: Brill, 1968-.

Published for the Union académique internationale, the *Corpus* provides texts in French and original language; vol. 3 (1983) covers Cuba.

64a. *Constitutions of African States*, by the Secretariat of the Asian-African Legal Consultative Committee. Dobbs Ferry, NY: Oceana, 1972, 2 vols.

English texts of some 40 African constitutions.

—b. *Constitutions of Asian States*, by the Secretariat of the Asian-African Legal Consultative Committee. Bombay: Tripathi, 1968.

65a. *Konstitutsii sotsialisticheskikh gosudarstv: sbornik v dvukh tomakh*. Moskva: IUridicheskaia Literatura, 2 vols.

See also *Durdenevskiĭ, V. N., *Konstitutsii stran narodnoĭ demokratii*. Moskva, 1958.

—b. Simons, W. B., *The constitutions of the Communist world*. Alphen a/R: Sijthoff & Noordhoff, 1980, 644 pp.

Contains texts in English of European and some Asian socialist countries' constitutions. Supersedes Triska, J., *Constitutions of the Communist Party States*. Stanford, CA: Hoover Institution on War, Revolution and Peace, 1968.

—c. Feldbrugge, F. J. M., *The constitution of the USSR and the Union Republics*. Alphen a/R: Sijthoff & Noordhoff, 1979.

66. Roberts, J. E., *A guide to official gazettes and their contents*. Washington, DC: Library of Congress, 1985. 204 pp.

Based on the extensive holdings of the US Library of Congress. *See also Government gazettes: an annotated list of gazettes held in the Dag Hammarskjöld Library*. New York: UN, 1964, 50 pp. (UN document ST/LIB/SER.B/10); *Analysis of materials published regularly in official gazettes*. Geneva: UNOG Library, 1958, 38 pp. (The Library's Miscellaneous Bibliographies. New Series, 1). *See also* [72b].

67a. Cherns, J. J., *Official publishing: an overview. An international survey and review of the role, organisation and principles of official publishing*. Oxford: Pergamon, 1979, 527 pp. (Guides to Official Publications, 3).

Examines various aspects of official/governmental publishing in 20 countries in Europe, North America and Asia, as well as by selected IGOs (this information is updated in [631b]).

—b. Pemberton, J. E., *The bibliographic control of official publications*. Oxford: Pergamon, 1982. 172 pp. (Guides to Official Publications, 11).

See also Survey on the present state of bibliographic recording in freely available printed form of government publications and those of intergovernmental organizations, prepared by F. Sinnaswamy for the International Congress on National Bibliographies, Paris, 1977. Paris: UNESCO, 1977, 160 pp. (UNESCO document PGI.77/UBC/Ref.4) covering 87 countries, 42 IGOs; Meyriat, J., *A study of current bibliographies of national official publications: a short guide and inventory*. Paris: UNESCO, 1958, 260 pp. (UNESCO Bibliographical Handbooks, 7).

68a. *Guides to official publications*. Oxford: Pergamon, 1975-. Editor of the series J. E. Pemberton.

Individual volumes deal with the publishing [67a] and bibliographic control [67b] of official materials in general, as well as in selected countries (*see also* [69, 70, 71]).

—b.   Hernon, P. and McLure, C.R., *Public access to government information*, 2nd edn. Norwood, NJ: Ablex Publishing, 1988, 524 pp.

Chapter 19 concerns materials issued by IGOs (updating information in [631b]).

—c.   *Government publications review: international journal of issues and information resources*. Elmsford, NY: Pergamon, 1974–, 1–, bimonthly.

Contains information on current national and international official publications developments.

—d.   *Availability and use of official publications in libraries*. Paris: UNESCO/PGI and UNISIST, 1983, 140 pp. (UNESCO document PGI-83/WS/30).

69a.   Johansson, E. (ed.), *Official publications of Western Europe*. London: Mansell, 1984–, 1–.

Vol. 1 covers official/governmental publications in Denmark, Finland, France, Ireland, Italy, Luxembourg, the Netherlands, Spain and Turkey. For each country it contains information on: the structural outline of its government; main categories of official (and/or legislative) publications; the publishing and acquisition of such publications; bibliographical notes. Vol. 2 covers official publications in Austria, Belgium, FRG, Greece, Norway, Portugal, Sweden, Switzerland and the UK.

—b.   Englefield, D., *Parliament and information: the Westminster scene*. London: The Library Association, 1981, 132 pp.

Complements Pemberton, J.E., *British official publications*, 2nd edn. London, 1974.

70.   Walker, G. (ed.), *Official publications of the Soviet Union and Eastern Europe, 1945–1980: a select annotated bibliography*. London: Mansell, 1982, 620 pp.

71.   Schwarzkopf, L.C. (comp.), *Government reference books: a biennial guide to US government publications*. Littleton, Co: Libraries Unlimited, 1984, 394 pp.

Complemented by Schwarzkopf, L.C., *Government reference serials*. Englewood, CO: Libraries Unlimited, 1988, 344 pp.
See also Federal information sources and systems: a directory issued by the Comptroller General, US General Accounting Office. Washington, DC: GPO, 1980, 1,178 pp. (Congressional Sourcebook series, PAD-80-50).

72a.   *Annuaire de législation française et étrangère*. Paris: CNRS, 1954–, annual (since 1979 twice a year).

Superseded *Annuaire de législation étrangère*. Paris: Société de législation comparée, 1872–1938. The new series, begun in 1954, provides information (for the periods 1938–49, 1950–) on legislative evolution worldwide, with special reference to different fields of law and/or legal procedures.

—b.   Reynolds, T.H. and Flores, A.A., *Foreign law: current sources of codes and basic legislation in jurisdictions of the world*. Littleton, CO: F.B. Rothman, 1989–, 1– (AALL Publications series, 33).

This documentary guide (to be published in three volumes by 1991) provides bibliographic citations to primary materials including legislation, codes, official gazettes, etc.; references to available English translations and/or secondary resources (in English) are also indicated. Vol. 1, *Western Hemisphere* (1989); vol. 2, *Europe (Eastern, Western and European Communities)* (1990): vol. 3, *Africa, Asia, Australia* (1991).

73a. *Encyclopedia of Arab legislation*. Cairo: The Arab League, 1978-, 1-, loose-leaf. In Arabic. *See also* [429d].

—b. *Collected legislation of the USSR and the constituent Union Republics*. Editor W. E. Butler. 1978-, 1-, loose-leaf.

Contains texts in English of selected Soviet (federal, republic) constitutional and legislative documents.

ii. SECONDARY RESOURCES

a. Treatises, manuals, textbooks

74. Williams, J. W., 1984, International law textbooks: a review of materials and methods. *International Lawyer*, **18**(1), pp. 173-250.

An analysis of Anglo-American PIL textbooks considered in terms of their traditional (casebooks, hornbooks/treatises, manuals) and contemporary (problem-solving, case studies) forms and functions. For a similar review of mostly pre-1960s PIL textbooks predominantly by North American authors *see* Falk, R., in [500c].

75. *Manuel d'initiation de l'Unesco au droit international public*, sous la direction de M. Bedjaoui. Paris: UNESCO Press, in press. The English edition, *Unesco handbook on public international law*, is in preparation.

The handbook contains contributions by PIL scholars throughout the world on various, sometimes controversial, topics and aspects of PIL.

76. Sørensen, M. (ed.), *Manual of public international law*. London: Macmillan, 1968, 930 pp. Reprinted in 1978.

This is a collection of essays on different PIL aspects and topics by PIL scholars throughout the world. Issued under the auspices of the Carnegie Endowment [381], the contributions include: C. Parry on the law of treaties; M. Virally on PIL sources; N. Mujerva on PIL subjects; A. el-Erian on the legal organization of international society; B. G. Murty on the settlement of disputes, etc. For bibliography *see* [333].

Africa

With the exception of works, mostly inaccessible, in Arabic in North Africa and in Afrikaans or English in South Africa, as far as could be ascertained treatises and manuals on general PIL appear rarely to have been published in newly independent African countries. However, several scholars from Africa have contributed to the contemporary perception of the dynamic development of international law. Mention should be made in particular of the writings (published mostly outside of Africa) of two ICJ justices, T.O. Elias of Nigeria and M. Bedjaoui of Algeria. The endeavours of the latter have brought about, among many other PIL works, the *UNESCO handbook on public international law* [75]. For other contributions by scholars from or relating to Africa on various specialized aspects of PIL *see* [482a, 486].

The Americas

Canada

77. Williams, S.A. and de Mestral, A.L.C., *An introduction to international law: chiefly as interpreted and applied in Canada*. Toronto: Butterworth, 1979, 338 pp. (Butterworth Basic Text series). Published in French as *Introduction au droit international public*, 1981, 340 pp.

78. Cassel, J.-G., *International law, chiefly as interpreted and applied in Canada*, 3rd edn. Toronto: Butterworth, 1976, 1,268 pp. (Canadian Legal Casebook series). 1st edn 1965.

79. Morin, J.-Y., *Cours de droit international public*. Montréal: Librairie de l'Université de Montréal, 1972, 3 vols.

For references to further treatises and other material published in Canada *see* [348a].

United States of America

80. McDougal, M.S. and Reisman, W.M., *International law in contemporary perspective: the public order of the world community, cases and materials*. Mineola, NY: Foundation Press, 1981, 1,584 pp. (University Casebook series).

The textbook (intended for a 14 week course) illustrates McDougal's conceptual framework (the world order/community) and interdisciplinary approach (linking PIL with international relations). The focus is on the 'process of authoritative decisions' relative to the strategies by which participants (mainly states) in the world order shape and share material, military and legal power. Complementing this textbook are various world order studies [445a–c,] and contributions in [507b].

81. Weston, B.H., Falk, R.A. and D'Amato, A.A., *International law and world order*. St Paul, MN: West Publishing, 1980.

Accompanied by a separate, chronologically arranged collection of *Basic documents in international law and world order*, this teaching manual outlines selected PIL issues and problems within the context of a dynamic international legal community. *See also* D'Amato, A.A., *International law: process and prospect*. Dobbs Ferry, NY: Oceana/Transnational, 1986, 250 pp. This work is a collection of the author's articles, with a postscript on the undervalued role of PIL in American legal education.

82. Rhyne, C. S., *International law*. Washington, DC: CLB Publishers, 1971, 685 pp.

The author, president of the World Peace through Law Center [388], approaches PIL and international organization in terms of their combined role in the furtherance of peace and disarmament.

83. Sweeney, J. M. et al., *The international legal system: cases and materials*. Mineola, NY: Foundation Press, 1981, 1,371 pp. (University Casebook series).

Continues the PIL casebook approach perfected in the USA by Hudson, M. O., *Cases and materials on international law*, 3rd edn. St Paul, MN: West Publishing, 1951; Bishop, W. W., *International law: cases and materials*, 3rd edn. Boston: Little, Brown & Co., 1971; and Henkin, L. et al., *International law: cases and materials*. St Paul, MN: West Publishing, 1980. *See also* note 7, p. 29.

Cuba

84a. D'Estefano Pisani, M. A., *Fundamentos del derecho internacional público contemporáneo*. La Habana, 1938, 2 vols (Ministerio de educación superior. Cursos dirijidos). Earlier editions (with slight title variations) published in 1965 and 1980.

Vol. 1 includes chapters on decolonization, underdevelopment, the international community and the process of 'regionalization'; vol. 2 deals with international relations in general, and neutrality and war in particular. Includes cases and bibliographies. *See also* his *Cuba, Estados Unidos y el derecho internacional contemporáneo*. La Habana: Editorial de ciencias sociales, 1938, 348 pp.

—b. de Bustamente y Sirven, A. S., *Derecho internacional público*, 2nd edn. La Habana, 1938-9, 2 vols.

An abridged, updated version was published as *Manual de derecho internacional público*, 4th edn. La Habana: Mercantil, 1947, 765 pp.

Dominican Republic

85. *Arias, L., *Derecho internacional público*. Santo Domingo, 1984, 684 pp.

Mexico

86. *Sepúlveda, C., *Derecho internacional*, 11th edn. Mexico, DF: Porrua, 1980.

87. *Seara Vazquez, M., *Derecho internacional público*, 8th edn. Mexico, DF: Porrua, 1982.

88. *Szekely, A., *Instrumentos fundamentales de derecho internacional público*. Mexico, DF: Universidad Nacional Autónoma de México, 1981, 482 pp.

Nicaragua

89.   Arguello, A. M., *Manual de derecho internacional*. Managua, 1969, 226 pp.

Includes an analysis of the Latin American doctrine of the recognition of states or governments, and a selection of Nicaraguan PIL cases.

El Salvador

90.   *López Jiménez, R., *Tratado de derecho internacional público*. San Salvador, 1970, 2 vols.

Argentina

91.   *Moncayo, G. R. et al., *Derecho internacional público*. Buenos Aires: V. D. de Zavalia, 1977.

92.   Ruda, J. M., *Instrumentos internacionales*. Buenos Aires: Tipografía Editora Argentina, 1976, 787 pp.

Arranged under broad PIL topics, this is a selection of basic post-1945 PIL texts in Spanish, including: the UN and OAS charters; the Law of the Sea Convention of 1958 (supplemented by the 1970 Lima and Montevideo declarations); the Vienna conventions (on the law of treaties; diplomatic relations); documents of the OAU and the Arab League; the Antarctic Treaty; and a selection of 'problemas internacionales argentinos' on pp. 721–760. Texts on the law of war are excluded. Contains a detailed subject index.

93.   Halajczuk, B. T. and del R. Moya-Dominguez, M. T., *Derecho internacional público*. Buenos Aires: EDIAR, 1972, 740 pp.

In addition to traditional PIL topics, Chapter 6 deals with controversial aspects of sanctions and war. The extensive bibliography includes references to Argentinian PIL scholars on pp. 699–711.

Mention should also be made of the nineteenth century classic, C. Calvo (of the Calvo doctrine and clause on the elimination of diplomatic protection in contractual claims), notably his *Le droit international théorétique et pratique, précédé d'un exposé historique des progrès de la science du droit des gens*, 5th edn. Paris: Rousseau, 1888–96, 6 vols. The Spanish edition was published in Paris, 1868.

Brazil

94.   Trindade, A. A. C., *Princípios do direito internacional contemporâneo*. Brasilia: Editora Universidade de Brasilia, 1981, 268 pp.

95.   Accioly, H. P. P., *Manual do direito internacional público*, 11th edn. São Paulo: Saraiva, 1978, 401 pp.

The *Manual* (revised by G. E. do Nascimento Silva) is an abridged version of Accioly's *Tratado do direito internacional público*, 2nd edn, Rio de Janeiro, 1956, 3 vols; the 1st edn, 1933–5, was translated into French and Spanish.

Chile

96. *Llanos Mansilla, H., *Teoría y práctica del derecho internacional público*. Santiago de Chile: Editorial Jurídica de Chile, 1983, 3 vols.

97. Benadava, S., *Derecho internacional público*. Santiago de Chile: Editorial Jurídica de Chile, 1976, 448 pp.

The traditional outline of PIL is concluded with 'el sistema inter-americana', reproducing excerpts from texts relative to selected Latin American, OAS treaties. For a nineteenth-century classic *see* Bello, A. (who was born in Venezuela, and undertook diplomatic and teaching activities mainly in Chile), *Principios de derecho internacional*. Madrid, 1883, 2 vols.

Colombia

98. *Gaviria Lievano, E., *Derecho internacional público*, 2nd edn. Bogotá: Universidad Externado de Colombia, 1985, 565 pp.

99. Camargo, P. P., *Tratado de derecho internacional*. Bogotá: Temis, 1983, 2 vols.

Based on the author's *Derecho internacional*, 1973-5, 3 vols, the *Tratado* centres on international legal issues of the world community at the close of the twentieth century. Vol. 1 deals with the evolution and content of general PIL; vol. 2 with specialized aspects of PIL, including 'el derecho de la sociedad internacional'.

Peru

100. *Solari Tudela, L., *Derecho internacional público*. Lima, 1983, 245 pp.

Uruguay

101. Jiménes de Arechaga, E., *El derecho internacional contemporáneo*. Madrid: Tecnos, 1980, 379 pp. (Semilla y surco: Colección de ciencias sociales. Serie de relaciones internacionales).

Based on his earlier *Curso de derecho internacional público*. Montevideo: Centro Estudiantes de Derecho, 1959-60, 2 vols. *See also* his International law in the past third of a century. *RCADI*, 1978/I, **159**, pp. 1-344.

Venezuela

102. Toro Jiménez, F., *Manual de derecho internacional público*. Caracas: Facultad de Ciencias Jurídicas y Políticas, Universidad Central de Venezuela, 1982, 2 vols.

Asia

People's Republic of China

103. *Zhou Gengsheng [*Public international law*]. Beijing, 1981, 815 pp. In Chinese.

104. Pan Baocun, Z. G. [*Chinese theories of international law*]. Beijing, 1988. 220 pp. Reviewed by R. Heuser in *Archiv für Volkerrecht*, 1989, **27**(2), pp. 218-223. Cf. [36c].

See also [36a,b].

India

105. *Kapoor, S. K., *A textbook of international law*, 6th edn. Foreword by N. Singh. Allahabad: Central Law Agency, 1985, 722 pp.

106. Hingorani, R. C., *Modern international law*, 2nd edn. Dobbs Ferry, NY: Oceana, 1984, 472 pp. 1st edn, *Studies in international law*. Dobbs Ferry, NY: Oceana, 1981, 115 pp.

The author, dean of the Law Faculty at Patna University, approaches traditional PIL issues from the perspectives of the Third World; section 3 discusses recent PIL trends, including humanitarian law, terrorism, multinationals, environmental law, etc.

107. *Tandon, M. P. and Tandon, R., *An introduction to international law*. Allahabad: Allahabad Law Agency, 1982. Earlier edition in 1961.

See also *Bhattacharya, K. K., *Public international law*, 5th edn, with supplement by S. N. Misra. Allahabad: Central Law Agency, 1976.

Japan

108. Takano, Y., *Einführung in das Völkerrecht*. Köln: Heymanns, 1979-84, 2 vols.

The German translation of all but Chapter 4 in vol. 2 (Dispute settlement) of the original second Japanese edition (1969-82); reflects the 'classical' textbook approach to PIL, including the law of international organization.

Sri Lanka

109. *Amerasinghe, C. F., *Studies in international law*. Colombo: Lake House Investments Ltd, 1969, 321 pp.

Eastern Europe

Albania

110. *Puto, A., *E drejta ndërkombëtare publike* [Public international law]. Tirana, 1985-6, 3 vols (vol. 3 by Puto, A. and Krisafi, K.).

For extensive German commentaries *see* Frenzke, D., Das albanische Völkerrechtslehrbuch. *Osteuropa Recht*, 1987, **33** (2), 134-156; **33** (3), 214-238; 1988, **34** (4), 279-292.

Bulgaria

111a. Kamenov, E. *et al.*, *Georgi Dimitrov i niakoĭ problemi na mezhdunarodnoto pravo i mezhdunarodnie otnosheniia*. Sofiia: Bulgarskata Akademiia na Naukite, 1977, 217 pp.

An outline of PIL within the context of peace and security, mainly in terms of socialist internationalism.

—b. *Sbornik dokumenti i normativni materiali do mezhdunarodno publichno pravo. Sofii͡a: Sofiiski Univerzitet, 1974-, 1-.

Selection of basic PIL texts, periodically updated.

112. Genovski, M., *Osnovi na mezhdunarodnoto pravo*, 3rd edn. Sofii͡a: Nauka i Izkustvo, 1969, 454 pp. 1st edn 1956; 2nd edn 1966.

The textbook contains a traditional PIL outline and includes a French summary. The bibliography provides references mostly to Soviet authors or to Russian translations of East European PIL publications.

Czechoslovakia

113. Potocny, M., *Mezinárodni právo veřejné*, 2nd rev. edn. Praha: Panorama, 1978, 451 pp. 1st edn 1973.

The textbook provides a traditional PIL outline, including the law of international organization. Contains a bibliography and subject index.

114a. Srnska, M. and Toman, J., *Uvod do mezinárodního práva veřejného*. Praha: Statni Pedagogické Nakladatelstvi, 1968-71, 2 vols.

An introduction to PIL, it exists also in English and French translations (both published in 1971).

—b. Outrata, V., *Mezinárodni právo veřejné*. Rev. edn. Praha, 1969, 291 pp. 1st edn 1960.

115. *Dokumenty ke studiu mezinárodního práva a politiky*. Praha: Státni Naklad. Polit. Lit., 1982. Earlier editions published in 1977, 1965, 1963 and 1957.

A selection of basic texts concerning PIL and international relations; may be complemented by Outrata, V., *Dokumenty ke studiu mezinárodního práva a politiky*. Praha, 1963-70, 3 vols.

German Democratic Republic

116. Graefrath, B. (ed.), *Probleme des Völkerrechts*. Berlin: Akademie-Verlag, 1987, 360 pp.

Published under the auspices of the Akademie der Wissenschaften der DDR, Institut für Theorie des Staates und des Rechts, this collection of essays contains socialist perceptions of contemporary PIL presented within the context of international relations. Continues and updates *Probleme des Völkerrechts: Beiträge*. Berlin: Akademie-Verlag, 1985, 334 pp.

117. Oeser, E. and Peggel, W. (eds), *Völkerrecht: Grundriss*, 2nd edn. Berlin: Staatsverlag der DDR, 1988, 287 pp. 1st edn 1983.

This outline of PIL is complemented by Kröger, H. (ed.), *Völkerrecht: Lehrbuch*, 2nd edn. Berlin: Staatsverlag der DDR, 1981-2, 2 vols, published under the auspices of the Akademie für Staats- und Rechtswissenschaften der DDR, Institut für internationale Beziehungen, Arbeitsgemeinschaft für Völkerrecht.

118. Morgenstern, P. (comp.), *Völkerrecht: Dokumente*, 2nd edn. Berlin: Staatsverlag der DDR, 1980, 3 vols.

A collection of basic PIL texts published under the auspices of the Akademie für Staats- und Rechtswissenschaft der DDR, Institut für Internationale Beziehungen, Arbeitsgemeinschaft für Völkerrecht.

Hungary

119. Harászti, Gy., Herczeg, Gy. and Nagy, K. (eds), *Nemzetközi jog*. Budapest: Tankönyvkiadó, 1983, 490 pp. (Egyetemi tankönyv).

A periodically updated traditional PIL outline; the 4th edn, 1968, was edited by L. Buza and Gy. Hajdú.

120. Posta, I. (comp.), *Nemzetközi jogi dokumentgyüjtemény*. Budapest: Tankönyvkiado, 1984, 456 pp.

A selection of basic PIL texts.

Poland

121. Goralczyk, W., *Prawo międzynarodowe publiczne w zarysie*, 3rd edn. Warszawa: Pánstwowe Wydawnictwo Naukowe, 1983, 408 pp.

A periodically updated traditional PIL outline. Reviewed by D. Frenzke in *Osteuropa-Recht*, 1984, **30**(3/4), pp. 304-306. See also D. Frenzke's review of Gelberg, L., *Zarys prawa międzynarodowego*, 3rd edn, 1983, in *Osteuropa-Recht*, 1986, **32**(3), pp. 221-223.

122. Klafkowski, A., *Prawo międzynarodowe publiczne*, 5th edn. Warszawa: Pánstwowe Wydawnictwo Naukowe, 1979.

For the older classical treatise *see* Ehrlich, L., *Prawo międzynarodowe*, 4th edn. Warszawa: Wydawnictwo Prawnicze, 1958, 749 pp. 1st edn 1928.

123. Kocot, K. and Wolfke, K. (eds), *Wybór dokumentów do nauki prawa międzynarodowego*, 3rd edn. Warszawa: Pánstwowe Wydawnictwo Naukowe, 1976, 665 pp.

A selection of basic PIL texts.

Romania

124. Geamanu, G., *Drept international public*, 3rd edn. București: Editura Didactica, 1981-3, 2 vols.

A traditional treatise on general PIL. *See also* his *Théorie et pratique des négotiations en droit international*. *RCADI*, 1980/I, **166**, pp. 365-440.

125. Moca, G., *Dreptul international*. București: Ed. Politică, 1983, 467 pp.

A traditional PIL textbook. For a comparative review of Moca's work (the 1977 edition) and that of Takács, L. and Niciu, M.I., *Drept international public*. București: Editura Didactica, 1976, *see* Cismarescu, M., 1979, *Osteuropa Recht*, 25(2), pp. 123-125.

USSR

126. Kozhevnikov, F.I. (ed.), *Mezhdunarodnoe pravo: Uchebnik*. Moskva: Mezhdunarodnye Otnosheniia, 1987, 590 pp.

Periodically updated, this textbook deals with general PIL, including the socialist periodization of PIL, peaceful co-existence, national liberation movements, international organizations and conferences. Contains an extensive bibliography of Soviet PIL materials (primary, secondary and reference) in a broad subject arrangement.

127. Blatova, N.T. (ed.), *Mezhdunarodnoe pravo*, 2nd edn. Moskva: IUridicheskaia Literatura, 1987, 544 pp. 1st edn 1979, edited by N.T. Blatova and L.A. Modzhorian.

This textbook is patterned after Kozhevnikov [126] but without its research apparatus. Includes (pp. 518-525) several charts relating to the UN system, the Warsaw Pact, categories of treaties, etc.

128. Tunkin, G.I. *et al.*, *Mezhdunarodnoe pravo: Uchebnik dlia VUZov*. Moskva: IUridicheskaia Literatura, 1982, 566 pp. English translation: Tunkin, G.I. (ed.), *International law: a textbook*. Moscow: Progress Publishers, 1986, 546 pp.

In addition to the traditional PIL outline, the textbook includes chapters on PIL and the international system, the law of international security, international relations among socialist states and bourgeois concepts of international economic law. Contains a bibliography (but in the English edition titles are listed in English translation only). *See also* Tunkin, G., International law in the international system. *RCADI*, 1975/IV, **147**, pp. 1-218, which includes outlines of the Marxist-Leninist theory of society and PIL, socialist internationalism, and universalism and regionalism in PIL.

129. Chkhikvadze, V.M. (ed.), *Kurs mezhdunarodnogo prava v shesti tomakh*. Moskva: Nauka, 1967-73, 6 vols. 1st edn 1964.

Provides an extensive analysis of the theory and practice of contemporary PIL; vols 1 and 6 emphasize socialist perceptions of and approaches to PIL.

130. Blatova, N.T. (comp.), *Mezhdunarodnoe pravo v dokumentakh*. Moskva: IUridicheskaia Literatura, 1982, 853 pp.

A collection of basic PIL texts. *See also* Sobakin, V.K. (comp.), *Sovremennoe mezhdunarodnoe pravo: sbornik dokumentov*. Moskva: IMO, 1964, 666 pp.

For references to other PIL textbooks published in the USSR *see* [353].

Yugoslavia

131. Andrassy, J., *Međunarodno pravo*, 9th edn. Zagreb: Školska Knjiga, 1987, 656 pp. (Udžbenici Sveučilista u Zagrebu/Manualia Universitatis Studiorum Zagrabiensis). 1st edn 1949.

Regularly updated, this textbook presents a traditional outline of general PIL.

132. Janković, B.M., *Međunarodno javno pravo*, 5th edn. Beograd: Naučna Knjiga, 1983, 411 pp. (Univerzitetski Udžbenici). English translation: Janković, B.M., *Public international law* [translated by M. and B. Milosavljević]. Dobbs Ferry, NY: Oceana/Transnational, 1984, 423 pp. 1st edn 1959.

In addition to this periodically updated textbook *see also* the older PIL treatise by Bartoš, M., *Međunarodno javno pravo*. Beograd: Kultura, 1954-8, 3 vols.

133. Avramov, S. and Kreća, M., *Međunarodno javno pravo* [Rev. 9th edn]. Beograd: Naučna Knjiga, 1988, 582 pp. 1st edn 1963.

Periodically updated, the textbook is intended mainly as a teaching manual in the SR of Serbia. *See also* Mangovski, P., *Meǵunarodno javno pravo*. Skopje: Kultura, 1975, 311 pp., which is intended mainly as a teaching manual in the SR Macedonia.

134. Vukas, B. (comp)., *Međunarodno javno pravo: izbor dokumenata*, 2nd edn. Zagreb: Pravni Fakultet. Institut za Međunarodno Pravo i Međunarodne Odnose, 1977, 276 pp. (mimeographed). 1st edn 1975.

A selection of basic PIL texts.

Scandinavia
Denmark

135. Ross, A., *Laerobog i folkeret*. København, 1976. 1st edn 1946. English translation: Ross, A., *A textbook of international law*. New York: Longmans, Green, 1947, 312 pp. German translation in 1951.

Finland

136. Broms, B., *Kansainvälinen oikens*. Helsinki, 1978, 570 pp. (Suomalainen Lakimiesyhdistys, Helsinki. Julkaisuja. B-sarja, 182).

See also [184].

Norway

137. Castberg, F., *Folkerett*, 2nd edn. Oslo: Lindkvist, 1948, 242 pp.

Sweden

138. Sundberg, H.G., *Folkrätt*, 2nd edn. Stockholm: Institutet för Offentlig och Internationell Rätt, 1950, 398 pp.

Western Europe

Austria

139. Verdross, A. and Simma, B. (eds), *Universelles Völkerrecht: Theorie und Praxis*, 3rd edn. Berlin: Duncker & Humblot, 1984, 956 pp.

Verdross, a prominent member of the Vienna school of normative law, uses the constitutional law approach in his PIL treatise, first published in 1937 (Vienna, Springer) and periodically updated until 1964; thereafter it has been edited by B. Simma.

140. Seidl-Hohenveldern, I., *Völkerrecht*, 5th edn. Köln: Heymann, 1984, 467 pp. 1st edn 1965.

This periodically updated traditional PIL textbook may be complemented by the author's *Praktische Fälle aus dem Völkerrecht*, Wien, 1958, and [620c].

141. *Österreichisches Handbuch des Völkerrechts*. Wien, 1983, 2 vols.

A textbook including examples of Austrian international state practice.

Belgium

142a. de Visscher, C., 1954/II, Cours général de principes du droit international public. *RCADI*, **86**, p. 522.

Illustrates the socio-humanistic approach to PIL.

—b. de Visscher, P. 1972/II, Cours général de droit international public. *RCADI*, **136**, pp. 1–202.

143. van Bogaert, E.R.C., *Volkenrecht*. Brussel: Elsevier/Sequoia, 1973, 602 pp.

A traditional PIL textbook intended mainly for use by Flemish-speakers.

Federal Republic of Germany

144. von Münch, I., *Völkerrecht, ohne internationale Organisationen und Kriegsvölkerrecht, in programmierter Form mit Vertiefungshinweisen*, 2nd edn. Berlin: W. de Gruyter, 1982, 484 pp.

A textbook of general PIL (excluding the law of war or international organization) with extensive bibliographic references.

145. Berber, F., *Lehrbuch des Völkerrechts*, 2nd edn. München: Beck, 1969–77, 3 vols.

This general PIL treatise consists of vol. 1 on the law of peace, vol. 2 on the law of war and vol. 3 on the settlement of disputes and prevention of war.

146. Kimminich, O., *Einführung in das Völkerrecht*, 2nd enlarged edn. München: Saur, 1983, 548 pp. (UTB für Wissenschaft: Uni-Taschenbücher, 469). 1st edn 1975.

An introductory (pocket) textbook of general PIL.

France

147. Nguyen Quoc Dinh, Daillier, P. and Pellet, A., *Droit international public*, 6th edn. Paris: LGDJ, 1987, 1,189 pp. 1st edn 1975.

Midway between a treatise and a textbook, this is an analysis of PIL with reference to international relations within the world community of states and international organizations. The extensive bibliography contains: monographs published worldwide in the pre-1914, 1919–45 and post-1945 periods; a chronological list of commemorative essays; and the titles of individual courses in *RCADI* [220a] for the period 1929–83. Reviewed by Chemilier-Gendreau, M., 1988, *Journal du droit international*, **115**, pp. 91–99.

148. Carreau, D., *Droit international*. Paris: Pédone, 1986, 612 pp.

This textbook of general PIL emphasizes the dynamic process in the formation, application and control of international legal rules (both conventional and 'soft law').

149. Rousseau, C.E., *Droit international public. Avec chapitre supplémentaire sur la protection internationale des droits de l'homme, par P.-M. Dupuy*, 10th edn. Paris: Dalloz, 1984, 433 pp. (Précis Dalloz).

This regularly updated textbook of general PIL is based on the author's *Traité de droit international public*, Nouvelle édition. Paris: Sirey, 1970–82, 5 vols. Considered by G. Fitzmaurice in [206] as Rousseau's 'opus doctissimum', the *Traité* deals with the international law of peace; complemented by the author's *Le droit des conflits armés*, Paris, 1983 [593c].

150. Thierry, H. *et al.*, *Droit international public*, 4th edn. Paris: Montchréstien, 1984, 799 pp. 1st edn. 1975.

Regularly updated with extensive bibliography. The 3rd edn (1981) was considered as 'l'un des meilleurs manuels existants en droit international public'. Reviewed in *RGDIP*, 1982, **86**, p. 193.

151. Colliard, C.-A., *Institutions des relations internationales*, 8th edn. Paris: Dalloz, 1985, 991 pp. 1st edn 1956.

82   EVIDENTIARY STATUS OF MATERIALS

The treatise examines PIL within the context of international relations conducted by states and state-like entities. Part 1 deals with the international community in terms of such phenomena as domination and association, intervention, and interdependence. Part 2 deals with the law of international organization. Includes extensive bibliographies.

152. Dreyfus, S., *Droit des relations internationales*, 3rd edn. Paris: Cujas, 1987, 490 pp. 1st edn 1978.

An introductory PIL manual, each section of which contains an 'annex pédagogique' with concepts, practical exercises and bibliographies. The concluding 'annex documentaire' contains samples of basic PIL documents. The 2nd edn (1981) was considered as 'la meilleure introduction que puissent utiliser les étudiants pour l'approche du droit international'. Reviewed in *RGDIP*, 1982, **86**, p. 441. *See also* Pinto, R., *Le droit des relations internationales*. Paris: Payot, 1972, 372 pp.

153. Thierry, H. (comp.), *Droit et relations internationales; traités, résolutions, jurisprudence: textes choisis*. Paris: Montchréstien, 1984, 696 pp.

Selection of basic texts.

154. Colliard, C.-A. and Manin, A. (comps), *Droit international et histoire diplomatique: documents choisis*, 3rd edn/série. Paris: Publications de la Sorbonne, 1979, 2 vols.

Contains selected basic texts relative to PIL and international relations during 1815-1978. 1st edn/série, Paris: Montchréstien, 1948, 1 vol. (period covered 1815-1948); 2nd edn/série, Paris: Montchréstien, 1970-1, 2 vols (period covered 1815-1970); 3rd edn/série, 1979, 2 vols (period covered 1971-8). Vol. 1 contains general texts, vol. 2 texts relative to Africa, America and Asia. *See also* [8d].

Italy

155. Barile, G., *Lezioni di diritto internazionale*, 2nd edn. Padova: CEDAM, 1983.

A traditional PIL textbook. For an older treatise *see* Balladore-Pallieri, G., *Diritto internazionale publico*, 8th edn. Milano, 1962.

156. Monaco, R., 1968/II, Cours général de droit international public. *RCADI*, **125**, pp. 93-335.

Netherlands

From Grotius on Dutch PIL scholarship has been continuous and prolific. Twentieth-century 'transnational' publishing, especially by Nijhoff and Sijthoff & Noordhoff, accounts for numerous Dutch imprints of PIL works, many by non-Dutch authors.

157. Verzijl, J.H.W., *International law in historical perspective*, Leiden: Sijthoff, 1968-72, 9 vols.

A collection, in English, of the author's principal works written between 1919 and 1956 in various languages. The volumes include 'analytical and descriptive juristic expositions with historical surveys' of various PIL topics and aspects, dealt with in a predominantly Eurocentric vein. Vol. 1, 1968, contains chapters on 'Panorama of the law of nations' and 'Research into the history of the law of nations'.

158. François, J.P.A., *Grondlijnen van het Volkenrecht*. Zwolle: W.E.J. Tjeenk Willink, 1954, 947 pp. (Publiek- en Privaatrecht, 28).

An abridged version of his *Handboek van het Volkenrecht*, Zwolle, 1931-3, 2 vols.

Portugal

159. *Azevedo Soares. *Liçoes de direito internacional público*, 3rd edn. Coimbra, 1987.

160. *Silva Cunha. *Direito internacional público*, 3rd edn. Lisboa, 1981-4, 2 vols.

161. **Principais textos de direito internacional*. Lisboa, 1981, 326 pp.

Spain

162. Gonzales Campos, J., Sanchez Rodriguez, L.I. and Saenz de Santa Maria, P.A., *Curso de derecho internacional público*, 3rd edn. Oviedo: Universidad de Oviedo, 1983.

This textbook reflects a socio-historical approach to PIL. The *Curso* is complemented by *Materiales de prácticas de derecho internacional público*, 3rd edn. 1984, 844 pp., which contains selected basic PIL texts in broad topical arrangement.

163. Diez de Velasco Valleja, M., *Instituciones de derecho internacional público*, 6th edn. Madrid: Tecnos, 1983-6, 2 vols.

This PIL treatise deals (in vol. 1) with the legal status and competences of the international community and (in vol. 2) with the law of international organization. Contains extensive bibliographies, systematically arranged.

164. Miaja de la Muela, A., *Introducción al derecho internacional público*, 7th edn. Madrid: Atlas, 1979.

Periodically updated introductory PIL textbook.

165. Remacha, J.R. (comp.), *Derecho internacional codificado: derecho de gentes, recopilación sistemática de textos y tratados*. Pamplona: Editorial Aranzadi, 1984, 1,136 pp.

A selection of basic PIL texts in broad topical arrangement, with alphabetical subject index.

Switzerland

166. Müller, J. P. *et al.*, *Praxis des Völkerrechts*, 2nd rev. enlarged edn. Bern: Stämpfli, 1982, 639 pp.

Essentially a textbook of general PIL, the work uses the casebook approach and illustrates mostly twentieth-century international legal practice with reference to selected cases of customary and treaty law in a topical arrangement. Part 4 deals with PIL and municipal law with emphasis on Swiss international legal practice. A list of cases arranged by international and municipal (also Swiss) courts and a subject index conclude the work. Contains end-bibliographies.

167. Guggenheim, P., *Traité de droit international, avec la mention de la pratique internationale et suisse*, 2nd edn. Genève: Georg, 1967, 2 vols. 1st edn 1953-4.

The *Traité* represents the French translation of Guggenheim's classic textbook, *Lehrbuch des Völkerrechts, unter Berücksichtigung der internationalen und schweizer Praxis*. Basel: Verlag für Recht und Gesellschaft, 1948-51, 2 vols.

United Kingdom

168. Shaw, M. N., *International law*, 2nd edn. Cambridge: Grotius Publications Ltd, 1986, 627 pp. (paperback). 1st edn Hodder & Stoughton, 1977.

Midway between a treatise and a PIL textbook, the work covers major areas of international law within the international political, economic and cultural context. Shaw examines emerging concepts of contemporary PIL (e.g. world community) and outlines the trends of modern PIL theories and interpretations (e.g. systems analysis, weakening of Eurocentrism). Contains bibliographic notes and subject index.

169. Starke, J. G., *Introduction to international law*, 9th edn. London: Butterworth, 1984, 664 pp.

Regularly updated textbook of general PIL. *See also* an introductory essay by the ICJ justice Jennings, R. Y., 1984, International law. *Enc. PIL*, 7, pp. 278-297.

170. Akehurst, M., *Modern introduction to international law*, 5th edn. Reading: Allen & Unwin, 1984, 310 pp.

An outline of PIL within the contemporary political context. For a similar approach *see also* Brownlie, J., *Principles of public international law*, 3rd edn. Oxford: Clarendon Press, 1979, 743 pp.

171. Schwarzenberger, G., *A manual of international law*, 6th edn. Abingdon: Professional Books Ltd, 1976, 612 pp. 2nd impression, 1978. 1st edn 1947.

The *Manual*, an outcome of 'study outlines' as taught at the New Commonwealth Institute in London, has since set teaching and research standards for PIL textbooks (especially in common law countries). Reflecting the author's inductive approach [495b], the *Manual* consists of four sections: (i) elements of international law; (ii) (didactic) study outlines; (iii) 'for further references', a bibliography of PIL works published worldwide up to the mid-1950s; and (iv) glossary of terms and maxims. A subject index concludes the work. *See also* his The fundamental principles of international law. *RCADI*, 1955/I, **87**, pp. 195-383, which includes the 'seven pillars of international law'.

172. Brierly, J. L., *The law of nations*, 6th edn [edited by C. H. M. Waldock]. Oxford: Clarendon Press, 1963.

A PIL treatise with emphasis on obligation as the basis of international law. *See also* his *The basis of obligation in international law*. Selected and edited by H. Lauterpacht and C. H. M. Waldock. Oxford: Clarendon Press, 1958, 387 pp.

173a. Oppenheim, L., *International law: a treatise*, 8th edn. London: Longmans, 1962, 2 vols. 1st edn 1905-6. 4th edn edited by Lord McNair; 5th to 8th edns edited by H. Lauterpacht.

This treatise (also in Russian, Serbo-Croat and Spanish translations) is considered a twentieth-century classic, not least because of the author's clear, if 'traditional', presentation of PIL, complete with extensive bibliographic references to worldwide imprints. Vol. 1, *Peace*; vol. 2, *Disputes, war and neutrality*.

—b. Lauterpacht, H., *International law, being the collected papers of H. Lauterpacht, systematically arranged and edited by E. Lauterpacht*. Cambridge: Cambridge UP, 1970-8, 4 vols.

Vol. 1 (1970) contains the updating which was foreseen for a 9th edn of Oppenheim's treatise [173a].

174. Brownlie, I., *Basic documents in international law*, 3rd edn. New York: Clarendon Press, 1983, 406 pp.

Reviewed in *AJIL*, 1985, **79**(4), pp. 1,130-1,131. *See also* Harris, D. J., *Cases and materials on international law*, 3rd edn. London: Sweet & Maxwell, 1983, 810 pp. Reviewed in *Cambridge law journal*, 1984, **43**, pp. 199.

b. Commemorative essays

The section includes commemorative essays specific to general PIL published mostly in the 1980s; the bibliographies of general and legal essays [175a-c, 176] concern mostly imprints through the 1970s.

175a. Roberts, L. M., *A bibliography of legal Festschriften*. The Hague: Nijhoff, 1972, 177 pp.

Includes legal (and a few PIL) commemorative essays published worldwide between 1868 and 1968. No subject index. Complementing this bibliography are the following two entries.

—b. Tearle, B. (ed.), *Index to legal essays: English language legal essays in Festschriften, memorial volumes, conference papers and other collections, 1975–1979.* Compiled for the British and Irish Association of Law Librarians. London: Mansell, 1983, 430 pp. Provides a content analysis of English-language commemorative legal essays (listed on pp. 186–8) regardless of the country of publication. Topically arranged.

—c. Dau, H. (comp.), *Bibliographie juristischer Festschriften und Festschriften-Beiträge: Deutschland, Schweiz, Österreich.* Karlsruhe: Müller, 1962–77, 3 vols; Berlin: Berlin Verlag A. Spitz 1981-4, 2 vols, and 1989, 629 pp.

The six volumes spanning the period 1864–1987 list German-language legal (including PIL) commemorative essays and indicate titles of individual contributions therein.

176. Leistner, O., *Internationale Bibliographie der Festschriften von den Anfängen bis 1979, mit Sachregister/International bibliography of Festschriften from the beginnings until 1979, with subject index*, 2nd enlarged edn. Osnabrück: Biblio Verlag, 1984, 2 vols. 1st edn 1976, 893 pp.

Lists Festschriften, mélanges, commemorative essays etc. in all fields published worldwide between 1850 and 1979. Vol. 1 is an alphabetical listing of scholars honoured, vol. 2 a subject index to the essays listed (several devoted to PIL scholars). *See also* New York Public Library. The Research Libraries. *Guide to Festschriften. The retrospective Festschriften collection of the New York Public Library, materials cataloged through 1971.* Boston, MA: G.K. Hall, 1977, 2 vols. Lists some 6,000 titles (of essays and contributions therein) including numerous PIL ones.

177. *New directions in international law: essays in honour of Wolfgang Abendrot . . .* edited by R. Gutierrez Girardot *et al.* Frankfurt a/M: Campus Verlag, 1982, 592 pp.

Includes contributions mainly on international developmental law, by Agrawala, Anand, Corea, Herczeg, Okeke and Syatauw.

178. *Le droit international à l'heure de sa codification; études en l'honneur de Roberto Ago/Il diritto internazionale al tempo della sua codificazione: studi in onore di Roberto Ago/International law at the time of its codification: essays in honour of Roberto Ago.* Milano: Giuffrè, 1987, 4 vols.

Vol. 1 contains contributions by G. Abi-Saab, Bos, Brownlie, Dupuy, Lachs [317a], McWhinney [462e], Sette-Camara, Zemanek and others on the codificatory aspects of PIL principles and sources. Vols 2 and 3 contain contributions by Bedjaoui, Broms, Colliard, Degan, Šahović, Singh, Oda and others on codificatory cooperation in terms mainly of international economic law. Vol. 4 concerns the codification mostly of private international law.

179. *Mélanges offerts à Juraj Andrassy/Essays in international law in honour of Juraj Andrassy/Festschrift für Juraj Andrassy.* Texte rédigé par V. Ibler. La Haye: Nijhoff, 1968, 365 pp.

The contributors include: M. Bartoš, Transformation des principes généraux en règles positives du droit international; R. Bierzanek, Le statut juridique des partisans et des mouvements de résistance armée; and P. Guggenheim, La souveraineté dans l'histoire du droit des gens.

180. *Studi in onore di Giorgio Balladore Pallieri.* Milano: Giuffrè, 1978, 2 vols.

181. *Droit public interne et international: études et réflexions: recueil publié en hommage à la mémoire de George Berlia.* Avant-propos de G. Vedel et J. Robert. Paris: LGDJ, 1980, 521 pp.

Part 2 deals with PIL and international relations.

182. *Festschrift für Rudolf Bindschedler.* Herausgegeben von E. Diez *et al.* Bern: Stämpfli, 1980, 638 pp.

The contributions on various aspects of PIL include those by Dominicé (definition of PIL); Marek (history of PIL); el-Erian, Reuter and de Visscher (law of international organization); Verdross and Skubiszewski (municipal law/PIL); Caflisch [546b].

183. *Liber amicorum Elie van Bogaert.* Antwerpen: Kluwer Rechtswetenschapen, 1985, 339 pp.

The contributors include: J. Salmon, La jurisprudence belge en matière de reconnaissance; E. Suy, The status of the Antarctic (in Flemish); and B. Cheng, Flight from justiciable to auto-interpretative international law.

184. *Essays in honour of Erik Castren, celebrating his 75th birthday, March 20, 1979.* Editorial board E. J. Manner *et al.* Helsinki, 1979, 254 pp. (Publications of the Finnish branch of the ILA, 2).

The contributors include: A. Rosas, International law and the use of nuclear weapons; and H. Rotkirch, The socialist (Soviet) concept of international law.

185. *Le droit des peuples à disposer d'eux-mêmes: méthodes d'analyses du droit international; mélanges offerts à Charles Chaumont.* Paris: Pédone, 1984, 595 pp.

Among the contributions honouring Chaumont, a representative of the French Marxist school of PIL at the Université de Reims, should be mentioned: S. Bastid, Les droits des peuples dans le plan à moyen terme (1984–1989) de l'UNESCO; M. Bennouna, Réalité et imaginaire en droit international du développement; R. Charvin, Le droit international tel qu'il a été enseigné. Notes critiques de lecture des traités, manuels; P. F. Gonidec, Dialectique du droit international et de la politique internationale; M. Lachs, Le droit international, l'ordre mondial et les Nations Unies; and J. A. Salmon, Le raisonnement par analogie en droit international public.

186. *Droit et libertés à la fin du XXe siècle: influences et données économiques et technologiques; études offertes à C. A. Colliard.* Paris: Pédone, 1984, 655 pp.

Mostly on international developmental law, the contributors include A. Kiss, Activités scientifiques et techniques et devoir d'information en droit international public; M. Bedjaoui, Les négotiations globales; R.-J. Dupuy, La notion de patrimoine commun de l'humanité appliquée aux fonds marins; M. Benchikh, Le transfert de technologie dans les résolutions des organisations internationales; and G. Feuer, Technique juridique et valeurs morales en droit international du développement.

187. *Modern problems of international law and the philosophy of law: miscellanea in honour of D. S. Constantopoulos.* Thessaloniki: Institute of International Public Law and International Relations, [1977], 636 pp. (Thesaurus Acroasium, 4).

Part 1 concerns the history and evolution of PIL (including contributions by Münch on the history of the law of the sea and Hambro on Antarctic perspectives); part 4 deals with international relations; part 6 examines the problem of international and comparative law. *See also Grundprobleme des internationalen Rechts/Problèmes fondamentaux du droit international/Fundamental problems of international law.* Festschrift für Jean Constantopoulos. Bonn: Schimmelbusch, 1957, 471 pp.

188. *Mélanges Fernand Dehousse.* Paris: Nathan, 1979, 2 vols.

Vol. 1 includes contributions by: A. el-Erian, La Commission du droit international et le sujet des organisations internationales; E. Hambro, Codification of international law under the League and the UN; J. J. A. Salmon, Quelques observations sur la qualification en droit international; and P. de Visscher, *see* [378d]. Vol. 2 concerns European legal issues.

189. *Essays on international and comparative law in honour of Judge Erades.* Presented by the Board of the *Netherlands International Law Review.* The Hague: Nijhoff, 1983, 273 pp. (T. M. C. Asser Institute).

Includes contributions by M. Bos, Prolegomena to the identification of custom in international law, and A. J. P. Tammes, Soft law.

190. *Jus et societas. Essays in tribute to Wolfgang Friedmann, with an introduction by P. C. Jessup.* Principal editor G. M. Wilner. The Hague: Nijhoff, 1979, 381 pp.

Includes contributions by: Boutros-Ghali and Falk (the future of world order); Garcia-Amador (Andean economic integration); Jennings (treaties as 'legislation'); Schachter (international social justice); Tunkin (the new system of international law).

191. *Essays in honour of B. Godenhielm (70 years); E. Manner (70 years) and S. von Numers (80 years).* Editorial board B. Broms *et al.* Helsinki, 1984, 109 pp. (Publications of the Finnish Branch of the ILA, 3–4).

192. *The relevance of international law: essays in honor of L. Gross.* Edited by K. Deutsch and S. Hoffman. Cambridge, MA: Schenkman, 1968, 280 pp.

Includes contributions by Falk, Kelsen and Fried (orphan, harlot, jailer theories of PIL). *See also* Gross, L., *Essays on international law and organization*. The Hague: Nijhoff; Ardsley-on-Hudson, NY: Oceana/Transnational, 1984, 2 vols (reviewed in *CYIL*, 1984, **22**, pp. 442-444). The *Essays* (omitting Gross's writings in German) deal with the development of PIL, evidence of customary law (the essay served as the basis for [31]), auto-interpretation of PIL by states, and a critical appraisal of Kelsen's works. Note also Gross, L., *International law in the twentieth century*. New York: Appleton-Century-Croft, 1969, 1,011 pp., which is a selection of Gross's articles previously published in *AJIL* [227] or used in his PIL course at Harvard University.

193. *Recueil d'études de droit international en hommage à Paul Guggenheim.* Genève: Faculté de droit/Institut universitaire de hautes études internationales, 1968, 901 pp.

Includes contributions by Bastid (on the progressive development of PIL), Blondel (on the general principles of law and the ICJ), Cahier (on the behaviour of states as a legal source) and Tunkin [474d].

194. *Transnational law in a changing society: essays in honor of Philip C. Jessup.* Edited by W.G. Friedmann *et al.* New York: Columbia UP, 1972, 324 pp.

The contributors on the 'transnational' aspect of PIL (a concept introduced by Jessup) include Lachs (on the substance and form of international law), Bastid (on the UN administrative Tribunal and the development of PIL), Visscher (on stages in the codification of PIL), Deak (neutrality revisited) and el-Erian (on international law and developing countries).

—a. *Festschrift für Hans Kelsen zum 90. Geburtstag.* Herausgegeben von A.J. Merkl *et al.* Wien: Deuticke, 1971, 326 pp.

See also: *Law, state and international legal order; essays in honor of H. Kelsen.* Edited by S. Engel *et al.* Knoxville: University of Tennessee Press, 1964, 365 pp.; Fouilloux, G., 1981, Kelsen et le droit international public (conférence du 9 février 1981). **Revue de la recherche juridique du droit prospectif* (Marseille), **6**(11), pp. 317-326.

195. *Essays in international law in honour of Judge Manfred Lachs.* Edited by J. Makarczyk. The Hague: Nijhoff, 1984, 760 pp. (Institute of State and Law of the Polish Academy of Sciences).

The essays commemorate the ICJ justice's seventieth birthday and include contributions by: Tunkin, Nahlik and Virally (on the theory of PIL), Elias, Monaco and Mosler (on the ICJ and the peaceful settlement of disputes), Bokor-Szegö, Franck and Schwebel (on the law of international organizations), Jimenez de

Arechaga, Oda and Vignes (on the law of the sea), and Röling (on the law of arms control and disarmament). *See also Essays in honour of Professor Manfred Lachs*. Warsaw, 1964.

196. *Multum non multa. Festschrift für Kurt Lipstein aus Anlass seines 70. Geburtstages.* Herausgegeben von P. Feuerstein und C. Parry. Heidelberg: C.F. Müller, 1980, 383 pp.

The contributions include critical reviews by R.J. Dupuy and McWhinney of current PIL theories, proposals for the application of new paradigms (e.g. the T.S. Kuhn model) in international developmental law, Ginther on Systemwandel und Theoriendynamik im Völkerrecht and J. Collier on the status of an international corporation.

197. *Toward world order and human dignity: essays in honor of Myres S. McDougal.* Edited by W.M. Reisman and B.H. Weston. New York: The Free Press/Macmillan, 1976, 603 pp.

The contributions on PIL in the context of 'world order' (a concept introduced by McDougal and developed in the Yale University/New Haven Studies in International Law and World Public Order) include essays on the jurisprudential and institutional aspects of PIL, e.g. R. Higgins, Interpretations of authority and control: trends in the literature of international law and international relations (a historiographical assessment of world order studies at Princeton, Columbia and Yale Universities in the USA); V. Raman, Toward a general theory of international customary law (in terms of the communication/prescription process). *See also* B. Rosenthal, *Etude de l'œuvre de Myres Smith McDougal en matière de droit international public*. Paris: LGDJ, 1970, 218 pp. (Bibliotheque de droit international, 53), as well as M.S. McDougal, *Studies in world public order*. New Haven, CT: New Haven Press; Dordrecht: Nijhoff, 1987, 1,058 pp. (The New Haven Studies in International Law and World Public Order), a revised reprint of McDougal's writings (between 1943 and 1959) first published in 1960.

198. *Estudios de derecho internacional: homenaje al professor Miaja de la Muela.* Madrid: Tecnos, 1979, 2 vols.

Vol. 1, on general PIL, includes contributions by Ago and Truyol y Serra (on the evolution of PIL), Salmon ('Les contradictions entre fait et droit en droit international'), Sperdutti (on dualism/monism in PIL), Bos, McWhinney and Mosler (on sources of PIL). Vol. 2 deals with specialized PIL, including essays on the law of the sea, international organization and international economic law.

199. *Völkerrecht als Rechtsordnung. Internationale Gerichtsbarkeit. Menschenrechte. Festschrift für Hermann Mosler*. Berlin: Springer, 1983, 1,057 pp. (Beiträge zum ausländischen öffentlichen Recht und Völkerrecht, 81).

Includes contributions by Bastid (La mise en œuvre d'un recours concernant les droits de l'homme dans le domaine relevant de la compétence de l'Unesco), Elias

(The limits of the right of intervention in a case before the ICJ), Gros (La recherche du consensus dans les décisions de la CIJ), McWhinney (The legislative role of the World Court in an era of transition) and Schermers (International organizations as members of other international organizations).

200. *Essays on the development of the international legal order in memory of H. F. van Panhuys.* Edited by F. Kalshoven *et al.* Alphen a/R: Sijthoff & Noordhoff, 1980, 226 pp. (T.M.C. Asser Instituut).

Includes contributions by Lachs (The revised procedure of the ICJ), Kiss (Mechanism of supervision of international environmental rules), Riphagen (Environmental rules in the future law of the sea) and Lammers (General principles of law recognized by civilized nations).

201. *Du droit international au droit de l'intégration: liber amicorum Pierre Pescatore.* Herausgegeben von F. Capotorti *et al.* Baden Baden: Nomos, 1987, 869 pp.

The focus is on European Community law but the essays include Reuter (La conférence de Vienne sur les traités des organisations internationales), Riphagen (The second round of treaty law: on fictions and abstractions in the Vienna conventions), Rodriguez Iglesias (on municipal law before the ICC).

202. *Idee und Realität des Rechts in der Entwicklung internationaler Beziehungen: Festgabe für Wolfgang Preiser.* Herausgegeben von A. Böhm *et al.* Baden Baden: Nomos, 1983, 213 pp.

The contributions concern mainly historical aspects of PIL, including Grewe's Was ist 'klassisches', was ist 'modernes' Völkerrecht?

203. *Essays on international law, in honour of Krishna Rao.* Edited by M. K. Nawaz. Leiden: Sijthoff, 1976, 362 pp.

The contributors include Lachs (on science and technology and international law), Jenks (on idealism in international law), McWhinney (on the problem-solving approach to PIL), R.J. Dupuy (Coûtume sage et coûtume sauvage) and Tunkin (International law: the contemporary and classic).

204. *Mélanges offerts à Paul Reuter. Le droit international: unité et diversité.* Paris: Pédone, 1981, 584 pp.

The contributors include Rousseau (Les conceptions nationales du droit des gens), Virally (A propos de la *lex ferenda*), Furukawa (on the ICJ and international organizations) and Daoudi [570b].

205. *Declarations on principles: a quest for universal peace. Liber amicorum discipulorumque B. V. A. Röling.* Edited by R.J. Akkerman *et al.* Leiden: Sijthoff, 1977, 402 pp.

Sociologically weighted, the contributors include G. Abi-Saab (Wars of national liberation and the development of humanitarian law) and R.J. Dupuy [519e].

206. *Mélanges offerts à Charles Rousseau: la communauté internationale.* Paris: Pédone, [1974], 346 pp.

The contributors include Chaumont (Recherche d'un critère pour l'intégration de la guérilla au droit international humanitaire contemporain), Virally (La notion de fonction dans la théorie de l'organisation internationale), Wengler (La crise de l'unité de l'ordre juridique internationale), Fitzmaurice (The problem of *non liquet*: prolegomena to a restatement) and R.J. Dupuy [519f].

207. *Staatsrecht, Völkerrecht, Europarecht: Festschrift für Hans-Jürgen Schlochauer zum 75. Geburtstag* . . . Herausgegeben von I. von Münch. Berlin: W. de Gruyter, 1981, 1,023 pp.

The contributors include Münch (on the study and teaching of PIL), Grewe (the post-1945/American period of PIL), Suy (legal aspects of the UN Security Council) and Kewening (on the common heritage of mankind).

208. [No entry].

209. *Contemporary issues in international law: essays in honor of L. B. Sohn.* Edited by T. Buergenthal. Kehl/Strasbourg: N.P. Engel, 1984, 571 pp.

The contributors include Buergenthal ('The advisory jurisdiction of the Inter-American Court of Human Rights'), Chiu ('The 1982 UN Convention on the Law of the Sea and the settlement of China's maritime boundary dispute'), Nafziger ('The writing style of the ICJ') and Choi ('Judicial review of international administrative tribunal judgements').

210. *Studi in onore di Giuseppe Sperdutti: fonti internazionali e rapporti fra ordinamenti l'individuo nel diritto internazionale, altri contributi.* Milano: Giuffrè, 1984, 857 pp.

Includes contributions by Panebianco (the theory of PIL sources in the Latin American doctrine), Reuter (the notion of international practice by international organizations), Ferrari-Bravo (diplomatic practice of states) and R.J. Dupuy (on the universality of human rights).

211. *Ius humanitatis: Festschrift zum 90. Geburtstag von Alfred Verdross.* Herausgegeben von H. Miehsler *et al.* Berlin: Duncker & Humblot, 1980, 755 pp.

The contributors are mainly concerned with European Community law but also include Uibopuu (International law and municipal law in Soviet doctrine and practice) and Zemanek (The Vienna convention and succession to treaties). *See also Internationale Festschrift für Alfred Verdross zum 80. Geburtstag.* Herausgegeben von R. Marcic *et al.* München: Fink, 1971, 596 pp. including contributions by Tunkin (General principles of law), Schwarzenberger (World law and world order) and Guggenheim (Der Neutralitätsbegriff). *See also Völkerrecht und rechtliches Weltbild: Festschrift für Alfred Verdross.* Herausgegeben von F.A. Heydte *et al.* Wien: Springer, 1960, 345 pp., including contributions by Tunkin (The role of international law in international relations); Seidl-Hohenveldern (Die Rolle der Rechtsvergleichung im Völkerrecht); Castberg (Die Erklärung der Menschenrechte im Licht der Geschichte); Bindschedler (Zum Problem der Grundnorm); and Zemanek (on dualism in PIL).

212. *Völkerrecht und Rechtsphilosophie: internationale Festschrift für Stephan Verosta.* Herausgegeben von P. Fischer *et al.* Berlin: Duncker & Humblot, 1980, 523 pp.

Includes contributions by: Tunkin (the Soviet theory of PIL sources), Degan (international conciliation), Messner (the evolution of natural law) and Lachs (judiciary powers within the UN).

213. *Symbolae Verzijl: présentées au Professeur J. H. W. Verzijl à l'occasion de son 70. anniversaire.* La Haye: Nijhoff, 1958, 453 pp.

The contributors include Verdross (on neutrality within the UN framework), Lord McNair (on treaties and sovereignty), Röling (on defining aggression) and Fitzmaurice (on formal sources of PIL).

See also Varia jus gentium [289].

c. Dissertations

214. *Bibliotheca Visseriana dissertationum ius internationale illustrantium.* Leiden: Brill, 1923-80, 21 vols. Indexes in vols 10 and 20.

This series, sponsored by the Legatum Visserianum, contains the texts of outstanding PIL dissertations defended at the Universitas Lugduno-Batave, Leiden. Of continued, if historical, interest are: P. Vinogradoff, Historical types of international law (1923); C. de Visscher, La responsabilité des Etats (1924); M. van Blankenstein, Le role des conférences d'après-guerre dans le fonctionnement de l'organisme mondiale (1926); J. H. W. Verzijl, Un projet d'encyclopédie de droit international public et privé (1931); and J. ter Meulen and P.J.J. Diermanse [465c].

215. *Dissertation abstracts international.* Ann Arbor, MI: University Microfilms, 1938-, 1-, monthly.

The section on humanities and social sciences includes law and PIL dissertations defended at universities worldwide, but especially in North America from 1861 on. Complementing the abstracting service is the *Comprehensive dissertation index.* Ann Arbor, MI: University Microfilms, 1937, 37 vols (vol. 27 concerns law and politics). *See also Guide to the availability of theses.* München: Saur, 1981, 443 pp. (IFLA Publications, 17).

d. Periodicals, yearbooks

216a. Ulrich's *international periodicals directory*, 28th edn 1989-90. New York: Bowker, 1989, 3 vols.

The *Directory* incorporates the formerly separate 'Irregular serials and annuals' and provides bibliographic annotations to over 10,000 periodicals and serials published worldwide. Vols 1 and 2, classified list of serials (vol. 2 pp. 2,157-2,165, international law; pp. 3,022-3,045, international relations); vol. 3, serials available online, cessations, serial publications of international organizations and an alphabetical title index to vols 1 and 2.

—b. *World list of social science periodicals*, 5th rev. edn. Paris: UNESCO, 1980, 447 pp.

Produced in cooperation with the International Committee for Social Science Information and Documentation, this periodically updated list of some 3,000 social science (including law and PIL) periodicals is generated by the computerized UNESCO/DARE system. The arrangement is by countries, with a separate section on serial publications by international organizations. Kept up to date in the *International social science journal* (UNESCO).

See also Periodical title abbreviations, 4th edn. Detroit, MI: Gale, 1983, 2 vols, as well as Leistner, O., *Internationale Titelabkürzungen* (*ITA*). Osnabrück: Biblio, 1977, 1,137 pp.

217. Wypyski, E.M., *Legal periodicals in English*. Dobbs Ferry, NY: Oceana/Glanville, 1975-, 1-, four loose-leaf binders with index and supplements.

218. Stepan, J. and Chapman, F.C., 1980, National and regional yearbooks of international law and relations: a brief survey. *IJLL*, **8**(1), pp. 19-26.

A tabulated presentation of nineteen PIL yearbooks (excluding the *Yearbook of the ILC*).

General

219a. *International legal materials*. Washington, DC: American Society of International Law, 1962-, 1-, bimonthly.

Although necessarily selective, *ILM* is the only regularly issued periodical publication which provides speedy access to full or lengthy excerpts of texts in English of current primary PIL materials, notably treaties, final acts of international conferences and declarations by IGOs. *ILM* often reproduces such texts (mostly by photo-offset from the official documents or unofficial typescript) before these are published in other PIL documentary sources (e.g. *UNTS* [2]). At the end of each issue references to titles of recent relevant documents are listed. An annual table of contents and subject index are published in the November issue of *ILM*.

—b.   *Documents juridiques internationaux*. Montréal: Thémis/Société québécoise de droit international, 1982-, 1-, 2 or 3 numbers per year.

Patterned upon (and where relevant with cross-references to) *ILM*, *DJI* reproduces in French the texts of selected primary PIL materials, notably of treaties, international and state judicial acts, declarations and unilateral acts.

220a.   *Recueil des cours de l'Académie de droit international de La Haye/The Hague Academy of International Law. Collected courses*. La Haye/The Hague: Nijhoff, 1929-, 3 to 5 volumes per year. Indexes.

RCADI contains the texts, in English or French, of postgraduate courses on (mainly general) private and public international law given since 1923 each summer at The Hague Academy of International Law [380a] by eminent international legal scholars, notably W. E. Butler (1985/I), F. Castberg (1973/I), C. Chaumont (1970/I), R.-J. Dupuy (1979/IV), G. Fitzmaurice (1957/II), W. Friedmann (1969/II), E. Jiménez de Arechaga (1978/I), M. Lachs (1957/II), C. Rousseau (1958/I), G. Schwarzenberger (1955/I), G. Scelle (1933/I), G. Tunkin (1975/IV), A. Verdross (1935/III), M. Virally (1983/V), C. de Visscher (1954/II) and P. de Visscher (1972/II). *Index général . . ./General index . . .*, vols 1–101, 1923-60. Leiden: Sijthoff, 1968, 369 pp.; vols 102-125, 1961-8. Leiden: Sijthoff, 1973, 185 pp., vols 126-151, 1969-76. Alphen a/R: Sijthoff & Noordhoff, 1980, 280 pp. The cumulative indexes include: chronological lists of courses (per volume; *see also* [147, 335, 344]); alphabetical index of authors; systematic index (according to English and French subject headings and contents); separate alphabetical indexes of French and English-language courses; and separate tables of cases, as referred to in the French and English courses. Bio-bibliographies precede each course.

—b.   *The Hague Academy of International Law Workshops*, 1st-, 1968-. Dordrecht: Nijhoff, 1971-, annual.

The published contents of the *Workshops* (in English or French, with bilingual titles since 1981) deal with various specialized aspects of PIL, e.g. international environmental law (1973, 1984) [714]; international economic law (1979) [722a]. *See also* [459, 548a, 648b].

221.   *Grotiana: a journal under the auspices of the Foundation Grotiana*. Assen: Van Gorkum, 1980-, 1-, new series, twice yearly.

Established in 1916, the Foundation for the Publication of the Works of Grotius, until 1947 edited a publication entitled *Grotiana*; issued every two years the publication contained studies in English, French and Dutch on or of Grotius. Published semi-annually since 1980, *Grotiana* deals with the historical, legal and theological aspects of Grotius's life and promotes studies (including bibliographies) about Grotius and his relevance to present-day thinking about PIL and world problems. *See also* [465e].

Africa

Egypt

222. *Revue égyptienne de droit international.* Cairo: Société égyptienne de droit international, 1945-, 1-, annual.

Text in Arabic with occasional French or English summaries.

Nigeria

223. *Nigerian annual of international law.* Lagos: Nigerian Society of International Law, 1980-, 1-, annual.

Republic of South Africa

224a. *The comparative and international law journal of Southern Africa.* Pretoria: University of South Africa, 1968-, 1-, three times yearly.

Formerly entitled *South African journal of comparative and international law.*

—b. *South African yearbook of international law/Suid-Afrikaanse Jaarboek vir Volkereg.* Pretoria: University of South Africa, V. van Themat Centre for Public International Law, 1975-, 1-, annual.

See also African law digest. Addis Ababa: University of Addis Ababa, 1966-, 3 times yearly (includes summaries of selected African legislative texts and inter-African treaties); *Journal of African law.* London: University of London, School of Oriental and African Studies, 1956-, 1-, semi-annual.

The Americas

Canada

225. *Canadian yearbook of international law/Annuaire canadien de droit international.* Vancouver, BC: University of British Columbia Press, 1963-, 1-, annual.

Published under the auspices of the Canadian Branch of the ILA. *See also* Cohen, M., 1987, The *Canadian Yearbook* and international law in Canada. *CYIL*, **25**, pp. 3-27.

226. *Revue québécoise de droit international.* Montréal: Thémis, 1984-, 1-, annual.

Published in French under the auspices of the Société québécoise de droit international.

USA

Given the numerous legal and PIL periodicals published throughout the USA, only the most outstanding or regionally representative PIL journals are listed below. Except for [228, 238] student-edited PIL journals are excluded.

227. *American journal of international law (AJIL)*. Washington, DC: American Society of International Law, 1907-, 1-, quarterly. Editor since 1985 T.M. Franck.

Between 1970 and 1973 included the *Proceedings* of ASIL [387a]. Vols 29 (1935) and 33 (1939) contain supplements on 'Research in international law under the auspices of the Faculty of the Harvard Law School' [389b]. *AJIL* carries a regular column on the 'Contemporary practice of the United States relating to international law', which supplements the annual *DUSPIL* [34]. Cumulative author and subject indexes cover periods 1907-20, 1921-40, 1941-60, 1961-70 and 1971-80 (this cumulation includes an index to the *Proceedings* of ASIL).

228. *ASILS international law journal*. Washington, DC: Association of Student International Law Societies, 1977-, 1-, annual.

Student edited, the journal includes the P.C. Jessup International Law Moot Court Competition problems. *See also* Kearley, T., 1983, US law school international, transnational and comparative law reviews. *IJLI* 11 (1/2), pp. 26-28, listing 29 student-edited PIL journals. *See also The American University journal of international law and policy*. Washington, DC: 1986-, 1-, twice yearly. Student edited, the journal includes a section on 'Recent developments in international organizations' (mostly located in Washington, DC).

229. *California Western international law journal*. San Diego, CA: California Western School of Law, 1969-, 1-, three times yearly.

230. *Case Western Reserve journal of international law*. Cleveland, OH: Case Western Reserve University, 1968-, 1-, three times yearly.

231. *Columbia journal of transnational law*. New York: Columbia University, 1961-, 1-, three times yearly.

Founded by W. Friedmann [190] the journal reflects P.C. Jessup's [194] 'transnational' approach to PIL. *See also* Essays on international law: from the *Columbia law review*. New York: 1965, 435 pp. *See also* [242].

232. *Cornell international law journal*. Ithaca, NY: Cornell University Law School, 1968-, 1-, twice yearly.

233. *Denver journal of international law and policy*. Denver, CO: Colorado University, Denver College of Law, 1971-, 1-, twice yearly.

234. *Georgia journal of international and comparative law*. Athens, Georgia: University of Georgia School of Law, 1970-, 1-, three times yearly.

235. *Harvard international law journal*. Cambridge, MA: Harvard Law School, 1967-, 1-, three times yearly.

Formerly entitled *Harvard international law bulletin* (1959-62) and *Harvard international law club journal* (1963-6).

236. *International law perspective.* Washington, DC, 827 15th St NW, 1975-, 1-, monthly.

Reports information on US court and congressional activities with an impact on international legal issues.

237. *The international lawyer.* Houston, TX: American Bar Association. Section of International Law, 1966-, 1-, quarterly.

Topically arranged, the quarterly issues contain articles on mostly private and public international law, as well as a regular feature on 'Selected readings on foreign and international law'.

238. *Journal of international law and economics.* Washington, DC: George Washington University, The National Law Center, 1971-, 1-, three times yearly. Title varies.

Edited by, and for, graduate students, the journal emphasizes aspects of international economic law and from time to time provides bibliographic surveys of PIL materials: *see* [328]. Between 1966 and 1982 entitled *Journal of law and economic development*; since 1982 entitled *George Washington journal of international law and economics*.

239. *New York University journal of international law and politics.* New York: New York University School of Law, 1968-, 1-, quarterly.

240. *Stanford journal of international law.* Stanford, CA: Stanford University School of Law, 1966-, 1-, twice yearly.

241. *Texas international law journal.* Austin, TX: University of Texas School of Law, 1965-, 1-, three times yearly.

242. *Vanderbilt journal of transnational law.* Nashville, TN: Vanderbilt University School of Law, 1967-, 1-, quarterly. *See also* [231].

243. *Virginia journal of international law.* Charlottesville, VA: University of Virginia School of Law, 1960-, 1-, quarterly.

244. *The Yale journal of international law.* New Haven, CT: Yale University, 1974-, 1-, twice yearly.

Until 1983 entitled *The Yale studies in* (also *journal of*) *world public order.*

See also Inter-American law review. Coral Gables, FL: University of Miami School of Law, 1969-, 1-, three times yearly.

Argentina

245a. *Anuario de derecho internacional público.* Buenos Aires: Universidad de Buenos Aires, Facultad de derecho y ciencias sociales, Instituto de derecho internacional público, 1981-, 1-, annual.

—b. **Revista de derecho internacional y ciencias diplomáticas.* Rosario: Instituto de Derecho Internacional, 1949-, 1-, semi-annual.

Cuba

246. *Revista de derecho internacional*. Habana: Instituto Americano de Derecho Internacional, 1922-, 1-.

Ecuador

247. *Anuario ecuatoriano de derecho internacional*. Quito: Instituto de Investigaciones Internacionales, 1964-, 1-, annual.

Peru

248. *Revista peruana de derecho internacional*. Lima: Sociedad Peruana de Derecho Internacional, 1941-, 1-, semi-annual.

Uruguay

249. *Anuario uruguayo de derecho internacional*. Montevideo, 195?-, 1-.

Asia

China, People's Republic

250. Chinese yearbook of international law. Beijing, 198?-, 1-, annual.

In Chinese, with contents also in English. Contains articles, book reviews and references to PIL-related laws, statutes, as well as a special feature, 'Study of international law in China.' See also *Selected articles from the Chinese yearbook of international law. Beijing: Translation and Publication Corp., 1983, 308 pp.

Taiwan

251. Chinese yearbook of international law and affairs. Taipei: Chinese Society of International Law/Taiwan Branch of the International Law Association, 1981-, 1-, since 1985 every two years.

Includes articles, book reviews and notes on recent (mostly private international law) developments, as well as references to bilateral treaties concluded by Taiwan in a given year.

India

252. Indian yearbook of international law. Madras: Indian Study Group of International Affairs, 1952-, 1-, annual.

253. Indian journal of international law. New Delhi: Indian Society of International Law, 1960-, 1-, quarterly.

Contains a section on international law in India.

254. Eastern journal of international law. Madras: Eastern Centre of International Studies, 1969-, 1-, quarterly.

The contents of these and other relevant periodicals are usually analysed by the *Index to Indian legal periodicals*. New Delhi: Indian Law Institute, 1963-, 1-, twice yearly.

Japan

255. [No entry].

256. *Kokusaiho gaiko zassi/Journal of international law and diplomacy*. Tokyo: Faculty of Law, University of Tokyo, 1903-, 1-, bimonthly.

In Japanese with English summaries, the journal is published under the auspices of the Japanese Association of International Law.

Korea, South

257. *Korean journal of international law*. Seoul: Korean Association of International Law, 1956-, 1-, twice yearly.

Since 1975 entitled *Journal of international law*. Contains articles (in Korean with English summaries) on Far Eastern, including Korean, international legal matters.

Malaysia

258. *Survey of Malaysian law*. Kuala Lumpur: Faculty of Law, University of Malaya, 1977-, 1-.

Includes articles on PIL. See also *Malaya law review*, which regularly contains a section entitled on 'Singapore and international law'.

Philippines

259. *Philippine yearbook of international law*. Quezon City: Philippine Society of International Law, 1974-, 1-, annual.

Thailand

260. **Law of the Marut Bunnag International Law Office*. Bangkok, 195?-, 1-.

Australia

261. *Australian yearbook of international law*. Sydney: Chattwood/Butterworth, 1965-87, vols 1-10.

Contained articles on current problems of private and public international law, with a section on 'Australian practice in international law for the year . . .'. Included table of cases, statutes and treaties. Vol. 10 (1987) covered the period 1981-3 and included Crawford, J. R., Teaching and research in international law in Australia, pp. 176-201. Vol. 9 (1985) contained a collection of the proceedings of the Seminar on the Protection of the Human Being in Armed Conflict, Canberra, 1983.

For the contents of this and other relevant periodicals in the region *see Current Australian and New Zealand legal literature index*. North Ryde, NSW, The Law Book Co. Ltd, 1974-, 1-, quarterly.

Europe, Eastern

Bulgaria

262.   **Trudove po mezhdunarodno pravo.* Sofiia, 197?-, 1-.

See also **Droit international: privé et public*. Sofia: Association bulgare de droit international, 1978-, 1-.

Czechoslovakia

263a.   **Studie z mezinarodniho prava.* Praha: Nakl. Československe Akademie Vĕt, 1955-, 1-, irregular.

—b..   **Zbornik prace z medzinarodneho prava.* Bratislava: Slovenska Spolecnost pre Medzinarodne Pravo, 195?-, 1-, irregular (Acta Facultatis Juridicae, Universitas Comenianae).

German Democratic Republic

264.   *Staat und Recht.* Berlin: Staatsverlag der DDR, 1952-, 1-, monthly.

Hungary

265a.   *Questions of international law.* Budapest: Akadémiai Kiadó; Leiden: Sijthoff, 1962-, 1-, irregular. New series 1977-. Editors Gy. Harászti (1962-85), H. Bokor-Szegö (1986-).

Contains English translations of selected articles on private and public international law written by members of the Hungarian Branch of the ILA. The new series include contributions by Gy. Herczeg (International humanitarian law, in vol. 1; International law in a multicultural world, in vol. 3); L. Válki (Social functions of international law, in vol. 3); and I. Szabó (Human rights and socialism, in vol. 2).

—b.   *Allam és jogtudomány/Political science and jurisprudence.* Budapest: Magyar Tudományos Akadémiai Allam és Jogtudományi Intézet, 1957-, 1-, quarterly.

Poland

267.   *Polish yearbook of international law.* Wrocław: Publishing House of the Polish Academy of Sciences, 1966-, 1-, annual.

Contains a section on 'Polish bibliography of international law'.

268.   *Panstwo i prawo.* Warszawa: Polska Akademia Nauk, Instytut Panstwa i Prawa, 1946-, 1-, monthly.

Romania

269. *Studii cercetari juridice.* București: Academia de Stiinte Sociale si Politica, 1955-, 1-, quarterly.

See also *Revue roumaine d'études internationales.* Bucarest: Association de droit international et relations internationales, 1967-, 1-, 6 times yearly. There is also an English edition.

USSR

270. *Sovetskiĭ ezhegodnik mezhdunarodnogo prava (SEMP)/Soviet yearbook of international law.* Moskva: Sovetskai͡a Assot͡siat͡sii͡a Mezhdunarodnogo Prava/Soviet Association of International Law, 1958-, 1-, annual.

Includes bibliographies of Soviet works on PIL.

271. *Sovetskoe gosudarstvo i pravo.* Moskva: Institut Gosudarstva i Prava, 1927-, 1-, monthly.

Soviet law and government is an English translation of selected articles by the International Arts and Sciences Press, New York, 1962-, quarterly. See also **Voprosy mezhdunarodnogo prava.* Moskva: Institut Gosudarstva i Prava, 1961-197?, continued as **Aktual'nye problemy sovremennogo mezhdunarodnogo prava.* Moskva: Institut Mezhdunarodnykh Otnoshenii͡a, 197?-, irregular.

Yugoslavia

272. *Jugoslovenska revija za međunarodno pravo.* Jugoslovensko Udruženje za Međunarodno Pravo, 1954-, 1-, 3 times a year.

Contains English or French summaries. Includes references to treaties, book reviews and occasionally bibliographies of Yugoslav periodical articles on PIL (e.g. vol. 25, 1977, contained such a bibliography for 1971-9).

The following selected periodical titles are published outside Eastern Europe and deal with various aspects, including PIL ones, of socialist law.

273a. Kavass, I.I., 1982, Selected Soviet and Eastern European periodicals of special interest to lawyers and legal scholars. *IJLI*, **10**(3), pp. 102-114.

—b. *Review of socialist law.* Dordrecht: Nijhoff, 1974-, 1-, quarterly. Editor F.J.M. Feldbrugge.

Published under the auspices of the Documentation Office for East European Law [397a], the *Review* includes English translations of selected official legal texts, the state of the art of law and PIL in socialist countries, and book reviews.

—c. *Yearbook on socialist legal systems.* London: University of London, Centre for the Study of Socialist Legal Systems [397c], 1986-, 1-, annual.

—d. *Bulletin on current research in Soviet and East European law.* Toronto: University of Toronto, Centre for Russian and East European Studies, 1970-, 1-, irregular.

Reports on English-language publications and legal activities relative to Eastern Europe.

—e. *Jahrbuch für Ostrecht.* Köln: Bundesanzeiger Verlag, 1960-, 1-, annual.

Published under the auspices of the Institut für Ostrecht, München.

—f. *Osteuropa-Recht.* Stuttgart: Deutsche Verlagsanstalt, 1955-, 1-, semi-annual.

Published under the auspices of the Deutsche Gesellschaft für Osteuropakunde, Stuttgart, the journal contains extensive reviews of PIL textbooks [110].

Scandinavia

274. *Nordisk tidskrift for international ret og jus gentium/Acta scandinavica juris gentium.* Copenhagen: Redsvidenskabeligt Institut, 1930-, 1-, quarterly.

Since 1986 titled *Nordic journal of international law.*

275. *Scandinavian studies in law.* Stockholm: University of Stockholm, Stockholm Institute for Scandinavian Law, 1957-, 1-, annual. Cumulative subject index for vols 1-16.

Contains articles in English by Scandinavian legal scholars on various aspects of law, including PIL.

Europe, Western

Austria

276. *Österreichische Zeitschrift für öffentliches Recht und Völkerrecht.* Wien: Springer, 1971-, 1-, irregular.

Includes surveys of Austrian judicial decisions relating to PIL.

Belgium

277. *Revue belge de droit international/Belgian review of international law.* Bruxelles: Bruylant, 1965-, 1-, semi-annual.

Published under the auspices of the Société belge de droit international. Superseded *Revue de droit international et de législation comparée* (1908-64).

Federal Republic of Germany

278. *German yearbook of international law/Jahrbuch für internationales Recht.* Berlin: Duncker & Humblot (since 1976), 1948-, 1-, annual.

Published under the auspices of the Universität Kiel, Institut für internationales Recht, *GYIL* superseded the *Jahrbuch des Völkerrechts*, founded in 1913 by T. Niemeyer and K. Strupp.

279. *Zeitschrift für ausländisches öffentliches Recht und Völkerrecht.* Berlin, 1927-42 (Editor V. Bruns); New series, Stuttgart: Kohlhammer, 1950-, 1-, quarterly.

Superseded *Zeitschrift für Völkerrecht*, Breslau, 1907-26. Contains articles on private and public international law, book reviews and a bibliographic section, 'Zeitschriftenschau'.

280. *Archiv des Völkerrechts.* [New series] Tübingen: Mohr, 1948-, 1-, quarterly.

From time to time includes lists of PIL dissertations, e.g. Die völkerrechtlichen Dissertationen an den Universitäten der Bundesrepublik Deutschland und von West-Berlin, 1981, **19**(2), pp. 214-240, for the period 1970-9.

281. *Internationales Recht und Diplomatie/Droit international et diplomatie/International law and diplomacy/Mezhdunarodnoe pravo i diplomatiĩa.* Köln: Verlag für Wissenschaft und Politik, 1956-, 1-, irregular. Editor S. Constantopoulos.

Founded by R. von Laun, the journal (last known volume published in 1980) is issued under the auspices of the Institut für Ostrecht [397b].

France

282. *Annuaire français de droit international.* Paris: CNRS, 1955-, 1-, annual. Indexes. Editorial board S. Bastid, D. Bardonnet and J. Combacau.

The regular features of *AFDI* include: 'Les conventions internationales conclues par la France et publiées au *Journal officiel*'; 'Jurisprudence française du droit international'; and 'Bibliographie systèmatique des ouvrages et articles relatifs au droit international public publiés en langue française'. *AFDI* also: lists PIL dissertations (many on international economic law and/or by candidates from the Third World) at French universities; summarizes proceedings and reports of PIL conferences, notably the *Colloques* of the Société française de droit international [403]; and contains book reviews in the extensive section 'Bibliographie critique'. Each volume has a subject, name and geographical index (edited by P.M. Eisenmann), cumulated as follows: *Tables quinquennales*, 1970- (covering 1965-9, 1970-4 and 1975-9) and *Tables décennales*, 1978- (covering 1965-74, published in 1978, and 1975-84, published in 1988).

283. *Revue générale de droit international public.* Paris: Pédone (avec concours de CNRS), 1894-, 1-, quarterly. Indexes.

Between 1894 and 1948 subtitled 'Droit des gens, histoire diplomatique, droit pénal, droit fiscal, droit administratif', *RGDIP* has been edited by prominent French legal scholars, including La Pradelle, Politis, Virally and Rousseau. The regular features of *RGDIP* include: 'Chronique des faits internationaux'; 'Jurisprudence française en matière de droit international'; book reviews in a section called 'Bibliographie'; and an index to selected PIL articles in a section called 'Publications périodiques'. The section 'Documents' contains texts in French of selected current primary PIL materials; the information is similar to that in [219a,b].

284. *Journal du droit international*. Paris: Editions techniques, 1874-, 1-, quarterly. Indexes.

Founded by E. Clunet, the *Journal* contains articles mostly on private international law. Its regular features include 'Chronique de jurisprudence administrative internationale', and Chronique de la jurisprudence de la CIJ' (edited by R. Pinto). There are cumulative author and subject indexes for the periods 1874-1904, 1905-25 and 1925-55.

Greece

285. *Revue hellénique de droit international*. Athens: Hellenic Institute of International and Foreign Law, 1948-, 1-, quarterly.

Contains articles in English, French and German.

Italy

286. *Italian yearbook of international law*. Napoli: Editoriale Scientifica, 1975-, 1-, annual.

The last known volume was 6-7, published in 1983 and covering the period 1980-1. The volumes include a section 'Italian bibliographical index of international law'. *See also Annali di diritto internazionale*. Milano: Istituto per gli Studi di Politica Internazionale, 1945-, 1-.

287. *Rivista di diritto internazionale: jus gentium*. Milano: Casa Editrice Dott; Padua: Casa Editrice Milani, 1906-, 1-, 3 times a year.

The contents of these and other relevant periodicals are usually analysed by the *Dizionario bibliografico delle riviste giuridiche italiane*. Milano: Giuffrè, 1980-, 1-, annual. Compiler V. Napoletano.

Netherlands

288. *Netherlands yearbook of international law*. Dordrecht: Nijhoff, 1970-, 1-, annual. Since 1978 published by Sijthoff & Noordhoff, Alphen a/R. Indexes.

Published under the auspices of the T.M.C. Asser Institute [406], the *NYIL* includes information on Dutch PIL practice, with selected texts of relevant judicial decisions, treaties, etc. Contains a section called 'Dutch literature in the field of PIL' (formerly included in the NILR [289]). Each volume has a detailed PIL classification scheme and an index, cumulated for vols 1-10, 1970-9 (published in 1983).

289. *Netherlands international law review*. Alphen a/R: Sijthoff & Noordhoff, 1953-, 1-, 3 times a year.

Published under the auspices of the T.M.C. Asser Institute [406], the *NILR* contains articles on private and public international law, as well as comparative law. *NILR* used to include bibliographic surveys of international law literature [339b]; since the 1970s such surveys have been included in *NYIL* [288]. A special issue of *NILR* contains the commemorative essay for J.P.A. François, subsequently published as *Varia jus gentium*. Leiden: Sijthoff, 1959, 427 pp.

Spain

290. *Anuario de derecho internacional*. Pamplona: Facultad de Derecho. Universidad de Navarra, 1975-, 1-, annual.

Switzerland

292. *Schweizer Jahrbuch für internationales Recht/Annuaire suisse de droit international*. Zürich: Editions polygraphiques (Schultheiss), 1944-, 1-, annual.

ASDI regularly contains: 'La pratique suisse en matière de droit international public'; 'Bibliographie du droit international public'; and 'Parti documentaire' (includes references to and/or texts of relevant acts and treaties). *See also* [449f].

293. [No entry].

United Kingdom

294. *British yearbook of international law*. London: Oxford UP, 1920-76, vols 1-46; Oxford: Clarendon Press, 1977-, vol. 47-. Editors (since 1983) I. Brownlie and D.W. Bowett; H. Lauterpacht (1944-53).

Published under the auspices of the Royal Institute of International Affairs, *BYIL* regularly contains a survey of British Court decisions affecting public and private international law, and book reviews and bibliographies of UK literature on PIL.

295. *International and comparative law quarterly*. London: British Institute of International and Comparative Law, 1952-, 1-, quarterly.

ICLQ incorporates the *Transactions* of the Grotius Society [465e] and the *Quarterly* of the Society of Comparative Legislation and International Law. *ICLQ* superseded the *International quarterly* (London, 1947-51). The focus of *ICLQ* is on Commonwealth and European Community legal and PIL issues.

Middle East

296. *Palestine yearbook of international law*. Nicosia, Cyprus: el-Shaybani Society of International Law, 1984-, 1-, annual.

The articles and English translations of relevant judicial decisions and legislative acts pertaining to the region aim to render accessible a variety of scattered legal and PIL materials chiefly concerning the Israeli-Palestinian conflict. *See also Journal of Palestine studies*, a quarterly on Palestinian Affairs and the Arab-Israeli conflict. Washington, DC: Institute for Palestine Studies, 1971-, 1-, quarterly.

e. Encyclopaedias, dictionaries

Monolingual
Chinese
See [36b].

English

297. *Encyclopedia of public international law.* Amsterdam: North-Holland, 1981-, 1-.

Published under the auspices of the Max-Planck Institute for Comparative Public Law and International Law [402a], under the direction of R. Bernhardt. Foreseen as having twelve volumes (vol. 11 was published in 1989). Each volume contains articles on a broadly conceived PIL domain: vol. 1, Settlement of disputes; vol. 2, Decisions of international courts, tribunals and international arbitrations; vols 3 and 4, Use of force, war and neutrality, peace treaties; vol. 5, International organizations in general; vol. 6, Regional cooperation, organizations, problems; vol. 7, History of international law, foundations and principles of international law, sources of international law, law of treaties; vol. 8, Human rights and the individual in international law; vol. 9, International relations and legal cooperation in general, diplomacy and consular relations; vol. 10, States, responsibility of States, international and municipal law; vol. 11, Law of the sea, air and space; vol. 12, Geographical coverage. Cumulative index.

Prominent international legal scholars and specialists have contributed some 45 to 180 articles (complete with extensive bibliographic notes) per volume of the *Encyclopedia*. The English-language *Encyclopedia* is patterned after the German-language *Wörterbuch des Völkerrechts* [303]. For a review of vols 1-7 of the *Encyclopedia* see *AFDI*, 1984, **30**, pp. 1073-1074.

298a. Parry, C., Grant, J.P., Parry, A. and Watts, A.D. (eds), *Encyclopaedic dictionary of international law.* Dobbs Ferry, NY: Oceana, 1986, 654 pp.

Patterned after the the German-language *Wörterbuch des Völkerrechts* [303] and the French-language *Dictionnaire diplomatique* [573c], this one-volume English-language work is midway between being a dictionary (explaining the meaning of words) and an encyclopaedia (containing substantive information on given topics) with the focus on the law of peace. The coverage of the history of PIL, of the law of armed conflict or of international organization is little more than sketchy. Decisions of municipal courts relating to PIL have ben omitted and the bio-bibliographical information is rather selective.

—b. Bledsoe, R.L. and Boczek, B.A. (eds), *The international law dictionary.* Santa Barbara, CA: ABC-Clio Press, 1987, 422 pp. (Clio Dictionaries in Political Science).

Provides historical and current explanations of selected general PIL terms (e.g. act of state doctrine, claims commission, non-combatants, responsibility) in a broad systematic arrangement.

299. Gamboa, M., *A dictionary of international law and diplomacy*. Quezon City, Philippines: Central Law Book Publishing, 1973, 351 pp.

Supersedes the author's *Elements of diplomatic and consular practice*, 1966.

See also PIL glossary in [171].

Czechoslovak

300. **Slovnik verejného prava československeho*. Editors A. Hobza *et al*. Brno: Nakl. Polygraphia R.M. Rohrer, 1929-47.

French

301a. *Juris-classeur de droit international*. Paris: Editions techniques, 1966-, 1- (Collection des juris-classeurs).

The individual binders of the loose-leaf *Juris-classeur* provide a dictionary-type approach to private and public international law topics in general and French international legal practice in particular. Vol. 1, analytic, alphabetic table, as well as general theory of international organization; vols 2 and 3, universal, regional international organizations; vol. 4, international (and French) fiscal law; vols 5 and 6, international criminal law; vol. 7, international private law; vol. 8, international labour law, etc.; vol. 9 (published in 1987), international social security. Supersedes La Pradelle, A.G. de and Niboyet, J.P., *Encyclopédie juridique: répertoire de droit international*. Paris: Sirey, 1929-34, 11 vols. New series, Paris: Dalloz, 1968-9, 2 vols. Editor P. Franceskakis. *See also* Calvo, C., *Dictionnaire de droit international public et privé*. Berlin: Puttkammer & Mühlenbrecht, 1885, 2 vols, in which the Argentinian scholar lists, in French, concepts reflecting the traditional (Eurocentric) approach.

—b. *Encyclopédie juridique de l'Afrique*. Abidjan: Nouvelles éditions africaines, 1982, 10 vols.

Directed by P.-F. Gonidec (head of the Centre d'études des problèmes juridiques et politiques du Tiers-Monde, Paris), the individual volumes of the *Encyclopédie* deal with different legal (and a few PIL) issues specific to Africa. Vol. 2 (Editor S. Camara, Minister of Justice, Guinea), *Droit international et relations internationales*; includes contributions by African legal scholars on the formation and interrelations of African states, Inter-African organizations, human rights issues, etc.

—c. *Encyclopédie de l'Islam*. Nouvelle édition. Leiden: Brill; Paris: Maisonneuve, 1954-, 1-. Editor J.J. Kramers.

The last known fascicule (of vol. 4, to the letter *Kha*) was published in 1977/8. Published under the auspices of the Union académique internationale, the *Encyclopédie* contains long, signed scholarly articles on various aspects of Islam.

The new French edition is based on the English *Encyclopaedia of Islam*. Leiden: Brill, 1913–36, 4 vols. *See also Enzyklopaedie des Islam: geographisches, ethnographisches und biographisches Wörterbuch der muhamedanischen Völker*. Leiden: Brill, 1908.

German

302. Seidl-Hohenveldern, I., *Lexikon des Rechts: Völkerrecht*. Neuwied/Darmstadt: Luchterhand, 1985, 369 pp.

The first volume of a general *Ergänzbares Lexikon des Rechts*, projected in 18 (loose-leaf) parts. Systematically arranged, the first (PIL) part outlines traditional and contemporary concepts and issues. Includes bibliographies and cross-references to relevant information in other parts of the *Lexikon*.

303. Strupp, K. and Schlochauer, H., *Wörterbuch des Völkerrechts*, 2nd edn. Berlin: W. de Gruyter, 1960–2, 3 vols + index.

Contains expository signed articles on PIL concepts and topics, as well as selected ICJ decisions. Includes English and French tables of contents and bio-bibliographical notes. Reviewed by Suy, E., 1966, *Revue belge de droit international* 2, pp. 606–607. The first edition, begun by J. Hatschek and edited by K. Strupp (Leipzig: W. de Gruyter, 1924–9, 3 vols) emphasized PIL within the context of German political affairs.

Polish

304. Klafkowski, A. *et al., Encyklopedia prawa międzynarodowego i stosunków międzynarodowych*. Warszawa: Wieza Powszechna, 1976, 472 pp.

For an older, extensive, but incomplete work (to the letter P) *see* Cybichowski, Z., *Encyklopedia podreczna prawa publicznego: konstytucyjnego, administracyjnego i międzynarodowego*. Warszawa, 1929–35.

Portuguese

305. *Ferreira de Mello, R., *Dicionario de direito internacional público*. Rio de Janeiro, 1962, 369 pp.

Romanian

306. Cloşca, I., *Dictionar de drept international public*. Bucureşti: Ed. Ştiintifica şi Enciclopedica, 1982, 318 pp.

Includes summaries of international treaties from 1864 to 1978.

Russian

307. Klimenko, B.M. *et al.*, *Slovar' mezhdunarodnogo prava*, 2nd rev. edn. Moskva: Mezhdunarodnye Otnosheniĩa, 1986, 432 pp. 1st edn 1982.

An alphabetical list of contemporary PIL concepts and topics with the emphasis on the law of peace and Soviet international legal practice. The 1st edn was translated by M. Saifulin into English as *A dictionary of international law*. Moscow: Progress, 1986, 291 pp.

Serbo-Croat

308. Ibler, V., *Rječnik međunarodnog javnog prava*, 2nd edn. Zagreb: Informator, 1987, 368 pp. 1st edn 1972.

Spanish

309. *Vasco, M., *Diccionario de derecho internacional*. Quito, 1963.

Multilingual

310. Paenson, I., *Manual of the terminology of public international law (law of peace) and of international organizations: English, French, Spanish, Russian*. Bruxelles: Bruylant, 1983, 846 pp.

The third volume in a series of multilingual terminologies, the *Manual* lists in a systematic arrangement PIL terms in English with French, Spanish and Russian equivalents. The annotations refer to the (textual and ideological) sources of the terms. A bibliography of the sources cited concludes the manual.

311. Gilbertson, G., *Harrap's German and English glossary of terms in international law*. London: G.G. Harrap, 1980, 355 pp.

Based on some 200 international treaties and many authoritative PIL treatises the glossary consists of terms relating to the theory, codification and practice of PIL. The first, German–English, section contains terms, derived phrases and contextual examples; the second section provides excerpts from primary and secondary PIL sources (fully cited), illustrating the terms listed in the first section; the third section is a register of some 12,000 English terms listed in the first and second sections.

312. Basdevant, J. (comp.), *Dictionnaire de la terminologie du droit international*. Publié sous le patronage de l'Union académique internationale. Tables en anglais, espagnol, italien, allemand. Paris: Sirey, 1960, 755 pp.

Although it was published 30 years ago, this remains an outstanding multilingual dictionary of private and public international law. The French terms, with English, German, Italian and Spanish equivalents, are illustrated with examples from international legal primary and secondary sources.

313. *Terminologjia e së drejtës ndërkombëtare: shqip, rusisht, frenjisht, anglisht*. Tirana: Univ. Shtetëror, 1970, 282 pp. (Fjalor i terminologjise tekniko-shkencore).

A glossary of international law terms in Albanian, with Russian, French and English equivalents.

For references to further vocabularies, glossaries, etc. (including legal and PIL terms) *see Bibliography of mono- and multilingual vocabularies, thesauri, subject headings and classification schemes in the social sciences*. Prepared by the Aslib Library in collaboration with J. Aitchison and C. G. Allen. Paris: UNESCO, 1982, 101 pp. (Reports and Papers in the Social Sciences, 54). French edition, 1984. Arranged according to the Universal Decimal Classification (UDC: Law/340) the bibliography has author, database and subject indexes. *See also* Riggs, F. W., *Interconcept report: a new paradigm for solving the terminology problems of the social sciences*. Paris: UNESCO, 1981, 49 pp. (Reports and Papers in the Social Sciences, 47).

f. Conferences, colloquia

Bibliographic lists, calendars

315. *International congress calendar*. Brussels: Union of International Associations (UIA), 1960/1-, 1-, annual.

Lists forthcoming conferences and meetings convened under the auspices of governmental and non-governmental international organizations. Arranged in geographical, chronological and subject organization sections (the latter provides references to a few outstanding conferences on or relating to international law). For retrospective lists of conferences *see Les congrès internationaux de 1681 à 1899; liste complète*. Brussels: UIA, 1960, 76 pp. and Gregory, W. (ed.), *International congresses and conferences, 1840-1937*. New York: H. W. Wilson, 1938, 229 pp. Since the Second World War the proliferation of conferences has led to various (often abortive) attempts to provide subject access to the increasingly specialized conferences. In PIL terms this has led mainly to (methodological) analyses [317-319] of the types and contents of relevant conferences rather than their bibliographic control.

316. *Bibliographic guide to conference publications*. Boston, MA: G. K. Hall, 1975-, annual.

Lists published conference proceedings available in and catalogued by the Research Libraries of the New York Public Library and the US Library of Congress. Arranged alphabetically by subjects, including law and international law.

Topical, regional aspects

317a. Lachs, M., La diplomatie par les conférences et le droit, pp. 331-340 in [178].

The focus is on the role of multilateral negotiations in the creation of international legal rules.

—b. Rosenne, S., 1986, International conferences and congresses. *Enc. PIL*, **9**, pp. 27-32.

Analyses conferences, mainly UN ones, according to their category, legal status and substantive or documentary outcome.

318. Pambou Tchivounda, G., *La conférence au sommet: contribution à l'étude des institutions des relations internationales.* Paris: LGDI, 1980, 425 pp. (Bibliotheèque de droit international, 85).

319. *Ashavskiĭ, B. M., *Mezhpravitel'stvennye konferentsii: mezhdunarodno-pravovye voprosy.* Moskva, 1980.

See also chapters on international conferences in [116, 126].

320. The following conferences were convened under the auspices of, and/or their proceedings were published for, the Carnegie Endowment for International Peace [381].

—a. *The process of change in international law, Menton, 1964.* Edited by R. Zacklin. Geneva, 1965.

—b. *The newly independent states and international law, Geneva, 1963.* Edited by G. Abi-Saab. Geneva, 1964.

—c. *The international conferences of American states, 1826–1929.* Edited by J. B. Scott. New York: Oxford UP, 1931.

1st supplement for period 1933–40 (1940); 2nd supplement for period 1938–42 (1943). Subsequent supplements have been published by the Pan-American Union/OAS [688].

—d. *A guide to the practice of international conferences.* Edited by V. Pastuhov. Washington, DC, 1944.

—e. *Inter-American conferences, 1826–1954: history and problems.* Edited by S. G. Inman. Washington, DC, 1965.

321. The Société française pour le droit international [403] has since 1971 annually convened PIL colloquia, subsequently published by Pédone, Paris, 1972–. Known by the name of the French city in which they were held, the colloquia expertly review developments in contemporary general and specialized PIL, e.g. Colloque de Montpellier, 1972, *Actualité du droit de la mer* [542a]; Colloque de Bordeaux, 1976, *Régionalisme et universalisme dans le droit international contemporain* [478c]: Colloque de Poitiers, 1979, *La frontière* [534b]; Colloque de Lyon, 1986, *La juridiction internationale permanente* [667b].

322. The Centre d'études des relations internationales, Reims, has since 1973 (irregularly) convened and published the outcome of PIL meetings titled *Rencontres de Reims* (part of the series *Annales*, Université de Reims, Faculté de droit et sciences économiques). The proceedings (sometimes titled Actes or Rapports sur discussion) have so far been published as:

—a. *Les méthodes d'analyse en droit international. Actes* de la 1ère Rencontre de Reims, 1973.

—b. *Réalités du droit international contemporain.* [*Rapports*] de la 2ème et 3ème Rencontres de Reims, 1974-5.

—c. *Les relations du droit international avec la structure économique et social.* [*Actes*] de la 4ème Rencontre de Reims, 1977.

—d. *Discours juridique et pouvoir dans les relations internationales: l'exemple des sujets de droit.* [*Actes*] de la 5ème Rencontre de Reims, 1980.

The contributions represent a French Marxist (mainly methodological) approach to PIL issues.

323. [No entry].

324a. *Deutsch-polnisches Völkerrechtskolloquium, 1972. Referate deutscher und polnischer Völkerrechtler . . . mit Beiträgen von R. Schroers.* Frankfurt a/M: Athenäum, 1972, 90 pp. (Völkerrecht und Aussenpolitik, 16).

—b. *Anglo-Polish legal colloquia, London, 1982-*, contributions to which are published in [273c]; *see also* [428a].

325. **African Conference on international law and African problems, Lagos, 1967.* Lagos, 1967, 106 pp.

326a. *Conference on problems of international law in the Western Hemisphere, New York, 1971.* The Hague: Nijhoff, 1974, 199 pp.

—b. **El derecho internacional en los congresos ordinarios.* Córdoba: Asociación Argentina de Derecho Internacional, 1981. *See also* [320c,d].

iii. REFERENCE AIDS

a. Guides to research

327. Miskin, C., *International law and organization*, pp. 437-487, in [411a, 2nd edn].

Analyses PIL primary (including national and international official materials), secondary and auxiliary sources and resources (mainly in English) and outlines reference methods relating to general and PIL case law. Updates and complements Parsons, K.O., *Public international law*, pp. 337-353, in [411a, 1st edn].

328. Williams, J.W., 1986, Guide to international legal research. *George Washington journal of international law and economics*, **20**(1/2), 413 pp.

Represents the first updating (to be repeated every five years) of the author's 'Research tips in international law: bibliographical notes'. *JILE*, 1981, **15**(1), 321 pp. (itself a cumulation of the author's surveys published in *JILE*, 1972-9).

The work contains: a discussion of basic concepts of private and public international law, along with relevant research and reference steps; a documentary typology of (mostly English language) PIL materials, i.e. primary sources (codified and case law), secondary resources (including analytical tools, e.g. treatises, digests, serials) and research tools (including handbooks, bibliographies, directories).

329. Schwietzke, J., 1985, The availability of research tools in public international law, especially for documents and publications of intergovernmental organizations. *IJLL*, **13**(5/6), pp. 1-48.

Originally presented at the IALL [415a] Round Table, Chicago, 1985, the article deals with selected PIL primary (mainly treaties) and auxiliary (mainly bibliographic) materials; part 6 deals with UN and SA materials relative to PIL.

330. Kleckner, S.-M., *Public international law and international organization: international law bibliography*. Dobbs Ferry, NY: Oceana, 1988, 126 pp. (Collection of Bibliographic and Research Resources [1]). 1st edn 1984.

The guide contains references to some 1,300 PIL monographs published worldwide. Included are: treaty collections; materials on international legal practice by states and IGOs; judicial decisions; writings (in English, in topical arrangement) on PIL; periodicals; reference aids. No index. The 1984 edition superseded the author's *Public international law and international organization: a basic selective bibliography* [compiled] 'at the request [in 1976] of a Permanent Mission to the United Nations, to assist . . . in establishing basic libraries in the field of international law and organization'. New York: UN, DHL, 1982, 102 pp. (UN document ST/LIB/38, 1982).

331a. Mostecky, V., International law, pp. 638-691, in Cohen, M.L. and Berring, R.C., *How to find the law*, 8th edn. St Paul, MN: West Publishing, 1983.

Discusses PIL primary sources (treatises, judicial decisions) and secondary resources (treaties, periodicals, bibliographies), as well as selected UN and SA materials relating to PIL. The research and reference methods outlined elsewhere in the Cohen and Berring work complement Mostecky's guide to PIL materials.

—b. Bernal, M.-L., 1983, Reference sources in international law. *Law library journal*, **76**(3), pp. 427-435.

An analysis of selected reference aids, notably bibliographies and dictionaries.

—c. Szepesi, J., *International law: selected sources of information*. Ottawa: Carleton University Library, Social Sciences Division, 1979, 29 pp.

An outline mostly of secondary PIL resources (treatises, periodicals, bibliographies) and a few documents relating to international affairs.

332. *Sbornik mezhdunarodno-pravovoĭ dokumentatsii, neobkhodimoĭ dlia studentov-praktikantov po spetsial'nosti 'Mezhdunarodnoe pravo'. Moskva: Universitet P. Lumumba, 1974, 242 pp.

A documentary guide intended for PIL study and teaching.

333. Kasme, B., General bibliography on primary sources of international law, pp. 855-892 in [76]. Also separately published: Geneva, 1966, 56 pp.

Discusses PIL primary sources (treaties, judicial decisions, state practice and materials of international organizations), including treatises, etc., published worldwide before the mid-1960s.

334. Robinson, J., *International law and organization: general sources of information*. Leiden: Sijthoff, 1967, 560 pp.

Preceded by introductory notes, the six chapters contain references to secondary and auxiliary resources of general PIL, published mainly in Europe and the Americas between the 1850s and 1950s. Included are: encyclopaedias; treatises (by country of publication), including 'classics'; bibliographies; biographical information; serials, including yearbooks; works on study, teaching and research, including directories. Occasional annotations refer to analytical indexes, tables of cases, historical surveys and book reviews. An author and subject index concludes the guide.

335. Morgenstern, P., *Einführung in die Bibliographie und das Schrifttum zum Völkerrecht*. Göttingen: Institut für Völkerrecht. Universität Göttingen, 1963, 47 pp. (Reihe Allgemeines Völkerrecht, 7).

Discussed are PIL auxiliary resources (mainly bibliographies), secondary resources (treatises, periodicals, etc.) and primary sources (treaties, materials of international organizations). Includes a chronological list of PIL courses in *RCADI* [220a] for the period 1929-61.

b. Bibliographies, indexing journals

Bibliographies of PIL bibliographies

336a. Dag Hammarskjöld Library. United Nations, New York. *Bibliographies*. New York: UN, DHL, 1949-, 1-, mimeographed (UN document ST/LIB/Ser.B/1-).

Includes several bibliographies specific to general [330] and specialized PIL, the latter including: succession of states in respect of treaties [530c]; law of the sea [559a]; NIEO [729a]. The topical (PIL) bibliographies range from 10 to 90 pages and contain references to monographs and periodical articles published worldwide (usually excluding UN, SA materials). *See also* [618b, 652d].

—b. United Nations Organization at Geneva. Library. *Bibliographies*. Geneva: UNOG Library, 1970- (UN document ST/Geneva/LIB/Ser.B/Ref. 1-), 1-, mimeographed.

Includes bibliographies on territorial asylum [702d], the Third World and PIL [486].

337a. Besterman, T., *Law and international law: a bibliography of bibliographies*. Totowa, NJ: Rowman & Littlefield, 1971, 436 pp.

A separately published section from the author's *World bibliography of bibliographies*, 4th edn. Lausanne: Societas bibliographica, 1965-6, 5 vols. The 1971 reprint (of vol. 2, 4th edn) includes mainly general legal bibliographies, published in separate monographic form before 1963; pp. 3069-3087 concern PIL bibliographies proper. For a critical review *see* [372c].

—b. *A collection of bibliographic and research resources*. Dobbs Ferry, NY: Oceana, 1984-, 1-, irregular.

The series includes bibliographies relative to PIL, e.g. [330, 559c, 578b, 614b, 736b].

Library catalogues

338a. Moody, M. (ed.), *Catalog of international law and relations*. Cambridge, MA: Harvard Law School Library, 1965-7, 20 vols. Microfiche edition, München: Saur, 1984.

The *Catalog* is a segment of the overall Harvard Law School Library collection [417b]. Probably one of the most important retrospective bibliographies in the field, the *Catalog* comprises over 80,000 (main entry) references to monographs and serials published worldwide (but especially in North America) between 1817 and 1960, relating to (private and public) international law, relations and organizations. Based on some 360,000 library catalogue cards, the *Catalog* is an alphabetical list of authors, subjects and titles. *See also* [345].

—b. *Annual legal bibliography*. Cambridge, MA: Harvard Law School Library, 1962-81, 21 vols. Edited by V. Mostecky (vols 1-8); M. Moody (vols 9-21). Microfiche edition, München: Saur, 1984.

ALB is the annual cumulation of the monthly *Current legal bibliography* (CLB, 1962-81), and both reflect the acquisition objectives of the Harvard Law School Library. *ALB* and *CLB* contain references to monographs and periodical articles published worldwide in the broad area of law; excluded are references to primary source materials. In *ALB*'s systematic topical arrangement, sections C and D refer to private and public international law, respectively. Each annual volume also contains: a classified list of subjects; an alphabetical subject index (the 'Sachverzeichnis' and 'Table alphabétique' represent subject headings in German and French translations respectively); and a geographical index. Titles of periodicals indexed by *ALB* are listed in its vol. 3. The microfiche edition provides bibliographic access to works on law (including PIL) catalogued by the Harvard Law School Library [417b] between 1963 and 1981.

—c. *Law books, 1876–1981: books and serials on law and related subjects*. New York: Bowker, 1981, 4 vols.

Based on the Bowker American Book Publishing Record Database, *Law books* represents a retrospective bibliography containing some 130,000 references to monographs and serials in law (including PIL) published worldwide during the period 1876-81 and part of the major US law library collections (including those of the Library of Congress and the Universities of California, Chicago, Columbia, Harvard and Yale). Systematically arranged, the references include, where relevant, the LC call number. Based on the Bowker Serials Bibliography Database, *Law books* lists in subject arrangement some 4,000 legal serial titles, including relevant abstracting/indexing services thereto. A list of law book publishers and distributors concludes the bibliography. *See also* [366a,b].

339a. *Catalogue de la Bibliothèque du Palais de la Paix/Catalogue of the Peace Palace Library* [PPL]. Leiden: Sijthoff, 1966, 5 vols with supplements. Microfiche edition München, Saur, 1980.

The systematically arranged PPL *Catalogue* represents a retrospective bibliography of some 64,000 titles of monographs and serials, published worldwide between 1916 and 1952, predominantly in international and comparative law, as well as peace research and international relations. Edited by E. E. Kuehl, the microfiche edition includes acquisitions of the PPL through the 1970s and is based on over 350,000 PPL catalogue cards, including references to periodical articles, brochures.

—b. Landheer, B. and van Essen, J. L. F., *Fundamentals of public international law*. Leiden: Sijthoff, 1953, 85 pp. (Selective Bibliographies of the Library of the Peace Palace).

Based on the PPL international law collection, the Landheer and Essen bibliography was annually updated under the title 'Survey of literature on public and private international law: a selection from the catalogues of the Peace Palace Library', published during 1956-70 in [289].

340. *Catalogue of international law*. Compiled by M. A. Lekner under the direction of W. A. F. P. Steiner. Dobbs Ferry, NY: Oceana, 1972, 4 vols.

The *Catalogue* represents a retrospective bibliography of some 32,000 titles of private and public international law monographs and serials published worldwide through 1970. The arrangement is alphabetically by authors (vols 1 and 2) and systematic (vols 3 and 4). Updated to 1973, the contents of the 4 vols of the *Catalogue* were subsequently incorporated into the *Law catalogue* (Dobbs Ferry, NY: Oceana, 1974-5, 14 vols) of the University of Cambridge Squire Law Library. Vol. 1 of the *Law catalogue* contains the systematic classification scheme of which class F outlines the classified subject divisions of international law and relations, while vol. 11 is an alphabetical list of subject (including PIL) headings. This information in the *Law catalogue* is also contained in vol. 3 of the *Catalogue*.

Retrospective bibliographies

341. Merrills, J.G., *A current bibliography of international law*. London: Butterworth, 1978, 277 pp.

Contains often briefly annotated references to mostly secondary materials (monographs and periodical articles) relating to private and public international law published in English between 1960 and 1975. Systematically arranged. Author index. Reviewed in *Harvard international law journal*, 1980, **21**, p. 467.

342. Delupis, I., *Bibliography of international law*. London and New York: Bowker, 1975, 670 pp.

Contains references mainly to secondary materials (monographs and some periodical articles) published worldwide from 1920 to the 1970s relating to private and public international law. The bibliography is systematically arranged in 14 sections, each preceded by introductory notes, including concepts, interpretations and important scholars in the given field. Author index. Reviewed by Sprudzs, A., 1976, *IJLL*, **4**, p. 160.

343. Gould, W.L. and Barkun, M., *Social science literature: a bibliography for international law*. Published for the American Society of International Law. Princeton, NJ: Princeton UP, 1972, 541 pp.

A companion volume to *International law and the social sciences* (published for ASIL by Princeton UP in 1970), the annotated bibliography contains over 2,800 references to periodical articles and monographs in private and public international law published between 1955 and 1965, 'when experimentation with new social science methods was gaining momentum'. Systematically arranged. Author index. *See also* Schwerin, K. and Gould, W.L., *International law*. South Hackensack, NJ: F.B. Rothman, for the Association of American Law Schools, 1968, 246 pp. (Law Books Recommended for Libraries, 46).

344. Strupp, K., *Bibliographie du droit des gens et des relations internationales*. Leiden: Sijthoff, 1938, 521 pp.

Contains nearly 2,800 references mostly to private and public international law monographs published during 1933-6. Arranged in four parts: part 1 includes extensive critical reviews of some sixty international law treatises and a survey of courses in *RCADI* [220a], parts 2-4 take geographical, systematic and alphabetical approaches to the bibliography. Critically reviewed by Kunz, J.L., 1939, *AJIL*, **33**, p. 613.

345. Olivart, Ramon de Dalman y Olivart, Marquis, *Bibliographie du droit international. Catalogue d'une bibliothèque du droit international et sciences auxiliaires*, 2nd rev. edn. Paris: Pédone, 1905-10, 2 vols. 1st edn 1899.

The systematic catalogue of the international law collection gathered by the Spanish diplomat, Marquis de Olivart. At the time probably the world's most comprehensive, the collection (containing over 14,000 volumes) included primary PIL sources such as treaty texts (Olivart's *Colección de los tratados, convenios y documentos internacionales . . . desde el reinado de Doña Isabel II hasta nuestros dias . . .* Madrid: Progreso Editorial, 1890–1911, 14 vols), documents of international disputes, arbitration, etc., as well as standard works published worldwide on private and public international law. The Harvard Law School Library [417b] acquired the Olivart collection in 1911, developing it and its original classification scheme. The contents of the *Bibliographie* were eventually incorporated into the dictionary card catalogue (1947–63) of the Harvard Law School Library. Since 1983 Inter-Documentation Co., Zug, Switzerland, has undertaken a microfiche edition (Editor W.E. Butler, University College, London) of the volumes in the Olivart collection. So far, some 2,000 titles have been microfiched. *See also* [338a, 417b].

346. Vergé, C., Bibliographie raisonnée du droit des gens. In Martens, G.F., *Précis du droit des gens* . . . Paris: Guillaumin, 1864, vol. 2, pp. 387–441.

A classified bibliography of primary and secondary international law materials (mostly nineteenth-century European imprints).

347. Ompteda, D.H.L., *Literatur des gesamten sowohl natürlichen als positiven Völkerrechts*. Regensburg: J.L. Montag, 1785, 688 pp. Continued by Kamptz, K.A., *Neue Literatur von 1784 bis 1794*, Berlin, 1817, 384 pp. Reprinted by Scientia Verlag, Aalen, in 1963 and 1965 respectively.

An annotated classified bibliography of some 1,000 international law monographs published in Europe during the seventeenth and eighteenth centuries. Ompteda's compilation is midway between a bibliography and a history of ideas (tracing the ascendancy of positive over natural law). The work includes long critical reviews, especially of PIL classics, and discusses the concepts and purpose of PIL (with emphasis on its customary aspects within the context of international relations).

The Americas

Canada

348a. Wiktor, C.L., *Canadian bibliography of international law*. Toronto: Toronto UP, 1984, 767 pp.

Contains some 9,000 references to general and specialized PIL monographs and periodical articles published in or pertaining to Canada from the mid-eighteenth century to 1982. Part 1 concerns the doctrine and institutions of PIL; part 2 refers to legal implications of international relations and specialized PIL areas. Classified arrangement. Alphabetical author and subject index. Reviewed in *CYIL*, 1984, **22**, pp. 457–458.

—b. Langlois, M., *Canadian bibliography on international law/Bibliographie canadienne en droit international*. Ottawa: Conseil canadien de droit international, 1978, 53 pp.

Covers Canadian PIL publications issued between 1967 and 1977.

Latin America

349. Villalón-Galdames, A., *Bibliografía jurídica de América Latina, 1810-1965*. Santiago de Chile: Ed. Jurídica de Chile, 1969, 2 vols.

Vol. 1 includes an outline of general legal bibliographies worldwide, and relating to Argentina and Bolivia in particular; vol. 2 includes a classified index.

Asia

People's Republic of China

350. Pinard, J. L., *The People's Republic of China: a bibliography of selected English language legal materials*. Washington, DC: The Law Library, Library of Congress, 1985, 108 pp.

Supersedes and complements Ho, P., *The People's Republic of China and international law: a selective bibliography*. Washington, DC: The Law Library, Library of Congress, 1972, 45 pp. *See also* [36a,b].

Europe, Eastern

Bulgaria

351. **Bibliografiia na bŭlgarskata pravna literatura [vyp.]* 5. *Mezhdunarodnopravni nauki, 1944-1976*. Sofiia, 1977.

Bibliography of Bulgarian PIL works published during 1944-76.

Hungary

352. *Allami-és jogtudományi bibliográfia*. Budapest: Közgazdasági és Jogi Könyvkiadó, 1954-82; Budapest: Országgyülési Könyvtár, 1983-, biennial. Edited by A. Orosz (since 1980).

The general legal bibliography of Hungarian monographs and periodical articles published since 1945 includes an extensive section on PIL. The volume for the period 1945-51 was published in 1957. Based on the biennial publication is *A magyar állam- és jogtudományi irodalom bibliográfiája/Bibliographia iuridica hungarica/Hungarian legal bibliography/Vengerskaia iuridicheskaia literatura* [selected by] Nagy, L. and Balázsné Veredy K. and published since 1982 in *Acta iuridica* (Budapest: Academia Scientiarum Hungarica, 1959-, 1-, quarterly).

USSR

353a. Fel'dman, D.I. (ed.), *Mezhdunarodnoe pravo: bibliografiia, 1973–1985*. Moskva: Mezhdunarodnye Otnosheniia, 1987, 357 pp.

This classified bibliography of over 5,000 references concerns mostly secondary PIL resources published in the USSR during 1973-85. Section 1 includes PIL bibliographies, mainly published in *SEMP* [270]; section 2 contains treaty collections and official documents; section 3 includes treatises, commemorative essays (including Tunkin, Kozhevnikov, etc.) and directories; section 9 refers to Soviet reviews of non-Soviet PIL works; sections 10-21 concern works on general PIL; sections 23-33 concern specialized PIL areas (but only selectively cover the law of the sea); section 34 refers to PIL publications and contributions of Soviet scholars outside the USSR.

Preceding the 1973-85 bibliography is Kurdiukov, G.I. (comp.), *Mezhdunarodnoe pravo: bibliografiia, 1917–1972*. Moskva: IUridicheskaia Literatura, 1976, 597 pp., itself superseding Durdenevskiĭ, V.V. (ed.), *Sovetskaia literatura po mezhdunarodnomu pravu: bibliografiia, 1917–1957*. Moskva: IUridicheskaia Literatura, 1959, 302 pp. (includes select articles in PIL periodicals, a list of which is appended).

—b. Grabar [sometimes cited as Hrabar], V.E., *Materialy k istorii literatury mezhdunarodnogo prava v Rossii, 1647–1917*. Edited by V.V. Durdenevskiĭ. Moskva: Akademiia Nauk SSSR, 1958, 490 pp.

Each of the five chronological periods (seventeenth century; first and second halves of the eighteenth century; first half of nineteenth century; 1856-1917) contains: the Russian development of PIL of the period; a bibliography of Russian PIL works (including Russian translations of western treatises); bio-bibliographies of Russian PIL scholars; Russian study and teaching of PIL of the period; and PIL classifications. *See also* reference to Grabar's PIL scholarship in *SEMP*, 1985, p. 245.

354. Butler, W.E., *Writings on Soviet law and Soviet international law: a bibliography of books and articles published since 1917 in languages other than East European*. Cambridge, MA: Harvard Law School Publications, 1966, 165 pp.

This systematically arranged bibliography contains references to monographs, periodical articles on international law (pp. 122-144) in English, French, German, Spanish, Turkish, Hebrew, Japanese, Chinese, etc. published from 1917 to the mid-1960s, mainly in the USA, Europe and Asia.

355. Meissner, B., *Sowjetunion und Völkerrecht, 1917 bis 1962: eine bibliographische Dokumentation*. Köln: Wissenschaft und Politik, 1963, 622 pp.

Contains an analysis of PIL developments in the USSR (pp. 11-102), followed by parallel texts (pp. 103-421) in German and Russian of Durdenevskiĭ's bibliography [353a]. A bibliography of PIL works published in the USSR during the period 1958-62, compiled by A. Uschakow (pp. 422-599), concludes the work, itself continued by Meissner, B., Frenzke, D. and Chilecki, E., *Sowjetunion und Völkerrecht, 1962-1973.* Köln, 1977, 575 pp. Together the 1963 and 1977 bibliographies, published in the FRG, essentially contain references to Soviet PIL works as listed in Kurdiukov's bibliography [353a], published in the USSR.

Yugoslavia

356. Ibler, V., *Bibliographie des jugoslawischen Schrifttums zum Völkerrecht, 1945-1968.* Hamburg: Hansischer Gildenverlag, 1970, 380 pp. (Universität Kiel, Institut für internationales Recht, Bibliographien, 2).

See also [272].

Scandinavia

357. Hummerhielm, R., *Nordisk folkrättslig litteratur, 1900-1939/Bibliographie de droit international des pays du nord, 1900-1939.* [Edited by] N. N. Stjernquist. Uppsala: Ohlsson, 1942, 266 pp. (Svenska Institutet för internationell Rätt, Universitet Uppsala. Skrifter, 6).

358. *Bibliographia juridica fennica.* Helsinki: Suomalen Lakimiesyhdistys, 1951-, 1-, irregular.

A bibliography of Finnish legal monographs and periodical articles. Vol. 1 (published in 1951) covers the period 1809-1941; vols 2-5 cover the period 1945-81. Since 1982 published annually. The bibliography's chapter 24 concerns private and public international law.

359. *Svensk juridisk literatur.* Stockholm: Norstedts Juridik, 1957-, 1-, irregular.

A bibliography of Swedish legal monographs and periodical articles, with a section 'Internationell Rätt'. Vol. 1 (published in 1957) covers the period 1865-56; vol. 2 (1979) 1957-70; vol. 3 (1988) 1971-86.

Europe, Western

360. Rauschning, D., *Bibliographie des deutschen Schrifttums zum Völkerrecht, 1945-1964.* Hamburg: Hansischer Gildenverein, 1966, 569 pp. (Universität Kiel, Institut für internationales Recht. Bibliographien, 1).

A supplement for the period 1965-70 was compiled by J. R. Gascard, Hamburg, 1972, 414 pp.

Indexing journals

361. *Public international law: a current bibliography of articles/Völkerrecht: laufende Bibliographie der Aufsatzliteratur/Droit international public: bibliographie périodique d'articles/Derecho internacional público: bibliografía periódica de artículos.*

Berlin: Springer, 1975-, 1-, twice yearly. Editor R. Bernhardt, Compiler W. Morway.

Published under the auspices of the Max-Planck Institute for Comparative Law and International Law [402a], this semi-annual service indexes nearly 1,000 periodicals and yearbooks, as well as selected commemorative essays published worldwide in the field of international law and relations. Annually *PIL* lists some 4,000 references, of which about 600 are specific to public international law. Each issue contains the classification scheme in English, French, German and Spanish. The second issue of each year includes author and subject indexes; a cumulative index exists for vols 2-6, 1976-80. There is a lag of some 12 to 18 months for the articles published (especially in African and Asian countries) and reported by *PIL*.

362. *Bibliographie Völkerrecht und internationale Beziehungen*. Potsdam-Babelsberg: Akademie für Staats- und Rechtswissenschaft der DDR, 1972-, 1-, bi-weekly.

Superseded *Referatezeitschrift Völkerrecht und internationale Beziehungen*. Berlin: Informationszentrum Staat und Recht, 1965-71. Systematically arranged, the *Bibliographie* lists annually some 4,000 references to monographs and periodical articles, as well as selected primary PIL official materials, published predominantly in (mainly European) socialist countries. For a critical review *see* [371b].

363. *Bibliografija odabranih članaka iz međunarodnog prava, objavljenih u domaćim i inostranim periodičnim publikacijama/Bibliography of selected articles on international public law, published in Yugoslav and foreign periodicals*. Beograd: Institut za Međunarodnu Politiku i Privredu, Centar (Odeljenje) za Međunarodno Pravo/Institute of International Politics and Economy, International Law Dept, 1967-, 1-, annual.

Intended for the use by Yugoslav faculties of law and PIL, *Bibliografija* indexes 60 periodicals and yearbooks published worldwide in the field of PIL. Systematically arranged, with author and subject indexes.

364a. *Index to legal periodicals*. New York: H.W. Wilson, 1908-, 1-, monthly.

Since 1928 published in cooperation with the AALL [415b] and between 1964-80 in cooperation with the Institute of Advanced Legal Studies [409]. *ILP* indexes over 400 English-language legal periodicals published mainly in the USA, UK and British Commonwealth countries; the references include book reviews but exclude contributions to commemorative essays. Annually and triennially cumulated with corresponding author and subject indexes, *ILP* also includes a list of periodicals indexed, a book review index and a table of cases cited.

See also Drummond, F.S., 1956, The history of the *ILP. Law library journal*, **49**, pp. 148-156; Mersky, R.M. and Jacobstein, J.M., *30-year index to periodical articles related to law*. Dobbs Ferry, NY: Oceana, 1989. Cumulates for the period 1958-88 references to English language legal and PIL articles scattered in non-legal periodicals (and not indexed by *ILM*).

—b. *Index to foreign legal periodicals: a subject index to selected international and comparative law periodicals and collections of essays*. London: Institute of Advanced Legal Studies, 1960–83. Editor W. A. Steiner; Berkeley, CA: University of California Press, 1984–, quarterly, triennial cumulations. Editor T. H. Reynolds.

Since 1984 *IFLP* has been published in cooperation with the AALL [415b]. *IFLP* indexes annually about 50 collections of essays and some 450 periodicals published worldwide (but generally excluding those from countries with common-law tradition) and relating to municipal, comparative and international private and public law. Systematically arranged (section IX, international law), the quarterly issues include a list of subject headings in English, French, German and Spanish, and author, subject and book review indexes. The annual cumulative index is contained in the July–September issue of each year. For a comparative review of *ILP* and *IFLP* see [371b].

—c. *Novaia inostrannaia literatura po obshchestvennym naukam: Gosudarstvo i pravo*. Moskva: Akademiia Nauk SSSR. Institut Nauchnoĭ Informatsii po Obshchestvennym Naukam, 1973–, 1–, monthly.

Formerly titled *Novaia literatura po gosudarstvu i pravu za rubezhom*, *NILON/GiP* lists, very selectively, references mainly to monographs in the fields of law (occasionally PIL) and government, published mostly in European countries. This indexing journal of non-Soviet legal materials should be used in conjunction with *Novaia sovetskaia literatura po gosudarstvu i pravu: bibliograficheskiĭ biulleten'* (Moskva, 1973–, 1–, monthly). Note also that *Pravovedenie* (Moskva, bimonthly) contains a bibliographic section concerning East European legal publications.

365. *Current law index and legal resource index*. Menlo Park, CA: Information Access Corp., 1980–, 1–, 8 times a year, annually cumulated.

This online indexing service consists of two parts: the computer-produced *CLI* indexes some 700 legal and PIL periodicals (mainly published in countries with common-law tradition), selected by the AALL [415b]; and the quarterly *LRI* in microfiche form. Both parts consist of sections on subject areas, authors and titles, and cases.

366a. *National legal bibliography*. Buffalo, NY: W. S. Hein, 1984–, 1–, monthly (since 1987). Editor P. D. Ward.

The computer-produced *NLB* combines the features of a bibliography and acquisitions list (formerly entitled *Law acquisition national*). *NLB* lists references (sometimes annotated) to monographs, serials, documents and dissertations published worldwide since 1980, and acquired by major law libraries in the USA, including the Library of Congress and the Universities of California, Chicago,

Columbia, Harvard and Yale. Systematically arranged, *NLB* includes selected references to PIL works. The 'index to jurisdictions and systems' provides geographical access to countries and systems of law. The annual cumulations consist of: part 1, Recent acquisitions of major legal libraries: part 2, Government documents from official and commercial sources.

—b. *Bibliographic guide to law*. Boston, MA: G.K. Hall, 1976-, 1-, twice-yearly.

A combined bibliographic and acquisition record, *BGL* lists legal monograph and serial titles published worldwide, and acquired and catalogued since 1980 by the Research Libraries of the New York Public Library (NYPL) and by the Library of Congress [417a]. Authors, titles and subjects (including PIL) are listed in one alphabetical order. The time lag of some three years between the imprints and their records in *BGL* is offset by the detailed bibliographic citation (including NYPL and LC call numbers) of the references listed. *See also* [338c].

367. *Karlsruher juristische Bibliographie: Systematischer Nachweis neuer Bücher und Aufsätze in monatlicher Folge aus Recht, Staat, Gesellschaft*. München: Beck, 1965-, 1-, monthly. Indexes.

KjB indexes legal and PIL periodicals and relevant commemorative essays published worldwide; section 15 concerns PIL. There are monthly and annually cumulated indexes.

368a. *Monthly bibliography/Bibliographie mensuelle*. Geneva: League of nations; UNOG Library, 1920-, 1-, bimonthly (since 1986 monthly) (UN document LIB/SER.B/9-).

MB consists of two parts: I. *Books, official documents, serials/Livres, documents officiels, publications en série*, 1928-, 1-; II. *Selected articles/Articles sélectionnés*, 1929-, 1-. *MB* is a selective acquisition record of national and international publications and official documents (Part I), as well as an index to articles (Part II) selected from some 900 periodicals available in the UNOG Library [419a]. *MB I-II*, with its unbroken coverage since 1920 of materials in law, economics, international relations, represents a continuous bibliographic service in general, while geared to the interests of the UNOG Secretariat in particular. Specifically in PIL terms, *MB I-II* annually records some 200 monographs and about 1,000 periodical articles. Note also *LoN and UN Monthly list of selected articles: cumulative, 1920-1970*. Editor N.S. Field. Dobbs Ferry, NY: Oceana, 1972, 14 vols (Political, legal and economic questions). Arranged chronologically by five-year periods, the cumulative index *Legal questions* deals with public and private international law (vol. 1) and municipal law (vol. 2). Computer-produced since 1986, *MB I-II* contains monthly and annual indexes.

—b. *Current bibliographic information*. New York: UN, DHL, 1971-, 1-, monthly.

CBI, like *MB I-II* [368a], is a combined acquisition record and index of periodical articles, primarily of interest to the UN Secretariat at New York. Computer-produced since 1979, *CBI* has monthly and annual indexes.

See also Schmittroth, J., *Abstracting and indexing services directory*. Detroit, MI: Gale, 1982 (some 1,500 services are listed).

c. Abbreviations, reviews, series, etc.

369. *A uniform system of citation*, 14th edn. Cambridge, MA: Harvard Law Review Association, 1986, 237 pp.

Referred to as the 'Bluebook'. The citator (revised every five years) provides standards for citing references to (mainly) Anglo-American case law, constitutions, statutes, legislative documents and published and unpublished materials (including periodicals). Includes a section on international law citations. *See also* Teitelbaum, G.W., 1983, The periodical section of the *Uniform system of citation*. 13th edn.: a review and some suggestions. *Law library journal*, **76**(2), pp. 264–98.

370a. Raistrick, D., *Index to legal citations and abbreviations*. Abingdon, Oxon.: Professional Books, 1981 (Law Reference Library, 3).

Lists some 20,000 abbreviations relating mainly to Anglo-American legal usage. *See also* Bieber, D.M., *Dictionary of legal abbreviations used in American law books*. Buffalo, NY: W.S. Hein, 1985, 490 pp. Includes abbreviations of legal periodical titles; *Shepard's law review citations: a compilation of citations to law reviews and legal periodicals*, 2nd edn. Colorado Springs, CO: Shepard, 1974.

—b. Kirchner, H. and Kastner, F., *Abkürzungsverzeichnis der Rechtssprache*, 3rd edn. Berlin: W. de Gruyter, 1983, 412 pp.

—c. Gendrel, M., *Dictionnaire des principaux sigles utilisés dans le monde juridique, de A à Z*. Paris: Les Cours de droit/Montchréstien, 1980, 171 pp.

See also Caparros, E. and Goulet, J., *La documentation juridique: références et abréviations*. Québec: Presses universitaires de Laval, 1973, 182 pp.

Reviews, reprints

371a. *Law books in review: a quarterly journal of reviews of current publications in law and related fields*. Dobbs Ferry, NY: Oceana/Glanville, 1974–, 1–, quarterly.

Continues, as a separate publication, to record information which until 1973 was included in [414b]. Book reviews are carried in some indexing journals [364a,b] and many PIL periodicals [250, 282, 414a, etc.].

—b. Gödan, J.C., *Die internationalen allgemeinjuristischen Fachbibliographien: aktuelle Bücher, Zeitschriften- und Zeitschrifteninhaltsverzeichnisse; ein kritischer Bericht*. Frankfurt a/M: Klostermann, [1975], 131 pp. (*Zeitschrift für Bibliothekswesen und Bibliographie*. Sonderheft, 20).

Contains extensive and critical reviews of legal and PIL retrospective and current bibliographies and indexing journals, notably [62a, 338b, 362, 364a,b, 432d]. A tabulated survey of the works reviewed concludes the essay. *See also International bibliography of book-reviews*. Edited by O. and W. Zeller. München: Saur, 1970-83, 13 vols.

372. *Law books in print. Books in English published throughout the world and in print through 1986*, 5th edn. Compiled and edited by N. Triffin. Dobbs Ferry, NY: Oceana/Glanville, 1987, 6 vols. 1st edn 1957.

Vols 1 and 2, authors and titles; vol. 3, series; vols 4 and 5, subjects; vol. 6, publishers. Previous editions (edited by J.M. Jacobstein and M.G. Pimsleur): 1982, 5 vols; 1976, 4 vols; 1971, 3 vols; 1965, 2 vols. For reviews *see IJLI* 1987, **15**, pp. 285-286, and 1983, **11**, pp. 89-90.

See also International bibliography of reprints. München: Saur, 1976, 2 vols in 4 parts; *International books in print: English language titles published outside the USA and the UK*. München: Saur, 1979-, 1-, (in two parts: Part 1, authors and titles; Part 2, classes, includes 340/Law). 7th edn 1988.

Series

373a. *International law studies/Blue book series*. Newport, RI: [US] Naval War College, 1901-, 1-; New series 1968-, 1-, annual.

—b. *Studies in Transnational Legal Policy*. Washington, DC: ASIL, 1972-, 1-.

—c. *Studies on a just world order*. Boulder, CO: Westview Press, 1982- (formerly *World order studies*, by the Center of International Studies, Princeton, NJ). *See also* [381].

—d. *Developments in international law*. Dordrecht: Nijhoff, 1980-.

—e. *Grotius Classic Reprints*. Cambridge: Research Centre for International Law, 1987-, 1-.

—f. *Hersch Lauterpacht memorial lecture series*. Cambridge: Research Centre for International Law, 1987-, 1-.

—g. *Melland Schill monographs in international law*. Under the auspices of the University of Manchester; published by Oceana, Dobbs Ferry, NY.

—h. *Bibliothèque de droit international*. Paris: LGDJ, 1957-, 1-. Editor C. Rousseau. Published under the auspices of the Institut de hautes études internationales, Paris. *See also* [623b].

—i. *Schweizer Studien zum internationalen Recht/Etudes suisses de droit international*. Zürich, Schultheiss, 1975-, 1-.

Published under the auspices of the Schweizerische Vereinigung für internationales Recht/Société suisse de droit international, the series supersedes *Zürcher Studien zum internationalen Recht*. *See also* [407a].

—j. Schwerin, K., *Bibliographie rechtswissenschaftlicher Schriftenreihen*. München: Verlag Dokumentation, 1978, 383 pp.

A bibliography of German-language institutional and publisher's series, in which the individual titles in the series are also indicated. Sections A, B, S and V contain PIL series and individual titles therein. *See also* [402a].

374a. *Nogueira Porto, L. de A., *Atlas de direito internacional público*. Preface by H. Accioly. Rio de Janeiro, 1953, 22 maps.

See also Winch, K. L., *International maps and atlases in print*, 2nd edn. London: Bowker, 1976, 882 pp. Contains annotated references to over 8,000 maps and atlases published worldwide; arranged by continents, countries, with index of geographical names. *See also* [488c].

—b. *Names of countries and adjectives of nationality/Noms des pays et adjectifs de nationalité/Nombres de países y adjectivos gentiliciosos*. New York: UN, 1984, 61 pp. (*Terminology Bulletin* No. 328; UN document ST/CS/SER.F/328; UN sales no. E/F/S.84.I.8).

d. Directories (biographical, institutional)

Biographical information

375. Kuehl, W. F. (ed.), *Biographical dictionary of internationalists*. Westport, CT; London: Greenwood Press, 1983, 934 pp.

BDI defines internationalists as 'transnational thinkers propounding intellectual and other forms of co-operation extending beyond national boundaries', and includes individuals with leading positions in functional international and national bodies, or persons whose writings or activities have gained them professional or academic recognition. *BDI* provides signed biographical sketches for internationalists in the period 1815-1975. Arranged in three sections, *BDI* provides geographical career and subject approaches to internationalists, including some 90 prominent (for the most part deceased) PIL scholars and practitioners, e.g. A. Alvarez, T. M. C. Asser, J. Basdevant, C. Calvo, C. J. Hambro, Hsu Mo, H. Kelsen, H. Lauterpacht and C. de Visscher. *See also International who's who*, 59th edn. London: Europa, 1988-9; note 2, Part I/A.iii.d.

Institutional information

376a. Rhyne, C. S. (ed.), *Law and judicial systems of nations*, 3rd edn. Washington, DC: World Peace through Law Center, 1977, 919 pp. 1st edn 1965.

Essentially a directory, this work contains facts about judicial systems in some 145 countries as well as information concerning names of incumbent chief justices of the highest national courts and lists of lawyers, bar associations, law schools and curricular.

—b. *Kime's international law directory [for the year]: a list of solicitors in Gt Britain, together with a selected list of trustworthy legal practitioners in most of the principal towns throughout the civilised world, established by P. G. Kime.* London: Butterworth, 1920-, 1-, annual.

—c. Wasserman, S. et al., *Law and legal information directory. A guide to national and international organizations, bar associations . . . law schools . . . special libraries . . . research centers*, 4th edn. Detroit, MI: Gale, 1986, 813 pp.

Regularly updated. The focus of the directory is mainly on North American professional, academic and research bodies in the field of law (marginally on PIL).

377. *Directory of teaching and research institutions in international law/Répertoire des institutions d'enseignement et de recherche en droit international.* Paris: UNESCO, 1986, 280 pp. (Reports and Papers in the Social Sciences/Rapports et documents de sciences sociales, 56).

Issued in cooperation with the Société française de droit internationale, the *Directory* reflects the endeavours by UNESCO to promote the teaching and research of general and specialized private and public international law. With a view to furthering inter-university cooperation, notably the comparability of degrees [499h], the *Directory* lists names, addresses and dates of establishment of selected legal and PIL institutes and university faculties at the international, regional and national level. Information on some 60 institutions in 45 countries (mostly in Europe and Latin America) includes: names of senior international law staff; publications; research and academic degree programme; admission requirements. Several institutions are concerned with human rights and international economic law. The *Directory*'s somewhat uneven geographic coverage may be complemented with analogous information worldwide contained in *World of learning*, 39th edn. London: Europa, 1989.

378. *Institute of international law/Institut de droit international (IDI)/Instituto de derecho internacional/Institut für internationales Recht/Institut Mezhdunarodnogo Prava.* Since 1981, 22, ave. W. Favre, 1207 Geneva, Switzerland (previously in Paris and Brussels).

Founded in 1873 (in Ghent, Belgium), IDI is an international non-governmental organization whose members through their personal views and research examine and develop various aspects of private and public international law as it affects the international legal order in times of peace and/or war. IDI holds biennial meetings, the proceedings of which are published in the *Annuaire de l'Institut de droit international*. Basel: Karger, 1877-, 1-, annual. IDI's resolutions (often normative appraisals of extant principles of international law and/or methodological proposals for its development) were published as *Resolutions of the Institute of International Law, dealing with the law of nations*, with a historical introduction and explanatory notes, collected and translated under the supervision of and edited by J. B. Scott. New York: Oxford UP, 1916, 265 pp. (Carnegie Endowment for International Peace, Division of International Law). This contained the English text of resolutions dating from 1873-1913. The French text was published as *Tableau général des travaux* [de l'Institut], 1873-1913, préparé sous la direction de J. B. Scott. New York: Oxford UP, 1920, 366 pp. (Dotation Carnegie pour la paix internationale, Division de droit international). An updated French edition was compiled by Wehberg, H., *Tableau général des résolutions, 1873-1956*. Basel: Verlag Recht und Gesellschaft, 1957, 404 pp. (Resolutions 1-81 concern PIL.)

For a survey of the Institute's activities *see*:

—a. *Livre centenaire, 1873-1973. Evolution et perspectives du droit international*. Basel: Karger, 1973, 473 pp.

Includes contributions by C. Visscher, 'La contribution de l'Institut . . . au développement du droit international'; G. Fitzmaurice, 'The future of PIL and of international legal system in the circumstances of today'; and O. Schachter, 'The role of the Institute . . . and its methods of work'.

—b. Fitzmaurice, G., 1973/I, The contribution of the Institute of International Law to the development of international law. *RCADI*, **138**, pp. 205-259.

—c. Koretskiĭ, V. M., Akademik V. P. Bezobrazov v Institute Mezhdunarodnogo Prava: k stoletiŭ Instituta, 1973. In *SEMP*, 1972, pp. 190-197.

—d. de Visscher, P., L'Institut de droit international et le principe de non-intervention dans les guerres civiles. In [188, vol. 1], pp. 39-44.

—e. Münch, F., 1986, Institut de droit international. *Enc. PIL*, **9**, pp. 172-174.

379. *International Law Association* (ILA). Three Paper Buildings, Temple, London EC4Y 7EU, UK.

Like the IDI, whose activities it complements, ILA is an international non-governmental organization, founded in Brussels in 1873 as the Association for the Reform and Codification of the Law of Nations. Its name was changed to ILA in 1895. Its nearly 4,500 individual members spread among some 40 ILA branches (the first created in 1910 in the Netherlands) elucidate the advancement of private and public international and comparative law, and propose solutions for the unification of these areas of law; ILA membership and branches are listed in its *Conference reports* (*see below*).

ILA's objectives are pursued mainly through the work of its 19 International Committees (on, among other research topics, the Formation of rules of customary general international law; Legal aspects of a NIEO; International medical and humanitarian law; Space law) whose reports are examined in ILA's biennial conferences held worldwide. [ILA] *Conference reports*, London, 1873-, 1-, biennial, include conference proceedings and texts of resolutions, as well as

ILA membership lists. An 'Index of Conference reports, 1873-1972' was published in 1975 (between 1873 and 1924 the ILA issued *Transactions*). The *Conference reports* may include restatements of a given law, draft provisions of a treaty or convention and reviews of recent developments in international legal theory and practice. The *Conference reports* are often commented on in legal and PIL periodicals, and may be referred to in materials preparatory to judicial opinions or treaties. The results of the research work by ILA's International Committees may in part be reflected in relevant rules and principles, e.g. Helsinki rules on the use of the waters of international rivers; draft statutes for an International Criminal Court; rules of international law applicable to international terrorism, etc.

Among publications issued under the auspices of ILA mention should be made of *The effect of independence on treaties* (1965); *Extra-territorial application of laws and responses thereto* [seminar proceedings] (1984); *Liber amicorum* (1987) in honour of Lord Wilberforce [621b], former chairman of ILA. See also ILA branch publications [225, 265a]. For a survey of ILA activities see [379a,b].

—a. Bos, M. (ed.), *The present state of international law and other essays: written in honour of the centenary celebration of the International Law Association, 1873-1973*. Deventer: Kluwer, 1973, 392 pp.

Consists of: Part 1, International Law Association; Part 2, general and specialized aspects of international (public and private) law. Includes contributions by O'Connell [531e], Voncken (international medical law), Cheng, Austin and Goedehuis (law of outer space) and Manner (pollution of waterways). *See also* [615].

—b. Stödter, R., 1986, *The International Law Association. Enc. PIL*, **9**, pp. 182-183.

See also Singh, N., 1979, *Raison d'être* of national associations of international law and the need for their development. *Indian journal of international law*, **19**(2), pp. 149-156 (with focus on the Indian Association); Perez Gonzales, M., 1977, En torno al 'status' de las asociaciones internacionales en derecho internacional y en derecho de gente. *Revista española de derecho internacional*, **30**(2/3), pp. 315-338.

380a. *The Hague Academy of International Law/Académie de droit international de La Haye*. Peace Palace/Vreedespaleis, Carnegieplein 2, 2517 KJ The Hague, Netherlands.

Founded in 1923 (following a 1907 project) with the support of the Carnegie Endowment for International Peace [381]. Annually since 1923 summer courses in English or French [220a] have been conducted at the Academy by outstanding scholars and specialists in international public and private law. Participants who successfully pass the course examination are awarded a diploma and have their names listed in the Academy's *Bulletin* (The Hague, 1930-, 1-, annual).

Since 1957 the *Centre for Studies and Research in International Law and Relations/Centre d'études et de recherche de droit international et de relations internationales* has formed a part of the Academy's teaching programme. The Centre is open only to a limited number of qualified graduate or doctoral students who are expected effectively to contribute to the Centre's group research on international law. Since 1968 the Academy has sponsored *workshops* [220b] on various aspects of international law. Since 1969 the *external programme* has enabled young teaching staff (often from Third World countries) to conduct annual international law courses (always in and of interest to Third World countries). The Academy's *Bulletin* gives information on the Academy sponsored research and teaching.

The Academy's activities are surveyed in Dupuy, R.-J. (ed.), *Livre jubilaire/Jubilee book.* Leiden: Sijthoff, 1973, 313 pp.; Dupuy, R.-J., 1973/I, La contribution de l'Académie au développement du droit international. *RCADI*, **138**, pp. 45-73; Schlochauer, H.J., 1986, Académie de droit international. *Enc. PIL*, 9, pp. 1-2.

—b. *Association of Attenders and Alumni of the Academy/Association des auditeurs et anciens de l'Académie.* Peace Palace/Vreedespaleis, Carnegieplein 2, 2517 KJ The Hague, Netherlands.

Founded in 1923 (independently from the Academy), the AAA organizes annual congresses and publishes the *Annuaire de l'AAA/Yearbook of the AAA.* The Hague, 1923-, 1-, annual. Between 1923 and 1929 titled *Bulletin*, not to be confused with the Academy's *Bulletin* [380a]. Proceedings of AAA congresses may be separately published, e.g. *Aktuelle Probleme des internationalen Rechts. Vorträge des VII. Kongresses der AAA in Deutschland.* Berlin: W. de Gruyter, 1957, 216 pp.

381. *Carnegie Endowment for International Peace.* 11 Dupont Circle NW, Washington, DC 20036, USA.

Founded in 1910, the Endowment is an operating (rather than grant-making) foundation, which conducts its own research programmes in international affairs and law, with particular reference to American foreign policy. Initially the Endowment emphasized research on the role of international law for the advancement of peace, especially in terms of study and teaching; this was illustrated by the Endowment's support towards the founding of The Hague Academy of International law [380a], and that of the Graduate Institute of International Studies [407a], as well by the *Conference of teachers of international law and related subjects*, convened under the Endowment's auspices during 1914-46 (1st to 8th Conferences). From 1945 to the 1960s the Endowment's focus was on the development of IGOs, notably the UN. The renewed emphasis of the Endowment on international law since the 1960s, has resulted among other PIL research on the publication of the *Manual of PIL* [76]. Note that the Endowment's library collection (rich in PIL materials) was absorbed by the Jacob Burns Law Library at the George Washington University, Washington, DC.

The Endowment's Division of International Law issued (through the Oxford

UP, New York, mainly in the period before 1944) numerous primary and secondary PIL materials; in addition to the Endowment's 'Monograph' and 'Pamphlet' series mention should be made of the series *Studies in the administration of international law and organization* (nos 1-9, 1944-8), and of the reprint series *Classics of international law* [463a]. For conferences convened under the auspices of the Endowment *see* [320a-e].

See also Macalister-Smith, P., 1986, Carnegie Endowment for International Peace. *Enc. PIL*, **9**, pp. 17-18; Lysen, A., *History of the Carnegie Foundation and of the Peace Palace at The Hague*. Leiden: Brill, 1934, 188 pp. (Bibliotheca Visseriana).

382. *International Association of Legal Sciences/Association internationale des sciences juridiques*. c/o International Social Science Council, UNESCO House, 1, rue Miollis, 75730 Paris 15, France.

Founded (as an NGO) in 1950 under the auspices of UNESCO, the objective of the Association has been the development of the legal sciences by means of comparative methods (reflected in the name of its Executive Committee: Comité international de droit comparé/International Committee of Comparative Law). The Association promotes international legal cooperation through conferences and publications, mostly by way of existing national institutions. The Association holds worldwide colloquia on specific legal topics and co-sponsors the international congresses of comparative law [432a]. Among the publications issued or sponsored by the Association mention should be made of *The university teaching of social sciences: international law* [499g], *A register of legal documentation in the world* [62a] and a number of legal bibliographies in given countries. For the membership (including many national comparative law bodies) of the Association, as well as its research and publication programme, the Association's annual booklet (14th edn 1989) should be consulted.

Regional, national

383. *Asian-African Legal Consultative Committee*. 27 Ring Road, Lajpat Nagar IV, New Delhi 24, India.

Founded in 1956. Its members include the governments of Burma, India, Indonesia, Iraq, Japan, Sri Lanka and Syria. The Committee elaborates on international legal questions common to its members. The Committee's *Quarterly bulletin*, New Delhi, 1975-, 1-, reports on the activities of the Committee and treaties concluded by its members. The Committee publishes from time to time special *Reports and papers*; under its auspices have been published the constitutions of Asia and Africa [64a,b]. *See also* Jahn, E., 1986, Asian-African Legal Consultative Committee. *Enc. PIL*, **9**, pp. 8-10.

384. *International African Law Association*. Faculty of Law, University of Ghana, PO Box 70, Legon, Ghana.

Promotes the study of African legal systems, with special reference to African customary law.

The Americas

385. *Instituto Hispano-Luso-Americano de derecho internacional.* c/o Instituto de derecho internacional, Duque de Medinaceli 4-6, Madrid 14, Spain.

Promotes research of international law relative to the Iberian Peninsula and Latin America. Publishes *Anuario*, 1976-, 1- (vol. 6, 1981, contains the institute's statutes).

Canada

386. *Canadian Council on International Law/Conseil canadien de droit international.* 236 Metcalfe St, Ottawa, Ontario, Canada K2P 1R3.

Established in 1972, the Council promotes scholarly studies of international law with a view to its progressive development, and acts as a centre for the collection, dissemination of PIL information in Canada and elsewhere; to this end it publishes a *Quarterly bulletin*. The Council holds annual conferences on 'International law and Canadian foreign policy', the topics of which have included human rights (1973, 1978), international economic law (1979) and peaceful settlement of disputes (1984), reported in *Proceedings of the Annual Conference/Travaux du congrès annuel*. The Council encourages the study and teaching of international law, and plays an active part in the organization of the P. C. Jessup International Law Moot Court Competition [387b].

USA

387a. *American Society of International Law.* 2223 Massachusetts Ave. NW, Washington, DC 20008, USA.

Founded in 1906, ASIL with its extensive research and publishing activities contributes to the development and study of private and public international law in general, and in the USA in particular. ASIL holds annual meetings, topical discussions of which are reported in its *Proceedings* (1908-, 1-, annual; during 1970-3 included in *AJIL* [227]). ASIL issues a *Newsletter* (1970-, 1-, bimonthly; available to ASIL members only) which contains information on forthcoming meetings, fellowship programmes and ASIL activities in general. Under the auspices of ASIL are published *AJIL* [227] and *ILM* [219a].

—b. *Association of Student International Law Societies.* c/o ASIL [387a].

Conducts for law school students in the USA the annual P. C. Jessup International Law Moot Court Competition, based on hypothetical problems in international law as drawn up by international legal scholars. Information of the competition is contained in the *ASILS International law journal* [228] and in the *ASIL newsletter* [387a].

—c. *John Bassett Moore Society of International Law.* University of Virginia Law School, Charlottesville, VA, USA.

Publishes the *Directory of opportunities in international law*. 7th edn 1984.

388. *World Peace through Law Center*. 1000 Connecticut Ave. NW, Suite 800, Washington, DC 20036, USA.

Founded in 1963, the Center holds biennial conferences worldwide, and contributes to the advancement of global peace through research on law and PIL. The panels of its 13th conference, Seoul, 1987 included papers on international terrorism, human rights, NIEO and non-western law in western legal education. The Center's activities are reported in *World jurist* (1964–, 1–, bimonthly); the Center also issues the quarterly journal *Law/Technology*.

389a. *Association of American Law Schools*. One Dupont Circle, Washington, DC 20036, USA.

Publications prepared by or published for AALS include *International legal education newsletter* (1973–, 1–, superseded the *Journal of legal education*, 1948–71), *Law books recommended for libraries* (South Hackensack, NJ: Rothman, 1967–76, 47 fascicules, *see* [343]) and the annually updated *Directory of law schools* (includes international law teaching and research programmes at North American law schools and universities).

—b. *Harvard [University] Law School International Legal Studies Program*, Cambridge, MA, USA.

The Program in part supersedes the *Harvard Law School, Research in International Law*, established in 1927 under the direction of M. O. Hudson; *see* Kenny, J. T., 1977, Manley O. Hudson and the Harvard research in international law, 1927–1940. *International lawyer*, **11**(2), pp. 319–329. The pre-second World War research dealt with diplomatic privileges and immunities, piracy laws, competence of courts in regard to foreign states, etc. The resulting draft conventions were preparatory to the First Conference on the Codification of International Law [673a]; the research findings were published as supplements to *AJIL* [227]. Many of the topics of the Harvard research have since been examined and updated by the International Law Commission [662a]. The focus of the current Harvard International Legal Studies Program is on regional legal systems, including publications in the Harvard Studies in East Asian Law series.

Argentina

390. *Instituto [argentino] de derecho internacional. Centro de derecho internacional público*. Universidad de Buenos Aires, Facultad de derecho y ciencias sociales.

Holds biennial conferences and publishes the proceedings in *Documentos de trabajo*; *see also* [245].

Brazil

391. *Sociedade brasileira de direito internacional.* Palacio Itamaraty, Rio de Janeiro.

Publishes *Boletim*, 1945-, 1-, twice yearly.

See also ILA [379] for its branches in Argentina, Chile, Mexico and Paraguay.

Asia

People's Republic of China

392. *Chinese Society of International Law.* 24 Zhan Lan Road, Beijing.

Publishes [250].

Taiwan

393. *Chinese Society of International Law.* Taiwan Branch of ILA [379], Taipei.

Publishes [251]. *See also European Association for Chinese Law.* 7, Sq. de la Quiétude, 1150 Brussels, Belgium.

India

394. *Indian Society of International Law.* 7-8 Scindia House, Kasturba Gandhi Marg, New Delhi 11000.

Affiliated to the Society is the Indian Academy of International Law and Diplomacy, which has since 1979 conducted courses and awarded diplomas in the fields of its competence. Publishes [253].

See also ILA [379] for its branches in Bangladesh, Hong Kong, Japan, Korea, Nepal, Pakistan, Philippines and Singapore.

Europe, Eastern

Romania

395. *Association de droit international et relations internationales.* 48, Chaussée Kiseleff, Bucarest.

Founded in 1965. Publishes *Revue roumaine d'études internationales* [269] (which published *Deux décennies d'activités de l'Association*, 1985, **19**(6), pp. 507-512).

Yugoslavia

396a. *Institut za Međunarodnu Politiku i Privredu/Institute of International Politics and Economy.* Makedonska 25, 11000 Beograd.

The Institute's activities (largely in the field of international law) are published in its *Godišnjak* (195?-, 1-, annual); also publishes [363].

—b. *Institut za Međunarodno Pravo i Međunarodne Odnose.* Ćirilometodska 4, 41000 Zagreb.

See also ILA [379] for its branches in Bulgaria, Czechoslovakia, the German Democratic Republic, Hungary, Poland, the USSR and Yugoslavia.

The following institutions in Western Europe conduct research on East European law and PIL.

397a. *Documentation Office for Eastern European Law*. Hugo de Grootstraat 32, 2311 Leiden, Netherlands.

Founded in 1953. The principal aim of the Office has been the collecting of legal and PIL materials especially relating to the USSR, as well as (mainly European) socialist countries. The Office analyses these materials and contributes relevant references to *IFLP* [364b]. In addition to maintaining a research library and conducting study programmes, the Office publishes monographs, e.g. [65c] and the *Review of socialist law* [273b].

—b. *Institut für Ostrecht*. Ubierring 53, Köln, FR Germany.

Its research library contains an extensive collection of legal and PIL materials from (mainly European) socialist countries, especially PIL textbooks published in these countries since the 1950s. On the basis of these materials the Institute contributes various historiographical surveys and book reviews to *Osteuropa-Recht* [273f].

—c. *Centre for the Study of Socialist Legal Systems*. Faculty of Law, University College, 4–8 Endsleigh Gardens, London WC1H 0EG, UK.

The Centre convenes conferences and symposia, especially relating to PIL and comparative law [428a]. It publishes the *Yearbook on socialist legal systems* [273c], and sponsors translations and reprints of selected primary legal source materials (mainly from the USSR).

Scandinavia

398. *Institut for international Ret og Europaret*. Skt. Peders Straedel 19, København, Denmark.

399. *Svenska Institutet för internationell Rätt*. Universitet Uppsala, Trädgårdgatan 18, Uppsala 75220, Sweden.

Convenes law and PIL colloquia [460] and publishes a series 'Skrifter'.

See also ILA [379] for its branches in Denmark, Finland, Norway and Sweden.

Europe, Western

Austria

400a. *Institut für Völkerrecht und internationale Beziehungen*. Universitätsstr. 2, 1090 Wien.

—b. *Institut für Völkerrecht und ausländisches öffentliches Recht.* Weiserstr. 22, 5020 Salzburg.

See Cichocki, P. F., Das Salzburger Institut für Völkerrecht. In Schreuer, C. H. (ed.), *Autorität und internationale Ordnung.* Berlin: Duncker & Humblot, 1977, pp. 229-237.

Belgium

401a. *Centre Charles de Visscher pour le droit international.* 2, Place de Montesquieu, 1348 Louvain.

—b. *Institut de droit international.* Université libre de Bruxelles, 50, ave. F. D. Roosevelt, 1050 Bruxelles.

Federal Republic of Germany

402a. *Max-Planck Institut für ausländisches öffentliches Recht und Völkerrecht/Max-Planck Institute for Comparative Public Law and International Law.* Berlinerstr. 48, 6900 Heidelberg.

Founded in Berlin in 1924 by V. Bruns within the framework of the Kaiser-Wilhelm-Gesellschaft zur Förderung der Wissenschaften. Reorganized and transferred to Heidelberg in 1949, the Institute conducts research in and advises national and international law-makers on questions mainly of PIL.

The extensive resources of its Library (over 300,000 monographs and some 4,000 serial titles) enable the Institute to prepare the indexing journal *PIL* [361] and the journal *ZaöRV* [279], as well as the specialized PIL and comparative law monographs in its series *Beiträge zum ausländischen öffentlichen Recht und Völkerrecht* (Berlin: Springer, 1927-40; new series 1951-, 27-). The Institute prepares the digest of international and German judicial decisions, *Fontes juris gentium* [49a, 58] and the *Encyclopedia of public international law* [297]. The Institute also convenes international law conferences and colloquia, proceedings and/or (national) reports of which may be published in its series *Beiträge* (above).

To commemorate the 50th anniversary of the Institute's foundation a colloquium was held in 1975, entitled *International law as legal order/Völkerrecht als Rechtsordnung,* reports of which were published in vol. 36 of *ZaöRV* [279]. *See also* Steiner, O., 1981, Juristische Dokumentation im Max-Planck Institut. *Datenverarbeitung im Recht* (Berlin), **10**(1/2), pp. 129-131.

—b. Gödan, J. C., 1983, Foreign and international law research centres in West Germany: the Max-Planck institutes. *Law library journal,* **76**(3), pp. 464-481.

Provides a comparative review of six Max-Planck institutes relating to PIL (Heidelberg), private international law (Hamburg), European legal history (Frankfurt a/M), international criminal law (Freiburg i/B), international patent law and international social law (both in Munich). For references to further law/PIL institutes in the FRG consult *Vademecum: Lehr und Forschungsstätten*, Essen. 7th edn 1978.

France

403. *Société française pour le droit international*. c/o Centre d'études internationales et européennes, Faculté de droit, Place d'Athènes, Strasbourg.

Founded in 1967, the Société holds annual colloquia in France on different aspects of general and specialized PIL [321]. Summaries of the colloquia are included in the yearbook *AFDI* [282], itself published under the auspices of the Société.

404. *Institut de hautes études internationales*. 12, Place du Panthéon, 75006 Paris.

Founded in 1921 as part of the Faculté de droit, Université de Paris II, IHEI is a research and teaching institute in the field of international studies with its focus on international law. Several bibliographic and documentary sections in the journal *RGDIP* [283] are contributed by the IHEI, based on the extensive resources of its Library.

Greece

405. *Institute of International Public Law and International Relations*. V. Constantinou Ave. 39, Thessaloniki.

Founded in 1966, the Institute convenes conferences, holds seminars and publishes monographs [434a, 534a, 561d, 702a, 715a] in its series *Thesaurus Acroasium*, Thessaloniki, 1974-, 1-.

Netherlands

406. *T. M. C. Asser Interuniversitair Instituut voor international Recht/Interuniversity Institute for International Law*. Alexanderstraat 20-22, 2514 The Hague.

Founded in 1965 jointly by eight Dutch universities, the Institute conducts research and engages in documentary and publishing activities in the fields of private and public international law, as well as European Community law. Under the auspices of the Institute are published the yearbook *NYIL* [288], the periodical *NILR* [289] and PIL readers and case materials in the teaching series 'collegemateriaal' and 'afstudeerscripties'. Mention should also be made of specialized PIL monographs published under the auspices of the Institute, notably in its series *Internationaal economisch Recht* (1977-) and *Cornelis van Vollenhoven Memorial Lectures* (1979-, in cooperation with the Cornelis van Vollenhoven Stichting, Leiden).

See also [380a,b].

Spain

See [385].

Switzerland

407a. *Institut universitaire de hautes études internationales/Graduate Institute of International Studies.* 132, rue Lausanne, Geneva.

Founded in 1927 with the support of the Carnegie Endowment for International Peace [381], IUHEI is an interdisciplinary research and teaching institute, with special focus on international law, politics and economics. IUHEI convenes conferences and symposia. It conducts a diplomacy training programme in cooperation with the University of Kenya, and carries out many publishing activities. IUHEI publications include doctoral dissertations and results of research (notably volumes in the series *Répertoire des décisions . . . de la Cour internationale* [49b]). For a complete list of materials published by IUHEI see *Publications*, an annual catalogue which includes titles in the Institute's series (Collections) commercially published and distributed.

For a survey of IUHEI activities *see* its annual *Rapport administratif*, which includes titles of doctoral dissertations; the annex indicates the geographical distribution of students (in 1986 one-fifth of its 415 students were from Third World countries). The extensive collection of the IUHEI library is especially rich in private and public international law materials, many with imprints going back to the 1920s.

—b. *Association des anciens étudiants de l'Institut universitaire de hautes études internationales.* c/o IUHEI [407a].

The Association publishes *Annales/Annals* [449d], which contains articles on international law and relations.

UK

408. *British Institute of International and Comparative Law.* Charles Clore House, 17 Russell Square, London WC1B 5DR.

In 1962 the Institute incorporated the *Grotius Society* [465e] and the *Society of Comparative Legislation and International Law.* The independent, self-governing Institute conducts research and documentary activities in international private and public and comparative law, with emphasis on the practical application of law and PIL to contemporary international problems. The Institute also provides a Commonwealth Legal Advisory Service, and holds meetings and workshops.

The Institute publishes the *International and comparative law quarterly* [295] and the *Bulletin of legal developments* (1965-, 1-, biweekly; the news service reports legal events worldwide, based on newspapers, official gazettes, etc.), as well as specialized monographs in the fields of its competence. A catalogue of the Institute's publications (from 1960 onwards) is in preparation.

409. *Institute of Advanced Legal Studies. University of London.* Charles Clore House, 17 Russell Square, London WC1B 5DR.

Founded in 1946 the IALS provides extensive research facilities in municipal and international private and public law to legal practitioners, scholars and graduate students. IALS is associated with the awarding of the George Schwarzenberger Prize in International Law (established in 1981). Between 1960 and 1983 IALS published the *IFLP* [364b], to which it continues to contribute. On the basis of the considerable resources of its library (some 145,000 volumes, over 2,400 serial titles in law and PIL) the IALS from time to time issues subject bibliographies, union lists of legal periodicals, etc. *See also* [497b].

    410. *Research Centre for International Law*. University of Cambridge, Faculty of Law, 5 Cranmer Road, Cambridge CB3 9BL.

Founded in 1983. The Centre's research activities are geared to the development of international law within the context of international relations. The Centre prepares for publications basic primary PIL materials (including commentaries on multilateral treaties, diplomatic correspondence, etc.) and publishes these under the imprint Grotius Publications. They include *International law reports* [50] since 1987 (vol. 73-), and monographs on various international legal topics in the series *Hersch Lauterpacht Memorial Lectures* and *Grotius Classic Reprints* [373e,f].

See also ILA [379] for its branches in Austria, Belgium, Luxembourg, France, FRG, Ireland, Italy, Netherlands, Spain, Switzerland and the UK.

e. Librarianship, publishers

    411a. Moys, E. (ed). *Manual of law librarianship*, 2nd edn. Aldershot: Gower, 1987, 915 pp. 1st edn. London: André Deutsch, 1976.

Outlines primary, secondary and auxiliary sources and resources relating to common law and other legal systems, as well as international law [327]. Part 4 (2nd edn) includes an analysis of official legal materials, classifications of law and law library practice in general.

    —b. Mueller, H. P. and Kehoe, P. E., *Law librarianship: a handbook*. Littleton, CO: Rothman (for the AALL), 1983, 2 vols.

Vol. 1 deals with different aspects of traditional law library practice; vol. 2 discusses modern library technologies and information retrieval in general. Lists legal publishers, professional organizations and law libraries in North America and the UK.

    —c. Marke, J.J. (ed.), *Law library information reports*. Dobbs Ferry, NY: Oceana/Glanville, 1981-, irregular. Series 1 vols 1-6; Series 2 vols 7-.

The individual volumes deal with special aspects of law librarianship, e.g. vol. 6 (1985), *Planning the law library as a legal information center*; vol. 7 (1986), *Automation in the law school, including law libraries*.

    412a. Bing, J. *et al.*, *Handbook of legal information retrieval*. Amsterdam: North-Holland, 1984, 580 pp.

Contains theoretical considerations underlying the legal decision and communication processes, aspects of (legal) text retrieval and an international survey of computerized legal information systems. *See also* Kavass, I. I. and Hord, H. A., 1983, Computerized legal databases: an international survey. *IJLI*, **11**(3/4), pp. 115-129.

—b. Weill, G., *The admissibility of microforms as evidence: a RAMP study*. Paris: UNESCO/PGI, 1981.

—c. Burton, W. C. *et al.*, *Legal thesaurus*. New York, 1980, 1057 pp.

Reviewed in *IJLL*, 1981, **9**(5), p. 242. *See also* Thesaurus problems as exemplified by the *Index to legal periodicals* [364a]. *IJLL*, 1974, **2**(1), pp. 5-13.

413. Sprudzs, A., *International legal perspectives*. Buffalo, NY: W. S. Hein, 1988, 154 pp.

Contains a selection of writings (several on researching international law, especially treaties [24a]) by A. Sprudzs, honouring his work in international legal librarianship, at the University of Chicago Law School and within IALL [415a].

414a. *International journal of legal information*. Washington, DC: IALL, 1982-, 10-, 3 times yearly. Superseded *International journal of law libraries*, vols 1-9, 1973-81.

Published under the auspices of IALL [415a], the journal is an invaluable documentary resource reporting on current legal and PIL developments and publications worldwide; contains bibliographic surveys [631a], book reviews and professional news.

—b. *Law library journal*. Chicago: AALL, 1907-, 1-, quarterly. Cumulative indexes.

Contained until 1973 a book review section, Current publications in the legal and related fields, since separately published [371a]. Includes papers of the International Law Symposium (1983, **76**(3), pp. 421-570) and Zagayko, F. F., Guide to a basic library in international law (1960, **53**, pp. 118-128).

—c. *Legal reference services quarterly*. New York: Haworth Press, 1981-, 1-, quarterly.

—d. *Mitteilungen der Arbeitsgemeinschaft für juristisches Bibliotheks- und Dokumentationswesen*. Augsburg: AJBD, 1971-, 1-, 3 times yearly.

415a. *International Association of Law Libraries*. PO Box 5709, Washington, DC 10016, USA.

Founded in 1959, IALL holds annual conferences worldwide concerning the exchange of information on legal systems and relevant literature. Since 1966 IALL has organized (usually every other year) law librarianship and bibliography seminars and workshops with topics including Legal literature and documentation (in developing countries, Lausanne, 1976; in socialist countries, Budapest, 1977), International law library cooperation (Brussels, 1977) and Access to information in international legal research (Chicago, 1985). These and other relevant contributions are usually published in *IJLI* [414a]. *See also* Sprudzs, A., 1984, The IALL and its 25 years of activities. *Law librarian*, **15**, pp. 50-53 (reprinted in [413]); *Gerichte, juristische Bibliotheken und juristische Information in einer sich ändernden Welt: 25. Jahrestag der IALL.* Freiburg i/B, 1984, 187 pp.

—b. *American Association of Law Libraries.* 53 W. Jackson Blvd, Chicago, IL 60604, USA.

Founded in 1906, AALL sponsors legal documentation activities [364a,b], including conferences and workshops. Contributions to such conferences may be published in the *Law library journal* [414b], issued on audio-cassettes or referred to in the *AALL Newsletter* (1969-, 1-, 10 issues per year). AALL also publishes the *Biographical directory of law librarians* (last edition 1984, out of print). The Foreign, Comparative and International Law Special Interest Section (part of AALL since 1947) holds annual meetings on topics such as Taking the mystery out of foreign and international research (1982) and Peaceful settlement of international disputes (1985). *See also* p. 34, note 4.

Libraries

416a. Moys, E. M. (ed.), *European law libraries guide/Guide européen des bibliothèques de droit.* Prepared by the IALL [415a] under the auspices of the Council of Europe. London: Morgan-Grampian, 1971, 678 pp.

Lists over 500 law libraries (30 with outstanding PIL collections) in 18 countries (excluding the socialist countries of Eastern Europe).

—b. Ash, L., *Subject collections: a guide to special book collections and subject emphases as reported by university college, public and special libraries and museums in the United States and Canada*, 5th rev. edn. New York: Bowker, 1978. *See also* [376c].

—c. Lewanski, R. C., *Subject collections in European libraries*, 2nd edn. New York: Bowker, 1978.

—d. Zidouemba, D. and de Grolier, E., *Directory of documentation library and archives service in Africa*, 2nd rev. edn. Paris: UNESCO, 1977, 311 pp. (Documentation, Libraries, Archives: Bibliographies and Reference Works, 5).

Lists (national, public etc.) libraries and archives in 40 African countries. English and French subject indexes. *See also World guide to special libraries/Internationales Handbuch der Spezialbibliotheken.* Edited by H. Lengenfelder. München: Saur, 1983. The section 'Social sciences' includes law and PIL libraries.

In addition to the aforementioned directories of law libraries, as well as references to PIL collections in selected institutions [381, 397a,b, 402, 407a, 409], the extensive PIL collections in the following libraries merit special mention.

417a. *Law Library of the Library of Congress.* Washington, DC, USA.

The origin of the Law Library (chartered in 1832) goes back to the personal library of Thomas Jefferson. In 1985 the law collection (Class K) consisted of some 515,000 titles in over 1,670,000 volumes; the international law collection (Class JX) is part of the political science collection (Class J), comprising in 1985 some 210,000 titles in over 640,000 volumes. Bibliographic access to these collections is made possible up to 1981 by way of the card and published volumes of the LC *Catalog*, and thereafter by way of SCORPIO and MUMS files of LC's computerized record retrieval. *See also* *Bernal, M.-L. H., 1986, Research in international law at the Library of Congress. *Law library lights*, 30(2), pp. 11-13; Melville, A. (comp.), *Special collections in the Library of Congress; a selective guide.* Washington, DC: LC, 1980, 464 pp.; [366a,b].

—b. *Harvard Law School Library.* Langdell Hall, Cambridge, MA 02138, USA.

Founded in 1817, the Library acquired in 1911 the international law collection of the Marquis de Olivart [345]. In 1989, out of the Library's total holdings of nearly 1.5 million volumes, some 200,000 concerned international law. Bibliographic access to the Library's holdings in general is possible by way of the microfiche catalogue (published in 1984, it permits a retrospective approach to materials acquired until 1981) and, since 1982, the Harvard On-Line Library Information System (HOLLIS) for current access. For the Library's international law collection *see* [338a].

418. *Peace Palace Library.* Peace Palace/Vreedespaleis, Carnegieplein 2, 2517 KG The Hague, Netherlands.

Following the 1899 and 1907 peace conferences held at The Hague, the Peace Palace (*see also* Lysen in [381]) was built with funds provided by Andrew Carnegie in 1903. In addition to housing the Permanent Court of Arbitration, the Peace Palace in 1913, at the initiative of F. de Martens, housed the Library. *See* ter Meulen, J., La bibliothèque du Palais de la Paix. In *Grotius: annuaire international* (reports for 1918, 1925-7 and 1933 concern the Peace Palace Library developments).

In 1988, out of the Library's total holdings of some 700,000 volumes, nearly 100,000 volumes concerned international private and public law, with many complete sets from the 1920s on of PIL primary and secondary materials (including the works of PIL classics). Bibliographic access to the Library's holdings is made possible up to 1970 by way of the published *Catalogue* [339a] and selected bibliographies [289], up to 1983 by way of the card catalogue, and thereafter through computerized retrieval. Note that the Carnegie-Stichting (separate from the Carnegie Endowment [381]) administers the Peace Palace and the institutions therein.

419a. *United Nations Office at Geneva (UNOG) Library*. Palais des Nations, door 20, Geneva, Switzerland.

Established in 1946, the UNOG Library incorporates the collections of the League of Nations Library (founded in 1920 with Rockefeller funds). Of the UNOG Library's nearly 1 million volumes (of monographs and serials) the municipal and international law collection in 1988 contained 300,000 volumes; the many complete sets of primary and secondary legal materials (often from the 1920s on) are complemented by extensive official national and international materials published worldwide (especially since the 1950s). See also Ross, B.I., 1973, The legal section of the UN Geneva library. *Law librarian*, 4, p. 3. The Library's card catalogue (to 1986), the *Monthly bibliography I–II* [368a] and, since 1987, computerized retrieval provide bibliographic access to the UNOG Library holdings.

—b. *Dag Hammarskjöld Library*. United Nations, United Nations Plaza, New York, NY 10017, USA.

Founded in 1946, DHL serves primarily the needs of the UN Secretariat in New York, in particular those of the UN Office of Legal Affairs and the International Law Commission [662a]. DHL has developed and continues to develop the United Nations Bibliographic Information System (UNBIS), by-products of which are *Current bibliographic information* [368b], selected subject bibliographies [336a], *UNDOC* and *UNBIS Thesaurus* [660c]. DHL has also elaborated criteria for the depository libraries within the UN system intended to make globally accessible selected materials generated by the UN and SAs.

See also *DUNDIS* [632a].

Publishers

420a. Sweet & Maxwell. *Then and now, 1799–1974: commemorating 175 years of law bookselling and publishing*. London, 1974.

—b. *Oceana Publications*, Dobbs Ferry, NY.

Periodically issues a *Checklist of loose-leaf services*, and a series *Collection of bibliographic and research resources* [337b], both reporting on law and PIL publications by Oceana.

—c. M. Nijhoff, Dordrecht (formerly of The Hague).

Issues the series *Developments in international law* [373d]; titles in the latter along with relevant PIL titles published by Sijthoff & Noordhoff, Alphen a/R, and the Kluwer Rechtsgroep, Deventer, represent the (often English language) 'transnational' publishing by selected Dutch publishers.

—d. Librairie générale de droit et jurisprudence, Paris.

Issues the series *Bibliothèque de droit international* [373h]. Paris-based publishers like Pédone, Dalloz, Thémis (also in Montreal) issue mainly law and PIL textbooks.

—e. For a list of German-language legal publishers (and their series) *see* [373j].

West Berlin-based publishers Duncker & Humblot, W. de Gruyter and Springer (also in Heidelberg and New York) issue mainly legal and PIL treatises; Beck in Munich issue many PIL textbooks.

—f. IUridicheskaía Literatura and Mezhdunarodnye Otnosheniia, both in Moscow.

Issue many legal and PIL treatises and textbooks.

See also Internationales Verlagsadressbuch/Publishers' international directory, 5th edn. München: Verlag Dokumentation, 1972–; *500 hard to find publishers and their addresses*, 2nd edn. Reading, UK: Armstrong, 1984; *International directory of scholarly publishers*, Paris: UNESCO; Toronto: International Association of Scholarly Publishers, 1977, 66 pp.; [372, vol. 6].

PART II

Substantive Aspects of PIL Materials.
A Selected Subject Bibliography:
Topical Approach

II/A. Interdisciplinarity

i. PIL AND MUNICIPAL LAW

421a. International law and municipal law. *Enc. PIL*, 1987, **10**, pp. 238-257 (K.J. Partsch); pp. 257-262 (P. Rambaud).

—b. *International law and municipal law: Proceedings of the German-Soviet Colloquy on International Law at the Institut für internationales Recht, Kiel, 1987*. Edited by G.I. Tunkin and R. Wolfrum. Berlin: Duncker & Humblot, 1988, 210 pp. (Veröffentlichungen des Instituts, 103).

—c. Cassese, A., 1985/III, Modern constitutions and international law. *RCADI*, **192**, pp. 331-475.

See also Weisbaum, E., 1983, Domestic sources of international law. *Law library journal*, **76**(3), p. 436 (examines constitutions, legislative, executive etc. materials for their PIL content); Ruzié, D., 1975, La constitution française et le droit international. *Journal du droit international*, **102**(2), pp. 249-268; Oliver, C.T., 1955/II, Historical developments of international law ... *RCADI*, **88**, pp. 439-452 (analyses the constitutional restrictions on state powers in the USA, France and Scandinavian countries in respect of concluding international treaties).

422a. Lowenfeld, A.F., 1979/II, Public law in the international arena: conflict of laws, international law and some suggestions for their interaction. *RCADI*, **163**, pp. 311-445.

—b. *De conflictu legum*. Leiden: Sijthoff, 1962, 554 pp.

The commemorative essays in honour of R.D. Kollewijn and J. Offerhaus contain articles on municipal (Riphagen), private (Erades [427b]) and comparative (M. Ancel) law.

423a. *Survey on the ways in which States interpret their international obligations/Enquête sur la manière dont les Etats conçoivent leurs obligations internationales.* Paris: UNESCO, 1955, 21 pp. (Reports and Papers in the Social Sciences, 1).

The 'General Report' of the International Committee of Comparative Law presented by P. Guggenheim. The survey concerns the legal, administrative and social responsibilities of states in terms of their respective municipal provisions for incorporating international customary law into municipal law.

—b. Falk, R.A., *The role of domestic courts in the international legal order.* Syracuse, NY: Syracuse UP, 1964, 184 pp. (Procedural aspects of international law series).

—c. Lauterpacht, H., *Private law sources and analogies of public international law*, 1927. Reprinted in [173b, vol. 2].

See also [428a].

ii. PRIVATE AND PUBLIC INTERNATIONAL LAW

424. *The Hague Conference on Private International Law.* [Permanent Office], Javastraat 2, 2583 AM The Hague, Netherlands.

First convened in The Hague in 1893, mainly on T.M.C. Asser's initiative, the Conference meets every four years (16th session, 1988) with a view to examining and applying convention rules on the unification and codification of international private law. Since 1955 the Conference has the status of a multilateral treaty.

425a. *UNIDROIT. International Institute for the Unification of Private Law.* Via Panisperna 28, Roma, Italy.

Established in 1926 under the auspices of the LoN, UNIDROIT convenes (often codificatory) conferences and sponsors research with a view to advancing the unification of given aspects of law in general, and of private international law in particular.

—b. *UNIDROIT yearbook.* Dobbs Ferry, NY: Oceana, 1973-, 1-, annual; [UNIDROIT] *Proceedings and papers.* Rome, 1928-, 1- (1928-81 in microfiche edition by Oceana, Dobbs Ferry, NY).

For an analysis of UNIDROIT conferences held until 1970 *see* van Hoogstraten, M.H., pp. 3-39 in [379a]; *see also International uniform law in practice* [Reports of the 1987 Conference in Rome]. Dobbs Ferry, NY: Oceana, 1988, 650 pp.

426a. Drobnig, L., 1987, Private international law. *Enc. PIL*, **10**, pp. 330-335.

Discusses the interfacing of PIL with private international law.

—b. Kahn-Freund, O., 1974/III, General problems of private international law. *RCADI*, **143**, pp. 139-474.

Outlines the choice of private international law methods and spheres of application.

—c. Müllerson, R.A., in [428a], examines Soviet positions concerning private international law and advances a 'polysystemic' model of interaction between private and public international law. *See also* Khrabskov, V.G., 1977, Problemy sootnosheniia mezhdunarodnogo publichnogo i mezhdunarodnogo chastnogo prava. *SEMP*, pp. 117-126.

For a description of the Max-Planck Institute for Private International law *see* [402b].

427a. *Festschrift für K. Zweigert zum 70. Geburtstag.* Edited by H. Bernstein *et al.* Tübingen: Mohr, 1981, 941 pp.

Part 1 deals with private international law, with contributions by H. Batiffol, B. Blagojević and K. Lipstein; Part 2 concerns comparative law.

—b. Erades, L., Application of private international law by the ICJ, pp. 145-153 in [422b].

In Erades's view the ICJ does not possess a *lex fori* nor can it rely on the concept of 'ordre public' as this may be applied in the conflict of given municipal laws.

iii. PIL AND COMPARATIVE LAW

428a. Butler, W.E. (ed.), *International law and the international system.* Dordrecht: Nijhoff, 1987, 208 pp.

The papers in this collection originated in the *First Anglo-Soviet Symposium on Public International Law*, University College, London, 25-27 April 1986, under the auspices of the Centre for the Study of Socialist Legal Systems [397c] and the Soviet Association of International Law. Most papers were first published in *Coexistence: a review of East-West and developmental issues* (Glasgow), 1987, **24**, nos 1 and 2. The Symposium examined the role of resolutions of international organizations in the creation of international norms (contributions by Tunkin, Higgins, Delupis and Lukashuk), the relationship between PIL and other systems of law (Butler, Müllerson [426c] and Rubanov on PIL and municipal law) and selected PIL issues, e.g. E.T. Usenko, The norm-creating activity of COMECON and A.P. Movchan, The concept and meaning of modern international law and order (*see also* [493]). Concluding the contributions on the comparative law approach is the text of 'The syllabus on international law for law faculties of universities and judicial institutions' in the USSR (English translation by W.E. Butler). *See also Materials on comparative approaches to international law*, a microfiche edition of materials (some unpublished) previously used in PIL courses at University College, London.

—b. Butler, W. E., 1985/I, Comparative approaches to international law. *RCADI*, **190**, pp. 13-89.

Updates and complements his *International law in contemporary perspective*. Alphen a/R: Sijthoff & Noordhoff, 1980, 315 pp. Information contained in the 1985 and 1980 works is summarized by Butler, W. E., 1987, Comparative law and international law. *Enc. PIL*, **10**, pp. 49-52. The emphasis in both works is on comparative legal methods applicable to legal systems *per se* and/or to their inter-relationship, but especially in terms of elucidating substantive, historical, regional and ideological aspects of PIL. The 1980 collection of essays contains contributions on the Comparative method in international law (Kiss, Dutoit, Harászti and Baskin; *see also* [493]), international legal history in comparative perspective (Schwarzenberger and Connelly [456a,b]), and a selective bibliography (arranged according to regional and ideological subsystems).

429a. David, R., *Les grands systèmes de droit contemporain*, 8th edn. [Edited by] C. Jauffert-Spinosi. Paris: Dalloz, 1982, 655 pp.

Frequently updated, the treatise provides a comparative outline of legal systems worldwide, with reference to their substantive, historical and regional aspects. Extensive bibliographic references, index.

—b. Derrett, J. D. M., *An introduction to legal systems*. London: Sweet & Maxwell, 1968, 203 pp.

An outline of Roman, Jewish, Islamic, Hindu, Chinese, African legal systems. *See also* [431, vols 1 and 2].

—c. Salacuse, J. W., *An introduction to law in French-speaking Africa*. Charlottesville, VA: The Michie Co., 1969-75 (The Legal Systems of Africa series).

Vol. 1, *Africa south of the Sahara*; vol. 2, *North Africa*. *See also* University of Virginia series *The legal systems of Africa*, 1970-.

—d. Hassan, F., *Legal systems of Islamic countries*. Dobbs Ferry, NY: Oceana, 1988, 2 vols.

A comparative analysis of four Islamic countries, members of the Arab League or the Islamic Conference, with reference to their procedural and criminal law, etc. *See also* [73a].

430. *Festschrift für Imre Zajtay/Mélanges en l'honneur d'Imre Zajtay*. Hrsg. R. H. Graveson *et al*. Tübingen: Mohr, 1982, 594 pp.

The contributors (M. Ancel, M. Matteuci, K. Zweigert *et al.*) focus on 'la relation entre l'emploi de la méthode fonctionnelle et le problème de la comparabilité des droits' (p. 4). A renowned comparative legal scholar, Zajtay was the editor of *Annuaire de législation française et étrangère* [72a] and of *Revue internationale de droit comparé* [432b], as well as the Secretary-General of the International Association of Legal Sciences [382]. See also Fikentscher, W., *Die Methoden des Rechts in vergleichender Darstellung.* Tübingen: Mohr, 1975-7, 5 vols. Compares common and civil law methodologies (vols 1-3) and outlines comparative conceptual ('meta'-theoretical, etc.) approaches to law and PIL.

431. *International encyclopedia of comparative law.* Alphen a/R: Sijthoff & Noordhoff; Tübingen: Mohr, 1972-, 1-, Editor K. Zweigert.

Published under the auspices of the Max-Planck Institut für ausländisches und internationales Privatrecht (referred to in [402b]). Of the projected 17 volumes, so far have been published: vols 1 and 2 (legal systems of the world), 11 and 16, each concerned with a special aspect of comparative law.

432a. *Congrès international de droit comparé.* 1932-, 1st-.

Held every four years, the Congress is convened by the Académie international de droit comparé; the proceedings of the Congress are usually issued in the form of country reports, e.g. *Recueil des travaux suisses présentés au X. Congrès*, Budapest, 1978. Basel: Helbing, 1979 (includes Dutoit, B., Droit comparé et droit international, pp. 127-156; updated in [428b]).

—b. *Revue internationale de droit comparé.* Paris: Société de législation comparée, 1949-, 1-. Cumulative indexes 1949-73, 1974-88.

—c. *Comparative law yearbook.* Dordrecht: Nijhoff, 1976-, 1-, annual.

Published under the auspices of the Center for International Studies (PO Box 19, Salzburg, Austria), part of the McGeorge School of Law, University of the Pacific, Sacramento, CA.

—d. Szladits, C., *A bibliography on foreign and comparative law: books and articles in English.* Dobbs Ferry, NY: Oceana, 1955-, 1-, irregular. Since 1989 edited by V. Pechota.

The eight volumes published between 1955 and 1989 contain references to English-language publications issued worldwide from 1790 to 1983 relating to comparative law, private international law, etc. A cumulative edition for 1984-6 is in preparation, with yearly supplements to follow. Reviewed in [371b]. *See also* Norman, P., Comparative law, pp. 489-495, in [411a, 2nd edn].

433a. *Académie internationale de droit comparé.* 15, rue des Bigots, 92190 Meudon-Bellevue, France. See also [432a].

For selected national bodies concerned with comparative law *see* the Booklet issued by the International Association of Legal Sciences [382].

—b. *Institut suisse de droit comparé.* Université de Lausanne, Dorigny/Lausanne, Switzerland.

The Library of the Institute contains an extensive collection of municipal laws worldwide (mainly from 1945 onward).

—c. [Institute of Comparative Law] Waseda University, Tokyo, Japan.

Created in 1958, the Institute prepares *Hikakahogaku* [Comparative law review], 1964-, 1-; *see also Law in East and West; on the occasion of the 30th anniversary of the Institute.* Tokyo: Waseda UP, 1988, 1062 pp.

iv. PIL AND INTERNATIONAL RELATIONS

434a. Fundamental problems of international law and international relations. *Thesaurus Acroasium*, 1987, vol. 5.

—b. International relations and legal co-operation in general. *Enc. PIL*, 1986, 9.

Contains articles on co-existence, international control systems, disarmament and the sociology of international law.

—c. Fiedler, W., *Das Kontinuitätsproblem im Völkerrecht. Zum funktionalen Zusammenhang zwischen Völkerrecht, Staatsrecht und Politik.* Freiburg i/B: Alber, 1978, 148 pp.

—d. Giraud, C., 1963/III, Le droit international public et la politique. *RCADI*, **110**, pp. 419-809.

—e. McDougal, M. S., 1953/I, International law, power and policy. *RCADI*, **82**, pp. 133-258.
See also [80].

435. Midgley, E. B. F., *The natural law tradition and the theory of international relations.* New York: Barnes & Noble, 1975, 588 pp.

Reviewed in *BYIL*, 1979, **49**, pp. 242-246. See also Groom, A. J. R. and Taylor, P. (eds), *Functionalism: theory and practice in international relations.* New York: Crane, Russak, 1975, 354 pp.

436. Sheikh, A., *International law and national behavior: a behavioral interpretation of contemporary international law and politics.* New York: John Wiley, 1974, 352 pp.

The interdisciplinary approach includes a conceptual model for the study of international law and politics, as well as discussions on the impact of ideology on, the historical perspective of, and methodological variables applicable to, international law and relations.

437a. Tunkin, G., *Pravo i sila v mezhdunarodnoĭ sisteme.* Moskva: Mezhdunarodnye Otnosheniia, 1983. English translation: *Law and force in the international system.* Moscow: Progress Publishers, 1985, 338 pp.

Part 1, International system and international law (includes concept of international relations, principles of modern PIL, legal and non-legal behaviour in international relations); Part 2, Two socio-economic systems and two conceptual models (bourgeois, socialist) of the international system; Part 3, General democratic model of the international system (including an integrated socialist/bourgeois model) and the role of law and force therein. *See also* his International law in the international system. *RCADI*, 1975/IV, **147**, pp. 1-218, including dialectical materialism as an approach to international law and relations. *See also* Fawcett, J., *Law and power in international relations*. London: Faber & Faber, 1982, 140 pp. (Studies in International Politics).

—b. *Genov, I., *Mezhdunarodnoto pravo v sŭvremennite mezhdunarodni otnosheniia*. Sofiia, 1985, 193 pp.

438. Dupuy, R.-J., *La communauté internationale entre le mythe et l'histoire*. Paris: Economica/UNESCO, 1986, 182 pp. (Collection droit international).

Traces the evolution of international law at the close of the twentieth century with reference to extant doctrinal positions on (the harmony *v.* conflict underlying the concept of) international community. Advances two broad conceptual models of international community: one in terms of force (*pouvoir*) and law, the other in terms of power (*puissance*) and justice. Concludes with the projection (based on methodological considerations and examples from evolving specialized PIL) of 'a law of humanity' conditioned by the dynamism of a community spirit (*le mythe communautaire*). Dupuy develops similar tenets in his Communauté internationale et disparité de développement. *RCADI*, 1979/IV, **165**, pp. 12-231, and in *Ordre et désordre: textes des conférences et des entretiens organisés par les vingt-neuvièmes Rencontres internationales de Genève, 1983*. Neuchâtel: La Baconnière, 1984, pp. 33-54 (Dupuy considers the making of order (*faiseuse d'ordre*) as an attribute of the international community). *See also* Mayall, J. (ed.), *The community of states: a study in international political theory*. London: Allen & Unwin, 1982, 189 pp.

439. Mosler, H., *The international society as a legal community*. Alphen a/R: Sijthoff & Noordhoff, 1980, 327 pp.

The work is a revised version of his course (with the same title) published in *RCADI*, 1973/III, **140**, pp. 1-320. Mosler follows C. de Visscher's sociological approach [503a] by assigning to PIL the role of shaping international society into a cohesive legal community. *See also* Puig, J. C., *Derecho de la comunidad internacional*. Buenos Aires: Depalma, 1974, 319 pp. Essentially a PIL textbook but with the emphasis on the dynamic role of PIL in shaping the international community. *See also* [508b].

440. *Public international law and the future world order: liber amicorum in honor of A.J. Thomas, Jr.* Sponsored by the Southern Methodist University School of Law. Center for International Studies. Edited by J.J. Norton. Littleton, CO: Rothman, 1987, Various pagination.

The contributions on the impact of PIL upon the evolving world order include Rui Mu (Dean emeritus, Beijing University Law School), Chinese view on the future possibilities of international law and the world economic order; C. T. Oliver, The World Court and world order; T. C. van Boven, Human rights and world order; and R. Trejos, The law of the sea: the Latin American view.

    441.   Murphy, C., *The search for world order: a study of thought and action*. Dordrecht: Nijhoff, 1985, 192 pp. (Developments in International Law, 9).

Traces the evolution of the concept 'world order', from the Grotian vision thereof, through the nineteenth-century quest for perpetual peace, to the twentieth-century dilemmas of law and force. Concludes with reference to the potential impact of J. Rawls's *Theory of justice* (London: Oxford UP, 1973) upon world order images of the future.

    442.   Dolman, A. J., *Resources, régimes, world order*. New York: Pergamon, 1981, 411 pp. (Pergamon Policy Studies on International Development).

Published in cooperation with the Foundation Reshaping the International Order (RIO), the work defines world order as 'a pattern of power relations among international actors capable of ensuring the functioning of various activities according to a set of rules, written and unwritten' (p. 9). The work outlines institutional and research areas with an impact on the shaping of world order, notably its economic and developmental aspects (e.g. resources in terms of 'common heritage of mankind').

If world order studies 'keep alive the tradition of scholastic speculation on the future of international relations' (p. 49) in an age of uncertainty, the substantive ramifications as well as the great number of such studies (especially in North America) preclude the inclusion in the *Guide* of more than the following titles.

    443a.   McKinlay, R. D. and Little, R., *Global problems and world order*. London: Frances Pinter, 1986, 292 pp.

    —b.   Galtung, J., *The true worlds: a transnational perspective*. New York: Free Press, 1980, 469 pp. (Preferred Worlds for the 1990s).

    444.   McWhinney, E., *Conflict and compromise: international law and world order in a revolutionary age*. Toronto: CBC Merchandising; Alphen a/R: Sijthoff & Noordhoff, 1981, 160 pp.

Based on lectures given at the Centro de Relaciones Internacionales, Universidad Autónoma de México in 1978 and at the Institute of Law, Chinese Academy of Social Sciences, Beijing in 1980, the work represents a variant of McWhinney's *International law and world revolution*, in turn reflecting the texts (published in 1967) of his 1966/7 radio broadcasts in the series 'Ideas'. *Conflit idéologique et ordre public mondial*. Paris: Pédone, 1970, 159 pp. is based on McWhinney's lectures at the Institut de hautes études internationales, Paris, in 1968. In these lectures McWhinney examined transcultural implications for world order, foreshadowing his concept of PIL in the light of ideological pluralism [474a].

445a. Falk, R., Kratochwil, F. and Mendlovitz, S. H. (eds), *International law: a contemporary perspective*. Boulder, CO: Westview Press, 1985, 702 pp. (Studies on a Just World Order, 2).

Contains essays on contemporary PIL aspects, illustrating the world order context thereof. The essays grew out of Falk, R. A., Kim, S. S. and Mendlovitz, S. H. (eds), *Toward a just world order*. Boulder, CO: Westview Press, 1982, 652 pp. (Studies on a Just World Order, 1) with an emphasis on non-legal values (peace, humanity, etc.) underlying the interaction of PIL and international relations. For similar (textbook) approaches *see* [80, 81].

—b. Falk, R. A. and Black, C. E. (eds), *The future of the international legal order*. Princeton, NJ: Princeton UP, 1969–72, 4 vols.

Vol. 1, *Trends and patterns* (includes McDougal *et al.*, The world constitutive process of authoritative decision, and Stone, Approaches to the notion of international justice); vol. 2, *Wealth and resources*; vol. 3, *Conflict management*; vol. 4, *Structure of the international environment* (includes G. Gottlieb, The nature of international law with reference to the need for a horizontal systems, rather than vertical power, model). The emphasis is on the dynamics of PIL and on alternative methodological models applicable to an evolving world order. *See also World order models project* (WOMP). *ASIL Proc.*, 1972, **66**, pp. 244–278 (refers to publications connected with WOMP).

—c. Falk, R. A. and Mendlovitz, S. H. (eds), *Strategy of world order*. New York: World Law Fund, 1966, 4 vols.

Vol. 1, *Toward a theory of war prevention*; vol. 2, *International law*; vol. 3, *The United Nations*; vol. 4, *Disarmament and development*. Instrumental in the formulation of the integrative world order approach, the authors attempt to set international law and relations into an overall socio-economic, historico-political framework, in part reflecting the *World peace through law* approach by G. Clark and L. Sohn [cf. 209, 388]. For a critical review of vol. 2 *see* Leary, V., 1972, *Annales d'études internationales*. **3**, pp. 217–221.

446. Thompson, W. R. (ed.), *Contending approaches to world system analysis*. Beverly Hills, CA: Sage Publications, 1983, 311 pp. (Sage Focus Editions, 62).

Represents essays mostly by US proponents of the world order approach to international relations.

447a. Jankowitsch, O. and Sauvant, K. P. (eds), *The collected documents of the Non-aligned Countries*. Dobbs Ferry, NY: Oceana, 1978–84, 6 vols (The Third World without Superpowers).

Contains the text of documents of the Conferences of the heads of state or government, of the Bureau of the movements and of meetings held by groups of experts, for the period 1961–79, 1st–6th Conferences. For texts of subsequent Conferences see [447b]. A bibliography of (secondary source) materials relating to the movement is included in vol. 4. *See also* [720b].

—b. *ECDC handbook: documents of the Movement of Non-aligned Countries and the Group of 77*, [8th edn]. New Delhi: Ministry of External Affairs, 1983, 679 pp.

The handbook (on economic cooperation among developing countries, ECDC) complements [447a] in providing the text of documents for the period 1961-83, 1st-8th Conferences, as well as texts relative to Asian-African conferences for the period 1955-60, and selected UN and UNCTAD texts on economic development. Member States of the Group of 77 and/or of the non-aligned movement are listed on p. 652.

—c. *Two decades of non-alignment: documents of the gatherings of the Non-aligned Countries, 1961-1982.* New Delhi: Ministry of External Affairs, 1983, 593 pp.

Contains commentaries on reports of 33 meetings held by heads of state, ministers of foreign affairs, etc.

448a. Singham, A. W. and Hune, S., *Non-alignment in an age of alignments.* London: Zed Books, 1986, 124 pp.

Traces the history and evolution of non-alignment as a concept and movement from the Bandung Conference, 1955 on. Includes references to the movement's role in developing PIL.

—b. Köchler, H. (ed.), *The principles of non-alignment: the Non-aligned Countries in the eighties, results and perspectives.* London: Third World Centre for Research and Publishing; Vienna: International Progress Organization, 1982, 281 pp. (Studies in International Relations, 7).

Contains papers of the Conference held in Baghdad, 1982, under the patronage of the International Progress Organization, Vienna. The contributors include K. P. Misra, Ideological bases of non-alignment: an overview; H. Gros Espiell, Los conceptos de soberanía e independencia y los principios del movimiento de los países no alienados; and K. Masmoudi, Le nouvel ordre international de l'information et de la communication: évolution et perspective.

—c. Bedjaoui, M., 1976/III, Non-alignment et droit international. *RCADI,* **151**, pp. 339-456.

See also his Non-aligned States. *Enc. PIL,* 1986, **9**, pp. 270-276, including bibliographic references to 1972-82 imprints on the subject.

—d. Tuzmukhamedov, R. A., *Dvizhenie neprisoedineniia v dokumentakh i materialakh,* 2nd edn. Moskva: Nauka, 1979, 430 pp. (Akademiia Nauk SSSR. Institut Afriki).

See also Benevolenskiĭ, V., *The non-aligned movement from Belgrade to Delhi.* Moscow: Progress, 1985, 134 pp.

449a. *International affairs*. London: Butterworth (for the Royal Institute of International Affairs), 1922–, 1– quarterly.

See also Yearbook of world affairs. London: Stevens, 1947–84, vols. 1–38. Published under the auspices of the London Institute of World Affairs (LIWA), the *Yearbook* contains articles on PIL, notably by Schwarzenberger and Verdross. Cumulative author and subject indexes in vol. 125, 1971 and vol. 38, 1984.

—b. *Foreign affairs*. New York: Council on Foreign Relations, 1922–, 1–, monthly.

Includes section 'Recent books [in English only] on international relations: source materials', a cumulation of which is contained in the *Foreign affairs bibliography*. Edited by J. Kreslins. New York: Bowker, 1976, 5 vols. For a selection of some 2,000 monographs *see The Foreign Affairs 50-year bibliography: new evaluation of significant books on international relations*, 1920–72. Edited by B. Dexter. New York: Bowker, 1972. *See also* [450b].

—c. *International affairs. Moscow*, 1955–, 1–, monthly.

The English edition of *Mezhdunarodnaĩa zhizn'*. Also exists in a French edition.

—d. *Annales d'études internationales/Annals of international studies*. Genève: Association des anciens étudiants de l'IUHEI [407b], 1970–, 1–, annual.

Each annual issue is generally devoted to one international law and relations topic, e.g. vol. 3, 1972, Les nouvelles formes de conflits; vol. 8, 1977, Droit humanitaire et protection de l'homme; vol. 13, 1983/4, Technologie et relations internationales; vol. 15, 1986, L'Etude des relations internationales: la nouvelle génération.

—e. *International Journal*. Toronto: Canadian Institute of International Affairs, 1946–, 1–, quarterly.

—f. *Revue de droit international, de sciences diplomatiques et politiques/The international law review*. 1211 Genève 12, Case postale 138, 1923–, 1–, quarterly.

—g. *Guoji wenti yanjiu/Journal of international studies*. Beijing: Tianjin People's Publishing House, 1983–, 1–, quarterly. In Chinese, with contents in English.

See also People's Republic of China yearbook. Beijing: Xinhua Publishing House; Hong Kong: New China News, 1981–, 1– , annual. Contains references in English to political military, economic and legal affairs of the People's Republic of China.

—h. *Revue interdisciplinaire d'études juridiques*. Bruxelles: Bruylant, 197?–, 1–, semi-annual.

Published under the auspices of the Université de Saint-Louis. Faculté des seminaires interdisciplinaires d'études juridiques.

For references to further political science/international relations periodicals, *see* [216a, vol. 2].

450a. Dimitrov, T. D., *World bibliography of international documentation*. [634a] vol. 2, *Politics and world affairs*.

Contains references to mostly post-1945 monographs in the field of politics, disarmament and peace-keeping operations. Includes a list of periodical titles in the field (pp. 263-295).

—b. *Catalog of the Foreign Relations Library*. Boston, MA: G. K. Hall, 1969, 9 vols.

Represents a retrospective bibliography based on the card catalogue of the holdings in the library of the Council on Foreign Relations. *See also* [449b].

—c. *International political science abstracts*. Oxford: Blackwell, 1950-, 1-, bi-monthly.

451a. Plano, J. C. and Olton, R., *The international relations dictionary*, 3rd edn. Santa Barbara, CA: ABC-Clio, 1982.

—b. Hänisch, W. et al., *Wörterbuch der Aussenpolitik und des Völkerrechts*. East Berlin: Dietz, 1980, 728 pp.

—c. Haentsch, G., *Wörterbuch der internationalen Beziehungen und der Politik, systematisch und alphabetisch: Deutsch, Englisch, Französisch, Spanisch/Dictionary of international relations and politics: systematic and alphabetical in four languages: German, English/American, French, Spanish*, 2nd edn. Amsterdam: Elsevier, 1975, 781 pp. 1st edn 1954 (includes diplomacy).

—d. *A dictionary of international relations: Arabic-French-English. News, economics, politics/Dictionnaire des relations internationales: arabe-français-anglais. Actualités, économie, politique*. Geneva: UNOG, 1986, 138 pp. (Arabic at the United Nations/L'Arabe aux Nations Unies).

See also *Sukkary, S., *A political and diplomatic dictionary*. Cairo: Mondiale Presse, 1980. (English-Arabic); el-'Adah, F., *A dictionary of diplomacy and international affairs: English, French, Arabic*. Beirut, 1974.

—e. *Key concepts in international relations*. Series editor P. Wilkinson. London: Allen & Unwin, 1983-, 1-.

The publications in the series review major international relations concepts, in terms of their origin, usage and variations, interdisciplinarity, etc. The volumes include references to authoritative sources on given concepts. *See* [627b].

—f. Ostrower, A., *Language, law and diplomacy: a study of linguistic diversity in official international relations and international law*. Philadelphia, PA: University of Pennsylvania Press, 1965, 2 vols.

Includes extensive bibliographic notes on linguistic problems relative to international agreements, conferences, etc.

452a. *The annual register: a review of public events at home and abroad.* London: Longman Group, 1761–, 1–, annual.

Gives a continuous coverage of international affairs from the mid-eighteenth century to date. *See also* Chronique des faits internationaux in [283].

—b. *Political handbook of the world.* Binghamton, NY: CSA Publishers, 1927–, 1– (since 1986 annual).

Contains country surveys (including political and economic aspects). *See also World bibliographical series.* Editor R. L. Collison. Santa Barbara, CA: ABC-Clio Press, 1983–. Contains annotated references to historical, political and legal aspects in over 100 countries.

—c. *The international yearbook and statesmen's who's who: statistical and historical annual of the states of the world.* New York: Macmillan; East Grinstead, West Sussex: Reed Information Services, 1864–, 1–, annual.

453. *International Political Science Association.* University of Ottawa, Ottawa, Canada K1N 6N5.

Convenes international conferences and sponsors publications. Note *Global problems of mankind and the state*, [Proceedings of the] 13th World Congress of IPSA, Paris, 1985. Edited by P. M. Fedoseev. Moscow: Social Science Today, 1985, 216 pp.

454a. Englefield, D. and Drewry, G., *Information sources in politics and political science: a survey worldwide.* London: Butterworth, 1984, 509 pp. (Butterworth's Guides to Information Sources).

The guide contains critical evaluations of mostly English-language post-1945 secondary resources concerning politics and government. Chapter 4, International politics and international relations; Chapter 13, International reference books; Chapter 24, International organizations.

—b. Holler, F. L., *Information sources of political science*, 4th edn. Santa Barbara, CA: ABC-Clio Press, 1986, 417 pp.

A frequently updated guide mainly to auxiliary resources published worldwide in the field.

—c. Finan, J. J. and Child, J., *Latin America: international relations, a guide to information sources.* Detroit, MI: Gale, 1981, 236 pp. (Gale/International Relations Information Guide series, 11).

II/B. Intradisciplinary aspects

i. HISTORY OF PIL

455a. History of the law of nations. *Enc. PIL*, 1984, **7**, pp. 126-273.

Contains: Basic questions and principles (Preiser); Ancient times to 1648 (Preiser, Verosta and Scupin); World War I to World War II (Grewe); since World War II (Kimminich). The articles trace the evolution of international legal institutions (e.g. recognition, control of navigation, etc.) in temporal and spatial (mostly European) terms.

—b. Grewe, W., *Epochen der Völkerrechtsgeschichte*. Baden Baden: Nomos, 1984, 897 pp.

The work traces six historical periods of PIL, the first four focusing on the role of European states in the development of PIL; the fifth period (1919-45) is viewed as the transition between classical and contemporary PIL, and the sixth period from 1945 on shows the emergence of a new 'universal' PIL influenced by Third World perceptions. Grewe's work is based on and supersedes Nussbaum, A., *A concise history of the law of nations*, rev. edn. New York: Macmillan, 1954, 376 pp. *See also* Vinogradoff, P. in [214].

—c. Paradisi, B., *Civitas maxima: studi di storia del diritto internazionale*. Firenze: Olschki, 1974, 2 vols.

Traces the evolution of selected PIL principles (e.g. sovereignty, pacifism, etc.). Includes extensive bibliographic notes.

—d. Levin, D. B., *Istoriia mezhdunarodnogo prava*. Moskva: Institut Mezhdunarodnykh Otnosheniia, 1962, 134 pp.

The work traces five Marxist periods of PIL. For further (pre-1917) references *see* [353b]. *See also* Butler, W. E., Some reflections on the periodization of Soviet approaches to international law. In Barry, D., Butler, W. E. and Ginsburgs, W. E. (eds), *Contemporary Soviet law: essays in honor of J. N. Hazard*. The Hague: Nijhoff, 1974, pp. 213-225.

—e. Strupp, K., *Urkunden zur Geschichte des Völkerrechts*. Gotha: Perthes, 1911, 2 vols. Rev. 2nd edn in French: *Documents pour servir à l'histoire du droit des gens*. Berlin: Sack, 1923, 5 vols.

A selection of texts from G. F. Martens [7] with a view to illustrating the historical development of PIL, mainly in terms of relevant treaties and agreements.

456a. Schwarzenberger, G., Historical models of international law: towards a comparative history of international law. In [428b, 1980] and in [495a].

Five historical PIL models are examined in the light of the 'seven pillars' of PIL (sovereignty, recognition, responsibility, self-defence, consent, good faith, freedom of seas). The methodological focus is on inter-disciplinary approaches, mainly to the history of state and judicial practice and away from the history of PIL doctrine.

—b. Connelly, A. M., The history of international law: a comparative approach. In [428b, 1980] and in *Yearbook of world affairs*, 1978, **32**, pp. 303-319.

A systems approach to the history of PIL; the proposed comparative methodology deals with PIL rules and concepts within the context of comparable legal systems.

—c. Preiser, W., *Die Völkerrechtsgeschichte, ihre Aufgaben und Methoden*. Wiesbaden: Steiner, 1964.

457a. History of the law of nations: regional developments. *Enc. PIL*, 1984, **7**, pp. 205-252.

The contributions by Elias, Miyazaki, Barberis and Singh trace the history of PIL in Africa, the Far East, Latin America and South/South-East Asia.

—b. Preiser, W., *Frühe völkerrechtliche Ordnung der aussereuropäischen Welt: ein Beitrag zur Geschichte des Völkerrechts*. Wiesbaden: Steiner, 1976, 184 pp.

Traces the history of PIL with reference to the pre-colonial periods in the Americas, Polynesia, Black Africa, the Indian subcontinent and China. *See also* Groening, I., *Bibliotheca iuris gentium exotica iuxta doctrinam Asiaticorum, Africanorum et Americanorum*. Hamburg, 1703 (disparagingly referred to by Ompteda [347], his item 19).

—c. Mensah-Brown, A. K. (ed.), *African international legal history*. New York:

UNITAR, 1975, 234 pp. (UNITAR/ST/9/1975: UN Sales publication E.76.XV/ST 9).

The historical 'welding' approach used in this work dwells on PIL rules as these emerged in Euro-African dealings in the colonial and post-colonial era. Part I examines treaties, boundaries and international relations relating to Africa; part II contains samples of PIL history in the Malagasy Monarchy, Zanzibar, Yoruba-Benin Kingdoms, Hausa-Fulani Emirates, etc.

—d. Alexandrowicz, C. H. (ed.), *Studies in the history of the law of nations*. The Hague: Nijhoff, 1970, 232 pp.

See also his The Afro-Asian world and the law of nations: historical aspects. *RCADI*, 1968/I, **123**, pp. 117-214.

ii. EVOLUTION of PIL

458a. Cassese, A. and Weiler, J. H. H., *Change and stability in international lawmaking*. Berlin: W. de Gruyter, 1988, 214 pp.

Part I, The classical 'sources' of international law revisited (includes Riphagen and Condorelli, The role of general principles and GA resolutions); part 2, Are we heading for a new normativity in the international community? (includes J. Brownlie, To what extent are the traditional categories of *lex lata* and *lex ferenda* still viable?; G. Arangio-Ruiz, Voluntarism versus majority rule; R. Falk, To what extent are international law and international lawyers ideologically 'neutral'?).

—b. Cassese, A., *International law in a divided world*. Oxford: Clarendon, 1986, 429 pp. Also in French: *Le droit international dans un monde divisé*. Paris: Berger-Levrault, 1986, 375 pp.

Part I, Origin and foundations of the international community (an historical and substantive approach); part 2, Creation and effectiveness of international standards; part 3, Critical issues of today (legal regulation of armed conflict; international protection of human dignity; law governing international economic relations).

—c. Carrillo Salcedo, J. A., *El derecho internacional en un mundo en cambio*. Madrid: Tecnos, 1984, 351 pp.

Concerns the dialectics of the contemporary international society and the need for new PIL structures, functions for overcoming the society's tensions.

459. *The future of international law in a multicultural world/L'Avenir du droit international dans un monde multiculturel*. The Hague Academy International Law Workshop, 1983. Edited by R.-J. Dupuy. Dordrecht: Nijhoff, 1984, 491 pp.

Jointly organized by the Hague Academy of International Law [380a] and the United Nations University [661d], the workshop was attended by six justices of the ICJ and numerous PIL scholars from the world over. Part I, Global approach; part 2, Comparative thematic approach; part 3, Future solutions. The interdisciplinary contributions focus on the sociological, philosophical and cultural aspects of PIL, including non-legal aspects thereof, e.g. N. Singh, The basic concept of universality and the development of international law; M. Flory, Le droit international est-il européen?; A. Bozeman, Cultural traditions of international law; A. Trapero-Ballestero, Le droit à l'éducation et le droit international; A. Cassese, The concept of law upheld by western, socialist and developing countries; and Sarin (*see* [483]). Reviewed in *AJIL*, 1985, **79**, pp. 1,091–1,093.

460. Grahl-Madsen, A. and Toman, J. (eds), *The spirit of Uppsala. Proceedings of the Joint UNITAR-Uppsala University Seminar on International Law and Organization for a New World Order* [IUS 81], *Uppsala 9–18 June 1981*. Berlin: W. de Gruyter, 1984, 601 pp.

The *Proceedings* reproduce but a fraction of the discussions held by international legal scholars from 50 countries, developed and developing. Arranged in nine sections, the contributions examine the changing concepts of PIL, often through the juxtaposition of the traditional/Eurocentric and modern/anthropocentric perceptions of the world order, e.g. B.J. Theutenberg, Changes in the norms guiding the international legal system: history and contemporary trends; V. Dimitrijević, A natural or moral basis for international law; and R. Dolzer, Universalism and regionalism; Puig, *see* [507c]. Section 5, International law in a multicultural world; section 6, Independence and interdependence; section 7, Sovereignty and humanity.

461a. Charnay, J.-P. et al., *De la dégradation du droit des gens dans le monde contemporain*. Paris: Anthropos, 1981, 218 pp. (Travaux du Centre d'études et de recherches sur les stratégies et les conflits. Université Paris I. Série contemporaine, 1).

Contains the proceedings of a symposium held at Unesco House, 2–3 March 1979.

—b. Carty, A., *The decay of international law: a reappraisal of the limits of legal imagination in international affairs*. Manchester: Manchester UP, 1986, 138 pp. (Melland Schill Monographs in International Law).

The author attributes the crisis in PIL methodology mainly to doctrinal preoccupation with the state as the chief actor in international relations, and customary law as the main PIL source. The extant PIL theory (in its predominantly Western/Eurocentric aspects) is questioned.

462a. Schachter, O., 1982/V, International law in theory and practice. *RCADI*, **178**, pp. 9–396.

—b. Lachs, M., 1980/IV, The development and general trends of international law in our time. *RCADI*, **169**, pp. 9–377.

—c. Elias, T.O., *New horizons in international law.* Alphen A/R: Sijthoff & Noordhoff, 1979, 260 pp.

—d. Tunkin, G., *Sovremennoe mezhdunarodnoe pravo.* French edition: *Droit international contemporain: recueil d'articles.* Moscou: Progrès, 1972. English edition: *Contemporary international law: collection of articles.* Moscow: Progress, 1969.

—e. McWhinney, E., Classical sources and the international law-making process of contemporary international law, pp. 341-353, in [178].

—f. Kunz, J. L., *The changing law of nations: essays on international law.* Columbus, OH: Ohio State UP, 1968, 970 pp.

Traces the evolution of PIL from 1914 to the 1960s. The work has been translated into many languages, including Russian and Chinese.

See also [209, 440, 507b].

iii. HISTORIOGRAPHY, DOCTRINAL SCHOOLS

463a. Scott, J. B., *Classics of international law.* Oxford: Clarendon, 1911-50. 22 vols in 39 (Publications of the Carnegie Endowment for International Peace, Div. International Law).

Three volumes in the series represent a photographic reproduction of the original texts and English translations with explanatory notes of works by fifteenth to eighteenth-century PIL scholars since usually referred to as 'classics'. In the 1960s Oceana Publications [420b] reissued the English translation parts of the series.

—b. *Die Klassiker des Völkerrechts in modernen deutschen Übersetzungen.* Tübingen: Mohr, 1950-, 1-.

464a. Scott, J. B., *The Spanish origin of international law. Lectures on Francisco de Vitoria (1480-1546) and Francisco Suarez (1548-1617).* Washington, DC: Georgetown University, 1928, 121 pp.

For an expanded version in French *see Vitoria et Suarez. Contribution des théologiens du droit international moderne.* Introduction par Y. de La Brière. Préface par J. B. Scott. Paris: Pédone, 1939, 279 pp. (Association internationale Vitoria-Suarez). *See also* Scott, J. B., *The Catholic conception of international law: F. de Vitoria . . . a critical examination and a justified appreciation.* Washington, DC: Georgetown University, 1934, 494 pp.

—b. *Miaja de la Muela, A., *Internacionalistas españoles del siglo XVI. Fernando Vázques de Menchaca (1512-1569).* Valladolid, 1932, 88 pp.

Note that the Asociación Francisco de Vitoria, Madrid envisaged the publication of a series *Biblioteca internacionalista clásica.*

465a. *International law and the Grotian heritage: a commemorative colloquium, held at the Hague on 8 April 1983 on the occasion of the fourth centenary of the birth of Hugo Grotius*. Organized by the Interuniversitair Instituut voor internationaal Recht, T. M. C. Asser, in cooperation with the Grotiana Foundation. The Hague: T. M. C. Asser Institute, 1985, 370 pp.

—b. *Grotius et l'ordre juridique international. Travaux du colloque Hugo Grotius, Genève, 10-11 novembre 1983.* Edited by A. Dufour, P. Haggenmacher and J. Toman, Lausanne: Payot, 1985, 140 pp. (Collection juridique romande. Etudes et pratique). *See also* [595b].

—c. ter Meulen, J. and Diermanse, P.J.J., *Bibliographie des écrits imprimés de Hugo Grotius.* The Hague: Nijhoff, 1950, 708 pp.

See also ter Meulen, J., *Liste bibliographique de 76 éditions et traductions du 'Du jure belli ac pacis'.* Leiden: Brill, 1925 (Bibliotheca Visseriana, 12).

—d. *Grotius reader: a reader for students of international law and legal history.* Edited by L. E. van Holk and C. G. Roelofsen. Published on the occasion of the fourth centenary of Hugo de Groot, 1583-1645. The Hague: T. M. C. Asser Institute, 1983, 244 pp.

Includes a bibliography of monographs, periodical articles relative to the life of Grotius and his legal writings.

—e. Grotiana Foundation. c/o Prof. E.J. Kuiper, University of Leiden, Netherlands.

The merger of various Grotius societies in the Netherlands eventually gave rise in 1980 to the Grotiana Foundation. The objective of the Foundation is to promote research into the thought of Grotius within the contemporary quest for a (new) world order. The Foundation publishes the journal *Grotiana* [221]. The British Institute of International and Comparative Law [408] in 1962 incorporated the Grotius Society (London). The latter published *Transactions* (vols 1-44, 1915-59) and *Papers: studies in the history of the law of nations.* Edited by C. H. Alexandrowicz. *See also* Interuniversity Institute for Documentation of Legal History, Oudezijds Achterburgwal 217-219, Amsterdam, Netherlands.

466a. Reibstein, E., *Völkerrecht: eine Geschichte seiner Ideen in Lehre und Praxis.* Freiburg i/B: Alber, 1958-63, 2 vols (Orbis academicus. Problemgeschichten der Wissenschaft in Dokumenten und Darstellungen).

Vol. 1 is a historiographical survey from Machiavelli to Vattel; vol. 2 examines the theories and methodologies of nineteenth- and twentieth-century PIL scholars within the relevant socio-political context. Extensive bibliography (pp. 710-764).

—b. de La Pradelle, A. G., *Maîtres et doctrines du droit des gens*, 2nd edn. Paris: Editions internationales, 1950, 440 pp. 1st edn 1939.

A historiographical analysis of works by PIL scholars divided into precursors (classics), moderns (Martens, Calvo, Lorimer *et al.*) and 'contemporaries' (Westlake, Fauchille, Le Fur, Politis *et al.*)

467a. *Puig, J. C., *Doctrinas internacionales y autonomía Latino-Americana*. Caracas, 1980, pp. 15-121.

—b. Jacobini, H. B., *A study of the philosophy of international law as seen in the works of Latin American writers*. The Hague: Nijhoff, 1954.

Chapter 4 concerns 'American international law' and the controversy attendant upon one of the earliest regional conceptions of PIL. *See also* Butler, W. E., 1976, Latin American approaches to international law. *International journal of politics*, **6**, pp. 50-105.

468a. *Das Naturrechtsdenken heute und morgen: Gedächtnisschrift für René Marcic*. Edited by D. Mayer-Maly and P. M. Simons. Berlin: Duncker & Humblot, 1983, 999 pp.

The contributions trace the history of natural law in general and its influence upon PIL scholars in particular, including a comparison of natural law and positivist methodologies. Concluding the volume is J. Stone, Natural law and human predicament in the age of technology.

—b. *Zhukov, G. P., *Kritika estestvennopravovykh teoriĭ mezhdunarodnogo prava*. Moskva: Gospolitizdat, 1961.

Marxist criticism of natural law in the conceptions of bourgois legal and PIL scholars.

—c. Ago, R., 1984, Positivism. *Enc. PIL*, **7**, pp. 385-393.

Traces *ius positivum* from its reaction to natural law, through positivist doctrinal variations in the nineteenth and twentieth centuries. *See also* Bos, M., 1982, Will and order in the nation-state system: observations on positivism and positive international law. *NILR*, **29**, pp. 3-31; Alexandrowicz, C. H., 1974/5, Empirical and doctrinal positivism in international law. *BYIL*, **47**, pp. 286-289; Erim, I. N., *Positivisme juridique et le droit international*. Paris: Sirey, 1939, 335 pp.

—d. Steiner, H. J., 1984, International law, doctrine and schools of thought in the twentieth century. *Enc. PIL*, **7**, pp. 297-309.

A historiographical survey of PIL doctrines in the works of twentieth-century scholars in Europe and North America (including positivist, analytical, jurisprudential, policy science and realist schools), the socialist countries and the Third World.

469a. McWhinney, E., 1988, Contemporary US theory of international law. *CYIL*, **26**, pp. 281-295.

Includes the appraisal of H. Lasswell and M. S. McDougal, as representatives of 'legal realism'. *See also* Tipson, F. S., 1977, From international law to world public order. *Yale studies in world public order*, **4**(1), pp. 39–88, based on his *Consolidating world public order: the American study of international law*, PhD thesis, University of Virginia, 1977.

—b. Falk, R.A., 1967, New approaches to the study of international law. *AJIL*, **61**, pp. 477–495.

A historiographical analysis of policy science, functionalism and systems theory approaches in the works of American PIL scholars.

470a. Adede, A.O., 1980, International law from a common law perspective. *Boston Univ. Law Review*, **60**(1), pp. 46–76.

—b. Higgins, A.P., 1932/II, La contribution de quatre grands juristes britanniques au droit international (Lorimer, Westlake, Hall, Holland). *RCADI*, **46**, pp. 705–826; see also R. Higgins in [197].

—c. Lauterpacht, H., 1931, The so-called Anglo-American and Continental schools of thought in international law. *BYIL*, **12**, 31.

471a. Klecatsky, H., Marcic, R. and H. Schambeck, H. (eds), *Die Wiener rechtstheoretische Schule. Ausgewählte Schriften von H. Kelsen, A.J. Merkl und A. Verdross*. Wien: Europa Verlag, 1968, 2 vols.

See also Kleinheyer, G. and Schröder, J. (eds), *Deutsche Juristen aus fünf Jahrhunderten: eine biographische Einführung in die Geschichte der Rechtswissenschaft*, 2nd edn. Heidelberg: C.F. Müller, 1983, 409 pp. (Uni-Taschenbücher, 578).

—b. Sereni, A.P., Dottrine italiane di diritto internazionale. In *Scritti di diritto internazionale in onore di T. Perassi*. Milano: Giuffrè, 1957, vol. 2, pp. 279–300.

—c. Stuyt, A.M., The science of public international law in the first century of the Kingdom of Netherlands, 1814–1914. pp. 167–193 in [45, vol. 1].

See also Strijbosch, A.K.J.M., *Juristen en de studie van Volksrecht in Nederlands-Indie en anglofoon Africa* . . . Nijmegen, 1980, 258 pp. (Publikaties over Volksrecht, 7). This PhD thesis examines customary law of the Dutch East Indies and British Africa in the perception of selected colonial Dutch and post-colonial British legal scholars. In Dutch with English summary.

472a. Butler, W.E., 1972, Eastern European approaches to public international law. *Yearbook of world affairs*, **26**, pp. 331–345.

See also Taube, M., 1926/I, Etudes sur le développement historique du droit international dans l'Europe orientale. *RCADI*, **11**, pp. 340–533.

—b. Hacker, J., 1986, Die Völkerrechtslehre der DDR . . . *Recht in Ost und West*, **30**(2), pp. 77–87; earlier version in *Friedens-Warte*, 1979, **62**, pp. 54–114.

—c. Frenzke, D., *Die Völkerrechtslehre in der ungarischen Volksrepublik* . . . Berlin: Berlin Verlag/A. Spitz, 1979, 176 pp.

—d. Uschakow, A., 1980, Die Völkerrechtswissenschaft in Polen. *Friedens-Warte*, **63**, pp. 133-153. See also [499c].

—e. Frenzke, D., 1976, Die neueste Entwicklung der rumänischen Völkerrechtslehre. *Osteuropa-Recht*, **22**(1), pp. 47-63; updated in *Friedens-Warte*, 1978, **61**, pp. 129-228.

—f. Dorsch, E., *Der gegenwärtige Stand der jugoslawischen Völkerrechtslehre*. Herrenalb (FRG), 1960, 104 pp.

473a. Schweisfurth, T., *Sozialistisches Völkerrecht*. Berlin: Springer, 1979, 615 pp. (Beiträge zum ausländischen öffentlichen Recht und Völkerrecht, 73).

Mainly a critical appraisal of the 'newer' Soviet approach to PIL; for the author's updated summary see Socialist conceptions of international law. *Enc. PIL*, 1984, **7**, pp. 417-424. For reviews see *ZaöRV,* 1980, **40**(3), pp. 661-663; *Panstwo i pravo*, 1980, **12**, pp. 134-135; see also [477].

—b. Butler, W. E., 1980, Anglo-American research on Soviet approaches to PIL. In [428b].

—c. Frenzke, D., 1979, Zur Entwicklung der sowjetischen Völkerrechtslehre. *Osteuropa-Recht*, **25**(4), pp. 262-299; for an updated version see *Recht in Ost und West*, 1985, **29**(1), pp. 7-21.

—d. Vamvoukos, A., 1979, Chinese and Soviet attitudes toward international law: a comparative approach. *Review of socialist law*, **5**(2), pp. 131-155.

—e. Erickson, R.J., *International law and the revolutionary state: a case study of the Soviet Union and customary international law*. Alphen a/R: Sijthoff & Noordhoff, 1973, 268 pp.

This historiographical analysis of selected Soviet works on PIL complements Grzybowski, K., *Soviet public international law: doctrines and diplomatic practice*. Leiden: Sijthoff, 1970, 544 pp.

—f. Lapenna, I., *Conception soviétique de droit international public*. Paris: Pédone, 1954, 324 pp. (Les systèmes de droit contemporain, 9).

For an abridged English summary see his The Soviet concept of socialist international law. *Yearbook of world affairs*, 1975, **29**, pp. 242-264.

—g. Calvez, J. Y., *Droit international et souveraineté en URSS: l'évolution de l'idéologie juridique soviétique depuis la Révolution d'octobre*. Paris: Colin, 1953, 229 pp. (Foundation nationale des sciences politiques. Cahiers, 48).

iv. IDEOLOGICAL, REGIONAL PERCEPTIONS

474a.   McWhinney, E., 1985, Regional ethnocentric or general universal international law. *International journal* (Toronto), **40**(3), pp. 398-422.

Includes his correlation of the 'fissiparous tendencies in international law doctrine' with the political breakdown of the old European concert of nations. See also his Ideological pluralism, chapters 9 and 10 in [648a].

—b.   Bedjaoui, M., 1970. *See* [531d].

Chapter 1 is a critical evaluation of European/bourgeois 'power-based' international law doctrines.

—c.   Chemillier-Gendreau, M., 1974, *La fonction idéologique du droit international public*, pp. 221-239, in [322b].

Considers the divergence between the 'is' and 'ought' of PIL, and the concept of an international community, as ideologically conditioned.

—d.   Tunkin, G., *Ideologicheskaîa bor'ba i mezhdunarodnoe pravo*. Moskva: Mezhdunarodnye Otnoshenîîa, 1967, 174 pp.

Represents a critical assessment of twentieth-century bourgeois approaches to PIL, juxtaposing these 'old' to 'new' socialist models. See also his Le conflit idéologique et le droit international contemporain, pp. 888-898, in [193].

—e.   Larson, A. and Jenks, C.W., (eds), *Sovereignty within the law*. Dobbs Ferry, NY: Oceana, 1965, 492 pp.

Includes surveys of Jewish (Rosenne), Islamic (Khaddduri), Hindu (Anantanarayanan), Socialist (Grzybowski), East European (Ramunde), Latin American (Garcia-Amador), African (Elias), Chinese (Leng) and Japanese (Tanaka) approaches to PIL.

475a.   Kooijmans, P.H., 1976/IV, Protestantism and the development of international law. *RCADI*, **152**, pp. 79-117.

—b.   de Riedmatten, H., 1976/III, Le catholicisme et le développement du droit international. *RCADI*, **151**, pp. 115-159.

See also [464a].

—c.   Iriye, K., 1967/IV, The principle of international law in the light of Confucian doctrine. *RCADI*, **120**, pp. 1-59.

—d.   Jayatilleke, K.N., 1967/IV, The principles of international law in Buddhist doctrine. *RCADI*, **120**, pp. 441-567.

—e.   Sastry, K.R.R., 1966/I, Hinduism and international law. *RCADI*, **117**, pp. 509-614.

See also [474e].

476a. el-Kosheri, A. G., 1984, History of the law of nations, regional developments: Islam. *Enc. PIL,* **7**, pp. 222-230.

An historical outline of PIL principles from the seventh to the twentieth centuries. Includes a historiographical appraisal of traditionalist/modernist Islamic legal scholars.

—b. Khadduri, M., 1983, International law, Islamic. *Enc. PIL,* **6**, pp. 227-233.

Discusses Islamic legal and political concepts such as *dar-al-Islam, siyar* and *jihad.* See also his *Islamic law of nations.* Baltimore, MD: Johns Hopkins UP, 1966 (essentially a translation of the section on *siyar* from the work of the eighth-century scholar el-Shaybani) and his *The law of war and peace in Islam: a study of Muslim international law.* London, 1962. 1st edn 1940.

—c. el-Ghunaimini, M. T., *Manual on international law of peace.* Alexandria: al-Maaref, 1982, 909 pp.

Represents an attempt to bridge the traditionalist teaching of ʿ*ulama* (based on divine revelation) and modernist PIL conceptions. Part 1 is an historical outline of Islamic PIL; part 2 is concerned with the Muslim legal legacy in general; part 3 deals with the mainly classical Muslim conception of PIL (the chapter is a summary of his *The Muslim conception of international law and the Western approach.* The Hague: Nijhoff, 1968, 288 pp.).

—d. *Hamidullah, M., *Muslim conduct of state, being a treatise on 'siyar', that is Islamic notions of public international law, consisting of the laws of peace, war and neutrality together with precedents from orthodox practice and preceded by a historical and general introduction*, 5th edn. Lahore: Ashraf, 1968, 379 pp.

See also Boisard, M.A., 1977, De certaines règles concernant la conduite des hostilités et la protection des victimes de conlits armée. *Annales d'études internationales,* **8**, pp. 145-158 (includes an analysis of Hamidullah, el-Gunaimini's views on war); *L'Islam dans les relations internationales.* Paris: Edisund, 1986.

—e. Kruse, H., *Islamische Völkerrechtslehre,* 2nd edn. Bochum (FRG): Brockmeyer, 1979, 252 pp.

Based on the author's PhD thesis (Göttingen, 1953), the work examines mainly eleventh- and twelfth-century Muslim state practice, with the focus on *siyar* as that PIL element which linked relations between Islamic and non-Islamic states. See also *Gaber, M.H.M., *The early Islamic state with special reference to the evolution of the principles of Islamic international law, 632-750 A.D.* Washington, DC, 1962.

477a. Kartashkin, V., The Marxist-Leninist approach: the theory of class struggles and contemporary public international law, pp. 79-109 in [507b].

—b. Starushenko, G.B., *Mirovoĭ revoliutsionnyĭ protsess i sovremennoe mezhdunarodnoe pravo.* Moskva: Mezhdunarodnye Otnosheniia, 1978, 328 pp.

See also [473].

—c. *Luk, I., Sotsializm i mezhdunarodnoe pravo. Moskva, 1977.

See also [473a].

—d. Krylov, S., 1947/I, La doctrine soviétique du droit international. RCADI, 70, pp. 411-475.

478a. Schindler, D., 1984, Regional international law. Enc. PIL, 7, pp. 404-409.

—b. *Voprosy universal'nosti i effektivnosti mezhdunarodnogo prava: mezhvuzovskiĭ sbornik nauchnykh trudov. Sverdlovsk: Sverdlovskiĭ IUridicheskiĭ Institut/ UrGU, 1981, 135 pp.

See also Likhachev, V. N., 1975, Mesto printsipa universal'nosti SEMP, pp. 100-109.

—c. Régionalisme et universalisme dans le droit international contemporain: Colloque, Bordeaux, 1976. Paris: Pédone, 1977, 358 pp. (Actes du 10. Colloque de la Société française pour le droit international).

—d. Butler, W.E., Regional and sectional diversities in international law, pp. 45-82, in [499b].

See also Wiek, K., 1978, International law and ideological realignment: universality re-examined. New York University journal of international law and politics, 10(3), pp. 463-490; Falk, R. A. and Mendlovitz, S. H. (eds), Regional politics and world order. San Francisco: W. H. Freeman, 1973, 475 pp. (chapters 4 and 6 on the concept of regionalism in international law/relations); Singh in [459], Galvez in [507b].

479a. Anghelov, S. et al., Socialist internationalism: theory and practice of international relations of a new type. Moscow: Progress, 1982, 507 pp. (Practice, Problems and Prospects of Socialism). Russian edition, 1979.

—b. Uibopuu, H.J., 1986, Socialist internationalism. Enc. PIL, 9, pp. 347-350.

480a. Tunkin, G., 1958/III, Co-existence and international law. RCADI, 95, pp. 5-79.

See also his Le droit international de la coexistence pacifique. In Mélanges offertes à Henri Rollin: problèmes de droit des gens. Paris: Pédone, 1964, pp. 407-418.

—b. Uschakow, A., Die sowjetische Konzeption der friedlichen Koexistenz und das Völkerrecht. Köln; Institut für Ostrecht, 1987.

481a. Barberis, J.A., 1984, American international law. Enc. PIL, 7, pp. 222-227.

—b. García-Amador, F. V., Sistema interamericana a través de tratados, convenciones y otros documentos. Washington, DC: Organización de los Estados Americanos, 1981, vol. 1, Asuntos jurídico-políticos.

English translation: *The Inter-American system: treaties, conventions and other documents.* Dobbs Ferry, NY: Oceana, 1983, vol. 1 in 2 parts, *Legal-political affairs.* See also García-Amador, F. V., *The Andean legal order: a new community law.* Dobbs Ferry, NY: Oceana, 1978, 423 pp.

—c. Sepúlveda, C., *Las fuentes del derecho internacional americano: una encuesta sobre los metodos de creación de reglas internacionales en el hemisferio occidental.* Mexico, DF: Porrua, 1975, 154 pp.

Based on his lectures in Madrid, 1966, and Paris, 1967. Traces the evolution of PIL principles in terms of Latin American doctrinal positions (including early twentieth-century controversies) and state practice in the Western Hemisphere. Includes an analysis of 'Conferencias internacionales americanas, 1889–1936'.

—d. Rodley, N.G. and Ronning, N. (eds), *International law in the Western Hemisphere: essays and commentaries.* The Hague: Nijhoff, 1974, 199 pp.

Contains the proceedings of the 'Conference of international law in the Western Hemisphere, 1971', held under the auspices of the New York University Center of International Studies. Includes contributions on regional water resources and superpower intervention.

—e. Caicedo Castillo, J.J., *El derecho internacional en el sistema interamericana.* Madrid: Cultura Hispánica, 1970, 606 pp. (Centro de estudios jurídicos hispano-americanos. Colección de monografías jurídicas).

—f. Alvarez, A., *Le droit international nouveau dans ses rapports avec la vie des peuples.* Paris: Pédone, 1959, 636 pp.

A revised version of the Chilean scholar's classic *Le droit international américain.* Paris: Pédone, 1910, 386 pp. Chapters 7 and 9 of the sociologically weighted 1959 work examine the Latin American PIL issues from 1939 on. *See also* his *International law and related subjects from the point of view of the American continent.* Washington, DC: Carnegie Endowment for International Peace, 1922, 93 pp. (Pamphlet series of the Endowment, 48).

482a. Anand, R.P., *International law and the developing countries: confrontation or co-operation?* Dordrecht: Nijhoff, 1987, 274 pp.

—b. Snyder, F.E. and Sathiratai, S., *Third World attitudes toward international law.* Dordrecht: Nijhoff, 1987, 850 pp.

See also Braillard, P. and Djalili, M.-R., *The Third World and international relations.* London: Frances Pinter; Boulder, CO: Lynne Rienner, 1986.

—c. *Agrawala, S.K. (ed.), *New horizons of international law and developing countries.* New Delhi: International Law Association, Indian Branch, 1983, 427 pp.

Contains articles contributed by Indian PIL scholars to seminars held under the auspices of the Indian Branch of the ILA. *See also* Wang Thieya in [507b].

—d. *Pays en voie de développement et transformation du droit international: Colloque, Aix-en-Provence, 1973.* Paris: Pédone, 1974, 315 pp. (Actes du 7e Colloque de la Société française pour le droit international).

See also [723e].

—e. *Razvivaiushchiesia strany i mezhdunarodnoe pravo.* Moskva, 1971.

See also [486].

483. Sarin, M.L., The Asian-African states and the development of international law, pp. 117-142, in [459].

Contains a historical survey of European and Afro-Asian relations; an analysis of the role of the Asian-African Legal Consultative Committee in the development of PIL; and an outline of traditional Asian customary international law.

484a. Ginther, K. and Benedek, W. (eds), *New perspectives and conceptions of international law: an Afro-European dialogue.* Wien, 1983, 261 pp. (Österreichische Zeitschrift für öffentliches Recht und Völkerrecht, 1983, suppl. 6).

See also [516b].

—b. Elias, T.O., *Africa and the development of international law.* Leiden: Sijthoff, 1972, 261 pp.

—c. Okoye, F.C., *International law and the new African states.* London: Sweet & Maxwell, 1972, 225 pp. (Law in Africa, 33).

—d. Yakemtchouk, R., *L'Afrique en droit international.* Paris: LGDJ, 1971, 319 pp.

Analyses recognition, succession, frontiers, etc. in African state practice, as well the Eurocentric approaches thereto.

—e. Bipoun-Woum, J.-M., *Le droit international africain.* Paris: LGDJ, 1970, 327 pp. (Toulouse, Faculté de droit et des sciences économiques, Bibliothèque africaine et malgache. Droit et sociologie politique, 5).

See also [325].

485a. Anand, R.P., *Asian states and the development of universal international law.* New Delhi: Vikas, 1972, 245 pp.

—b. Syatauw, J.J.G., *Some newly established Asian states and the development of international law.* The Hague: Nijhoff, 1961, 249 pp.

486. *The Third World and international law: selected bibliography 1955-1982/Le Tiers-Monde et le droit international: bibliographie sélective, 1955-1982.* Geneva: UNOG Library, 1983, 100 pp. (United Nations Library, Geneva, Publications Series C, Special bibliographies, répertoires and indexes, 5).

Contains references to periodical articles and monographs (excluding UN materials) reflecting in part doctrinal positions of PIL scholars from the Third World and, in part, perceptions of PIL in developing countries by scholars from developed countries. Parts 1-3 contain references mostly in English, French and Spanish to general and specialized aspects of PIL within the Third World context; part 4 lists relevant bibliographies. Excluded from the bibliography are studies on non-alignment, individual country and case studies and the history of international law in colonial times. An author index concludes the bibliography.

487a. Kurian, G. T., *Encyclopedia of the Third World*, 2nd edn. London: Mansell, 1982, 3 vols. 1st edn 1978.

Arranged alphabetically by countries, the *Encyclopedia* provides general and specialized (including legal) information about the countries selected, as well as regional organizations relating to the area. Vol. 3 contains an extensive bibliography and index.

—b. Gorman, G. E. and Mahoney, M., *Guide to current national bibliographies in the Third World*. München: H. Zell, 1983, 345 pp.

Arranged alphabetically by countries, the *Guide* lists available (general) national bibliographies.

—c. Duffy, J., Hevelin, J. and Österreicher, S., *International directory of scholars and specialists in Third World studies*. Honolulu, HI: Crossroads Press, 1981, 563 pp.

—d. Re Qua, E. G., *The developing nations: a guide to information sources*. Detroit, MI: Gale, 1965, 339 pp.

488a. *Annuaire du Tiers-Monde*. Paris: Berger-Levrault, 1976–, 1–, annual.

Published under the auspices of the Association française pour l'étude du Tiers-Monde, in cooperation with the Centre d'études politiques et juridiques du Tiers-Monde de l'Université de Paris I.

—b. *Jahrbuch Dritte Welt*. München: Beck, 1983–, 1–, annual.

Published under the auspices of the Deutsches Übersee-Institut, Hamburg.

—c. Crow, B. and Thomas, A. (eds), *Third World atlas*. Milton Keynes: Open University Press, 1983, 72 pp.

489. *Third World Centre for Research and Publishing*. 117 Piccadilly, London W1.

See also World Press Centre, 3 Parolles Rd, London N19 3RE, which acts as a clearing house of pre-publication (source) materials from the UN and SA concerning the Third World.

v. METHODOLOGY OF PIL

490. Bos, M., *A methodology of international law*. Amsterdam: North-Holland, 1984, 357 pp.

Published for the T.M.C. Asser Institute [406], the work dwells on methodological means for apprehending the 'process' of PIL, in terms of its genesis, recognized manifestation and application of its rules (a diagram of the three phases is on p. 16). The core of the work deals with the alleged and recognized manifestation of international law (RMIL), its identification, hierarchy and interpretation. Critical of the positivist methodological approach, Bos advances instead an 'analytical conceptualism' (pp. 28-32) for ascertaining the dynamics of the normative concept of law (NCL), itself considered the cornerstone for an acceptable theory on the binding force of PIL. *See also* [509c].

491. Rosenne, S., *Practice and method of international law*. Dobbs Ferry, NY: Oceana, 1983, 198 pp.

Midway between a reference guide to PIL documentary sources (with samples listed in the annexes) and an outline of PIL research methods. No index.

492. Bleckmann, A., *Grundprobleme und Methoden des Völkerrechts*. Freiburg i/B, München: Alber, 1982, 348 pp.

The work examines selected postulates of PIL within the structural context of the international community. Chapters 18 and 19 represent a methodological attempt to overcome the prevailing conceptual uncertainty of PIl, by bridging ideal/real, legal/non-legal (values/soft law, etc.) elements of international law. *See also* [461b, 509f].

493. Baskin, IU.IA. and Fel'dman, D.I., *Mezhdunarodnoe pravo: problemy metodologii, ocherki metodov issledovaniia*. Moskva: Mezhdunarodnye Otnosheniia, 1971, 175 pp.

Discusses materialist dialectics as a methodological approach to PIL; includes an analysis of (socialist and other) systems, models and cybernetics as PIL methodological means. For an updated summary *see* Baskin and Fel'dman, 1980, pp. 91-99, in [428b]. *See also* Butler, W.E., 1978, Methodological innovations in Soviet international legal doctrine. *Yearbook of world affairs*, 32, pp. 334-341.

494a. Vellas, P., *Droit international public. Institutions internationales. Méthodologie, historique, sources, sujets de la société internationale, organisations internationales*. Paris: LGDJ, 1970, 483 pp.

Part 1 contains PIL methodological considerations with reference to juridical logic, conceptual and terminological elements, problems of legal reasoning and the role of hypothesis and observation therein, and a review of PIL methods in selected doctrinal works. Part 2 is basically a traditional PIL treatise, complemented by selected texts in *Droit international et science politique: recueil des textes*. Paris: LGDJ, 1967, 343 pp.

—b. Castberg, F., 1933/I, La méthodologie du droit international public. *RCADI*, 43, pp. 313-383.

495a. Schwarzenberger, G., *The dynamics of international law*. Milton Keynes: Professional Books, 1976, 139 pp.

Intended as a companion volume to his *Frontiers of international law* (1962) and *International law and order* (1971), the work contains several of Schwarzenberger's essays previously published in the *Yearbook of world affairs* [449a] or *Current legal problems* (London: Sweet & Maxwell, 1948-, annual). Schwarzenberger examines selected PIL issues (e.g. equity, the law of armed conflict and 'civitas maxima') in the light of inductive, interdisciplinary methods. *See also* [456a].

—b. Schwarzenberger, G., *The inductive approach to international law*. London: Stevens; Dobbs Ferry, NY: Oceana, 1965, 209 pp.

Published under the auspices of the London Institute of World Affairs, the work posits empirical, dialectical tenets which constitute Schwarzenberger's inductive PIL methodology in response to his perceived shortcomings of deductive speculation; four PIL 'test cases' illustrate his inductive approach. For Bos [490], Schwarzenberger's inductive approach represents a 'consumer' interest in PIL sources, notably treaties.

A specific and largely North American methodological approach to PIL concerns the 'process of law', as opposed to the 'rule of law'; the interdisciplinary (PIL/international relations) methodology is in particular reflected in the world order and policy studies [80, 445b,c].

496a. *Tharp, P.A., *Systems analysis and international law*. Ann Arbor, MI: University Microfilms, 1980, 240 pp.

Based on PhD thesis, University of Wisconsin, 1969.

—b. Tunkin, G., Sistemnyĭ podkhod v nauke mezhdunarodnogo prava. In *Demokratiia i pravo razvitogo sotsialisticheskogo obshchestva*. Moskva, 1975, pp. 482-488.

—c. Fel'dman, D.F., Rol' sistemnogo podkhoda i issledovaniia sovremennogo mezhdunarodnogo prava. In *Mezhdunarodnoe pravo i sovremennost'*. Tbilisi, 1984, pp. 14-25.

See also [428b, 493].

497a. Verzijl, J.H.W., The systematization of public international law, pp. 337-345 in [157, vol. 1].

Provides a historical outline of PIL classification in substantive (hierarchy of states/community, war/peace, etc.) and doctrinal (Anzilotti, Guggenheim, Kelsen, Verdross) terms.

—b. Steiner, W.A., 1982, Some problems of classification in international and comparative law. *IJIL*, **10**(6), pp. 320-325.

Distinguishes between classification according to concepts and according to legal aspects of given topics; specialized PIL treatises tend to adopt the former, libraries the latter classification. The classification schemes used by the Institute of Advanced Legal Studies [409], the Squire Law Library [340], the European

University Institute, Florence and the Institut suisse de droit comparé [433b] are outlined.

—c. Moys, E. M., *Moys classification scheme for law books*, 2nd edn. *With a new index-thesaurus*. London: Butterworth, 1982, 344 pp. 1st edn 1968.

Divided into 8 tables, the scheme combines form (table 1 primary materials; table 8, journals, reference works, conferences, etc.) and conceptual (subjects and sources of law, common law jurisdiction etc.) elements and provides alternative notations, i.e. class K (patterned after the Library of Congress classification) and class 340 (decimal style). The section 'International law: KC-341' (pp. 34-51) in its subdivisions (primary reference materials, international law as a whole, PIL, international criminal, economic and social law, international relations, diplomacy and treaties, worldwide organizations, war, etc.) is more detailed than Schwerin [497d]. The bibliography contains references to law librarianship and classification schemes.

—d. Schwerin, K., *Classification for international law and relations*, 3rd edn. Dobbs Ferry, NY: Oceana, 1969, 130 pp. 1st edn 1947, 2nd edn 1958.

Schwerin's is essentially a library classification reflecting the form (treatises, official publications, periodicals) of PIL materials. The decimal system of the *Classification* is an expansion of the two-figure classificatory outlined by E. Basset (1942), as well as an adaptation of notations used in classifications of international law by the United Nations libraries in Geneva and New York, the Peace Palace Library, The Hague and the Columbia University Law Library, New York. Multiple notations and cross-references facilitate the use of the system. *See also* Zagayko, F. F., *International law: a classification for libraries*. Dobbs Ferry, NY: Oceana, 1965, 66 pp. Patterned on the Library of Congress [417a] Class JX, 'International law. Foreign relations. Diplomacy. International arbitration', Zagayko's system combines form (treatises, documentary sources, etc.) and conceptual (common law, conflict of law, etc.) elements, permitting the adaptation and expansion of the system's notations.

—e. Krieger, T., *Subject headings for the literature of law and international law, and index to LC 'K' schedules*, 3rd edn. Littleton, CO: Rothman, 1982, 356 pp. (AALL Publication series, 16). 2nd edn 1969, compiled by W. B. Ellinger.

Published for the AALL [415b], Krieger's work is based on the Library of Congress *Subject headings*, 10th edn. Washington, DC, 1986, 2 vols. The work includes LC call numbers and LC subject headings not officially authorized for use. *See also* Kimminich, O., 1983, Stichworte. *ZaöRV*, **43**, pp. 412-413.

498a. Bernhardt, R., 1984, Interpretation in international law. *Enc. PIL*, **7**, pp. 318-327.

Raises basic question of interpreting international law in general and treaties in particular; also refers to special problems of multilingualism and authenticity attendant upon interpretation of PIL texts.

—b. Sur, G., *L'Interprétation en droit international public*. Paris: LGDJ, 1974, 449 pp.

Part 1 deals with: definition and classification of interpretative approaches (especially in the works of Ehrlich, Rousseau and Siorat [509f]), as well as the competence of states and international institutions with reference to the evidence, applicability and validity of interpretation of PIL texts. Part 2 outlines a possible harmonization of interpretative methods. The bibliography also includes references to articles in *RCADI* [220a] concerning PIL methodology and interpretation.

—c. de Visscher, C., *Problèmes d'interprétation judiciaire en droit international public*. Paris: Pédone, 1963.

—d. McDougal, M.S. et al., *The interpretation of agreements and world public order: principles of content and procedure*. New Haven: Yale UP, 1967, 410 pp.

—e. Degan, V.D., *L'Interprétation des accords en droit international*. La Haye: Nijhoff, 1963, 176 pp.

Although mainly concerned with the interpretation of treaties, the work includes a section on general aspects of PIL interpretation, e.g. procedural, textual/functional and auxiliary interpretative methods. See also Sourioux, J.L. and Lerat, P., *L'Analyse de texte: méthode générale et application au droit*. Paris: Dalloz, 1980, 81 pp., on the distinction between legal analysis and commentaries on laws, based on samples of French laws.

See also [517e].

499a. *Consultation informelle sur l'enseignement et la recherche en droit international public, Paris (Maison UNESCO), 2-4 février 1987. Rapport final.* 19 pp. (UNESCO document SHS.87/WS/10).

Presided over by the ICJ justice, M. Bedjaoui, the consultation was attended by PIL scholars from developed and developing countries with a view to overcoming deficiencies in the study and teaching of PIL. Attention was drawn to the need for digests of state practice relating to Third World countries and postgraduate PIL seminars in African countries. The handbook on PIL discussed at the meeting is in the press [75].

—b. Cheng, B., *International law: teaching and practice*. London: Stevens, 1982, 287 pp.

The work grew out of a legal workshop organized in 1980 by the Institute of Advanced Legal Studies [409]. Contains articles on methodological aspects of PIL study and teaching (including analyses on 'rules versus process'), as well as surveys of PIL teaching in the UK, France and Austria (*see also* [499g]). The contributors include G. Schwarzenberger, International law and the contemporary problem of political world order: interdisciplinary working hypotheses and perspectives; T.O. Elias, Methodological problems faced by the ICJ in the application of international law; J. Brownlie, Problems of specialization;

R. Higgins, The identity of international law; and B. Cheng, On the nature of sources of international law. The appendix reprints Cheng, B., United Nations resolutions on outer space: 'instant' international customary law (first published in *Indian journal of international law*, 1965, **5**, pp. 23-48).

—c. Lachs, M., *The teacher in international law: teachings and teaching*. The Hague: Nijhoff, 1982, 236 pp.

A revised version of his Teachings and teaching of international law. *RCADI*, 1976/III, **151**, pp. 161-252. The work examines the contributions of PIL scholars (many from East Europe, especially Poland) to the methodology of PIL teaching.

—d. Bleckman, A., *Die Funktionen der Lehre im Völkerrecht: Materialien zu einer allgemeinen Methoden- und Völkerrechtslehre*. Köln: Heymann, 1981, 344 pp.

See also Bernhardt, R., *Das internationale Recht in der Juristenausbildung*. Heidelberg: Müller, 1981, 183 pp. (Berichte der deutschen Gesellschaft für Völkerrecht, 21).

—e. Simma, B., 1972, Völkerrechtswissenschaft und Lehre von den internationalen Beziehungen: erste Überlegung zur Interdependenz zweier Disziplinen. *Österreichische Zeitschrift für öffentliches Recht und Völkerrecht*, **23**, pp. 292-327.

—f. Fujita, H., 1978, Le Prof. Tabata et l'étude du droit international au Japon. *Revue de droit international, de sciences diplomatiques et politiques*, **56**(1), pp. 1-21.

See also Takano, Y., Post-war studies in international law in Japan. Paper submitted to the Conference on Innovation in International law, held at the Villa Serbellone, Italy, 9-15 September 1971, 41 pp.

—g. Dupuy, R.-J., *The university teaching of social sciences: international law/Les sciences sociales dans l'enseignement supérieur: droit international*. Paris: UNESCO, 1967, 152 pp. (Teaching in the Social Sciences).

Complements Eisemann, C., *The university teaching of social sciences: law*. Paris: UNESCO, 1954, 133 pp. (French edition published in 1972). Contributions in the 1967 work by Arangio-Ruiz, Boutros-Ghali, Harászti, Jiménez de Arechaga, Simmonds, Tunkin *et al.* survey PIL teaching in Egypt, France, Hungary, India, Italy, Japan, Latin America, Nigeria, Scandinavia, the USSR, the USA and Yugoslavia. Dupuy concludes the work with a summary of the teaching at the Hague Academy of International Law [380a].

—h. Dupuy, R.-J. and Tunkin, G., *Comparabilité des diplômes en droit international: étude structurelle et fonctionnelle*. Paris: UNESCO, 1972, 83 pp. English edition: *Comparability of degrees*, 1973, 75 pp. (Studies on International Equivalences of Degrees, 4).

The work analyses the structures and organization of PIl teaching, curricula and degrees (at the time first degrees in PIL were largely non-existent) and functional comparability of degrees (beyond equivalences). The appendix contains a 'Draft international passport for the accreditation of qualifications in international law'.

500a. Johnson-Champ, D. G., 1984, Bibliography: selected readings on teaching international law. *International lawyer*, **18**, pp. 197-200.

Contains references to monographs and articles (in English only) published during 1943-84.

—b. Cardozo, M. H., *The practical state of teaching and research in international law, 1974: a report*. Washington, DC: American Society of International law, 1977.

Of 150 accredited US law schools polled in 1974, 140 offered at least one course classifiable as 'international legal studies'. An inter-disciplinary study group was envisaged to overcome the persisting conflict between practitioners and professors of PIL, as well as that between procedural techniques and the academic/humanistic scope of PIL.

—c. Falk, R. A., New approaches to the study of international law. In Kaplan, M. (ed.), *New approaches to international relations*. New York: St Martin's Press, 1968, pp. 357-380.

Falk's contribution is based on his article in *AJIL*, 1967, **61**, pp. 477-495, and further developed in his New paradigm for international legal studies. *Yale law journal*, 1974/5, **84**, pp. 969-1021. To overcome the confusion between adversary presentation and academic assessment of PIL, Falk advocates an 'adjudicatory' scholarly approach.

—d. Rohn, P. H., Gordenker, L. and Miles, E. L., *Basic courses in international law: an anthology of syllabi*. Beverly Hills, CA: Sage, 1970, 127 pp.

See also Brown, C., 1978, The Jessup Moot Competition as a vehicle for teaching public international law. *CYIL*, **16**, pp. 332-341; Brecht, A., 1984/5, Changes in legal scholarship and their impact on law school library reference services. *Law library journal*, **77**(1), pp. 157-164 (on the need for identifying doctrinal ambiguities in teaching and research).

—e. Ignatenko, G. V. and Ostapenko, D. D., Mezhdunarodnoe pravo v sisteme iuridicheskogo obrazovaniia; v aspekte problemy vzaimodeistviia mezhdunarodnogo i vnutrigosudarstvennogo prava. In **Mezhdunarodnoe i vnutrigosudarstvennoe pravo: problemy sravnitel'nogo pravovedeniia*. Sverdlovsk, 1984, pp. 3-12.

—f. Butler, W. E., 1976, Soviet international legal education: the Pashukanis syllabus. *Review of socialist law*, **2**(2), pp. 79-102.

See also his: On the origins of international legal education in the Soviet Union: the Kravchenko syallabus. *Legal historical review*, 1975, **43**, pp. 297-305; English translation of the current PIL syllabus [428a].

—g.   Rivero, J., Réflexions sur l'enseignement du droit. In *Mélanges offerts à M. le Doyen L. Trotabas*. Paris: LGDJ, 1970, pp. 448-458.

In the light of the 1968 student unrest, Rivero suggests a shift of emphasis away from requiring law and PIL students to memorize rules towards teaching the evolution of rules by way of comparative study of primary legal sources. *See also L'enseignement et la recherche en droit international en France face aux besoins de la pratique; Actes du Colloque, 1967*. Paris: Dalloz, 1968, 91 pp. (Annales de la Faculté du droit et des sciences politiques et économiques, Strasbourg, 21).

—h.   Dreyfus, S., *La thèse et le mémoire de doctorat: étude méthodologique (sciences juridiques et politiques)*, 2nd edn. Paris: Cujas, 1984, 341 pp. 1st edn *La thèse et le mémoire de doctorat en droit*. Paris: Colin, 1971.

Outlines the drafting, writing and subsequent defence of dissertations in law and political science, mainly for French-speaking students. Annex C of the 1st edn lists titles of French doctoral dissertations in law and PIL during 1960-70.

501a.   Salmon, J.J.A. and David, E., *Méthodologie de la recherche en droit international public*. Bruxelles: Presses universitaires de Bruxelles, 1982, 131 pp.

Intended for students preparing PIL doctoral dissertations, the guide stresses research methods mainly in terms of primary PIL materials. Includes a list of Belgian libraries with extensive PIL collections. The annexes contain abbreviations of legal and PIL periodicals, and a bibliography of selected primary and secondary PIL materials. *See also* [500h].

—b.   Leurquin de Visscher, F. and Simonart, H., *Documentation et méthodologie juridiques*. Louvain: Bruylant, 1980, 330 pp.

Approaches legal research in terms of: Les sources normatives (où trouver la règle de droit? que dit la règle); Les sources jurisprudentielles; Les sources doctrinales; La mise en oeuvre des sources documentaires (including the right to and legal aspects of information).

—c.   Jacobstein, J.M. and Mersky, R.M., *Fundamentals of legal research*, 2nd edn. Mineola, NY: Foundation Press, 1981, 614 pp.

Includes a section on PIL research. *See also* [328].

502a.   Butler, W.E., 1985, *The language of international law*, pp. 57-71 in [428b].

Discusses the cultural context of PIL terminology and points to linguistic discrepancies (mainly in terms of treaty texts), translation problems (e.g. finding conceptual equivalents) and stylistic variants as a result of different methodological (inductive and teleological) approaches to PIL. *See also* Weisflog, W.E., Problems of legal translation. In *Rapports suisses présentés au XII. Congrès international de droit comparé, Sydney/Melbourne, 1986*. Zürich: Schulthess, 1987, pp. 179-218.

—b. Reuter, P., Quelques réflexions sur le vocabulaire du droit international, pp. 423-445 in *Mélanges Trotabas* [500g].

Raises the question of how best to arrive at substantive (legal) and linguistic equivalents.

—c. Bailey, J. F., 1976, Linguistic obstacles to the effective exchange of legal documentation. *IJLL*, 4(2), pp. 91-100.

See also Nafziger in [209] and [451f].

II/C. Public international law in general

i. THEORIES

503a. de Visscher, C., *Théories et réalités en droit international public*, 4th edn. Paris: Pédone, 1970, 451 pp. 1st edn 1953. English translation by P. E. Corbett of the 2nd (1955) French edition: *Theory and practice in public international law*. Princeton, NJ: Princeton UP, 1957, 381 pp.

Stresses the sociological context of PIL. Part 3 was also published separately as *Les effectivités du droit international public*. Paris: Pédone, 1967, in which the real rather than potentially normative binding force of PIL is examined. Review of English edn in *Harvard law review*, 1957, **70**, pp. 1331-1335. *See also* de Visscher, C., 1973/I, Méthode et système en droit international. *RCADI*, **138**, pp. 75-80.

—b. Kelsen, H., 1953/III, Théorie du droit international public. *RCADI*, **84**, pp. 1-203.

Presents the monist approach to PIL, deriving its supremacy over municipal law from a purely formal basic norm (*Grundnorm*). For criticism of Kelsen's approach *see* de Visscher [503a] or Gross [192].

—c. Johnston, D. M., 1988, Functionalism in the theory of international law. *CYIL*, **26**, pp. 3-60.

Compared to PIL theory as a 'framework of core concepts' or as doctrinal rationalization designed to advance (theoretical) consistency, functionalism is viewed as a 'theoretical orientation that treats society as if it were composed of mutually dependent and determinant parts'. *See also* [507b].

504a. Levin, D. B., *Aktualnye problemy teorii mezhdunarodnogo prava*. Moskva: Nauka, 1974, 262 pp.

—b. Tunkin, G., *Teoriia mezhdunarodnogo prava*, 2nd edn. Moskva: Mezhdunarodnye Otnosheniia, 1970, 511 pp. 1st edn *Voprosy teorii mezhdunarodnogo prava*. Moskva: IUridicheskaia Literatura, 1962, 329 pp. English translation of 2nd edn by W. E. Butler, *Theory of international law*. London: Allen & Unwin, 1974, 447 pp. (includes a bibliography of Tunkin's works published during 1938–73). French translation of 1st edn *Droit international public: problèmes théoriques*. Paris: Pédone, 1965. Arabic edition, Cairo, 1972.

Tunkin postulated the theory of 'the co-ordination of the wills of states' (the will of the 'ruling class' implicit therein), as underlying the international community and influencing the development of PIL. *See also* McWhinney, E., 1987, Contemporary Soviet general theory of international law: reflections on the Tunkin era. *CYIL*, **25**, pp. 187–217.

505a. *Sotirova, A. S., *Filosofski ananliz na suvremenoto mezhdunarodnoto pravo*. Sofiia, 1983, 182 pp.

—b. Válki, L., *A nemzetközi jog sajátos társadalmi természete, mibenléte, funkciója, értéktartalma és szankciórendszere*. Budapest: Akadémiai Kiadó, 1981, 128 pp. (Szociológiai tanulmányok, 24).

Surveys the sociological approaches by Hungarian (Hegedüs, Rozgony) and other (Ancilotti, McDougal) PIL scholars. Examines PIL in terms of its possible normative effect upon the regulation of international relations, but is critical of Kelsen's normative approach.

506a. Blenk-Knocke, E., 1986, Sociology of international law. *Enc. PIL*, **9**, pp. 351–354.

—b. Yakemtchouk, R., 1974, L'Approche sociologique du droit international. *RGDIP*, **78**, pp. 5–39.

—c. Landheer, B., *On the sociology of international law and international society*. The Hague: Nijhoff, 1966, 118 pp.

Traces the evolution from the nineteenth-century coercive political society to the twentieth-century world community whose egalitarian aspirations are furthered by PIL.

507a. Stone, J., *Visions of world order: between state power and human justice*. Baltimore, MD: Johns Hopkins UP, 1984, 246 pp.

Based in part on Stone's articles and Tagore lectures delivered at the University of Calcutta in 1968, *Visions* is less concerned with the technical precepts of existing

PIL than with the 'factual substratum' out of which PIL may arise and the relevance to such evolution of international justice. Sociologically weighted, the work includes chapters on International law and the limits of knowledge, Justice and equality among nations, and World order, economic justice and international law. See also his *A sociological perspective on international law*, 1983, a revision of his Problems confronting sociological enquiries concerning international law. *RCADI*, 1956/I, **89**, pp. 65-175.

—b. MacDonald, R. St J. and Johnston, D. M. (eds), *The structure and process of international law: essays in legal philosophy, doctrine and theory*. The Hague: Nijhoff, 1983, 1,234 pp.

Reviewed in *BYIL*, 1986, **57**, pp. 390-391. The work in part complements MacDonald, R. St J., Johnston, D. M. and Morris, G. L. (eds), *The international law and policy of human welfare*. Alphen a/R: Sijthoff & Noordhoff, 1978, 690 pp. The 1983 work is arranged in four sections: (1) Historiographical analysis of 'schools of jurisprudence' (natural law, positivism, Marxism, policy/world order); (2) International law from the perspective of the social sciences (international relations, economics, sociology, etc.); (3) Theoretical foundations of PIL (concepts such as statehood, recognition, custom, responsibility, etc.) and (4) Modern controversies relating to PIL (relation to municipal law; common interest; minimum legal standards; international organizations, etc.). The contributors include G. Schwarzenberger, The conceptual apparatus of international law; B. Cheng, Custom: the future of general state practice in a divided world; A. Pardo and C. Q. Christol, The common interest; S. G. Galvez, The future of regionalism in an asymmetrical society; S. Rosenne, The role of controversy in international legal development; C. T. Oliver, The future of idealism in international law; and Wang Thieya, The Third World and international law (based on his article in the *Chinese yearbook of international law*, 1982).

—c. Alibert, C., *Du droit de se faire justice dans la société internationale depuis 1945*. Paris: LGDJ, 1983, 732 pp. (Bibliothèque de droit international, 91).

See also Puig, J. C., International law and the categorical exigencies of a world in dramatic transition, pp. 133-145 in [460] (on justice and 'trialist' methodology); Schachter, in [190]; Bastid, S., La justice dans les relations internationales, In Aubenas, R. *et al.*, *La justice*. Paris: Presses universitaires de France, 1961, pp. 427-449; D'Amato, A., 1975, International law and Rawls's theory of justice. *Denver journal of international law and policy*, **5**(2), pp. 525-537 (*see also* [441]).

508a. Benchik, M. *et al.*, *Introduction critique au droit international*. Lyon: Presses universitaires de Lyon, 1986, 134 pp. (Collection critique du droit).

A critical appraisal by a French Marxist PIL scholar of the prevailing PIL theory (including *jus cogens*). *See also* La critique marxiste appliquée aux théories traditionnelles du droit international public, 1974, pp. 193-219 in [322b].

—b. Hernes, H. M., *Concepts of community in modern theories of international law*. PhD thesis, Johns Hopkins University, 1970, 517 pp. Produced by microfilm-xerography by University Microfilms International, Ann Arbor, MI, 1978.

A historiographical analysis of (mainly sociological) theories underlying the works of C. de Visscher, J. Stone, M. S. McDougal, etc.

   —c. *Droit et société: revue internationale de théorie et de sociologie juridique*. Paris: LGDJ, 1985–, 1–, nouvelle série.

Superseded *Revue internationale de la théorie du droit*, founded in 1926 by H. Kelsen and L. Duguit. Includes articles on conceptual, linguistic and methodological aspects of law and PIL.

ii. SOURCES

509a. van Hoof, G. J. H., *Rethinking the sources of international law*. Deventer: Kluwer, 1983, 322 pp.

Traces the evolution of PIL sources (in terms of article 38 of the ICJ Statute) in the light of contemporary societal changes; attempts to 'map out the legal implications of legally non-binding instruments . . . and their relation with full-fledged legal rules', including a discussion on the 'soft-law' aspects of PIL sources.

   —b. Bleckmann, A., *Die Aufgaben einer Methodenlehre des Völkerrechts: Probleme der Rechtsquellenlehre im Völkerrecht*. Heidelberg: Müller, 1978, 72 pp.

Views the analysis of sources (mainly the interpretation of treaties) as a methodological approach to PIL.

   —c. Jennings, R. Y., 1981, What is international law and how do we tell it when we see it? *ASDI*, **37**, pp. 59–88.

The focus is on the 'sources test' as the cornerstone of PIL. *See also* Bos, M., 1977, The recognized manifestations of international law: a new theory of 'sources'. *GYIL*, **20**, pp. 9–76 (further developed in [490]); Cheng in [499b]; Tunkin in [212].

   —d. *L'Elaboration du droit international public: Colloque de Toulouse, 1974*. Paris: Pédone, 1975, 224 pp. (Actes du 8. Colloque de la Société française pour le droit international).

   —e. Parry, C., *The sources and evidences of international law*. Manchester: Manchester UP, 1965, 122 pp. (Melland Schill Lectures).

Distinguishes between cause, basis, origin and evidence of PIL. Centres on primary PIL sources indicative of what PIL is, and on documentary records attesting to its evidence. Parry is critical of Kelsen's formal approach to sources, as well as of the overly general article 38 of the ICJ Statute. *See also* **Kennedy, D.**, 1987, The sources of international law. *American University journal of international law and politics*, **2**(1), pp. 1–96 (an analysis of the contemporary 'sources doctrine', mainly Verdross and Virally, with reference to the creation, categorization of 'authoritative' sources/norms).

—f. Siorat, L., *Le problème des lacunes en droit international: contribution à l'étude des sources du droit et la fonction judiciaire*. Paris: LGDJ, 1958, 479 pp. (Bibliothèque de droit international, 6).

Examines the role of international judges in overcoming PIL deficiencies and lacunae, especially through analogous interpretative methods. *See also* Fitzmaurice in [206].

510a. Jacqué, J.-P., *Eléments pour une théorie de l'acte juridique en droit international public*. Avant-propos de P. Reuter. Paris: LGDJ, 1972, 511 pp. (Bibliothèque de droit international [69]).

Examines the juridical act in the light of the will of international legal subjects intent on creating binding norms, and outlines various types of juridical acts (i.e. decisions of international tribunals, organizations; unilateral acts, etc.). *See also* **Corbu, A. C.**, *Essai sur la notion de règle de droit en droit international*. Paris: Pèdone, 1935, 119 pp., and [519c].

—b. Suy, E., *Les actes juridiques unilatéraux en droit international public*. Paris: LGDJ, 1962, 290 pp. (Bibliothèque de droit international, 23).

Based on his PhD thesis, Graduate Institute of International Studies, Geneva, 1962.

—c. *Vasilenko, V. A., *Mezhdunarodno-pravovye sanktsii*. Kiev, 1982.

—d. Tavernier, P., *Recherches sur l'application dans le temps des actes et des règles en droit international public*. Paris: LGDJ, 1970, 351 pp. (Bibliothèque de droit international, 55).

Distinguishes between the effect of acts, norms in time (i.e. when created) and the temporal validity of such instruments (i.e. when actually put into effect). *See also* **Chemillier-Gendreau, M.**, *Le rôle du temps dans la formation du droit international*. Paris: Pédone, 1987, 70 pp. (Cours et travaux, Institut des hautes études de Paris, 3).

511. Villiger, M. E., *Customary international law and treaties: a study of their interactions and interrelations with special consideration of the 1969 Vienna Convention on the Law of treaties*. Dordrecht: Nijhoff, 1985, 432 pp. (Developments in International Law).

Based on selected state practice, ILC materials and doctrinal studies, the work examines the development of treaty rules from international custom, as well as customary law generated by conventional rules. *See also* **Baxter, R.**, 1970/I, Treaties and custom. *RCADI*, **129**, pp. 25–106.

Treaties

512a. Bastid, S., *Les traités dans la vie internationale: conclusion et effets.* Paris: Economica, 1985, 303 pp. (Collection Droit international).

Essentially a commentary on the Vienna Convention on the Law of Treaties [1]. Includes bibliographical notes and an index. The annex contains the French text of the Vienna Convention and table of cases.

—b. Reuter, P., *Introduction au droit des traités.* Paris: Presses universitaires de France, 1985, 211 pp. (Publications, Institut universitaire de hautes études internationales, Genève).

A treatise on the 'phénomène conventionnel', including the role, classification, procedural aspects and effectivity of treaties. *See also* Reuter in [201].

—c. McNair, Lord A. D., *The law of treaties.* Oxford: Clarendon, 1961, 789 pp.

The classical treatise on the types, procedural aspects and interpretation of treaties and effects thereupon of state succession and war. Appendix B contains words and phrases related to national and international treaty contexts. An index and table of cases conclude the work. *See also* Bowett, D. W. *et al.*, *Cambridge essays in international law: essays in honour of Lord McNair.* London: Stevens, 1965, 186 pp.; McNair, Lord A. D., *Selected papers and bibliography.* Leiden: Sijthoff, 1974, 396 pp.

See also [297, vol. 7].

513. *Review of the multilateral treaty-making process/Réexamen du processus d'établissement des traités multilatéraux.* New York: United Nations, 1985, 521 pp. (UN document ST/LEG/SER.B/21; UN sales publication EF.83.V.8).

Examines the role of the United Nations in treaty-making; includes comments by national and international official bodies on the treaty-making process.

514a. Ul'ianova, N. N., *Obshchie mnogostoronnie dogovory v sovremennykh otnosheniiakh: nekotorye voprosy teorii.* Kiev: Naukova Dumka, 1981, 259 pp.

—b. Talalaev, A. N., *Pravo mezhdunarodnykh dogovorov.* Moskva, 1980, 311 pp.

Traces the history of Soviet treaty-making and outlines codificatory procedural aspects of the law of treaties in general (with emphasis on the consensual element). *See also* Filimonova, M. V., 1978, Osobennosti universal'nogo dogovora, kodifitsiruiushchego normy mezhdunarodnogo prava. *SEMP*, pp. 113-124.

—c. Vukas, B., *Relativno djelovanje međunarodnih ugovora.* Zagreb: Školska knjiga, 1975, 179 pp.

—d. Harászti, Gy., *Some fundamental problems of the law of treaties.* Budapest, 1973, 439 pp.

Considers treaties alone to be open to interpretation; customary law is applied, but not interpreted.

515a. Gomez Robledo, A., 1981/III, Le *jus cogens* international: sa genèse, sa nature, ses fonctions. *RCADI*, **172**, pp. 9-217.

Outlines the theoretical and procedural aspects of the concept and the doctrinal dialectics thereof; points up the antinomy between *jus cogens* and the principle of PIL effectivity. *See also* Alexidze, L. A., 1981/III Legal nature of *jus cogens* in contemporary international law. *RCADI*, **172**, pp. 219-270; Gaja, G., 1981/III, *Jus cogens* beyond the Vienna Convention. *RCADI*, **172**, pp. 271-316.

—b. *Shestakov, L. N., *Imperativnye normy v sisteme sovremennogo mezhdunarodnogo prava*. Moskva, 1981.

—c. Diaconu, I., *Contribution à une étude sur les normes impératives en droit international* (jus cogens). Bucarest, 1971, 185 pp.

—d. Nicoloudis, E. P., *La nullité de* jus cogens *et le développement du droit international public*. Athènes: Papazissi, 1974, 253 pp.

—e. *The concept of* jus cogens *in international law*. Papers and Proceedings of a Conference on International Law, Lagonissi (Greece), 3-8 April 1966, organized by the Carnegie Endowment for International Peace (European Centre). Geneva, 1967, 140 pp.

Includes E. Suy, The concept of *jus cogens* in public international law, pp. 17-77 (an analysis of the concept illustrated by state practice and activities of international organizations; extensive bibliography).

516a. *el-Kadiri, A., *La position des Etats du Tiers-Monde à la Conférence de Vienne sur le droit des traités*. Préface de M. K. Yasseen. Rabat (Maroc): Ed. Faculté des sciences juridiques, économiques, sociales, 1980, 347 pp.

—b. Alexandrowicz, C. H., *The European-African confrontation: a study in treaty making*. Leiden: Sijthoff, 1973, 176 pp.

Includes a list of treaties concluded from 1157 to 1912. *See also* [484a].

517a. *Yambusic, E. S., *World order through legal certitude: the 'norm' of treaty interpretation*. Ann Arbor, MI: University Microfilms International, 1985, 323 pp.

PhD thesis, Catholic University of America, Washington, DC, 1984.

—b. Yasseen, M. K., 1976/III, L'Interprétation des traités d'après la Convention de Vienne sur le droit des traités. *RCADI*, **151**, pp. 1-114.

See also Sohn, L., 1976/II, Settlement of disputes relating to the interpretation and application of treaties. *RCADI*, **150**, pp. 195-294.

—c. Bernhardt, R., *Die Auslegung völkerrechtlicher Verträge in der neueren Rechtssprechung internationaler Gerichte*. Köln: Heymann, 1963, 200 pp. (Beiträge zum ausländischen öffentlichen Recht und Völkerrecht, 40).

—d. *Evintov, V.I., *Mnogostazychnye dogovory v sovremennom mezhdunarodnom prave*. Kiev: Naukova Dumka, 1981, 132 pp.

—e. Rosenne, S., The meaning of 'authentic' text in modern treaty law, pp. 759-784 in [199].

—f. de Visscher, C., Remarques sur l'interprétation dite textuelle des traités internationaux. In *Varia juris gentium* [289].

518a. Blix, H., *The treaty-maker's handbook*. Uppsala: Almquist & Wiksell, 1973, 355 pp.

An *aide-mémoire* for the conclusion, application and interpretation of treaties, including the classification of treaty-like instruments (constitutions, declarations, etc.).

—b. *A selected bibliography on the law of treaties*. New York: UN, DHL, 1968, 150 pp. (UN document A/CONF.39/4).

Contains references to (mostly doctrinal) works on treaty-law published from 1945 to the 1960s worldwide.

Customary law

519a. Ferrari-Bravo, L., 1985/III, Méthodes de recherche de la coûtume internationale dans la pratique des Etats. *RCADI*, **192**, pp. 233-329.

Comments on the dynamism underlying state practice, and points to the dificiency of documentary records of such practice, especially in developing countries.

—b. van den Bergh, A.L., *Praktijk en internationale gewoonteregelvorming*. Hilversum: Ed. Rodopi, 1984, 113 pp.

Insists on the distinction between an international customary *rule* and a *customary* rule of international law and on the type of practice giving rise to the latter. *See also* Bos, M., 1982, The identification of custom in international law. *GYIL*, **25**, pp. 9-53 (especially on the proof of the elements of practice and *opinio juris*).

—c. Bernhardt, R., 1984, Customary international law. *Enc. PIL*, **7**, pp. 61-66.

Examines the formation (especially the time-factor therein) of customary law underlying the practice of the international community in general, and its newer members in particular.

—d. Gounelle, M., *Les motivations des actes juridiques en droit international*. Paris: Pédone, 1979, 292 pp.

Analyses the role of motivation and will in the formation and interpretation of customary rules of PIL.

—e. D'Amato, A.A., *The concept of custom in international law*. Foreword by R.A. Falk. Ithaca, NY: Cornell UP, 1971, 286 pp.

Critically appraises the traditional theory of *opinio juris* as insufficiently explaining the authoritativeness invested in customary law; suggests the reformulation of the concept with consensus as the basis of obligation, itself inductively approached. See also Raman in [197], as well as Part I/A.i.b, note 9.

—f. Dupuy, R.-J., Droit déclaratoire et droit programmatoire: de la coûtume sauvage à la soft law. pp. 132-148 in [509d].

English translation, pp. 247-257 in [205]. See also his Coûtume sage et coûtume sauvage, pp. 75-87 in [206]. Juxtaposes traditional and revisionist/revolutionary perceptions of the formation of customary rules and their interpretation; views resolutions of international organizations as evidence of an emerging 'coûtume contestataire'.

520a. Thirlway, H.W.A., *International customary law and codification: an examination of the continuing role of custom in the present period of codification of international law*. Leiden: Sijthoff, 1972, 158 pp.

—b. Movchan, A.B., *Kodifikatsiia i progressivnoe razvitie mezhdunarodnogo prava*. Moskva: IUridicheskaia Literatura, 1972, 216 pp.

—c. *Codification in the communist world: symposium in memory of Zs. Szirmai*. Leiden: Sijthoff, 1975, 353 pp.

The contributors include G. Brunner, Socialist constitutions: recent constitutional developments in East European States, and C. Osakwe, Soviet 'pactomania' and critical negativism in contemporary international law: an inquiry into the Soviet drive for a comprehensive codification of general international law.

—d. Dokhalia, R.P., *The codification of public international law*. Manchester: Manchester UP, 1970, 367 pp.

Traces the evolution of codification work, especially by inter-governmental organizations and in the perception (as a quasi-legislative process) by newly independent states. See also [178].

—e. Bünzli, K., *Der Beitrag der Schweiz zum Zustandekommen universeller Kodifikationen des Völkerrechts*. Zürich: Schulthess Polygraph Verlag, 1984, 321 pp. (Schweizer Studien zum internationalen Recht, 37).

—f. Alvarez, A., *La codificación del derecho internacional en América*. Trabajos de la Tercera comisión de la Asamblea de jurisconsultos reunida en Santiago de Chile. Santiago de Chile: Imprenta Universitaria, 1923, 144 pp. (Quinta Conferencia Internacional Americana. Publicaciones, 2).

—g. Internoscia, J., *New code of international law*. New York: The International Code Company, 1910.

An early twentieth-century codificatory attempt by an Italian lawyer, a member of the Bar of the Province of Quebec, the *New code* outlines the substance of international law 'as it should be', notably with a view to 'securing peace' through the cooperation of states in a projected 'International Assembly'.

General principles of law

521a. Mosler, H., 1984, General principles of law. *Enc. PIL*, **7**, pp. 89-105.

Defines the concept as recognized in municipal law and enumerates general principles of law with reference to PIL and international relations.

—b. Vitanyi, B., 1982, Les positions doctrinales concernant le sens de la notion de 'principes généraux de droit reconnus par les nations civilisées'. *RGDIP*, **86**, pp. 48-116.

Analyses the acceptance versus the rejection by PIL scholars (Bartoš, Guggenheim, Lauterpacht, Le Fur, Levin, Scelle, Tunkin, Visscher *et al.*) of the general principles of law as PIL sources. *See also* Bartoš, M. in [179]; Lammers in [200]; Tunkin in [211].

—c. Pellet, A., Recherche sur les principes généraux de droit en droit international. Paris, 1974, 504 pp. PhD Thesis, Université de Paris II.

—d. Šahović, M., 1972/III, Codification des principes du droit international des relations amicales et de la coopération entre les états. *RCADI*, **137**, pp. 243-310.

—e. Degan, V. D., *L'Equité et le droit international*. The Hague: Nijhoff, 1970.

—f. Cheng, B., *General principles of law as applied by international courts and tribunals*. London: Stevens, 1953, 490 pp. (Library of World Affairs, 21). Reprinted Cambridge: Grotius Publications, 1987.

Published under the auspices of the London Institute of World Affairs, the work, although out of date, remains an important treatise on the subject. Cheng perceives the general principles more as a methodological approach to, than as a source of, PIL.

Judicial decisions

522. Decisions of international courts, tribunals and international arbitrations. *Enc. PIL*, 1981, **2**.

See also Starzhina, Auxiliary sources of international law; Nawaz, Other sources of international law: are judicial decisions of the International Court of Justice a source of international law? *Indian journal of international law*, 1979, **4**, pp. 522-525 and 526-540 respectively; [667b].

523a. el-Ouali, A., *Effets juridiques de la sentence internationale: contribution à l'étude de l'exécution des normes internationales*. Paris: LGDJ, 1984, 321 pp. (Bibliothèque de droit international, 88).

Examines the nexus between politics and law in the application of international judgements, especially of the 'declaratory' type.

—b. Foda, E., *The projected Arab Court of Justice: a study in regional jurisdiction with specific reference to the Muslim law of nations*. The Hague: Nijhoff, 1957, 258 pp.

Deals with the peaceful settlement of disputes within the Arab League and the role of the projected Court within the League. Discusses the ideological role of the projected Court in applying Islamic international principles. Appendix B includes a proposed draft statute of the Court. Contains an index and bibliographic notes. *See also* [546c].

524a. Schwebel, S.M., *International arbitration: three salient problems*. Cambridge: Grotius Publications, 1987, 322 pp. (H. Lauterpacht Memorial Lectures, 4).

—b. Gebrehana, T., *Arbitration: an element of international law*. Stockholm: Almquist & Wiksell, 1984, 161 pp.

—c. Wetter, G.J., *The international arbitral process: public and private*. Dobbs Ferry, NY: Oceana, 1979, 5 vols.

Includes references to relevant primary arbitral materials.

—d. Seide, K. (ed.), *A dictionary of arbitration and its terms: labor, commercial, international; a concise encyclopedia of peaceful dispute settlement*. Dobbs Ferry, NY: Oceana, 1970, 334 pp.

Published for the Eastman Library of the American Arbitration Association.

iii. SUBJECTS

525a. Okeke, C.N., *Controversial subjects of contemporary international law: an examination of the new entities of international law and their treaty-making capacity*. Foreword by G. Fitzmaurice. Rotterdam: Rotterdam UP, 1974, 243 pp.

Outlines doctrinal positions on the concept of international personality and discusses it with reference mainly to unrecognized states, national liberation movements, and inter-governmental and non-governmental organizations.

—b. *Fel'dman, D.I. and Kurdiukov, G.I., *Osnovnye tendentsii razvitiia mezhdunarodnoĭ pravosub"ektnosti*. Kazan', 1975.

See also *Modzhorian, L.A., *Sub"ekty mezhdunarodnogo prava*. Moskva, 1958.

526a. Steinberger, H., 1987, Sovereignty. *Enc. PIL*, **10**, pp. 397–418.

Includes an extensive bibliography of works published worldwide from 1539 to 1982.

—b. Carrillo Salcedo, J.A., *Soberanía de estado y derecho internacional*, 2nd edn. Madrid: Tecnos, 1976, 448 pp.

Follows C. de Visscher's sociological perception of the state as the guardian of its subjects' interest and in this context examines the principle of self-determination and human rights.

—c. Kelsen, H., *Das Problem der Souveränität und die Theorie des Völkerrechts: Beitrag zu einer reinen Rechtslehre*, 2nd edn. Tübingen: Mohr, 1928, 320 pp. Reprinted in 1960.

Examines the concept in purely abstract, formal terms, contested in particular by PIL scholars of the sociological persuasion.

527a. *Materials on jurisdictional immunities of states and their properties/Documentation concernant les immunités juridictionnelles des Etats et leurs biens*. New York: UN, 1981, 656 pp. (UN document ST/LEG/SER.B/20; UN sales publication EF.81.V.10).

Contains texts of national legislations, decisions of national tribunals, UN official records and treaty provisions on the subject considered.

—b. Badr, M.G., *State immunity: an analytical and prognostic view*. Dordrecht: Nijhoff, 1984, 200 pp. (Developments in International Law, 5).

A historical and analytical study of state immunity, pointing up a gradual shift from absolute to restrictive doctrinal positions. Suggests criteria for distinguishing public from private acts of state, only the former considered to be covered by State immunity.

—c. Anand, R.P., 1986/II, Sovereign equality of states in international law. *RCADI*, **197**, pp. 9-228.

Traces the history of the concept in selected doctrinal perceptions and examines the equality of states within the context of an 'unequal' world. *See also* Klein, R.A., *Sovereign equality among states: the history of an idea*. Toronto: Toronto UP, 1974, which considers the concept a myth, given the contradiction between practical considerations of security and equality.

—d. *Baratashvili, D.I., *Printsip sovremennogo ravenstva gosudarstv v mezhdunarodnom prave*. Moskva, 1978.

528a. Spinedi, M. and Simma, B. (eds), *United Nations codification of state responsibility*. Dobbs Ferry, NY: Oceana, 1987, 418 pp.

Includes contributions by Atlam, international liberation movements and international responsibility, and Mohr, on ILC's distinction between 'international crimes' and 'international delicts'. The appendices contain draft articles on state responsibility adopted by ILC and a bibliography on the codification of state responsibility (including the relevant ILC activities as commented on in monographs and periodical articles).

—b. Zemanek, K., 1987, Responsibility of states. *Enc. PIL*, **10**, pp. 362-372.

Traces the evolution of the concept, including grounds for obligation owed by states to the international community. *See also* [571].

—c. Kolosov, IU.M., *Otvetstvennost' v mezhdunarodnom prave*. Moskva: IUridicheskaia Literatura, 1975.

—d. García-Amador, P.V., *The changing law of international claims*. Dobbs Ferry, NY: Oceana, 1984, 2 vols.

529a. Crawford, J., *The creation of states in international law*. Oxford: Clarendon Press, 1979, 498 pp.

Part 1 deals with the concept of statehood (including the controversial aspects of recognition); part 2 is concerned with the creation of states and state-like entities. Includes an extensive bibliography and index. Reviewed in *Harvard international law journal*, 1980, **21**(2), pp. 594–604. *See also* [320b].

—b. Schweitzer, M., 1984, New states and international law. *Enc. PIL*, **7**, pp. 349–353.

Examines the pattern of creating new states (secession, decolonization) and the effect upon them of anterior obligation. *See also* Syatauw, J.J.G., Old and new states: a misleading distinction for future international law and international relations. In *Le droit international demain/International law tomorrow*. Actes du 25. Congrès de l'AAA de l'Academie de droit international de la Haye, Neuchâtel, 28 mai à 2 juin 1973. Neuchâtel (Suisse): Ides et Calendes, 1974, pp. 67–83.

—c. Avakov, M.M. (ed.), *Pravopreemstvo osvobodivshikhsia gosudarstv*. Moskva: Mezhdunarodnye Otnosheniia, 1983, 190 pp.

530a. *United Nations Conference on Succession of States in Respect of Treaties*. New York: UN, 1979, 3 vols (UN document A/CONF.80/16; UN sales publication R.79.V.8-10).

Contains the proceedings and final act of the Conference, as well as the text of the Vienna Convention on Succession of States in Respect of Treaties, 23 August 1978.

—b. *Materials on succession of states in respect of matters other than treaties/Documentation concernant la succession d'états dans les matières autres que les traités*. New York: UN, 1977, 558 p. (UN sales publication E, F.77.V.9; UN document ST/LEG/SER.B/17).

—c. *A select bibliography on succession of states in respect of treaties*. New York: UN, DHL, 1977, 24 pp. *A select bibliography on succession of states in respect of State property, archives and debts*. New York: UN, DHL, 1983, 34 pp. (UN documents ST/LIB/SER.B/24 and 39).

See also Guide for the draft articles on succession of states in respect of state property, archives and debts. Prepared by the Codification Division of the Office of Legal Affairs. New York: UN, Office of Legal Affairs, 1983, 96 pp. (UN document ST/LEG/14, 8 February 1983).

531a. Gruber, A., *Le droit international de la succession d'états*. Préface G. Feuner.

Paris: Faculté de droit; Bruxelles: Bruylant, 1986, 354 pp. (Publications de la Faculté de droit, Université R. Descartes, Paris. Série: Sciences juridiques de développement).

Deals mainly with the position of new states on state succession under customary law, especially in respect of acquired rights and debts.

—b. Udokang, O., *Succession of new states to international treaties.* Dobbs Ferry, NY: Oceana, 1972, 525 pp.

Deals with the concept and theory of the succession of states newly independent in Africa and Asia. Includes succession to membership in IGOs.

—c. Mériboute, Z., *La codification de la succession d'états aux traités: décolonisation, sécession, unification.* Préface P. Cahier. Paris: Presses universitaires de France, 1984, 272 pp.

Traces past and present state practices relating to succession of states in respect of treaties; examines the concept of self-determination in conjunction with the 'tabula rasa' theory.

—d. Bedjaoui, M., 1970/II, Problèmes récents de succession d'états dans les états nouveaux. *RCADI*, **130**, pp. 455–586.

Contains a critical appraisal of different types of PIL (geographical/European, bourgeois/ideological, economic/power-based) against which background decolonization and the emergence of new states is examined.

—e. O'Connell, D. P., *State succession in municipal law and international law*, 2nd edn. Cambridge: Cambridge UP, 1967, 2 vols (Cambridge Studies in International and Comparative Law, 7). 1st edn 1956.

Examines the congruity of various theories and processes of state succession including the doctrine of acquired rights in the light of selected case studies. For an updated summary *see* [379a].

532a. Ginther, K., 1982, National liberation movements. *Enc. PIL*, **3**, pp. 245–249.

Examines the legal status (in terms of political representation and military conduct/*jus ad bellum*) and legitimacy of movements considered 'a major issue of diverging state practice and academic controversy'.

—b. Kim, G. F. *et al.* (eds), *Aktual'nye problemy ideologii natsional'no-osvoboditel'nogo dvizheniia v stranakh Azii i Afriki.* Moskva: Nauka, 1982, 445 pp.

—c. Hasbi, A., *Les mouvements de libération nationale et le droit international.* Rabat (Maroc): Editions Stouky, 1981, 540 pp.

On the basis of his PhD thesis, Nancy, 1978, Hasbi examines the status of the movements relative to states and inter-governmental organizations. However, in the words of C. Rousseau, 'ce travail manque de sérénité et de l'objectivité.' *See also* Abi-Saab, G., 1977, Les guerres de libération nationale et la Conférence diplomatique sur le droit humanitaire. *Annales d'études internationales*, **8**, pp. 63–78, who is critical of the implicitly traditional position of the Conference on wars of liberation as 'conflits armés n'ayant pas de caractère international'. English version in [205].

iv. JURISDICTION, COMPETENCE

533a. de La Pradelle, P.G., 1977, Notion de territoire et d'éspace dans l'aménagement des rapports internationaux contemporains. *RCADI*/IV, **157**, pp. 415–484.

—b. Klimenko, B.M., *Gosudarstvennaia territoriia: voprosy teorii i praktiki mezhdunarodnogo prava*. Moskva: Mezhdunarodnye Otnosheniia, 1974, 166 pp.

Defines the concept of territoriality in terms of political and economic jurisdiction (including the settlement of disputes over territorial changes, etc.); critically appraises bourgeois theories on the subject. *See also* *Volova, L.I., *Printsip territorial'noi tselostnosti i neprikosnovennosti v sovremennom mezhdunarodnom prave*. Rostov-na-Donu, 1981, on the integrity and inviolability of the territory in PIL.

—c. *Multi-system nations and international law: the international status of Germany, Korea and China; proceedings of a regional conference of ASIL*. Edited by H. Chiu and R. Downen. Baltimore, MD: School of Law, University of Maryland, 1981, 203 pp. (Occasional Papers, 8).

See also Klein, E., *Statusverträge im Völkerrecht: Rechtsfragen territorialer Sonderregime*. Berlin: Springer, 1980, 395 pp. (Beiträge zum ausländischen öffentlichen Recht und Völkerrecht, 76). Examines what formerly were termed international settlements or arrangements.

534a. National and international boundaries. *Thesaurus Acroasium*, 1985, vol. 14.

Contains papers of the 1983 session at the Thessaloniki Institute [405]. Includes G.J. Mangone, Unrecognized boundaries: the case of Antarctica.

—b. *La frontière: Colloque, Poitiers, 1979*. Paris: Pédone, 1980, 304 pp. (Actes du 13. Colloque de la Société française pour le droit international).

—c. Brownlie, I. and Burns, I.R., *African boundaries: a legal and diplomatic encyclopaedia*. London: Hurst, 1979, 1,355 pp. Maps, tables.

See also Allott, A., Boundaries in Africa: a legal and historical survey, pp. 69–86 in [457c].

535a. Joyner, C.C. and Chopra, S.K. (eds), *The Antarctic legal régime*. Published under the Antarctica Interest Group of ASIL. Dordrecht: Nijhoff, 1988.

See also Francioni, F. and Scovazzi, T. (eds), *International law for Antarctica*. Milano: Giuffrè, 1987.

—b. Bush, W. M., *Antarctica and international law: a collection of inter-state and national documents*. Dobbs Ferry, NY: Oceana, 1982-8. 3 vols + loose-leaf supplements.

Contains texts of national and international primary source materials relating to the legal aspects of Antarctic resource exploitation, scientific research, etc.

—c. *Symposium internacional sobre el desarrollo de la Antártica*/Obra editada bajo la dirección de F. Orrego Vicuña y A. Salinas Araya. Santiago de Chile: Editorial Universitaria, 1977, 305 pp. (Estudios internacionales, Instituto de Estudios Internacionales de la Universidad de Chile).

The contributions, in Spanish and French, concern mainly the economic development and natural resources of the Arctic region. *See also* Moneta, C., 1981, Antarctica, Latin America and the international system in the 1980s. Towards a new Antarctic order? *Journal of Inter-American studies of world affairs* (London), **23**(1), pp. 29-68; Pharand, D., 1984, The legal régime of the Arctic: some outstanding issues. *International journal* (Toronto), **29**, pp. 742-799.

536a. Zacklin, R. and Caflisch, L., *The legal régime of international rivers and lakes/Le régime juridique des fleuves et des lacs internationaux*. The Hague: Nijhoff, 1981, 415 pp.

Deals with the Canadian–American regime of international rivers, the conventional hydro-economy of Greece, Bulgaria, Turkey and Yugoslavia, and the effects of war on treaties concerning the Danube and Mekong.

—b. Vitanyi, B., *The international régime of river navigation*. Alphen a/R: Sijthoff & Noordhoof, 1979, 406 pp.

—c. *Utilization of international rivers for purposes other than navigation (including regulations of maintenance of rivers, establishment of special commissions)*. New York: UN Office of Legal Affairs, 1964, 934 pp. (UN document ST/LEG/SER.B/12).

Contains national legislative texts and treaty provisions on the subject.

—d. *Kolodkin, A. L. (ed.), *Pravovye i ekonomicheskie problemy regulirovaniia mezhdunarodnogo sudokhodstva*. Moskva, 1984.

Also translated into English as *Legal and economic aspects of regulating international navigation*. Moscow, 1985.

—e. Lammers, J. G., *Pollution of international watercourses: a search for substantive rules or principles of law*. Dordrecht: Nijhoff, 1984, 750 pp.

A comparative study concerning the legal aspects of river pollution, with reference to state responsibility in unlawful transborder water pollution.

a. Law of the sea

537a. *Third United Nations Conference on the Law of the Sea. Official Records.* New York: UN, 1975-82, 17 vols (UN sales publication E.75 [-84].V.3).

Contains the summary records of meetings and documents from the first session (Caracas, Venezuela, 1974) to the 11th session (Montego Bay, Jamaica, 1982) of UNCLOS III.

Facilitating the use of the *Official Records* is *Law of the sea: master file containing references to official documents of the UNCLOS III.* New York: UN, 1985, 176 pp. (UN sales publications E.85.V.9); French edition, *Le droit de la mer: Répertoire général des documents officiels de la 3. Conférence.* 1986, 183 pp. (Le droit de la mer, 1). Complementing the aforementioned international official materials is the commercially published *Third United Nations Conference on the Law of the Sea: Documents.* Edited by R. Platzöder. Dobbs Ferry, NY: Oceana, 1982-, 17 vols + index. This English-language publication is in part based on Platzöder, R. (comp.), *Dokumente der dritten Seerechtskonferenz der Vereinten Nationen, Genfer Session, 1980: Materialiensammlung für die deutsche Seerechts-delegation.* Ebenhausen/München: Stiftung Wissenschaft und Politik, Forschungsinstitut für internationale Politik und Sicherheit, 1980, 3 vols (SWP-2 2272/I-III).

—b. *United Nations Convention on the Law of the Sea.* New York: United Nations, 1983, 224 pp. (UN sales publication E.83.V.5). French edition, *Le droit de la mer: texte officiel de la Convention . . .* 1984, 267 pp.

The outcome of the Third United Nations Conference on the Law of the Sea (UNCLOS III), the Convention was signed in 1982. The UN publications contain the English and French texts of the Convention's 320 articles and nine annexes relating to control over navigation, fishing, deep-sea mining, pollution etc. in seas and oceans. The publications include the Final Act of UNCLOS III, a signed, official account of the proceedings leading to the adoption of the Convention, the text of the four resolutions adopted, and an outline of the history (by B. Zuleta) of the Conference.

538a. Nordquist, M. H., *United Nations Convention of the Sea 1982: a commentary.* Dordrecht: Nijhoff, 1985-, 1-.

Written by diplomats and scholars directly engaged in the negotiations leading to the Convention, the commentary provides the complete legislative history of each provision in the Convention, as well as information on the negotiating process and the work of the Drafting Committee.

—b. Evensen, J., 1986/IV, Working methods and procedures in the Third UN Conference on the Law of the Sea. *RCADI,* **199,** pp. 415-520.

Examines the procedures used at UNCLOS III with a view to determining the application of similar procedures at other international conferences. Discusses in particular the principle of consensus, the package deal, gentlemen's agreements and voting.

—c. *A quite revolution: the United Nations Convention on the Law of the Sea: a summary booklet on the Law of the Sea Convention and its accomplishments*. New York: UN, 1983 (UN sales no. E.83.V.7).

—d. el-Baradei, M. and Gavin, C., *Crowded agendas: crowded rooms; institutional arrangements at UNCLOS III. Some lessons in global negotiations*. New York: UN/UNITAR, 1981 (UNITAR/PE/3 = E.81.XV.PE/3).

539a. *National legislation and treaties relating to the law of the sea/Législation nationale et traités concernant le droit de la mer*. New York: UN, 1976-80, 2 vols (UN document ST/LEG/SER.B/19; UN sales publication EF.76.V.2; EF.80.V.3).

In addition to these two volumes another seven volumes issued during the period 1951-75 contain national legislation and treaty provisions relating to various aspects of the law of the sea. The texts (in country arrangement) deal with the regime of the high seas, territorial seas, contiguous zones, continental shelf, fishing and conservation of the living resources of the seas. *See also* [549a, 550a, 555, 556a].

—b. *Law of the sea: current developments in state practice*. New York: UN Office of the Special Representative of the Secretary-General for the Law of the Sea, 1987, 2 vols (UN sales publication E.87.V.3 and 7).

Contains texts of recent national legislation, treaty provisions and communications to the UN. Previously published in the *Law of the Sea Bulletin/Bulletin du droit de la mer/Boletín del derecho del mar*, nos 6-9, 1985-7, this material illustrates the national implementation of the 1982 Convention on the Law of the Sea [537b].

—c. *The law of the sea: multilateral treaties relevant to the UN Convention on the Law of the Sea*. New York: UN Office of the Special Representative of the Secretary-General for the Law of the Sea, 1985 (UN sales publication E.85.V.11). French edition, *Traités multilatéraux relatifs au droit de la mer*. (Le droit de la mer, 2).

A chronological list and index of multilateral treaties in force and touching upon issues covered by the 1982 Convention.

—d. *The law of the sea: maritime boundary agreements, 1970-1984*. New York: UN Office for Ocean Affairs and the Law of the Sea, 1987, 297 pp. (UN sales publication E.87.V.12).

See also [552].

—e. UN Office for Ocean Affairs and the Law of the Sea, United Nations, UN Plaza, New York, NY 10017, USA.

In 1988 superseded the UN Office of the Special Representative of the Secretary-General for the Law of Sea. The Office has the responsibility to ensure that state practice develops in a manner consistent with the provisions of the 1982 UN

Convention on the Law of the Sea [537b]. For publications by the Office *see* [539b,c,d, 550a]. *See also Study on the future functions of the Secretary-General under the Draft Convention and on the needs of countries, especially developing countries, for information, advice and assistance under the new legal régime.* Prepared by the Secretary-General in his capacity as Secretary-General of the 3rd UN Conference on the Law of the Sea. New York: UN, 1981, 46 pp. (UN document A/CONF.62/L.76). Also in French.

540a. Law of the sea. Air and space. *Enc. PIL*, 1989, **11**.

Contains 97 articles, mainly on law of the sea aspects, including admiralty law, the *Amoco-Cadiz* incident, fisheries, hot pursuit, straits and whaling regimes as well as articles on air and space law.

—b. Dupuy, R.-J. and Vignes, D. (eds), *Traité du nouveau droit de la mer*. Paris: Economica; Bruxelles: Bruylant, 1985, 1,447 pp. (Collection droit international).

Divided into four parts, the treatise contains contributions on the sources and codification of the law of the sea (H. Caminos), definitions of national competences, high seas, Antarctic/Arctic regions (A. van Essen), international marine resources, including the 'common heritage of mankind' (R.-J. Dupuy), the use of the seas, including navigation, fishing settlement of disputes, war (Ranjeva and Halkiopolous). Includes the French text of the 1982 UN Convention of the Law of the Sea and its status to 1984. An extensive, systematically arranged bibliography concludes the treaties.

—c. O'Connell, D. P., *The international law of the sea*. Oxford: Clarendon Press, 1982-4, 2 vols.

An English-language treatise similar to [540b].

—d. Lazarev, M. I., *Teoreticheskie voprosy sovremennogo morskogo prava*. Moskva, 1983, 270 pp.

Reviewed in *AJIL*, 1985, **79**(4), pp. 1087-1088. Exists in German translation (Berlin: Duncker & Humblot, 1985). *See also* Lazarev, M. I. (ed.), *Sovremennoe mezhdunarodnoe morskoe pravo: sotrudnichestvo sotsialisticheskikh stran: ekonomicheskaia zona; mezhdunarodnye organizatsii; razreshenie sporov* . . . Moskva: Nauka, 1984, 267 pp.

—e. Theutenberg, B. J., *The evolution of the law of the sea: a study of the resources and strategy with special regard to the polar regions.* Dublin: Tycooly International, 1984. (Natural Resources and the Environment, 17).

—f. *New directions in the law of the sea.* [Series published under the auspices of the] British Institute of International and Comparative Law, London, 1973-81, 11 vols. New series, Dobbs Ferry, NY: Oceana, 1983-, looseleaf. Editor K. R. Simmonds.

Based on primary sources (treaties, judicial decisions, etc.) the individual topical volumes examine current developments relating to the territorial sea, continental shelf, pollution, etc. *New directions* supersedes *Cases on the law of the sea*. Edited by K. R. Simmonds. Dobbs Ferry, NY: Oceana, 1976-84, 4 vols. Arranged in chronological order for the period 1800-1920, the work provides a historical perspective on representative aspects of the law of the sea. See also [558b,c].

541. *The law of the sea: essays in memory of Jean Carroz/Le droit de la mer: mélanges à la mémoire de Jean Carroz/El derecho y el mar: ensayos en memoria de Jean Carroz.* Rome: Food and Agriculture Organization, 1987, 281 pp.

The contributors include J.-P. Dolbert, Evolution of the treaty-making capacity of international organizations; A. G. Roche, A new intergovernmental fisheries organization/INFOFISH; Sucharitkul, Evolution continue d'une notion nouvelle: le patrimoine commun de l'humanité.

542a. *Actualités du droit de la mer: Colloque, Montpellier, 1972.* Paris: Pédone, 1973, 296 pp.; *Perspectives du droit de la mer à l'issue de la 3. Conférence des Nations Unies: Colloque, Rouen, 1983.* Paris: Pédone, 1984, 341 pp. (Actes du 6., 17. Colloque de la Société française pour le droit international).

—b. *Propos sur le nouveau droit de la mer: Colloque, Paris, 1983.* Paris: Pédone, 1985, 120 pp.

Organized by the Académie diplomatique internationale.

—c. *The new law of the sea: Athens Colloquium on the Law of the Sea, 1982.* Selected and edited by C. L. Rozakis and C. A. Stephanon. Amsterdam: Elsevier, 1983, 354 pp.

543a. Dipla, H., *Le régime juridique des îles dans le droit international de la mer.* Paris: Presses universitaires de France, 1984, 244 pp. (Publications, Institut universitaire de hautes études internationales, Genève).

The emphasis is on the legal aspects of natural resources, rather than sovereignty of islands. See also Bowett, D. W., *The legal régime of islands in international law.* Alphen a/R: Sijthoff & Noordhoof, 1979, 337 pp.

—b. *Jiménez Piernas, C. B., *El proceso de formación del derecho internacional de los archipiélagos.* Madrid: Universidad Complutense de Madrid, 1980, 2 vols.

Based on selected state practice, the work illustrates the dynamic approach to PIL in general, and archipelagos in particular; includes an extensive bibliography and maps.

—c. *International straits of the world.* Edited by G. J. Mangone. Alphen a/R: Sijthoff & Noordhoff, 1978-9; Dordrecht: Nijhoff, 1980-.

Vol. 1 in the Sijthoff series concerns the Northwest Arctic Passage (by W. E. Butler); vols 1-3 and 7-8 in the Nijhoff series concern the Northwest Passage, including the Arctic Straits (by D. Pharand). *See also* Koh, Kheng-lian, *Straits in international navigation: contemporary issues.* Dobbs Ferry, NY: Oceana, 1982, 219 pp.

—d. Strohl, M. P., *The international law of bays.* The Hague: Nijhoff, 1963, 440 pp.

544. Anand, R. P., *Origin and development of the law of the sea: history of international law revisited.* Dordrecht: Nijhoff, 1982, 249 pp. (Publications on Ocean Development, 7).

See also Scupin, H.-U., *Enc. PIL*, 1984, 7, pp. 187-193 (on the law of the sea between 1815 and 1914).

545. *Adjangba, M. A, *Inequality and a new maritime order: theories and issues of dependent development.* Tampere (Finland): University of Tampere, Dept of Political Science, 1985, 434 pp. (*Acta Univ. Tamperensis*, Ser. A, 189).

546a. Wasum, S., *Der internationale Seegerichtshof im System der obligatorischen Streitbeilegungsverfahren der Seerechtskonvention.* München: V. Florentz, 1984, 298 pp. (Europarecht-Völkerrecht: Studien und Materialien, 7).

Examines the implementation of the 1982 Convention [537b] in the light of the proposed International Tribunal for the Law of the Sea. *See also* [546c].

—b. Caflisch, L., Le règlement judiciaire et arbitral des différends dans le nouveau droit international de la mer, pp. 351-371 in [182].

—c. *Draft rules of the International Tribunal of the Law of the Sea.* [Established by the] Preparatory Commission for the International Sea-Bed Authority and for the International Tribunal for the Law of the Sea. New York: UN, 1983, 14 pp. (UN document LOS/PCN/28).

The Preparatory Commission [546d] in its sessions since 1983 has examined the practical arrangements for the establishment of the International Tribunal of the Law of the Sea, closely following the ICJ Statute for analogy. *See also* Oda, S., *The law of the sea in our time.* Alphen a/R: Sijthoff, 1977, vol. 2, The UN Seabed Committee, 1968-1973 (Publications on Ocean Development, 4).

—d. Preparatory Commission for the International Sea-Bed Authority and for the International Tribunal for the Law of the Sea. *The Law of the Sea Documents.* Edited by R. Platzöder. Dobbs Ferry, NY: Oceana, 1990, 10 vols.

Established by Resolution 1 (*see* Final Act of UNCLOS III [537b]), the Preparatory Commission held its first session in 1983, and has met twice yearly since. The *Law of the Sea Documents* contain for the period 1983-9 documents of the Commission (vols 1-7) and relevant press releases issued by the UN Dept of Public Information (vols 8-10). The publication is sponsored by the Stiftung Wissenschaft und Politik (Ebenhausen-München) and the International Ocean Institute [558].

547a. Kiss, A.C., 1982/II, La notion de patrimoine commun de l'humanité. *RCADI*, **175**, pp. 99-256.

Examines the legal content of the concept and its implications for international relations in general, and the legal régime of marine resources, the Antarctic, etc. in particular. *See also* Hoof, G.I.H., 1986, Legal status of the concept of the common heritage of mankind. *Grotiana*, **7**, pp. 49-79, which defines the concept in a general *res communis* rather than law of the sea context. Shraga, D., 1986, The common heritage of mankind. *Annales d'études internationales*, **15**, pp. 45-63, views the concept in terms of non-appropriation, peaceful uses of common or shared resources. Dowdy, W.L. and Trood, R.B. (eds), *The Indian Ocean: perspectives on a strategic arena*. New Delhi: Himalayan Books, 1987, 613 pp. discuss the expansion of navies as a threat to the security of Indian Ocean coastal states, and Kewening in [207].

—b. Pardo, A., *The common heritage: selected papers on oceans and world order, 1967-1974*. Valetta: Malta UP, 1975, 549 pp. (International Ocean Institute. Occasional Papers, 3).

In his statement to the 1st Committee of the UN General Assembly in November 1967, Pardo proposed that in the interest of mankind the traditional concept of the 'freedom of the sea' be replaced by that of the 'common heritage'.

548a. *The management of humanity's resources: the law of the sea/La gestion des ressources pour l'humanité: le droit de la mer*. The Hague Academy International law Workshop, 1981. Edited by R.-J. Dupuy. The Hague: Nijhoff, 1982, 433 pp.

The papers of the Workshop deal with mineral and biological resources of the sea and their management for international peace and security.

—b. Brownlie, I., 1979/I, Legal status of natural resources in international law. *RCADI*, **162**, pp. 245-318.

Discusses NIEO and sovereignty over natural resources in general, and existing versus potential models for resource allocation or sharing with reference to PIL principles in particular.

—c. Luard, E., *The control of the sea-bed: who owns the resources of the oceans*. London: Heinemann, 1977, 315 pp. 1st edn 1974.

Outlines basic international issues (militarization, pollution, oil production) of the deep sea-bed that are considered to be beyond national jurisdiction.

—d. Neubauer, R.D., *Establishing the non-seabed provisions of the UNCLOS III treaty as customary international law*. Dobbs Ferry, NY: Oceana, 1984, 148 pp. (University of Virginia School of Law, Center for Oceans Law and Policy. Ocean Policy Study Series).

549a. *The law of the sea: national legislation on the exclusive economic zone, the economic* zone and the exclusive fishery zone. New York: United Nations, 1986, 337 pp. (UN sales no. E.85.V.10).

—b. Attard, D.J., *The exclusive economic zone in international law*. Oxford: Clarendon Press, 1987.

—c. Orrego Vicuña, F., 1986/IV, La zone économique exclusive: régime et nature juridique dans le droit international. *RCADI*, **199**, pp. 9-170.

Defines the concept in the light of selected state practice and emerging relevant customary rules.

—d. Gründling, L., *Die 200 Seemeilen Wirtschaftszone. Entstehung eines neuen Régimes des Meeresvölkerrechts*. Berlin: Springer, 1983, 370 pp. (Beiträge zum ausländischen öffentlichen Recht und Völkerrecht, 83).

—e. Kovalev, F., 1979, The economic zone and its legal status. *International Affairs* (Moscow), **2**, pp. 58-64.

550a. *The law of the sea: National legislation on the continental shelf*. New York: UN Office for Ocean Affairs and the Law of the Sea, 1989, 289 pp. (UN sales publication E.89.V.5).

Based in part on relevant articles in the 1958 Geneva Convention on the Continental Shelf, as well as on articles in the 1982 UN Convention on the Law of the Sea.

—b. Vallée, C., *Le plateau continental dans le droit positif actuel*. Paris: Pédone, 1971, 359 pp. (RGDIP Publications, Nouvelle série, 14).

—c. Slouka, Z., *International custom and the continental shelf: a study in the dynamics of customary rules*. The Hague: Nijhoff, 1968, 186 pp.

551a. Sinjela, A.M., *Land-locked states and the UNCLOS régime*. Dobbs Ferry, NY: Oceana, 1983, 495 pp.

Examines claims by land-locked states to rights of transit through third states, as well as freedom of the high seas and resources of the territorial sea.

—b. Glassner, M.I., *Bibliography on land-locked states*, 2nd edn. Dordrecht: Nijhoff, 1986, 210 pp. 1st edn 1980.

See also his *Access to the sea for developing land-locked states*. The Hague: Nijhoff, 1970.

552. Jagota, S.P., *Maritime boundary*. Dordrecht: Nijhoff, 1985, 240 pp. (Publications on Ocean Development).

Deals with the delimitation of maritime boundaries between states with opposite or adjacent coasts, and the emergence of new maritime zones since 1945. *See also* [539d].

553. Rembe, N.S., *Africa and the international law of the sea: a study of the contribution of the African states to the Third UN Conference on the Law of the Sea*. Alphen a/R: Sijthoff, 1980, 272 pp.

554. *International Symposium on the New Law of the Sea in Southeast Asia: development effects and regional approaches.* Edited by D.M. Johnston, E. Gold and P. Tangsubkul. Halifax, Nova Scotia: Dalhousie Ocean Studies Programme, 1983, 239 pp.

Includes contributions on ocean management in new national jurisdictional zones, maritime boundary delimitations and regional cooperation in ocean development.

555. Nordquist, M.H. and Park, C.H. (eds), *North America and Asia-Pacific and the development of the law of the sea: treaties and national legislation.* Dobbs Ferry, NY: Oceana, 1981, 1 vol., loose-leaf.

556a. Szekely, A., *Latin America and the development of the law of the sea: regional documents, national legislation.* Dobbs Ferry, NY: Oceana, 1976-, loose-leaf.

—b. Hjersonsson, K., *The new law of the sea: influence of the Latin American states on recent developments of the sea.* Leiden: Sijthoff; Stockholm: Almquist & Wiksell, 1973, 187 pp.

—c. Morris, M.A. and Ferreira, P.S., 1981, Latin America, Africa and the Third UN Conference on the Law of the Sea: annotated bibliography. *Ocean development and international law*, 9(1/2), pp. 101-186.

See also *Vargas, J.A., *Repertorio bibliográfico: América Latina y la soberanía sobre sus recursos oceánicos: contiene una selección de obras sobre: derecho del mar, documentos oficiales, organismos internacionales y trabajos científicos.* Mexico, DF, 1976, 384 pp.

557a. *The USSR, Eastern Europe and the development of the law of the sea.* Compiled, translated and edited by W.E. Butler. Dobbs Ferry, NY: Oceana, 1983-, loose-leaf.

Continues Sebek, V., *Eastern European states and the development of the law of the sea.* Dobbs Ferry, NY: Oceana, 1976, 2 vols, loose-leaf. See also *The law of the sea and international shipping: Anglo-Soviet post-UNCLOS perspectives.* Edited by W.E. Butler. Dobbs Ferry, NY: Oceana, 1985, 432 pp. (Studies on Socialist Legal Systems. Faculty of Law, University College, London).

—b. Durante, F., *Western Europe and the development of the law of the sea.* Dobbs Ferry, NY: Oceana, 1979-, loose-leaf.

558a. *Ocean development and international law: the journal of maritime affairs.* New York: Taylor & Francis, 1973-, 1-, bimonthly.

—b. *Ocean policy study series.* Edited by the Center for Oceans Law and Policy, University of Virginia School of Law. Dobbs Ferry, NY: Oceana, 1984-, approximately 6 studies annually.

—c. *Publications on ocean development.* Edited by S. Oda. Alphen a/R: Sijthoff, 1977-1981; Dordrecht: Nijhoff, 1982-.

See also Oda, S., *The international law of ocean development: basic documents*. Leiden: Sijthoff, 1975, 2 vols, a selection of basic texts (mainly issued by the UN) on various aspects of the law of the sea.

—d. International Ocean Institute. PO Box 524, Valetta, Malta.

Founded in 1972, the Institute contributes to the development of the law of the sea through research and publications, notably the *Ocean yearbook*. Edited by E. M. Borgese, Chicago, IL: University of Chicago Press, 1978–, 1–, annual.

—e. *International organizations and the law of the sea: documentary yearbook*. Published for the Netherlands Institute for the Law of the Sea. London: Graham & Trotman; Dordrecht: Nijhoff, 1987–, 1–.

—f. *Law of sea terminology/Terminologie du droit de la mer/Terminología del derecho del mar*. New York: United Nations, 1975 (*Terminology Bulletin* no. 297/Rev. 1. UN document ST/CS/SER.F/297/Rev. 1; sales no. E/F/R/S.74.1.22).

559a. *The law of the sea: a select bibliography*. New York: United Nations Office of the Special Representative of the Secretary-General for the Law of the Sea, 1985–, 1– (UN document LOS/LIB/1–; UN sales no. E.85-V.2).

Continues *The sea: legal and political aspects, a select bibliography*. New York: UN Dag Hammarskjöld Library, 1974–80, 5 issues (UN sales nos: 74.I.9; 75.I.12; 76.I.6; 78.I.3; 80.I.6). The bibliographies exclude references to materials issued by IGOs.

—b. Papadakis, N. and Glassner, M. I., *International law of the sea and marine affairs: a bibliography*. Dordrecht: Nijhoff, 1984, 650 pp.

A supplement to the bibliography of the same title, published by Sijthoff & Nordhoff, Alphen a/R, 1980, 457 pp. Systematically arranged, the 1980 bibliography contains monographs and periodical articles published since 1945 in English and French, complemented in the 1984 bibliography by references to German, Italian, Spanish and Russian works. The appendices in the 1984 bibliography represent a documentary guide to auxiliary resources (bibliographies, directories, dictionaries, etc.) of the law of the sea.

—c. Kudej, B., *The new law of the sea: international law bibliography*. Dobbs Ferry, NY: Oceana, 1984, 156 pp. (Collection of Bibliographic and Research Resources).

Reviewed in *IJLI*, 1985, **12**(5/6), p. 270.

—d. Jenisch, U., *Bibliographie des deutschen Schrifttums zum internationalen Seerecht, 1945–1981*. Frankfurt a/M: A. Metzner, 1982, 141 pp. (Werkhefte, Institut für internationale Angelegenheiten, Universität Hamburg, 38).

—e. *Razumnyĭ, I.A., *Raboty sovetskikh avtorov po morskomu pravu: bibliograficheskiĭ ukazatel'*, *1917-1978*. Moskva: Morflot, 1981, 214 pp.

—f. Sybesma-Knol, N. and Regout, A., *Bibliografie van het nieuwe zeerecht: en keuze uit boeken en UNO dokumenten/Bibliography of the new law of the sea: a selective list of books and UN documents*. Brussel: Centrum voor de Studie van het Recht van de Verenigte Naties en van de gespecialiseerde Organisaties aan de Vrije Universiteit, 1976, 109 pp. Supplement 1977, 188 pp.

—g. Bermes, A. and Levy, J.-P., *Bibliographie du droit de la mer/Bibliography on the law of the sea*. Paris: Ed. techniques et économiques, 1974, 138 pp.

b. Air, space law

560a. *Space activities and resources: a review of the activities and resources of the United Nations, of its Specialized Agencies and other competent international bodies relating to the peaceful uses of outer space*. New York: UN, 1986, 301 pp. (UN document A/AC.105/358; UN sales publication E.86.I.2).

A directory of international (inter-governmental and other) organizations and their space activities.

—b. Lay, S.H. (ed.), *Air and aviation treaties of the world*. Dobbs Ferry, NY: Oceana, 1984–, loose-leaf.

Complements *Air laws and treaties of the world*. Washington, DC: GPO, 1965, 3 vols. The latter, compiled at the request of the US Congress Senate Committee on Commerce, contains texts of bi- and multilateral treaties concluded by some 120 countries and in force up to 1963.

—c. *UN treaties on outer space*. New York: UN, 1984, 37 pp. (UN sales publication E.84.I.10).

Contains English texts of three multilateral agreements and two conventions illustrative of the UN General Assembly 'Declaration of legal principles governing activities of states in the exploration of outer space'.

561a. Mateesco-Matte, M., *Le droit extra-atmosphérique et la course aux armaments: droit spatial ou droit aéro-orbital?* Paris: Pédone, 1984, 717 pp.

Published under the auspices of the Centre de droit maritime et aérien, Nantes, this is a collection of Mateesco's essays published between 1968 and 1983, including 'Spatialisme ou fictionalisme juridique?' presented at the Montreal symposium in 1981 [562a]. *See also* his *Space activities and emerging international law*. Montreal: Centre for Research of Air and Space Law, 1984, 627 pp., and his *Deux frontières invisibles: de la mer territoriale à l'air territorial*. Paris: Pédone, 1965, 294 pp.

—b. Christol, C.Q., *The modern international law of outer space* [second printing].

New York: Pergamon, 1984, 932 pp. (Pergamon Policy Studies on International Politics).

—c.   Jasentuliyana, N. and Lee, R. S., *Manual of space law*. Dobbs Ferry, NY: Oceana, 1979-81, 4 vols.

—d.   *Air and outer space law. Thesaurus Acroasium*, 1981, vol. 10.

—e.   *Movchan, A. P. (ed.), *Mezhdunarodnoe vozdushnoe pravo*. Moskva, 1980.

See also *Piradov, A. S., *Mezhdunarodnoe kosmicheskoe pravo*. Moskva, 1974. French translation, *Le droit international de l'espace*. Moscou: Progrès, 1976, 369 pp.; Kolosov, IU.M. and Stashevskiĭ, S.G., *Bor'ba za mirnyi kosmos: pravovye voprosy*. Moskva: Mezhdunarodnye Otnosheniia, 1984, 173 pp. (the 1968 edn contains 'kritika burzhuaznykh teoriĭ kosmicheskovo prava'); Zhukov, G.P., 1978/III, Tendances contemporaines du développement du droit spatial international. *RCADI*, **161**, pp. 229-328.

—f.   Lachs, M., *Law of outer space*. Leiden: Sijthoff, 1972, 196 pp.

See also Cheng and Goedhuis in [379a].

562a. *Earth-oriented space activities and their legal implications/Les activités spatiales au service de la Terre et leurs implications juridiques*. Proceedings of the Symposium [Montreal], October 15-16, 1981. Montreal: Centre for Research of Air and Space Law, McGill University, 1983, 366 pp.

The Symposium dealt with the legal aspects of broadcasting satellites, remote sensing energy from space, etc. *See also* [561a].

—b.   *Settlement of space law disputes: the present state of the law and perspectives of further development*. Edited by K.-H. Böckstiegel. Köln: Heymann, 1980, 415 pp.

The Proceedings of an International Colloquium, Munich, 1979, include contributions by I. H. P. Diederiks-Verschoor, Rules for dispute settlement in present space law, and S. M. Williams, Dispute settlement according to INMARSAT and INTELSAT. A bibliography and selected texts on dispute settlement (in general and space law) conclude the work. *See also* Heere, W. P., 1976, Desirability of an international court for aeronautical disputes. *Air law*, **1**(4), pp. 229-252.

—c.   Schwartz, M. D., *Space law perspectives: commentaries based on volumes 1-15, 1957-1972 of the Colloquia on the law of outer space*. Sponsored by the International Institute of Space Law of the International Astronautical Federation. South Hackensack, NJ: Rothman, 1976, 302 pp.

The commentaries are all the more useful since many of the initial volumes of the published proceedings of the Colloquia are out of print.

—d.   *Prevention of arms race in outer space: international law aspect*. Geneva: UNOG, 1986, 26 pp. (UNIDIR/86/08 = GV.E.86.02).

563a. *Yearbook of air and space law.* Montreal: McGill UP, 1965-, 1-, annual.

Part 1 contains articles on theoretical and procedural aspects of air and space law, while part 2 contains bibliographic references to the latest developments, including treaties, in the field.

—b. *Journal of space law.* University of Mississippi Law Center, Lamar Society of International Law, 1973-, 1-, semi-annual.

—c. *Annuaire de droit maritime et aérien.* Paris: Pédone, 1975-, 1,-, annual.

—d. *Zeitschrift für Luft und Weltraumrecht.* Köln: Heymann, 1952-, 1-, quarterly.

Under the auspices of the Institut für Luft und Weltraumrecht, Köln.

564. *International Institute of Space Law.* International Astronautical Federation, 250, rue St Jacques, 75005 Paris.

Conducts research on legal and sociological aspects of astronautics. Convened 'Colloquia on the law of outer space' [562c] and in the 1960s published *Worldwide bibliography of space law and related matters*, superseded by [565a]. See also [560a].

565a. Heere, W.P., *International bibliography of air law, 1900-1971.* Leiden: Sijthoff, 1972, 569 pp. Supplements, 1972-6 (1976); 1977-80 (1981); 1981-84 (1985).

Includes references to monographs, periodical articles and dissertations; excludes case law, treaties and legislation. Table of contents also in French and Spanish. Supersedes *Worldwide bibliography of space law and related matters* [564].

—b. *Outer space: a reference handbook.* Edited by C. Driscoll Sullivan. Santa Barbara, CA: ABC-Clio Press, 1989, 180 pp.

A guide to information sources concerning political, scientific and legal aspects of outer space.

v. REPRESENTATION, DIPLOMATIC PRACTICE

566a. *Vienna Convention on Diplomatic Relations, Vienna, 18 April 1961.* Texts of Convention and Optional Protocols. In *UNTS*, 1965, **500**, pp. 96-221 and 223-265 respectively.

Represents the codification of laws and regulations relating to the immunity of diplomatic missions, categories of diplomatic agents, etc. Complemented by *Laws and regulations regarding diplomatic and consular privileges and immunities*. New York: United Nations, 1958. (UN document ST/LEG/SER.B/7; UN sales publ. E, F.58. V.3), itself traceable to the 'Draft convention on diplomatic privileges and immunities' elaborated (in 1932) by the Harvard Research in International Law [389b].

—b.   Denza, E., *Diplomatic law: a commentary on the Vienna Convention on Diplomatic Relations*. Dobbs Ferry, NY: Oceana, 1976, 348 pp.

For a comparative historical survey *see* Michaels, D. B., International privileges and immunities. The Hague: Nijhoff, 1971, 249 pp.

567.   *Vienna Convention on Consular Relations, Vienna, 24 April 1963*. Texts of Convention and Optional Protocols. In *UNTS*, 1969, **596**, pp. 261-467 and 469-512 respectively.

Complemented by *Collection of bilateral consular treaties*. New York.

568.   Feller, A. H. and Hudson, M. O. (eds), *A collection of diplomatic and consular law and regulations of various countries*. Washington, DC: Carnegie Endowment for International Peace, 1933, 2 vols.

569.   *Handbuch der diplomatischen Korrespondenz der europäischen Staaten/Répertoire de la correspondance des Etats Européens/Digest of the diplomatic correspondence of the European States*. Berlin: Heymann, 1933, 790 pp. (*Fontes juris gentium*, Series B, Section I, vol. 1).

See also *Archives diplomatiques: recueil de diplomatie, d'histoire et de droit international*. Paris: Amyot, 1861-1914, 193 vols; *Annuaire diplomatique de l'Empire de Russie*, St Pétersbourg, 1861-1917.

570a. Diplomacy and consular relations. *Enc. PIL*, 1986, **9**.

—b.   Daoudi, R., La représentation en droit international public. pp. 205-219 in [204].

—c.   Florio, F., *Nozione di diplomatia e diritto diplomatico*, 2nd edn. Milano: Giuffrè, 1978, 386 pp.

The treatise traces the evolution of diplomatic practice, defines diplomatic functions, style (including language) and communication (correspondence, protocols, declarations, etc.) within the context of international relations, and concludes with a list of primary and secondary diplomatic materials.

—d.   Cahier, P., *Le droit diplomatique contemporain*. Genève: Droz, 1964, 534 pp. Reprinted in 1974.

—e.   Blishchenko, I. P., *Diplomaticheskoe pravo*. Moskva, 1972, 479 pp.

See also Levin, D. B, *Diplomaticheskiĭ immunitet*. Moskva, 1949, 414 pp.

571.   Przetacznik, F., *Protection of officials of foreign States according to international law*. Dordrecht: Nijhoff, 1983, 390 pp.

Examines the protection of such officials within the context of the host country's international responsibility.

572a. *Satow's Guide to diplomatic practice*, 5th edn. London: Longman, 1979, 544 pp.

Deals with the conduct of official/diplomatic relations, including the role therein of international organizations and conferences convened under their auspices. The appendix contains definitions, terminology, lists of conferences and specialized aspects of diplomacy.

—b. Sen, B., *A diplomat's handbook of international law and practice*, 2nd edn. The Hague: Nijhoff, 1979, 529 pp.

Deals more extensively than Satow's *Guide* [572a] with practical procedures of treaty-making, recognition of states, asylum, extradition and passports.

573a. *Diplomaticheskiĭ slovar'*, 4th edn. Moskva: Nauka, 1984–. 1st edn 1984–50, 3 vols, edited by A. A. Gromyko.

—b. Gamboa, M.J., *Elements of diplomatic and consular practice: a glossary*. Quezon City (Philippines), 1970, 489 pp.

—c. *Dictionnaire diplomatique*. Publié sous la direction de A.-F. Frangulis. Paris: Académie diplomatique internationale, 1933-68, 7 vols.

Contains articles on diplomatic practice, codification of international law and various aspects of international relations. Vol. 1 includes the history and activities of Académie diplomatique internationale; vol. 5 is a biographical dictionary of diplomats from the Middle Ages to the mid-twentieth century.

See also [451d].

vi. SETTLEMENT OF DISPUTES

574a. *A survey of treaty provisions for the pacific settlement of international disputes, 1949-1962*. New York: UN, 1966, 901 pp.

Updates the *Systematic survey of treaties for pacific settlement of international disputes, 1928-1948*. Lake Success, NY: United Nations, 1949, 1,201 p. The two surveys provide English texts of treaties (some of which are not included in either *UNTS* or *LoNTS*) and related materials on the peaceful settlement of international disputes.

—b. Oellers-Frahm, K. and Wühler, N., *Dispute settlement in public international law: texts and materials*. Berlin: Springer, 1984, 913 pp. (Publication of the Max-Planck Institute for Comparative Public Law and International Law).

A selection of English texts, complete with bibliographic reference relating to the settlement of disputes in general and specialized PIL (human rights; economic cooperation; disputes arising out of world wars, etc.); analyses arbitration and dispute settlement clauses in treaties. Subject index. *See also* [297, vol. 1].

575a. Merrills, J. G., *International dispute settlement*. London: Sweet & Maxwell, 1984, 211 p. (Modern Legal Series). Reviewed in *BYIL*, 1986, **57**, pp. 392-393.

Analyses the different means (mediation, arbitration, etc.) of, and the role of international organizations/conferences (ICJ, UNCLOS, etc.) in, the settlement of disputes, from the legal and non-legal perspective.

—b. Bowett, D.W., 1983/II, Contemporary developments in legal techniques in the settlement of disputes. *RCADI*, **180**, pp. 169-236.

The emphasis is on legal means of international dispute settlement, as well as the enforcement of international judicial, arbitral decisions.

—c. Oeser, E., *Der internationale Streit. Völkerrechtliche Regelungsbedingungen für die Staaten.* Berlin: Staatsverlag der DDR, 1987, 192 pp.

—d. Levin, D.B., *Printsip mirnogo razresheniia mezhdunarodnykh sporov.* Moskva: Nauka, 1977, 111 pp.

—e. *Entin, M.L., *Mezhdunarodnye sudebnye uchrezhdeniia: rol' mezhdunarodnykh arbitrazhnykh i sudebnykh organov v razreshenii mezhgosudarstvennykh sporov.* Moskva: Mezhdunarodnye Otnosheniia, 1984, 172 pp.

576a. Mosler, H. and Bernhardt, R. (eds), *Judicial settlement of international disputes; International Court of Justice, other courts and tribunals, arbitration and conciliation: an international symposium.* Berlin: Springer, 1974, 572 pp. (Beiträge zum ausländischen öffentlichen Recht und Völkerrecht, 62).

Contributions by H. Mosler, T.O. Elias, R.Y. Jennings, F.V. García-Amador and H. v. Mangoldt.

—b. *Complementary structures of Third Party settlement of international disputes.* New York: UN, 1975 (UNITAR/PS/3 = E.75.XV.PS/3).

577a. Mavungu, M.-di-N., *La contribution de la Cour internationale de justice au règlement pacifique des différends touchant les Etats africains.* Genève: Institut universitaire de hautes études internationales, 1987, 376 pp.

—b. Marotta Ranjel, V., 1986, Solução pacífica de controvérsia: o impacto dos organizações internacionais. *Anuario jurídico interamericano*, **36**, pp. 19-51.

—c. *Emory journal of international dispute resolution.* Emory University, School of Law, Atlanta, GA, 1986-, vol. 1-, semi-annual. Directed by T. Buergenthal.

The focus is on development of PIL by international tribunals and international commercial arbitration.

578a. Boulery, C., *Bibliography on the peaceful settlement of international disputes/Bibliographie sur le règlement pacifique des conflits internationaux.* Geneva: Henry-Dunant Institute, 1990.

Lists in systematic arrangement some 2,400 references to relevant materials published worldwide.

—b. Kleckner, S.-M., *Peaceful settlement of disputes in international law: a bibliography*. Dobbs Ferry, NY: Oceana, 1985, 96 pp. (Collection of Bibliographic and Research Resources).

vii. PEACE, WAR

a. Peace

579a. Use of force. War and neutrality. Peace treaties. *Enc. PIL*, 1982, 3 (A–M); 4 (N–Z).

The more than 90 essays examine aggression, the Geneva Red Cross Conventions, the Hague Peace Conferences, humanitarian law, neutrality, nuclear warfare, reparations, use of force, war and weapons.

—b. Rumpf, H., 1984, The concepts of peace and war in international law. *GYIL* 27, pp. 429–443.

Discusses the dualism of legal versus non-legal conceptual aspects mainly with reference to the UN Charter and resolutions.

580a. *Völkerrecht und Friede. Beiträge der Tagung 'Völkerrecht und Friede'*, Kreuth, 1984, Akademie für Politik und Zeitgeschehen der Hannes-Seidel-Stiftung. Heidelberg: Müller, 1985, 184 pp. (Heidelberger Forum, 37).

—b. Boasson, C., 1968, The place of international law in peace research. *Journal of peace research*, 5(1), pp. 28–42.

—c. Rikhye, I.J., *The theory and practice of peacekeeping*. London: Hurst, 1984, 255 pp.

Traces the evolution of peacekeeping and the role of the United Nations therein (UN Emergency Force, UN Peacekeeping Force in Cyprus, UN Interim Force in Lebanon, etc.).

—d. Avakov, M.M., (ed.), *OON kak instrument po podderzhaniiu i ukrepleniiu mira: mezhdunarodno-pravovye problemy*. [Under the auspices of] Diplomaticheskaia Akademiia SSSR. Moskva: Mezhdunarodnye Otnosheniia, 1980, 259 pp.

581a. Ferencz, B.B., *Enforcing international law: a way to world peace*. Dobbs Ferry, NY: Oceana, 1981, 2 vols.

Vol. 1 examines the application (including sanctions) of PIL; vol. 2 contains texts of primary and secondary (mainly post-1945) PIL materials meant to illustrate the enforcement of PIL. The work is the last part of Ferencz's trilogy, which includes *Defining international aggression; the search for world peace* (1975, 2 vols) and *An international criminal court: a step toward world peace* [704a].

—b. Israel, F.L., *Major peace treaties of modern history, 1648–1967*. With an introductory essay by A. Toynbee. New York: Chelsea House, 1967, 4 vols.

Contains annotated texts in English of selected peace treaties. *See also* [297, vol. 4].

582a. Laszlo, E. and Yoo, J.Y. (eds), *World encyclopedia of peace*. Oxford: Pergamon, 1986, 4 vols.

Vol. 3 includes texts of selected treaties geared to the maintenance of peace and a list and biographies of Nobel Peace Prize laureates. Vol. 4 lists institutes, periodicals and conferences (including the Pugwash Conferences) concerned with peace research.

—b. *Pugwash Conferences on Science and World Affairs*. 1957-, 1st-, annual. Permanent Offices in Geneva (11A, ave. de la Paix), London (63A Great Russell Street) and Rome (Via della Lungara 229).

The conferences take their name from the location of the 1st meeting held in 1957 in Pugwash, Nova Scotia, Canada. In addition to the annual Conferences, symposia and workshops are also held worldwide, several times a year, with a view to contributing to the maintenance of world peace. Participants, usually outstanding scientists, examine problems of security, disarmament, development, prevention of nuclear war, etc. *See Proceedings of annual Pugwash Conferences* (1957–85); Rotblat, J., *A history of the Pugwash Conferences*. Cambridge, MA: MIT Press, 1972; *Newsletter*, 1962-, 1-, quarterly.

—c. *Journal of conflict resolution: research on war and peace between and within nations*. Newbury Park, CA: Sage, 1957-, 1-, quarterly.

—d. *UNESCO yearbook on peace and conflict studies*. Westport, CT: Greenwood Press, 1980-, 1-, annual.

Part 1 contains substantive articles (including aspects of PIL); part 2 concerns peace activities and research, mainly by UNESCO.

583a. Woodhouse, T. (ed.), *The international peace directory*. Plymouth: Northcote House, 1988, 189 pp.

Arranged alphabetically by countries, the directory lists nearly 600 institutions (many from the 1970s on), as well as relevant periodicals, concerned with peace research; has bibliography and index.

—b. *World directory of peace research institutions*, 4th edn. Paris: UNESCO, 1981, 213 pp. (Reports and Papers in the Social Sciences, 49).

Produced by UNESCO's Social Science Documentation Centre with the collaboration of the Division of Human Rights and Peace, the directory lists 280 institutions.

—c. Carroll, B.A. *et al.*, *Peace and war: a guide to bibliographies*. Santa Barbara, CA: ABC-Clio, 1983, 580 pp. (The War/Peace Bibliography Series, 16).

An annotated list of some 1,400 bibliographies published from 1785 to 1980, in

b. Disarmament

the form of monographs, periodical articles and end-bibliographies; systematically arranged, with subject index.

584a. *Status of multilateral arms regulation and disarmament agreements*, 2nd edn. New York: UN, 1983, 176 pp. (UN sales no. E.83.IX.5).

Contains the text of 11 multilateral agreements and their status as of 31 December 1982. Compiled by the UN Department for Disarmament Affairs in cooperation with the UN Office of Legal Affairs. The information in this work is annually updated in the *UN Disarmament Yearbook* [584e].

—b. Goldblat, J., *Agreements for arms control: a critical survey*. London: Taylor & Francis, 1982, 387 pp.

Published on the occasion of the 1982 Special Session of the UN General Assembly and under the auspices of SIPRI [588a], the work outlines the scope of obligation in, and compliance with, bi- and multilateral arms control agreements (mostly since 1945); texts of relevant treaties are indicated on pp. 112-303.

—c. *The Conference on Disarmament*. Geneva: Committee on Disarmament, 1979-.

This multilateral disarmament negotiating body continues the work of the *Eighteen-Nation Conference(s) on Disarmament (ENCD)*, convened in Geneva from 1962 to 1978. The permanent agenda of the *Conference* is geared to the implementation of the international disarmament strategy (adopted by the Special Session of the UN General Assembly, 1982), including the verification and control measures relating to nuclear and other arms, and the linkage between disarmament and development. The annual *Report* [of the Conference] *to the UN General Assembly* (UN document CD/year) contains the organization, participants and activities of the Conference in a given year; the annexes include a list of documents issued by the Committee on Disarmament and a subject and country index of statements made to the *Conference*. For a brief description of the *Conference* see *Fact sheet No. 46*. New York: UN Dept of Disarmament Affairs, July 1986, 20 pp.

—d. *The United Nations and disarmament: a short history*. New York: UN Dept of Disarmament Affairs, 1988, 111 pp.

—e. *United Nations Disarmament Yearbook*. New York: UN Dept of Disarmament Affairs, 1976-, 1-, annual. (UN sales publication E.year.IX.number).

Complemented by *The United Nations General Assembly and disarmament*. New York: UN Dept of Disarmament Affairs, 1984-, 1-. *See also* [588a].

—f. *Terminology relevant to arms control and outer space*. Geneva: Committee on

Disarmament, 1986, 20 pp. (UN document CD/716; CD/OS/WP.15, 16 July 1986).

585a. Kalshoven, F., 1985/II, Arms, armaments and international law. *RCADI,* **191**, pp. 187-340.

A historical outline of wartime use of weapons from 1868 to 1934 and of relevant diplomatic conferences during 1974-7; reviews the law of disarmament within and outside the United Nations context.

—b. Israelian, V. L., *Organizatsiia Ob"edinënnykh Natsii i razoruzhenie.* Moskva: Mezhdunarodnye Otnosheniia, 1981, 230 pp.

See also [562d].

—c. Sheik R. Ali, *The peace and nuclear war dictionary.* Santa Barbara, CA: ABC-Clio Press, 1989, 350 pp. (Clio Dictionaries in Political Science).

Lists some 400 concepts, events, programmes, etc. relating to peace and war.

—d. Chilaty, D., *Disarmament: a historical review of negotiations and treaties.* Teheran, 1978, 404 p.

Published under the auspices of the Iran National University (printed in Switzerland), the work traces the evolution of disarmament in terms of its relevance to freely negotiated peace endeavours from 1899 to 1977, especially with reference to the Hague Peace Conferences, the London Naval Conference, conferences held under the auspices of the LoN and the UN and the Strategic Arms Limitation Talks.

—e. McWhinney, E., *The international law of détente: arms control, European security and East-West co-operation.* Alphen a/R: Sijthoff & Noordhoff, 1978, 272 pp.

Discusses disarmament within the PIL context since 1945 and with reference especially to NATO and the Warsaw Pact in their implications for peaceful co-existence, human rights, etc. Includes extensive bibliographic references to Western and socialist publications in the field.

586a. *Le droit international et les armes: Colloque, Montpellier, 1982.* Paris: Pédone, 1983, 366 pp. (Actes du 16. Colloque de la Société française pour le droit international).

—b. *Armes nucléaires et droit international/Nuclear weapons and international law.* Actes du Colloque, Genève, 1984, préparés par Z. Meriboute. Torino: A. Meynier, 1985, 189 pp.

Prepared under the auspices of the Geneva International Peace Research Institute (GIPRI), the work examines the control of nuclear arms in PIL terms.

—c. Shaker, M. I., *The nuclear non-proliferation treaty: origin and implementation, 1959-1979.* Dobbs Ferry, NY: Oceana, 1980-1, 3 vols.

587a. Blishchenko, I. P., *Obychnoe oruzh'e i mezhdunarodnoe pravo.* Moskva: Mezhdunarodnye Otnosheniia, 1984, 215 pp.

—b. Kaliadin, A. N., *Mezhdunarodnyĭ mekhanizm peregovorov po razoruzheniiu*. Moskva: Nauka, 1984, 100 pp. (ANSSSR. Nauchnyĭ Sovet po Issledoviŭniiu Problem Mira i Razoruzheniia. Mezhdunarodnyĭ mir i razoruzhenie, vyp. 21).

—c. *Assumptions and perceptions in disarmament: a documentary research study of Soviet and American images and conceptions*. Geneva: UN, 1984 (UN sales no. GV.E.84.0.4).

See also Rosas, A. in [184].

588a. *SIPRI yearbook: world armaments and disarmament*. Stockholm: Almquist & Wiksell; Oxford: Oxford UP, 1969–, 1–, annual.

Published under the auspices of the Stockholm International Peace Research Institute (SIPRI), the yearbook provides information on the trends in world military expenditures and arms race, as well as progress in disarmament. *See also UN Disarmament Yearbook* [584e].

—b. *Arms control: the journal of arms control and disarmament*. London: F. Cass, 1980–, 1–, three times yearly.

589a. [Cot, J.-P.], *Répertoire de la recherche sur le désarmement/Repertory of disarmament research*. Geneva: UN, 1982, 454 pp. (UN sales publication GV.E.82.0.2).

Produced by the UN Institute for Disarmament Research (UNIDIR) the work contains references to completed and ongoing disarmament research, as well as to auxiliary materials (bibliographies, official materials) in the field.

—b. Disarmament. *UN Terminology bulletin no. 335*. New York: UN, 1986, 315 pp. (UN document ST/CS/SER.F/335; UN sales publication MULT.86.I.14).

A multilingual (Arabic, Chinese, English, French, Russian, Spanish) glossary relative to disarmament terms used in UN conferences, documents. *See also Disarmament terminology* . . . by the Language Services Div. of the Foreign Office of the FR of Germany. . . . Berlin: W. de Gruyter, 1982, 645 pp. Based on the *UN Terminology Bulletin no. 310* (1978), this is a multilingual (English, German, French, Spanish, Russian) glossary of disarmament terms.

—c. Elliot, J. M. and Reginald, R., *The arms control, disarmament, and military security dictionary*. Santa Barbara, CA: ABC-Clio Press, 1989, 325 pp.

Includes definitions of détente, conventional weapons and nuclear strategy.

—d. Atkins, S. E., *Arms control and disarmament and military, international security, and peace; an annotated guide to sources*. Santa Barbara, CA: ABC-Clio Press, 1989, 411 pp.

Includes references to English-language materials (secondary, auxiliary) published since 1980.

c. Neutrality

590. Deak, F. and Jessup, P. (eds), *A collection of neutrality laws, regulations and treaties of various countries*. Washington, DC: Carnegie Endowment for International Peace, Div. International Law, 1939, 2 vols.

Prepared under the auspices of the Harvard Law School as part of its 'Research in international law' [389b], the *Collection* includes texts relating to neutrality contained in national official (legislative, treaty, etc.) materials for the period 1800-1938. Part 1, neutrality laws, regulations arranged by countries; part 2: treaty provisions concerning neutrality rights, duties.

591a. Bindschedler, R., 1982, Neutrality: concept and general rule. *Enc. PIL*, **4**, pp. 9-14.

—b. Nagore, A.P., 1977, The changing concept of neutrality and its significance under modern international law. *Lawyer* (Madras), **9**, pp. 179-182.

—c. The evolution of the notion of neutrality in modern armed conflict. In [604a].

—d. Ogley, F., *The theory and practice of neutrality in the twentieth century*. London: Routledge & Kegan Paul, 1970, 217 pp.

d. Use of force, war

592a. Levie, H.S., *The code of international armed conflict*. Dobbs Ferry, NY: Oceana, 1986, 2 vols.

Describes conventional and customary rules contained in various international/national materials. The work codifies the law of armed conflict in general, and of war in particular. Each of the 14 broad topical parts (definitions, warfare, persons, protective institutions, compliance with the law of war, etc.) contains relevant rules (or paragraphs or articles thereof) with regard not to their source but rather to their illustrative value in showing the substance in the given codificatory part. Each item in the code contains commentaries and source citations. An author and subject index concludes the work.

—b. Zourek, J., *L'Interdiction de l'emploi de force en droit international*. Leiden: Sijthoff; Genève: Institut Henry-Dunant, 1974, 155 pp.

Examines the limitation and/or prohibition of force in international relations, with the focus on *jus ad bellum*.

—c. Brownlie, I., *International law and the use of force by states*. Oxford: Clarendon Press, 1963, 532 pp.

593a. Calogeropoulos-Stratis, S., *Le recours à la force dans la société internationale*. Paris: LGDJ; Lausanne: Eds LEP, 1986, 191 pp.

Published with the aid of the Fondation Latsis Internationale, the work traces the history of the use of force, including war, on the basis of state practice and doctrinal perceptions. Chapters 6 and 8-10 concern the role of the UN with reference to international security and peacekeeping operations. Contains extensive bibliographic notes.

—b. Cassese, A. (ed.), *Legal restraints on the use of force forty years after the UN Charter: developments in international law*. Dordrecht: Nijhoff, 1986, 546 pp. For a similar earlier work *see* his *Current problems of international law: essays on UN law and the law of armed conflict*. Milano: Giuffrè, 1975, 375 pp.

—c. Rousseau, C., *Le droit des conflits armés*. Paris: Pédone, 1983, 629 pp.

Outlines concepts of war, belligerency, warfare, victims and neutrality, and compares the traditional law of war with contemporary regulation of the use of force in a system of collective security. *See also* [600d].

—d. *Menzhinskiĭ, V. I., *Neprimenenie sily v mezhdunarodnykh otnosheniiakh*. Moskva, 1976.

Interprets the use of force in terms of political, economic and military coercion rather than in the sense of the UN Charter's 'armed force'.

—e. Delivanis, J., *La légitime défense en droit international public moderne: le droit international face à ses limites*. Paris: LGDJ, 1971, 201 pp. (Bibliothèque de droit international, 59).

594a. Rifaat, A. M., *International aggression: a study of the legal concept, its development and definition in international law*. Stockholm: Almquist & Wiksell; Atlantic Highlands, NJ: Humanities Press, 1979, 355 pp.

Traces the evolution of the concept from earliest times to the mid-twentieth century.

—b. Broms, B., 1977/I, The definition of aggression. *RCADI*, **154**, pp. 299-400.

Traces the evolution of the concept within the context of the LoN and the UN General Assembly, Special Commission on the Question of Defining Aggression (Resolution 3314/XXIX, 1974).

—c. Schwebel, S. M., 1972/II, Aggression, intervention and self-defence in modern international law. *RCADI*, **136**, pp. 411-498.

—d. *Definition of aggression: a select bibliography*. New York: UN, DHL, 1976, 20 pp. (UN document ST/LIB/109).

See also [581a, 703a].

595a. Johnson, J. T., *Can modern war be just?* New Haven, CT: Yale UP, 1984, 215 pp.

—b. Haggenmacher, P., *Grotius et la doctrine de la guerre juste*. Paris: Presses universitaires de France, 1983, 682 pp. (Publications de l'Institut universitaire de hautes études internationales, Genève).

e. Humanitarian law

596a. Schindler, D. and Toman, J., *The laws of armed conflict: a collection of conventions, resolutions and other documents*, 3rd edn. Dordrecht: Nijhoff, 1988, 1,033 pp. 2nd edn. Alphen a/R: Sijthoff & Noordhoff, 1981, 933 pp.; 1st edn. Leiden: Sijthoff, 1973, 832 pp.

Published under the auspices of the Henry-Dunant Institute [611a] the 3rd edition contains texts mainly of multilateral conventions for the period 1863-1980 concerning *jus in bello*, i.e. the conduct of hostilities, means of warfare, protection of populations, victims of war, war crimes and neutrality. Systematically arranged with subject index.

—b. Friedman, L., *The law of war: a documentary history*. New York: Random House, 1972, 2 vols.

Contains relevant texts for the period 1856-1971, including the Hague Conventions, the Geneva Conventions and the Treaty of Versailles. Vol. 2 contains exclusively texts of war crimes trials.

—c. Roberts, A. and Guelff, R., *Documents on the laws of war*. Oxford: Clarendon Press, 1982, 498 pp.

Contains a selection of relevant texts for the period 1856-1981, including the Hague and Geneva Conventions, as well as several UN conventions on the subject. Chronologically arranged.

597. Perruchoud, R., *Les résolutions des conférences internationales de la Croix Rouge*. Genève: Institut Henry-Dunant, 1979, 470 pp.

Examines the legal nature and implementation of over 600 resolutions adopted between 1863 and 1977 by international conferences under the aegis of the International Committee of the Red Cross [610a]. On the basis of these resolutions it also traces the evolution of Red Cross activities. *See also* [610b].

598a. *Final Record of the Diplomatic Conference of Geneva of 1949*. Bern: Federal Political Dept, 1950, 3 vols. French edition, *Actes de la Conférence diplomatique de Genève de 1949*.

The Conference was convened at Geneva from 21 April to 12 August 1949 by the Swiss Federal Council for the purpose of revising the Xth Hague Convention of 18 October 1907 and the Geneva Convention of 27 July 1929, and to establish a convention for the protection of civilian persons in time of war. The *Final Record* includes the text of the four 1949 Geneva Conventions.

—b.   I. *Geneva Convention for the Amelioration of the Condition of the Wounded and Sick in Armed Forces in the Field.* II. *Geneva Convention for the Amelioration of the Condition of Wounded, Sick and Shipwrecked Members of Armed Forces at Sea.* III. *Geneva Convention Relative to the Treatment of Prisoners of War.* IV. *Geneva Convention Relative to the Protection of Civilian Persons in Time of War.*

The text of the four *Geneva Conventions of 12 August 1949* is contained in the *International Red Cross Handbook* [610b]. The International Committee of the Red Cross [610a] at regular intervals issues separate English (latest, 1986), French (latest, 1981) and Spanish (latest, 1981) editions of the *Conventions*; texts of the Conventions are also contained in [596a], and their official translations are referred to in [614a]. *See also* [599b].

—c.   *Les conventions de Genève du 12 août 1949: commentaire.* Publié sous la direction de J. Pictet. Genève: Comité international de la Croix Rouge, 1952-56, 4 vols.

Contains the commentaries on the four Geneva Conventions of 1949 [598b].

—d.   Toman, J., *Index of the Geneva Conventions for the Protection of War Victims of 12 August 1949.* Geneva: Henry-Dunant Institute; Leiden: Sijthoff, 1973, 194 pp.

The *Index* tabulates the rules of the 1907 Hague and 1949 Geneva Conventions applicable to civilian and military agents parties to armed conflicts. The alphabetical subject arrangement facilitates the identification of rules relevant to given practical aspects of (recognized) international armed conflicts. For an updated version of the *Index see* [600c].

—e.   Draper, G. I. A. D., 1965/I, The Geneva Conventions of 1949. *RCADI,* **114**, pp. 63-162.

—f.   de La Pradelle, P. G., *La Conférence diplomatique et les nouvelles conventions de Genève du 12 août 1949.* Paris: Editions internationales, 1951, 423 pp.

See also Scelle, G., *Jus in bello, jus ad bellum* in *Varia juris gentium* [289].

599a.   *Diplomatic Conference(s) on the Reaffirmation and Development of International Humanitarian Law Applicable in Armed Conflicts, Geneva, 1974-1977. Official records.* Bern: Federal Political Dept, 1978, 17 vols. Also in Arabic, French, Russian and Spanish editions.

The *Official records* contain the proceedings of the Conferences, as well as the texts of the *Protocols Additional to the Geneva Conventions of 12 August 1949* [599b].

—b.   *Protocols additional to the Geneva Conventions of 12 August 1949.* Geneva: International Committee of the Red Cross, 1977, 124 pp.

Contains the text of Protocol I Relative to the Protection of Victims of International Armed Conflict and of Protocol II Relative to the Protection of Victims of Non-International Armed Conflict. The provisions in the two Protocols of 8 June 1977 enlarge upon the material rules contained notably in the IVth Geneva

Convention Relative to the Protection of Civilian Persons in Time of War, and also with reference to belligerent occupation during land warfare. Protocol II develops the general principles contained in article 3 common to all four 1949 Geneva Conventions [598b]. For references to official translations of the Protocols *see* [614a].

600a. *Commentary on the Additional Protocols of 8 June 1977 to the Geneva Conventions of 12 August 1949.* Editors: Y. Sandoz, C. Swinarski, B. Zimmermann with the collaboration of J. Pictet. Dordrecht: Nijhoff; Geneva: ICRC, 1987. 1,625 pp. French ed. 1986. 1,646 p.

Contains the historical background and signed commentaries of legal opinions on each article of the two Protocols, taking into account the work of the 1977 Diplomatic Conference [599a] and other preparatory documents; p. xxviii defines humanitarian law in general, and with reference to the Protocols in particular. A bibliography and an index conclude the work.

—b. Bothe, M., Partsch, K. J., Solf, W. A. and Eaton, M., *New rules for victims of armed conflict: commentary on the two Protocols Additional to the Geneva Conventions of 1949.* The Hague: Nijhoff, 1982. 746 p.

The commentators participated as members of the Delegations of their countries, and in this capacity provide a guide to the drafting history of the Protocols.

—c. Solf, W.A. and Roach, J.A., *Index of international humanitarian law.* Revised edition. Geneva: ICRC, 1987. 283 pp.

The *Index* updates [598d] by tabulating in systematic order over 600 rules contained in the 1907 Hague, the four Geneva Conventions, and the two 1977 Protocols Additional to the Geneva Conventions.

—d. Schindler, D., 1979/II, The different types of armed conflicts according to the Geneva Conventions and Protocols. *RCADI,* **163**, pp. 117-164.

Whereas Schindler is more concerned with concepts (e.g. war versus use of force), Draper [598e] mainly discusses procedures used by 'the protecting power system', i.e. legal advisers, fact-finding commissions, etc. in monitoring observance of the law of war, or means for restoring observance when the law of war has been violated.

601a. Levie, H.S., *Protection of war victims: Protocol I to the 1949 Geneva Conventions.* Dobbs Ferry, NY: Oceana, 1979-81, 4 vols.

In systematic arrangement provides a cross-referencing to the official records and thereby traces the (1973-7) negotiating and drafting process underlying the individual articles of Protocol I.

—b. Levie, H.S., *The law of non-international armed conflict: Protocol II to the 1949 Geneva Conventions.* Dordrecht: Nijhoff, 1987, 635 pp.

Concerns the analysis of Protocol II, using a methodology similar to that in [601a].

—c. Abi-Saab, R., *Droit humanitaire et conflicts internes: origines et évolution de la réglementation internationale*. Paris: Pédone, 1986, 280 pp.

Covers the legislative history of article 3 common to all four 1949 Geneva Conventions (and as such at times referred to as a 'mini-convention' in itself), as well as the content of the rules in article 3 by the 1977 Protocol II concerning the protection of victims of non-international armed conflicts. Based on her PhD thesis, Graduate Institute for International Studies, Geneva, 1985.

602a. *Les dimensions internationales du droit humanitaire*. Paris: Pédone, 1986, 360 pp.

Published under the auspices of UNESCO and the Henry-Dunant Institute, the work commemorates the fortieth anniversary of UNESCO and the international year of peace, and is intended as a teaching manual. The contributions by Abi-Saab, Baxter, Blishchenko, Blix, Herczeg and Ruda, with an introduction by J. Pictet and conclusion by K. Vasak, concern the nature and development of humanitarian law in general, and the law of armed conflicts (international and non-international) in particular. An extensive bibliographic guide concludes the manual.

—b. Herczeg, Gy., *Development of international humanitarian law*. Translated by S. Simon. Budapest: Akadémiai Kiadó, 1984, 239 pp.

—c. Fahl, G., *Humanitäres Völkerrecht*. Berlin: Berlin Verlag, 1983, 390 pp.

—d. Pictet, J., *Développement et principes du droit international humanitaire*. Paris: Pédone, 1983, 99 pp.

Based on a course at the International Institute of Human Rights, Strasbourg, the essay traces the history of humanitarian thinking and its relevance to the Geneva Conventions and Additional Protocols. Exists in Arabic, English and Spanish editions. *See also* Coursier, H., 1960/I, L'Evolution du droit international humanitaire. *RCADI,* **99**, pp. 340-465.

—e. Rosenblad, E., *International humanitarian law of armed conflicts: some aspects of the principle of distinction and related problems*. Geneva: Henry-Dunant Institute, 1979, 200 pp.

Examines the obligation of belligerents at all times to observe a distinction between combatants and military objectives on the one hand, and civilians and civilian objectives on the other, as reflected in relevant treaties, customary rules, national regulations, etc.

603a. *Studies and essays on international humanitarian law and Red Cross principles/Etudes et essais de droit international humanitaire et de principes de la Croix-Rouge*. Edited by C. Swinarski. Dordrecht: Nijhoff, 1984, 1,200 pp.

Published under the auspices of the ICRC, the contributions by Abi-Saab, Perruchoud, Zimmermann *et al.* honour the work of J. Pictet and deal with the Geneva Conventions and Protocols, the International Red Cross, and the nexus between humanitarian law and human rights.

—b. *Im Dienst an der Gemeinschaft: Festschrift für D. Schindler zum 65. Geburtstag.* Herausgegeben von W. Haller *et al.* Basel: Helbing & Lichtenhahn, 1989, 826 pp.

604a. *VII. Congress of the International Society for Military Law and the Law of War, San Remo, 1976.* [Proceedings published in] *Revue de droit pénal militaire et de droit de la guerre (Bruxelles), 1978,* **17**(1), pp. 10–209.

—b. *Atti del Convegno internazionale di diritto umanitario/Actes du Congrès international de droit humanitaire/Proceedings of the International Conference on Humanitarian Law, San Remo, 1970.* Lugano: Grassi, 1971, 385 pp.

Contains contributions by Draper, McBride, Schwarzenberger *et al.* on the interdisciplinary aspects of humanitarian law.

—c. *Droit humanitaire et conflits armés.* [*Colloque, Bruxelles, 1970*]. Bruxelles: Ed. de l'Université de Bruxelles, 1976, 302 pp. (Bruxelles, Université libre, Institut de sociologie, Centre de droit international, 7).

The contributions by Draper, Farer, Zorgbibe *et al.* aim at defining armed conflicts, including civil war, and at categorizing combatants, including guerillas.

605a. Levie, H. S., *Prisoners of war in international conflict.* Newport, RI: Naval War College Press, 1979, 529 pp. (Naval War College, International Law Studies, 59).

Examines the status and treatment of prisoners of war, mainly with the focus on the Third Geneva Convention, 1949, devoted to this topic. Levie's is a presentation of pragmatic findings in a topical and functional arrangement based on relevant primary sources.

—b. Levie, H. S., *Documents on prisoners of war.* Newport, RI: Naval War College Press, 1979, 853 pp. (Naval War College. International Law Studies, 60).

A collection of primary sources including the Geneva Conventions. Chronologically arranged (1648–1977), the work represents the documentary background to [605a].

606a. Luard, D. E. T., *The international regulation of civil law.* London: Thames & Hudson, 1972, 240 pp.

—b. Falk, R. A. (ed.), *The international law of civil war.* Baltimore, MD: Johns Hopkins UP, 1971, 452 pp.

Mainly a political analysis of the American Civil War, the Algerian revolution and the post-independence wars in the Congo, Vietnam and Yemen, with reference to domestic conflict and foreign intervention.

—c. Pinto, R., 1965/I, Les règles du droit international concernant la guerre civile. *RCADI*, **114**, pp. 451-553.

607a. Suter, K., *An international law of guerrilla warfare: the global politics of law-making*. London: Frances Pinter, 1984, 192 pp. (Global Politics).

—b. Veuthey, M., *Guérilla et droit humanitaire*, 2nd edn. Genève: CICR, 1983, 451 pp. 1st edn 1976.

Examines the relevance of humanitarian law to national liberation movements, guerrilla warfare, terrorism, etc. Contains an extensive bibliography. *See also* Hentsch, T., 1977, Comment aborder le problème de la violence? *Annales d'études internationales*, **8**, pp. 159-170 (includes a critical review of the 1st edn. of Veuthey's work). *See also* Chaumont in [206].

608a. el-Kouhene, M., *Les garanties fondamentales de la personne en droit humanitaire et droits de l'homme*. Dordrecht: Nijhoff, 1986, 258 pp.

—b. Calogeropoulos-Stratis, A. S., *Droit humanitaire et droits de l'homme: la protection de la personne en période de conflit armé*. Alphen a/R: Sijthoff & Noordhoff, 1981, 258 pp. (Collection de droit international, 7).

609a. Nahlik, S. E., 1979/III, L'Extension du statut de combattant à la lumière du Protocole de Genève de 1977. *RCADI*, **164**, pp. 171-250.

—b. Khairallah, D. L., *Insurrection under international law, with emphasis on the rights and duties of insurgents*. Beirut: Lebanese University, 1973, 398 pp.

610a. *International Committee of the Red Cross/Comité international de la Croix-Rouge*. 17, ave. de la Paix, 1211 Geneva.

ICRC has convened international conferences since 1863. In addition to conference proceedings, reports and information booklets, ICRC regularly publishes various language editions of conventions, as well as a journal [613a], an *Annual report* (1925-, 1-) and a *Handbook* [610b].

—b. *The International Red Cross Handbook*, 12th edn. Geneva: ICRC/Henry-Dunant Institute, 1983, 744 pp. 1st edn 1889. Also in French and Spanish editions.

Part 1 includes the text of the 1949 Geneva Conventions and the 1977 Additional Protocols, as well as the texts of the 1864 Geneva Convention and of selected post-1970 conventions (before 1970 the *Handbook* contained the texts of all conventions concluded under the Red Cross aegis). Part 2 contains the statutes of the Red Cross, the rules of procedures of the League of Red Cross Societies, and regulations of various funds and institutes. Part 3 includes a selection of resolutions adopted at international conferences [597], a list of which is contained in the annexes (also including sessions of the Red Cross General Council and General Assembly).

—c. Willemin, G. *et al.*, *The International Committee of the Red Cross: international organization and the evolution of world society*. Dordrecht: Nijhoff, 1984, 300 pp.

Co-published with the Graduate Institute of International Studies, Geneva, the work examines the activities of the ICRC in terms of its institutional and political reactions to the evolving international society. *See also* Forsythe, D. P., *Humanitarian politics: the International Committee of the Red Cross*. Baltimore, MD: Johns Hopkins UP, 1977, 298 pp. (covers the period 1945-75); Freymond, J., *Guerres, révolutions, Croix-Rouge: réflexions sur le rôle du Comité international de la Croix-Rouge*. Genève: Institut universitaire de hautes études internationales, 1976, 222 pp. (Collection HEI-Presse, 3).

611a. *Henry-Dunant Institute*. 114, rue de Lausanne, 1202 Geneva.

Founded in 1965 under the auspices of the ICRD and with the aid of Swiss authorities, the activities of the Institute comprise research, study and teaching, publishing of substantive and documentary studies in the field of humanitarian law, and development within the context of peace. The Institute's Documentation Centre maintains a growing collection of primary and secondary materials on humanitarian law, human rights, the history of the Red Cross, etc., and provides computerized retrieval of information in the aforementioned subjects.

—b. *International Institute of Humanitarian Law/Istituto internazionale di diritto umanitario*. Villa Nobel, Corso Inglesi 352/A, 18038 San Remo, Italy.

Promotes the development of humanitarian law and to this end convenes international conferences [604b]; publishes a *Yearbook* (1984-, 1-).

612a. *Index on the teaching of international humanitarian law in academic institutions/ Répertoire sur l'enseignement du droit international humanitaire dans les milieux académiques/Repertorio de la enseñanza del derecho internacional humanitario en centros de enseñanza superior*. Geneva: Henry-Dunant Institute, 1987, looseleaf.

Arranged by countries and therein by institutions. Each entry provides information on the type of instruction (obligatory/elective; courses/seminars; teaching staff; number of students; titles of lectures/courses).

—b. *The war system: an interdisciplinary research*. Edited by R. A. Falk and S. S. Kim. Boulder, CO: Westview Press, 1980, 659 pp. (Westview Special Studies in Peace, Conflict and Conflict Resolution).

An anthology of the causes and the prevention of war. Using the systems/interdisciplinary approach, the work includes an inquiry into the role of international law for controlling the use of force (e.g. political and economic aggression as a cause of war).

—c. Verri, P., *Dictionnaire du droit international des conflits armés*. Genève: Comité international de la Croix Rouge, 1988, 142 pp.

Translated from Italian.

—d. Tabory, M., 1981, Language rights in international humanitarian law. *International Review of the Red Cross*, **21**(223), pp. 187-200.

613a. *Revue internationale de la Croix Rouge.* Genève: Comité international de la Croix Rouge, 1869–, 1–. English edition published since 1961, Spanish edition since 1976, Arabic edition in preparation.

—b. *Revue de droit pénal et de droit de la guerre.* Bruxelles: Palais de Justice, 1907–, 1–, monthly.

614a. *Bibliography of international humanitarian law applicable in armed conflicts*, 2nd edn. Geneva: ICRC/Henry-Dunant Institute, 1987, 605 pp. 1st edn compiled by H.T. Huynh, published in 1980, 389 pp.

Contains over 6,600 references to primary and secondary materials (including monographs, periodical articles, dissertations, selected commemorative essays and documents) published worldwide from the seventeenth century to the 1980s. Arranged in six parts concerned with: general studies, codification; international armed conflict (including wars of national liberation; status of combatants; means of warfare, protection of war victims); non-international armed conflict (including civil war, etc.); implementation of humanitarian law (including national military manuals; chapter 5 concerns war crimes); neutrality in time of war. Includes references to official translations of convention protocol texts. A keyword-in-titles index and an author index conclude the bibliography, preceded by English and French tables of contents. Complementing the two editions of the *Bibliography* is a *Basic bibliography of international humanitarian law.* Compiled by M. Severis and C. Seydoux. Geneva: Henry-Dunant Institute, 1985, 106 pp. (itself a continuation of *International humanitarian law: basic bibliography*, issued by the Institute in mimeographed form in 1977 and 1979). The 1985 *Basic bibliography* is restricted to recent English and French (secondary) materials selected from the extensive 1st (printed) 1980 edition of the *Bibliography.*

—b. Levie, H.S., *The law of war and neutrality: a selective English-language bibliography.* Dobbs Ferry, NY: Oceana, 1988 (Collection of Bibliographic and Research Resources).

Contains references to English-language publications, periodical articles concerned primarily with *jus in bello*; as such it complements in part [614a], notably with the section on different wars (Sino-Japanese, First and Second World Wars, Vietnam, Falklands, Iran–Iraq, etc.). Includes sections on military occupation, civil war, wars of national liberation, war crimes and neutrality. Arranged systematically, with an author index.

II/D. Specialized Aspects of PIL

615. Gupta, U.-N., *Developments on the frontiers of international law.* Allahabad, India: Allahabad Law Agency, 1983, 185 pp.

Outlines current developments in: the organizational base for international law; human rights in the contemporary international legal order; international economic law; international criminal law; and the new law of the sea. *See also* [379a] for developments up to the 1960s in the law of war, the law of the sea, international environmental law, international medical law, etc.

i. LAW OF INTERNATIONAL ORGANIZATION

a. General

616a. Kapteyn, P.J.G. (ed.), *International organization and integration: annotated basic documents and descriptive directory of international organizations and arrangements*, 2nd rev. edn. The Hague: Nijhoff, 1981-4, 2 vols in 5.

Published under the auspices of the Cornelis van Vollenhoven Foundation, Leiden, and the Foundation European Institute, Leiden, the work was first published in 1968, edited by H.F. van Panhuys and based on a collection of documents entitled *United Nations textbook* (1950). Contains in topical/subject arrangement constitutional texts and selected conventions related to intergovernmental organizations in the UN system, as well as other specialized, regional organizations. For a similar, older collection *see also* Peaslee, A.J. (ed.),

International governmental organizations; constitutional documents, 2nd edn. The Hague: Nijhoff, 1961, 2 vols. 1st edn 1956.

—b. *United Nations juridical yearbook*. New York: UN Office of Legal Affairs, 1963-, 1-, annual. (UN sales publication E, F.V.date; UN document ST/LEG/SER.C/1-). The separate French edition is titled *Annuaire juridique des Nations Unies*.

Published with a lag of several years (the 1983 *Yearbook* was published in 1990), the *Yearbook* consists of four parts: (1) Legal status of the UN and related intergovernmental organizations, based on national legislative texts relating to such status; (2) Texts of treaty provisions relating to the legal status (e.g. privileges, immunities; headquarter agreements, etc.) of the organizations; (3) Judicial decisions (by international and national tribunals) relating to the organizations; (4) Legal bibliography concerning the organizations in the UN system, as well as PIL relating to such organizations.

617a. *Legislative texts and treaty provisions concerning the legal status, privileges and immunities of international organizations/Textes législatifs et dispositions concernant le statut juridique, les privilèges et les immunités d'organisations internationales*. New York: United Nations, 1959-61, 2 vols (UN document ST/LEG/SER.B/10-11; UN sales publication EF.60.V.2; EF.61.V.3).

The work contains the legislative background and includes the texts of the *Convention on the privileges and immunities of the United Nations, 13 February 1946* (text also in *UNTS*, vol. 1, 1946/7, pp. 15-33) and of the *Convention on the privileges and immunities of the Specialized Agencies, 21 November 1947* (text also in *UNTS*, vol. 33, 1949, pp. 261-303). Several model text agreements (between the UN and SAs) are also appended. *See also* [641b].

—b. Duffar, J., *Contribution à l'étude des privilèges et immunités des organisations internationales*. Paris: LGDJ, 1982, 391 pp. (Bibliothèque de droit international, 83).

—c. Ahluwalia, K., *The legal status, privileges and immunities of the Specialized organizations*. The Hague: Nijhoff, 1964, 342 pp. Based on his PhD thesis, Columbia University, 1960.

Part 1 contains an analysis of the trend towards the abandonment of the theory of the absolute immunity of state (as part of the PIL tenet of privileges and immunities in general). Part 2 discusses the privileges and immunities of the UN and SAs in terms of 'functional necessity' rather than with reference to 'sovereign immunity'.

618a. *Vienna Convention on the Law of Treaties concluded between States and International Organizations and between International Organizations, 21 March 1986*. New York: UN, 1986, 60 pp. (UN document A/CONF.129/15). Also in Arabic, Chinese, French, Russian and Spanish editions.

Not yet in force; for commentaries *see* Reuter and Riphagen in [201]; Zemanek in [621a]. The *1986 Convention* codifies and complements the *Agreements between the UN and the SAs and the IAEA* (UN document ST/SG/14; UN sales publication EF 61.X.1) and the *Inter-Agency agreements and agreements between SAs and other intergovernmental organizations* (UN document ST/SG/3; UN sales publication EF 53.X.2).

—b. *A select bibliography on the law of treaties between States and International Organizations and between International Organizations*. New York: UN Dag Hammarskjöld Library, 1985, 33 pp. (UN document ST/LIB/SER.B/36).

Prepared for the UN Conference on the Law of Treaties concluded between States and International Organizations resulting in [618a].

619a. *Digest of legal activities of international organizations and other institutions*, 8th edn. Dobbs Ferry, NY: Oceana, 1988, loose-leaf. 1st edn 1970.

The outcome of a UNIDROIT [425a] decision in 1968, the *Digest* summarizes the legal activities of 38 international inter-governmental and non-governmental organizations. The arrangement is broadly by subjects and the slant is towards private international law. The *Digest* covers the activities, among others, of the Asian–African Legal Consultative Committee [383], the International Law Association [379], the International Association of Legal Sciences [382] and UNIDROIT [425a]. The information in the latest loose-leaf edition replaces the information in previous editions. *See also* [640b].

—b. United Nations Administrative Tribunal. *Judgements*. New York: UN Office of Legal Affairs, 1958-, 1- (UN document AT/DEC/1-).

Contains English and French texts of judgements in response to claims of UN and SA (except ILO) staff members mainly concerning reinstatements, terminations and pensionable remuneration aspects. Each volume contains texts of judgements (in 1990 up to judgement no. 501), a list of statutory provisions, rules referred to in the judgements, a table of cases/parties, a bibliography about the Tribunal, and a subject index. In the interval between the published volumes, *Judgements* are issued in abridged, mimeographed form, as are the verbatim records of the public hearings of the Tribunal. Summaries of the *Judgements* are also listed in [616b].

—c. de Vuyst, B.M., *Statutes and rules of procedure of international administrative tribunals*. Washington, DC: World Bank Administrative Tribunal, 1981, 2 vols.

Contains the Statutes and Rules of 12 international administrative tribunals and appeals boards concerned with settlement of disputes between staff and administrative bodies of intergovernmental organizations.

—d. Balladore-Pallieri, G., 1969/II, Le droit des organisations internationales. *RCADI*, **127**, pp. 1–36.

—e. Thompson, L. and Rodrigues, S., 1983, International administrative tribunals: current status and related bibliography. *IJLI*, **11**, pp. 130-142.

620a. Bowett, D.W., *The law of international institutions*, 4th edn. London: Stevens, 1982, 431 pp.

Published under the auspices of the London Institute of World Affairs the four parts of the work deal with: (1) global institutions, (2) regional institutions, (3) judicial institutions and (4) common institutional problems (e.g. international personality, treaty-making powers, responsibility and choice of law).

—b. Schermers, H.G., *International institutional law*. Leiden: Sijthoff, 1972-4, 3 vols.

Vol. 1, structure and classification of institutions; vol. 2, functioning and legal order of institutions; vol. 3, teaching and materials (including a methodological outline, bibliography and selected case materials).

—c. Seidl-Hohenveldern I., *Das Recht der internationalen Organisationen, einschliesslich der supranationalen Gemeinschaften*, 4th edn. Köln: Heymann, 1984, 420 pp. 1st edn 1967.

The work is intended for use in conjunction with the author's *Völkerrecht* [140].

—d. Monaco, R., 1977/III, Les principes régissant la structure et le fonctionnement des organisations internationales. *RCADI*, **56**, pp. 79-225.

See also a collection of the author's essays, *Scritti di diritto delle organizzazioni internazionali*. Milano: Giuffrè, 1981, 633 pp.

—e. *Shibaeva, E.A. and Potochnyi, M.V., *Pravovye voprosy struktury i deiatel'nosti mezhdunarodnykh organizatsiĭ*. Moskva, 1980. See also *Krivchikova, E.S., *Osnovy teoriĭ prava mezhdunarodnykh organizatsiĭ*. Moskva, 1979.

621a. *Völkerrecht, Recht der internationalen Organisationen, Weltwirtschaftrecht/Law of nations, law of international organizations, world's economic law. Festschrift für Ignaz Seidl-Hohenfeldern/Liber amicorum honouring Ignaz Seidl-Hohenfeldern*. Edited by K.K. Böckstiegel *et al.* Köln: Heymanns, 1988, 708 pp.

Includes contributions by C. Dominicé, La nature et l'étendu de l'immunité de juridiction des organisations internationales; C. Tomuschat, Jurisdictional immunities of states and their property. The draft Convention of the ILC; and K. Zemanek, The UN Conference on the law of treaties between states and international organizations or between international organizations. The unrecorded history of its general agreement.

—b. *Liber amicorum for the Rt Hon. Lord Wilberforce*. Edited by M. Bos and I. Brownlie. Oxford: Clarendon Press, 1987, 251 pp.

Includes contributions by R. Jennings, Universal law in a multicultural world;

T. O. Elias, The General Assembly and the problem of enhancing the effectiveness of the non-use of force in international relations; M. Mateesco-Matte: Global satellite telecommunications. Part III deals with arbitration and commercial law.

—c. *International collection of essays . . . in memoriam of Sir Otto Kahn-Freund.* München: Beck, 1980.

Includes N. Valticos, Le développement d'une jurisprudence internationale au sujet des normes établies par les organisations internationales, spécialement à propos des normes relatives au travail.

—d. *International organization: law in movement, essays in honour of John McMahon.* Edited by J. E. S. Fawcett and R. Higgins. London: Oxford UP, 1974, 182 pp.

Published for the Royal Institute of International Affairs, the essays include ones by I. Brownlie, The United Nations as a form of government, and R. Higgins, The desirability of third-party adjudication. *See also* Lachs, M., Le rôle des organisations internationales dans la formation du droit international. In *Mélanges offerts à H. Rolin* [480a].

622. Schreuer, C. H., *Decisions of international institutions before international courts.* Dobbs Ferry, NY: Oceana, 1981, 420 pp.

Examines the impact of IGO decision-making on litigation before municipal courts. *See also* [625a].

623a. Charpentier, J., 1983/IV, Le contrôle par les organisations internationales de l'execution des obligations des Etats. *RCADI*, **182**, pp. 143–246.

—b. *L'inspection internationale. Quinze études de la pratique des Etats et des organisations internationales.* Bruxelles: Bruylant, 1976, 521 pp. (Collection Organisation internationale et relations internationales).

The contributions by G. Fisher, D. Vignes, M. Bedjaoui *et al.* examine the means and types of control IGOs, notably the UN, may exercise over given state activities relating to the maintenance of peace, observance of (legal) rules in socioeconomic matters, etc. The activities of the UN and SAs are evaluated in documents periodically issued by the UN Joint Inspection Unit (UN document JIU/REP).

624a. Simon, D., *L'interprétation judiciaire des traités d'organisations internationales; morphologie des conventions et fonctions juridictionnelles.* Paris: Pédone, 1981, 936 pp.

—b. Lauterpacht, E., 1976, The development of the law of international organization by the decisions of international tribunals. *RCADI*, **152**, pp. 377–478.

—c. Rideau, J., *Juridictions internationales et contrôle du respect des traités constitutifs des organisations internationales.* Paris: LGDJ, 1969, 382 pp. (Bibliothèque de droit international, 47).

—d. Chiu, H., *The capacity of international organizations to conclude treaties and the special legal aspects of the treaties so concluded*. The Hague: Nijhoff, 1966, 242 pp.

See also Zemanek, *Das Vertragsrecht internationaler Organisationen*. Wien, 1957; [650a,c].

625a. Schwebel, S.M. (ed.), *The efffectiveness of international decisions. Papers of a Conference of the American Society of International Law and the Proceedings of the Conference*. Leiden: Sijthoff, 1971, 538 pp.

—b. Dupuy, R.-J., 1960/II, Le droit des relations internationales entre les organisations internationales. *RCADI*, **100**, pp. 457-589.

—c. Broms, B., The doctrine of equality of states as applied in international organizations. PhD thesis, Helsinki, 1959, 348 pp.

626a. Rouyer-Hameray, B., *Les compétences implicites des organisations internationales*. Paris: LGDJ, 1962, 111 pp. (Bibliothèque de droit internationale, 25).

—b. Radoĭnov, P., 1975, La compétence des organisations internationales: examen critique des principales théories doctrinales. *Droit international* (Sofia), pp. 213-242.

—c. Schermers, H.G., 1975, Succession of states and international organizations. *NYIL*, **6**, pp. 103-119.

—d. Boutros-Ghali, B., 1960/II, Le principe d'égalité des états et les organisations internationales. *RCADI*, **100**, pp. 5-73.

See also [182].

627a. Abi-Saab, G. (ed.), *The concept of international organization*. Paris: UNESCO, 1981, 245 pp. French edition *Le concept d'organisation internationale*.

This collection of ten articles, some of which were previously published in the *International social science journal* (Paris: UNESCO), traces the conceptual evolution (in international and national terms) of and methodological approach to international organization.

—b. Archer, C., *International organizations*. London: Allen & Unwin, 1983, 193 pp. (Key Concepts in International Relations, 1).

—c. *Kaliadin, A.N., *Aktual'nye problemy deĭatel'nosti mezhdunarodnykh organizatsiĭ: teoriĭa i praktika*. Moskva: Mezhdunarodnye Otnosheniĭa, 1982, 351 pp.

—d. Medina Ortega, M., *Teoria y formación de la sociedad internacional*. Madrid: Tecnos, 1983, 624 pp. (Semilla y surco: Colección de ciencias sociales. Serie de relaciones internacionales).

628a. International organizations in general. *Enc. PIL*, 1983, vols 5 and 6.

—b. *Les organisations internationales entre l'innovation et la stagnation . . . Colloque de Lausanne, 1984*. Textes rassemblés par N. Jéquier, et préfacés par F. Muheim. Lausanne: Presses polytechniques romandes, 1985, 271 pp.

The contributions by P. de Senarclens, T. van Boven, P. Braillard, etc. deal with multilateral diplomacy within the context of international organizations, as well as the need for their reforms.

—c. Bennett, A. L., *International organizations: principles and issues*, 3rd edn. Englewood Cliffs, NJ: Prentice-Hall, 1984, 498 pp.

Includes chapters on new (structural, functional) dimensions of IGOs, as well as retrospective and prospective assessments of their activities.

Auxiliary resources

629a. *Union of International Associations*. 1, rue aux Laines, 1000 Bruxelles, Belgium.

Serves as an information centre on international inter- and non-governmental organizations. Publishes the *Yearbook of international organizations* [630a].

—b. *International Association of Political Scientists for the United Nations*. PO Box 1219, Vienna International Centre, Vienna, Austria.

Founded in 1986, this NGO, independent of the United Nations, is concerned with the theory and practice of international organizations in general, and the application of United Nations tenets of internationalism, multilateralism and interdependence in particular. Publishes *IAPSUN reports*, 1988–, 1–, irregular.

—c. *Academic Council on the United Nations System*. ACUNS/United Nations Institute, Dickey Endowment, 207 Baker Library/Box 6025, Darmouth College, Hanover, NH 03755, USA.

Created in 1987, ACUNS is an international association of educational and research institutions, scholars and practitioners whose work is designed to prepare new teaching materials and enhance research and professional development within the context of the programmes and bodies of the United Nations system. Towards this end the Council maintains an annual review of programmes and policies within the UN system, sponsors the J.W. Holmes Memorial Lectures, and issues relevant publications [638a]. *See also* [638c].

630a. *Yearbook of international organizations*, 26th edn. Edited by the Union of International Associations [629a]. München: Saur, 1989/90. 1st edn 1948; annual.

The latest edition of the *Yearbook* consists of three volumes: vol. 1 contains names and descriptions of organizations; vol. 2 represents a country approach to organizations; vol. 3 is a classified subject directory of organizations in their 'global action networks'. Included are some 300 inter-governmental and over 3,000 non-governmental organizations, information about them regularly updated in the journal *Associations* (Bruxelles: UIA, 1955-, 1-, monthly). For a historical survey of IGOs and NGOs *see* Speeckaert, G. P., *The 1,978 international organizations founded since the Congress of Vienna*. Bruxelles: UIA, 1957.

—b. *International Geneva yearbook: organization and activities of international institutions in Geneva*. Dordrecht: Nijhoff, 1988-, 1-.

Part 1 contains articles and opinions (e.g. 1988: structural reform of the ILO and the codification of diplomatic law by ILC). Part 2 is an institutional guide to Geneva-based IGOs and NGOs.

—c. Chakhmakchev, A. G., *Nauchno-informatsionnaia deiatel'nost' mezhdunarodnykh organizatsii*. Moskva: Vsesoiuznyĭ Institut Nauchnoĭ i Tekhnicheskoĭ Informatsii (VINITI), 1977, 118 pp.

Provides brief information on (mostly documentary) activities by selected IGOs, mainly in the UN system, and a few NGOs.

—d. Bettati, M., Dupuy, P. M. and Beigbeder, Y., *Les ONG et le droit international*. Paris: Economica, 1986, 318 pp.

631a. Schaaf, R. W., 1986, International organizations documentation: serving research needs of the legal community. *Government Publications Review*, **13**(1), pp. 123-133.

See also his International organization documentation and international law collections. *Law library journal*, 1983, **76**(3), pp. 483-495 and his column 'International documentation' in [414a]; [659b].

—b. Hajnal, P. I. (ed.), *International information: documents publications, and information systems of international governmental organizations*. Englewood, CO: Libraries Unlimited, 1988, 339 pp.

Contributions by J.J. Cherns, P. Hernon, L. Marulli-Koenig, N. Leneman, C. Walker *et al.*, specialists in the field of international organization materials, examine the nature, availability and bibliographic control of publications and documents issued by international intergovernmental organizations, as well as problems of classification, citation form, computerization, reference and user services of international materials.

—c. *International documents for the '80s: their role and use*. Edited by T. D. Dimitrov. Proceedings of the 2nd World Symposium on International Documentation, Brussels, 20-22 June 1980. Berlin: W. de Gruyter, 1982, 570 pp.

—d. *Sources, organization and utilization of international documentation*. Proceedings of the [1st] International Symposium on the Documentation of the United Nations and Other Intergovernmental Organizations, Geneva, 21-23 August 1972. The Hague: Federation of International Documentation, 1974, 586 pp. (FID Publication 506).

Sponsored by UNITAR [672b], the 1972 and 1982 symposia address the problem of the growing output of international materials, especially in terms of their physical and bibliographic control.

632a. Advisory Committee for the Co-ordination of Information Systems (ACCIS), *Directory of United Nations databases and information systems (DUNDIS)*. New York: UN, 1984-, 1- (UN sales publ. GV.E.year.0.5).

First published by the Inter-Organization Board for Information Systems (IOB, Geneva). Computer-produced and regularly updated. Refers to databases containing materials issued by and/or relating to activities of inter-governmental organizations, as well as information systems permitting retrieval from the aforementioned databases in some 40 organizations in the UN system. Each entry contains the address of the organization, the types of (primary, secondary) holdings of the databases and their subject coverage (including relevant indexing tools) and printed computer outputs (handbooks, index to resolutions, etc.). A name or acronym, subject and geographical index conclude the work. *See also Providing access to United Nations databases: a guide for United Nations database producers*. Geneva: ACCIS, 1988, 90 pp., which contains guidelines and issues for consideration relating to databases in the UN system. *See also* [633a].

—b. Advisory Committee for the Co-ordination of Information Systems (ACCIS). *Directory of United Nations serial publications*. New York: UN, 1988, 500 pp. (UN sales publication GV.E.87.0.3).

Superseding the *Register of United Nations serial publications*. Geneva: Inter-Organization Board for Information Systems (IOB), 1982, the *Directory* lists some 4,000 current and non-current serial publications issued by some 40 organizations in the UN system; since 1987 such serials have carried the International Serials Data System (ISDS) number. Organization, subject and ISDS indexes complete the *Directory*.

—c. *International bibliography: publications of intergovernmental organizations*. Lanham, MD: UNIPUB, 1973-, 1-; New York: Kraus International Publ., 1988-, 16-, quarterly.

Superseding *International bibliography, information, documentation* (IBID), the quarterly issues of *International bibliography* provide summaries of selected current monographs and periodicals issued by the UN, SAs and regional intergovernmental organizations. Each issue contains a subject index (annually cumulated) and the contents of selected periodicals. *See also* the column by L. Marulli-Koenig, 'International documents round-up', in *Documents to the people*. Chicago, IL: American Library Association, Government Documents Round Table (GODORT), 1972-, 1-, bimonthly.

633a. *Directory of libraries and documentation centres in the UN system*. Geneva: UNOG Library, 1979, 84 pp. (Publications of the Library. Series E. Guides and Studies 1. UN sales publ. GV.E.79.I.9).

Superseded by *DUNDIS* [632a]; complemented by [633b].

240   SELECTED SUBJECT BIBLIOGRAPHY

—b.   *Guide to the archives of international organizations.* Paris: UNESCO, 1984, vol. 1, *The UN system*, 279 pp. (The preliminary version of April 1979 issued as UNESCO doc.PGI/79/WS).

See also Conseil international des archives. *Actes de la . . . Conférence internationale de la Table ronde des archives*, notably: 6. Varsovie, 1961, *Droit international des archives.* Paris: Imprimerie nationale, 1963, 160 pp. (Part 1 deals with international legal aspects of archives, i.e. safeguarding archival records during territorial changes, occupation, war); 17. Cagliari, 1977, *Constitution et reconstitution des patrimoines archivistiques nationaux.* Paris: CIA, 1980, 143 pp. (Includes definitions of archival sources; the annexes deal with LoN, UN archival records.) *See also* note 5, p. 43.

—c.   *Association of International Libraries.* c/o UNOG Library, Palais des Nations, door 20, Geneva, Switzerland.

Founded in 1963 in Sofia, AIL promotes cooperation among libraries mainly of IGOs, but also with libraries of recognized international character. AIL has held annual meetings through the 1970s, and has convened symposia [631c,d] directed to the control of and access to materials issued by IGOs. AIL also advances international library networking, especially with a view to rendering compatible extant computerized library and information systems.

634a.   Dimitrov, T.D. (comp.), *World bibliography of international documentation.* Pleasantville, NY: UNIFO; Berlin: W. de Gruyter, 1981, 2 vols.

This is an updated and expanded edition of the author's *Documents of international organizations: a bibliographical handbook.* Chicago: ALA, 1973, 301 pp. Compared to 2,300 references in the 1973 edition, some 9,000 references are contained in the 1981 edition. Vol. 1 deals mainly with materials issued by organizations in the UN system. For vol. 2 *see* [450a].

—b.   Hüfner, K. and Naumann, J., *The United Nations system: international bibliography.* München: Verlag Dokumentation, 1976-9, 3 vols, in 5.

Contains references (mainly in English, French and Spanish) to monographs and periodical articles relative to (but exclusive of materials issued by) the United Nations and selected SAs.

—c.   Atherton, A.L., *International organizations: a guide to information sources.* Detroit, MI: Gale, 1976, 350 pp. (International Relations Information Guide series, 1).

Part 1 contains references to auxiliary materials mainly relative to international organizations (including some of their publications). Part 2 is a topical bibliography of materials in English concerning the role of international organizations in world politics, economic welfare and international law (chapter 7). Author, subject and title indexes conclude the guide.

—d.   Haas, M., *International organization: an interdisciplinary bibliography.* Stanford,

CA: Hoover Institute Press, 1970, 944 pp. (Stanford University, Hoover Institute on War, Revolution and Peace, Bibliographic series, 14).

In topical arrangement contains some 8,000 references to monographs and periodical articles published mainly between the mid-nineteenth and mid-twentieth centuries; excludes IGO materials. The focus is on the history, structure and function of IGOs and their role in world political, socio-economic development. *See also* Speeckaert, G.P., *Bibliographie sélective sur l'organisation internationale, 1885-1964*. Bruxelles: UAI, 1965, 150 pp. (FID Publication, 361), which contains some 1,000 references, in chronological arrangement, with the focus on the historical evolution of IGOs and NGOs.

635. *Who's who in the UN and related agencies*. New York: Arno Press, 1975, 785 pp.

A biographical directory of top-level UN and SA officials up to the early 1970s; because out of date, the directory should be complemented by information in [375].

636a. Tabory, M., *Multilingualism in international law and institutions*. Alphen A/R: Sijthoff & Noordhoff, 1980, 284 pp.

Examines translation and authentication problems in multilingual texts, mainly with reference to official (working/final) documents and publications of IGOs, especially the UN, as well as relating to the lingustic and interpretative provisions in the 1969 Vienna Convention on the Law of Treaties [1].

—b. *Léxique général anglais-français avec supplements espagnol-français et russe-français*, 3rd edn. New York: UN, 1982, 886 pp. (UN document ST/DCS/1/rev. 2).

Contains French, Russian and Spanish equivalents of some 20,000 English terms of general and/or specific linguistic usage in the UN system, including names of international conventions and declarations. Supersedes *Glossaire juridique et technique à l'usage des interprètes et traducteurs*. Genève: UNOG, 1959. *See also* [310].

—c. *Glossary of conference terms: English-French-Arabic*, 2nd edn. Paris: UNESCO, 1980, 91 pp., 83 pp., 113 pp. respectively.

See also [Arabic manual for translators]. Vienna: UNIDO, 1989, 3 vols (UN document ID/352 + addenda 1, 2); contains Arabic terminology relative to activities and documentation (also legal) in the UN system.

—d. *Broad terms for UN programmes and activities*. Geneva: IOB, 1979, 187 pp.

Represents a thesaurus of some 2,500 English terms relating to programmes and activities of 28 organizations in the UN system.

—e. Cholganskaĩa, V.L. (comp.), *Kratkiĭ mezhdunarodnyĭ terminologicheskiĭ spravochnik*. Moskva: Nauka, 1981, 410 pp.

Published under the auspices of the Akademiĩa Nauk SSSR, Institut Nauchnoĭ

Informatsii po Obshchestvennym Naukam, the work provides a selection of general and specialized terms (in Russian) used in the UN system. *See also* the author's *Publikatsii OON i ee spetsializirovannykh uchrezhdenii; istochniko-vedcheskii obzor za 1945–1975 g*, 2nd edn. Moskva: Nauka, 1977, 504 pp., representing a survey of selected UN and SA materials, but without an index.

—f. *International Information Centre for Terminology*. c/o Österreichisches Normungsinstitut, Leopoldstr. 4, 1020 Wien 11, Austria.

Coordinates world terminological activities and promotes computerized retrieval of (mono-, multilingual) terms from international databases.

637. *Acronyms and abbreviations covering the United Nations system and other international organizations*. New York: United Nations, 1981, 405 pp. (UN publication E/F/R/S. 81.1.26).

Supersedes the [UN] *Terminology Bulletin*, no. 311, 1978 (ST/CS/SER.F/311/Rev.1); contains over 800 acronyms in Arabic, Chinese, English, French, Russian and Spanish relative to UN and SA programmes and activities.

638a. Lyons, G.M., *Teaching about international organizations*. Hanover, NH: ACUNS, 1989.

Complements and supplants Rohn, P.H., *Basic course in international organization: an anthology of syllabi*. Beverly Hills, CA: Sage, 1970.

—b. Approaches to the study of international organization. *International social science journal* (UNESCO), 1977, **29** (1, Special issue) 178 pp.

See also Morozov, G., 1976, The teaching of the general problems of international organisations. *Transnational Associations*, **28**(3), pp. 136–140.

—c. *Institute for the Study of International Organisation*. University of Sussex, Stanmer House, Falmer, Brighton BN1 9QA, UK.

Founded in 1968, the Institute provides teaching and research relative (mainly) to international organizations in the UN system. *See also* [629c].

—d. *Rule of Law Research Center*. Duke University, Durham, NC 27706, USA.

Conducts research on the law of international organization relevant mainly to peace, security and disarmament in general, and the law of the United Nations in particular.

—e. *International organization*. Boston, MA: World Peace Foundation, 1947-,1-, quarterly (since 1973 published in Madison, WI).

The quarterly reports mainly on the current activities of the UN and SAs, but may also provide in-depth analyses of substantive problems specific to international organization in general. Includes bibliographic surveys. *See also Transnational associations*. Brussels, 1949-, 1-, bimonthly.

b. United Nations

639. *UN Conference on international organization, San Francisco, 1945. Documents.* London: UN Information, 1945-6, 16 vols, supplements 17-22; New York: UN, 1954-5, 6 vols. Microfilm edition by Oceana, Dobbs Ferry, NY.

Contains the complete records, in English and French, of the Conference constitutive of the UN and its Charter.

640a. *Annual report on the work of the Organization.* New York: United Nations, 1947-, 1-, annual (UN documents *Official Records, A/session/suppl. 1*).

The Secretary-General annually reports to the UN General Assembly on the UN activities in the period of July of the past and June of the current year.

—b. *Yearbook of the United Nations.* New York: United Nations, Dept of Public Information, 1946/7-, 1-, annual (UN sales publication E.year/I.1).

Part 1 deals in topical arrangement with political, socio-economic and legal activities of the UN; part 2 summarizes activities of intergovernmental organizations in the UN system. Although published with a 2-3 year lag (vol. 36, covering 1982 activities, was published in 1986), the *Yearbook* contains an important section on international organizations and PIL (including references to titles of treaties deposited with the UN in a given year and draft rules of procedures for given conferences). The appendices include the Roster of the UN, texts of the UN Charter and ICJ Statute, and agendas of principal UN organs. Subject, name and resolution indexes complete the *Yearbook*.

—c. *Annual review of United Nations affairs.* Dobbs Ferry, NY: Oceana, 1949-, 1-, annual.

A commercially published digest of UN activities in general, the *Review* includes agendas of given UN meetings, texts of selected documents and resolutions. Supplementing the *Annual review* is Hovet, T. and Hovet, E., *A chronology and fact book of the United Nations, 1941-1985*, 7th edn. Dobbs Ferry, NY: Oceana, 1986, 364 pp.

641a. *Repertory of practice of the United Nations organs.* New York: UN Office of Legal Affairs, 1955, 4 vols + index vol. (published in 1957). Supplements 1-, 1973-.

The *Repertory* is a digest of intermediary and final decisions by principal and subsidiary UN organs, as well as of statements and proposals by UN representatives and officials related to the UN Charter provisions for which 'significant practice had developed . . . throwing light upon the interpretation or particular provision'. The *Repertory* serves as a preparatory work should a revision of the Charter be undertaken in accordance with its article 109. The initial 4 vols + index vol. exist also in the French and Spanish editions; supplements 1-3 exist in French, while only part of supplement 1 exists in Spanish.

—b. [UN] Committee on Relations with the Host Country. *Report.* New York: United Nations, 1946-, 1-, annual (UN document A/GA session/supplement 26/year).

The Report deals with security of missions and safety of their personnel, and host country legislation on matters relating to international organizations on its territory (staff travel, commissary, etc.).

642a. Goodrich, L. M., Hambro, E. and Simons, A. P., *United Nations Charter: commentary and documents*, 3rd edn. New York: Columbia UP, 1969, 732 pp.

—b. Cot, J.-P. and Pellet, A., *La Charte des Nations Unies: commentaire article par article*. Edited by P. Tavernier. Paris: Economica, 1985, 1,553 pp.

See also [652a-d].

643a. *Resolutions and decisions adopted by the General Assembly during its [ ] session.* New York: United Nations, 1946-, 1-, annual (UN document *Official Records*, A/session no./suppl. 49).

The annual volume, issued in English, French, Russian and Spanish editions, contains the text of resolutions adopted in the next to last GA session. The texts of resolutions adopted at the latest GA session are contained in UN press releases. *See also Index to resolutions of the General Assembly, 1946-1970.* New York: UN, DHL, 1972, 2 vols (UN document ST/LIB/SER.H/1). Part 1, numerical list; part 2, subject index to resolutions. References to current resolutions are included in the *Index to the Proceedings of the General Assembly.* New York: UN, DHL, 1973- (UN document ST/LIB/SER.B/A/session no.). *See also The use of the terms 'declarations and recommendations': a memorandum of the UN Office of Legal Affairs.* (UN document E/CN.4/L610, 2.4.62). *See also* [654a-b].

—b. Djonovic, D.J. (comp.), *United Nations resolutions.* Series 1: *Resolutions adopted by the General Assembly.* Dobbs Ferry, NY: Oceana, 1973-, 1-.

A commercial complement to [640a], the work contains the texts of GA resolutions in chronological arrangement. Vol. 16, published in 1984, covers resolutions adopted during 1976/7.

644a. *Répertoire of the practice of the Security Council.* New York: UN Dept of Political and Security Council Affairs, 1946-, 1-, irregular (UN document ST/PSCA; UN sales publ. year/VII/1). 6th supplement 1969-71, published in 1976, 246 pp.

An expository empirical survey of the Council's procedures. *See also* [656].

—b. Djonovic, D.J. (comp.), *United Nations resolutions.* Series 2: *Security Council.* Dobbs Ferry, NY: Oceana, 1988-, 1-.

Chronologically arranged. Includes a subject index, voting records and documents referred to in the resolutions.

645. *United Nations legislative series/Série législative des Nations Unies.* New York:

United Nations, 1951-, 1- (UN document ST/LEG/SER.B/1- ; UN sales publication: language/year/V/number).

The codificatory publications (also in microfiche form) in the series represent preparatory work towards the progressive development of PIL at the recommendations of the International Law Commission [662a]. In 1988 a total of 21 volumes published in the series included: diplomatic and consular privileges and immunities in general [566a] and those of inter-governmental organizations in particular [617a]; national legislation and treaties relating to the law of the sea [539a] (including the territorial sea and the continental shelf); the succession of states in respect of matters other than treaties [530b]; the multilateral treaty-making process [513]. The advantage of the series is that in its volumes is gathered substantive information otherwise scattered among different international and national primary source materials. Summaries of the PIL research contained in the series also are contained in the *UN Juridical Yearbook* [616b] and/or the *ILC Yearbook* [662b]. *See also* [659a].

646. Daudet, Y., *Les conférences des Nations Unies pour la codification du droit international*. Paris: LGDJ, 1968, 352 pp. (Bibliothèque de droit international, 43).

Discusses the techniques and procedures of codificatory conferences, rather than their actual contents.

647a. *Is universality in jeopardy?* Report of a symposium organized by the United Nations in connection with the commemoration of the fortieth anniversary of the Organization, Geneva, 16-17 December 1985. New York: UN Dept of Public Information, 1987, 177 pp. (UN sales publ. GV.E.86.0.3) French edition *L'universalité est-elle menacée?*

The contributions by M. Bertrand, G. Abi-Saab, P. de Senarclens and H.R. Brewster examine the historical evolution of the concept of universality and its institutionalization in the UN. P. Alston centres on the 'elliptical' notion of human rights in their universality.

—b. *Regionalism and the United Nations*. Dobbs Ferry, NY: Oceana, 1978, 603 pp. (Published for UNITAR).

—c. *Seminar on the role of the United Nations in the development of international law, Patna University, 1970*. [Papers] edited by R.C. Hingorani. Bombay: Tripathi, 1972, 202 pp.

The mostly Indian contributions examine PIL in terms of the UN role in decolonization, human rights (Afro-Asian attitudes), outer space and the peaceful use of the sea-bed. The Patna Declaration (pp. 201-202) sets forth Indian and Nepalese principles for teaching PIL.

—d. *Les Nations Unies face à un monde en mutation, Genève, 1970. Actes du colloque*. Genève: Université de Genève, Faculté de droit, Département de droit international public et organisation internationale, 1971, 112 pp. (Colloque de Genève, 1).

648a. McWhinney, E., *United Nations law making: cultural and ideological relativism and international law making for an era of transition.* New York: Holmes & Meier; Paris: UNESCO, 1984, 274 pp. (New Challenges to International law, 3). French edition *Les Nations Unies et la formation du droit,* 1986.

Critically reviewed in *AJIL,* 1985, **79**, pp. 1088-1089. McWhinney analyses the processes, arenas and actors involved in the law of, and by, the United Nations in 'an era of transition'. Among the 'relativist' problems examined are the spatial dimensions of PIL (including its regional manifestations in the western hemisphere the socialist systems), the inter-temporal aspects of PIL (in its classical and contemporary terms), 'soft' and 'hard' PIL, and alternative world constructs and corresponding axiological problems (value conflicts, etc.).

—b. *L'adaptation des structures et méthodes des Nations Unies/The adaptation of structures and methods of the United Nations.* The Hague Academy International Law Workshop, 1985. Edited by D. Bardonnet. Dordrecht: Nijhoff, 1986, 416 pp.

The contributors to the 1985 Workshop held under the auspices of the Hague Academy of International Law [380b] include T.M. Franck, The role and future prospects of the Secretary-General; A. Bolintineanu and M.L. Sarin, two articles on the role of the UN in peaceful settlement of disputes; and W.D. Verwey, on the development of NIEO law. Part 3 contains articles on transformation of control methods in the UN system.

—c. Rajan, M.S. et al., *The UN and the non-aligned.* Dobbs Ferry, NY: Oceana, 1987, 388 pp.

649a. Bokor, H. Szegö, *The role of the United Nations in international legislation.* Amsterdam: North-Holland, 1978, 192 pp.

Translated from the Hungarian, the work examines the legislative competences of IGOs, notably the UN, and their role in creating international customary rules.

—b. Yemin, E., *Legislative powers in the United Nations and Specialized Agencies.* Leiden: Sijthoff, 1969, 244 pp.

The focus of the work is on the constituent instruments of inter-governmental organizations in terms of the current and potential legislative aspects of such instruments.

650a. Kasme, B., *La capacité de l'ONU de conclure des traités.* Paris: LGDJ, 1960, 214 pp. (Bibliothèque de droit international, 12).

See also [624d].

—b. Combacau, J., *Le pouvoir de sanction de l'ONU: étude théorique de la coercion non-militaire.* Paris: Pédone, 1974, 394 pp.

—c. Schachter, O., *Towards wider acceptance of UN treaties*. New York: Arno Press, 1971, 190 pp.

—d. Higgins, R., *The development of international law through the political organs of the United Nations*. New York: Oxford UP, 1963, 423 pp.

Examines state practice in terms of votes cast and opinions expressed within the UN political organs, and the resultant development of PIL. *See also* Schachter, O., 1948, The development of international law through the legal opinions of the UN Secretariat. *BYIL*, **25**, pp. 91-132.

651a. Sohn, L.B. (ed.), *Cases on United Nations law*, 2nd edn. Mineola, NY: Foundation Press, 1967, 1,086 pp. 1st edn, 1956.

Supersedes the author's *Cases and other materials on world law* (1950) covering the period 1920-50. The 1967 edn contains selected UN case law and documents of the 1950 to mid-1960s period, with the focus on international peace and security. Contains a concise introduction to UN documents and publications (including symbols, indexes, etc.).

—b. *Carrillo Salcedo, J.A., *Textos básicos de Naciones Unidas*, 2nd edn. Madrid, 1981.

652a. Cros, G., *La notion de conflit de normes conventionnelles selon la Charte des Nations Unies*. Montpellier, 1981, 271 leaves. PhD Thesis, Université de Montpellier.

—b. Cahier, P., La Charte des Nations Unies et les Etats, pp. 81-105 in [593b, 1986].

—c. *Colloque [sur] l'application de la Charte des Nations Unies, Nice, 1971*. [Rapport]. Nice: Institut de droit de la paix et du développement. Université de Nice, 1971, 50 pp.

—d. *UN Charter: bibliography*. New York: UN, DHL, 1978 (UN document ST/LIB/SER.B/139).

653a. Finley, B., *The structure of the United Nations General Assembly: its committees, commissions and other organisms, 1946-1973*. Dobbs Ferry, NY: Oceana, 1977, 3 vols.

—b. *Fel'dman, D.I. and I͡Anovskiĭ, M.V., *General'nai͡a Assambleï͡a OON i voprosy razvitii͡a mezhdunarodnogo prava*. Kazan', 1974.

Examines GA decisions in terms of their (re)defining the concept of state responsibility.

—c. *Asamoah, O., *The legal significance of the decisions of the General Assembly of the United Nations*. The Hague: Nijhoff, 1966, 274 pp.

—d. Chaudhri, M.A., *The 6th Committee of the GA and international law*. Durham, NC, 1978, 336 pp.

Based on his PhD thesis, Duke University, 1962. Examines the legal and constitutional aspects of the GA's 6th (legal) Committee, in terms of its rules of procedures relating to requests to the ICJ for advisory opinions, reports to the ILC, etc.

654a. Castañeda, J., *Legal effects of the United Nations resolutions*. New York: Columbia UP, 1970, 255 pp.

Contains a legal analysis of six types of GA resolutions in terms of their 'true juridical effects'. *See also* the author's Valeur juridique des résolutions des Nations Unies. *RCADI*, 1970/I, **129**, pp. 207-331.

—b. Di Qual, L., *Les effets des résolutions des Nations Unies*. Paris: LGDJ, 1967 (Bibliothèque de droit international, 37).

655a. Arangio-Ruiz, G., *The United Nations declaration on friendly relations and the system of the sources of international law, with an appendix on the concept of international law and the theory of international organization*. Alphen a/R: Sijthoff & Noordhoff, 1979, 341 pp.

A revised version is published as The normative role of the GA . . . and the Declaration. . . . *RCADI*, 1972/III, **137**, pp. 419-742; for the author's summary see *Enc. PIL*, 1986, **9**, pp. 135-139.

—b. *An international law analysis of the major United Nations resolutions concerning the Palestine Question*. New York: United Nations, 1979, 60 pp. (UN sales publication E.79.I.19). Also French edition.

656a. Krökel, M., *Die Bindungswirkung von Resolutionen des Sicherheitsrates der Vereinigten Nationen gegenüber Mietgliedstaaten*. Berlin: Duncker & Humblot, 1977, 187 pp. (Schriften zum Völkerrecht, 56). PhD thesis, Universität Bielefeld.

—b. Nicol, D., Croke, M. and Adeniran, B., *The United Nations Security Council: towards greater effectiveness*. New York: UNITAR, 1982, 334 pp. (UN sales publication 1982.XV.CR/15).

Based on a UNITAR seminar, the document includes discussion with Presidents of the Security Council during 1977-80.

657a. Virally, M., Gerbet, P., Salmon, J. and Ghébali, V.-Y., *Les missions permanentes auprès des organisations internationales*. Bruxelles: Bruylant, 1971-6, 4 vols.

Vol. 1, permanent missions in Geneva; vol. 2, case studies (OECD, ILO, etc.); vol. 3, permanent missions to the UN, vol. 4, 'conclusions théoriques'. *See also* Pindic, D.D., *Stalne misije pri Ujedinjenim Nacijama*. Beograd, 1964, 254 pp. PhD thesis, Beograd, Pravni Fakultet.

—b. Sybesma-Knol, R.G., *The status of observers in the United Nations*. Brussel: Vrije Universiteit Brussel, Centrum voor de Studie van het Recht van de Verenigde Naties en de Gespecialiseerde Organisaties, 1981, 484 pp.

SPECIALIZED ASPECTS 249

—c.   *Bogdanov, O.V., *Shtab-kvartira OON v N'iu Iorke: mezhdunarodno-pravovye aspekty*. Moskva, 1976.

—d.   Smouts, M.-C., *Le secrétaire-général des Nations Unies*. Paris: Colin, 1971, 301 pp.

Auxiliary resources

658.   Osmanczyk, E.J., *The encyclopedia of the United Nations and international agreements*. Philadelphia, PA; London: Taylor & Francis, 1985, 1,059 pp.

Issued on the occasion of the 40th anniversary of the UN, the *Encyclopedia* is the English version of the author's Polish work, *Encyklopedia spraw międzynarodowych i ONZ*. Warszawa: Pánstwowe Wydawnictwo Naukowe, 1974, 1,102 pp. The 1985 work, complete with title-pages in French, Spanish and Russian, outlines general and legal activities of the UN, and contains relevant (some legal) concepts, terms and occasional texts of treaties and agreements.

659a.   Kleckner, S.M., 1981, Major publications of the UN Office of Legal Affairs. *Law library journal*, **74**(1), pp. 69–86.

Originally presented at the 2nd World Symposium on International Documentation [631c], the article provides concise information notably on *UNTS* [2], the *UN legislative series* [645], the *UN juridical yearbook* [616b], the *Repertory of practice of UN organs* [641a] and the work of ILC [662a].

—b.   Ross, D., 1985, Legal functions and initiatives of the UN: a document librarian's view. *Law librarian*, **16**(1), pp. 41–48.

See also Auburn, F.M., 1973, UN documentation and international law. *Law librarian*, **4**(3), pp. 37–39.

660a.   *United Nations publications catalogue*. New York: UN Dept Conference Services, Publishing Div. Sales Sect., 1945–55 (1st), since 1956–, annual (UN document ST/DCS/SS/Cat./year).

Represents an official (UN published) guide to UN publications in print only, arranged by subject categories, i.e. international law (V), disarmament (XIV), human rights (II.D), etc. The *Catalogue* also includes publications by ICJ, ILC, UNITAR, UNCTAD, etc., but does not include all *Official Records* of the UN. A title index, arranged by broad subjects, concludes the work. Note *United Nations official records, 1962–1981*. New York: UN, 1982, 154 pp. (printed by Renouf Publ. Co., Montreal) represents a cumulative list of UN *Official Records* through the 1970s. *See also United Nations documentation news*. New York: UN Dag Hammarskjöld Library, 1981–, 1–, irregular. Includes information on selected recent UN activities, materials and/or bibliographic aids thereto.

—b.   *United Nations editorial manual*. New York: UN Dept Conference Services, 1983, 524 pp. (UN sales publication E.83.I.16; UN document ST/DCS/2).

250   SELECTED SUBJECT BIBLIOGRAPHY

'A compendium of rules and directives on United Nations editorial style, publication policies, procedures and practice', to be followed in drafting, editing and reproducing UN documents, publications and other written materials, primarily in English. Article D of the *Manual* deals with the citation of reports of legislative bodies, GA decisions, resolutions, etc.

—c.   *United Nations documents: current index (UNDOC)*. New York: UN, 1979-, 1-, 10 times yearly.

Supersedes *United Nations documents index (UNDEX*: 1970-8), which in turn superseded *United Nations documents index (UNDI*: 1950-73). A by-product of UNBIS [419b], *UNDOC* represents a comprehensive check-list of UN ('main series') documents, official records and sales publications, facilitating their content analysis and bibliographic retrieval by means of subject, author and titles indexes (in each *UNDOC* issue, with annual cumulations). Because *UNDOC* encompasses UN activities and materials in general, the documentary access to the PIL aspects therein is necessarily selective. *See also UNBIS Thesaurus*. New York: UN, DHL, 1985; supplement 1989. Contains English, French and Spanish alphabetical and hierarchical terms used in the subject analysis (including law/PIL) of UN programmes and materials for subsequent retrieval through *UNDOC*. *See also United Nations document series symbols, 1946-1977; cumulative list with indexes*. New York: UN, DHL, 1978, 312 pp. (UN document ST/LIB/SER.B/5/Rev. 3); supplement 1978-84, published in 1986, 160 pp. Arranged by series symbol (alpha-numerical), subjects and bodies responsible for the symbols.

—d.   Hajnal, P., *Guide to United Nations organization, documentation and publishing*. Dobbs Ferry, NY: Oceana, 1978, 450 pp.

Analyses within the structural context of the UN the pattern of its publishing, as well as the acquisition, use and retrieval of UN published materials. Includes a bibliography of primary and secondary publications, documents issued by or relating to the UN. In part updated in [631b]. *See also* [651a].

—e.   Bibliography of guides to United Nations documentation issued by commercial publishers. In *United Nations documentation: a brief guide*. New York: UN, 1981 (UN document ST/LIB/34/Rev. 1), pp. 46-47.

661a.   *Terminology bulletin*. New York: UN Dept Conference Services. Translation Div., Documentation and Terminology Sect., 1948-, 1-, irregular.

Individual issues contain glossaries on given topics, e.g. the law of the sea [558f], disarmament [589b], geographical [374b] and institutional [661b,c] matters.

—b.   *Organs and instruments of the United Nations/Organes et instruments des Nations Unies/Organos e instrumentos de las Naciones Unidas*. New York: UN, 1981, 89 pp. (*Terminology Bulletin* No. 318; UN document ST/CS/SER.F/318).

Title and text also in Arabic, Chinese and Russian. *See also Broad terms for UN programmes* in [636d].

c. *United Nations functions and titles/Titres et fonctions aux Nations Unies/Cargos y functiones en las Naciones Unidas*. New York: UN, 1981, 278 pp. (*Terminology Bulletin* No. 319; UN document ST/CS/SER.F/319).

Title and text also in Arabic, Chinese and Russian.

—d. *United Nations University*. Toho Seimer Bldg, 15- Shibuya 2-chome, Shibuya-ku, Tokyo 150, Japan.

Established in 1973 by a UN.GA resolution; functions as an international community of scholars engaged in research, postgraduate training and dissemination of knowledge in furtherance of the purposes and principles of the UN Charter, notably peace and conflict resolution.

—e. World Federation of UN Associations. c/o UN Office at Geneva, Palais des Nations, Geneva, Switzerland.

International Law Commission

662a. The *International Law Commission* (ILC) was created by the United Nations in 1947, as a successor to the *League of Nations Committee of Experts for the progressive codification of international law* [673b]. ILC is composed of 34 (increased from 25 by GA resolution 36/39, 18 November 1981) prominent legal practitioners or scholars representing the principal legal systems of the world. Elected in their individual capacity by the UN General Assembly, the members of ILC direct their work towards the progressive development of international law in keeping with article 24 of the *ILC Statute* (UN sales publication E.82.V.8). To this end ILC, through the Secretary-General of the UN, may request governments to furnish texts of laws, judicial decisions, etc. relevant to given PIL topics and rules. On the basis of such materials the ILC *Committee on the Progressive Development of International Law and its Codification* prepares statements on the actual conditions of given PIL issues and proposals for overcoming gaps and inconsistencies therein. The Committee's research activities to some extent reflect those formerly conducted by the LoN Committee and/or the *Harvard Research in International Law Program, 1927–1940* [389b].

A nearly two-year delay between the actual ILC session and the publications of its records, the consecutive numbering of the (ILC) documents regardless of the subjects covered therein, and the lack of relevant indexes makes the full use of these documents difficult. The Kleckner article [659a] and the *Guide to the documents of the ILC, 1949–1969*. Geneva: UNOG Library, 1970, 50 pp. (UN document ST/Geneva/LIB/SER.B/ref. 2) in part provide guidance to ILC materials up to the 1970s.

—b. *Yearbook of the International Law Commission*. New York: UN Office of Legal Affairs, 1957–, 1–, annual (in 2 vols) (UN document

A/CN.4/SER.A/1949-; UN sales publication: language/year/V/1-). French edition, *Annuaire de la Commission du droit international*.

Vol. 1 contains the summary records of the ILC sessions. Vol. 2, part 1 includes reports of special rapporteurs and other documents considered during the session; vol. 2, part 2 contains the *Report* of the ILC to the General Assembly (also issued as UN document A/session of GA/10). The records of the first seven sessions (1949-55) of the ILC were retrospectively published; they contain the text of documents in the original language and summary records in English only, as well as names of members and officers of the ILC and titles of multilateral conventions to which reference is made in the volume. The records of the 38th ILC session in 1986 deal with jurisdictional immunities of States, status of the diplomatic courier, 'Draft Code of Offences against the Peace and Security of Mankind' and state responsibility.

663a. Sinclair, I., *The International Law Commission*. Cambridge: Grotius Publications, 1987, 185 pp. (H. Lauterpacht Memorial Lectures, 7).

—b. UNITAR, *The International Law Commission: the need for a new direction*. New York: United Nations, 1981 (UN sales publication E.81.XV.PE/1; UNITAR document PE/1).

—c. Briggs, H.W., *The International Law Commission*. Ithaca, NY: Cornell UP, 1965, 380 pp.

See also [178, vol. 1].

International Court of Justice

664a. *International Court of Justice yearbook*. New York: United Nations, 1946/7-, 1-, annual. French edition: *Cour internationale de justice. Annuaire*. (Distributed by the UN Sales Section without a UN sales number).

Prepared by the ICJ Registry, the *Yearbook* is issued in the 3rd quarter of each year; its eight chapters contain: (1) organization of the ICJ; (2) bio bibliographies of ICJ justices; (3) jurisdiction of the ICJ; (4) texts governing the ICJ's jurisdiction and relationship to the UN and SAs; (5) functions and practice of the ICJ; (6) work of the ICJ in a given year (the summaries of judgements and advisory opinions cannot be quoted against, nor do they constitute interpretations of the actual texts of the relevant judgements and opinions); (7) publications of the ICJ and PCIJ; official citation of judgements, abbreviations of pleadings; (8) finances of the ICJ. The *Report* of the ICJ to the General Assembly is issued as UN document A/session [of GA]/4.; the ICJ Statute is annexed to the UN Charter (by virtue of its article 92) and also published in [664b].

—b. *Acts and documents concerning the organization of the Court*. The Hague: ICJ, 1-, irregular.

The latest issue (no. 4) was published in 1978 and contains the text of the 'Rules of the Court' revised in 1978, as well as an analytical table of concordances between the 1946, 1972 and 1978 texts of the 'Rules'. No. 1 is out of print.

—c. *Bibliographie de la Cour internationale de Justice/Bibliography of the International Court of Justice*. The Hague: ICJ, 1964/5-, 1-, annual.

Nos 1-18, 1947/8-1962/3, formed chapter 9 of *ICJ Yearbook* [664a]. The *Bibliography* lists references to publications, documents and periodical articles (available at the ICJ Library) concerned with the structure, functions, and activities (including pleadings and case law) of the ICJ, and/or international law and organization issues related to ICJ. *See also Bibliography on the International Court including the Permanent Court, 1918-1964*. Leiden: Sijthoff, 1966, 387 pp; [665b].

665a. Rosenne, S., *Documents on the International Court of Justice*, 2nd edn. Alphen a/R: Sijthoff & Noordhoff, 1979, 497 pp. 1st edn 1974.

Contains a selection of texts concerning the ICJ statute, rules and case law, as well as UN resolutions relating to the ICJ and declarations on the compulsory jurisdiction of ICJ. As such, to some extent, it duplicates the information contained in the *ICJ yearbook* [664a]. Rosenne's 1979 work essentially expands the (documentary) appendices contained in vol. 2 of his *The law and practice of the International Court*. Leiden: Sijthoff, 1965, 2 vols.

—b. Eisenmann, P. M., Coussirat-Coustère, V. and Hur, P., *Petit manuel de la jurisprudence de la Cour internationale de justice*, 4th edn. Paris: Pédone, 1984, 394 pp.

Part 1 includes summaries of selected ICJ judgements and advisory opinions; part 2 includes texts of basic documents relating to the ICJ. Meant for teaching purposes, the manual also contains a systematic evaluative bibliography of works about ICJ.

666a. Rosenne, S., *A commentary on the 1978 Rules of the International Court of Justice*. The Hague: Nijhoff, 1983, 305 pp.

An article-by-article analysis of the latest (1978) revision of the ICJ rules; also includes the annotated ICJ Statute.

—b. Guyomar, G., *Commentaire du règlement de la Cour international de justice adopté le 14 avril 1978*. Paris: Pédone, 1983, 760 pp.

Comments on the 1978 revision of ICJ rules; complements her commentary (Paris: Pédone, 1973) on the 1972 ICJ rules.

667a. Damrosch, L. F. (ed.), *The International Court of Justice at crossroads*. Dobbs Ferry, NY: Oceana/Transnational Publishers, 1987, 511 pp.

Published under the auspices of ASIL, the work consists of four parts: (1) system of compulsory jurisdiction; (2) typology and content of disputes examined by the ICJ; (3) special problems (including evidence of proof of facts); (4) the USA and ICJ.

—b. *La juridiction internationale permanente: Colloque de Lyon, 1986*. Paris: Pédone, 1987, 439 pp. (Actes du 20. Colloque de la Société française pour le droit international).

Includes contributions by A. Pillepich, P, Coussirat-Coustère, L. Condorelli and P. Kahn on procedural and substantive matters relating to the ICJ.

—c. Elias, T. O., *The International Court of Justice and some contemporary problems: essays in international law*. The Hague: Nijhoff, 1983, 384 pp.

Gives the views of one of the ICJ justices.

—d. McWhinney, E., *The World Court and the contemporary international law-making process*. Alphen a/R: Sijthoff & Noordhoff, 1979, 219 pp.

668. Thierry, H., 1980/II, Les résolutions des organes internationaux dans la jurisprudence de la CIJ. *RCADI*, **167**, pp. 389-450. *See also* Lauterpacht, E., [624b].

669a. Fitzmaurice, G., *The law and procedure of the International Court of Justice*. Cambridge: Grotius Publications, 1986, 2 vols.

Based on Fitzmaurice's articles in the *BYIL* during 1950-63, the collection analyses the ICJ jurisprudence with a view to arriving at the 'general principles and rules of law' underlying the case work.

—b. Rosenne, G., *Procedure in the International Court*. The Hague: Nijhoff, 1983, 305 pp.

Reviewed in *CYIL*, 1984, **22**, pp. 447.

—c. de Visscher, C., *Aspects récents du droit procédural de la Cour international de justice*. Paris: Pédone, 1966, 219 pp.

Analyses selected ICJ decisions reflecting specific concepts, e.g. the political and judicial aspects of an international dispute, the admissibility of a request for ICJ judgement, etc.

—d. Lauterpacht, H., *The development of international law by the International Court*. London: Stevens, 1958, 408 pp. Reprinted Cambridge: Grotius Publications, 1982, 409 pp.

670a. Elkind, J. B., *Non-appearance before the International Court of Justice: a functional and comparative analysis*. The Hague: Nijhoff, 1984, 224 pp.

Examines the concept of default in municipal and international law, as well as interim measures of protection and the types of self-judgements by states. *See also* Elkind, J. B., *Interim protection: a functional approach*. The Hague: Nijhoff, 1981.

—b. *Finkel, G., *Les avis consultatifs et la justice internationale*. PhD thesis, Grenoble, 1969, 2 vols.

—c. Shihata, I.F.I., *The power of the International Court to determine its own jurisdiction: compétence de la compétence*. The Hague: Nijhoff, 1965, 198 pp.

671a. Sicart-Bozec, M., *Les juges du Tiers-Monde à la Cour internationale de Justice*. Paris: Economica, 1986, 326 pp. (Collection Coopération et développement, 11).

Published under the auspices of Centre d'études et de recherches internationales et communautaires, Université Aix-Marseille III, Faculté de droit et de science politique, the work examines the 're-reading' of traditional PIL rules by ICJ justices from the Third World. Includes tables of the justices' nationality, tenure and education, and the typology (conservative, progressive, extremist) of the justices' case law approaches.

—b. Hussain, I., *Dissenting and separate opinions at the World Court*. The Hague: Nijhoff, 1984, 325 pp.

The Pakistani author analyses the potential of dissenting or separate opinions by ICJ justices in overcoming the dialectical conflict between traditional and contemporary PIL. Based on his PhD thesis, Université de Nice, 1974 (in French).

—c. Isaïa, H., 1975, Les opinions dissidentes des juges socialistes dans la jurisprudence de la Cour international de justice. *RGDIP*, **79**(3), pp. 657–718.

UNITAR

672a. *United Nations Programme of assistance in teaching, study, dissemination and wider appreciation of international law. Report of the Secretary-General*. New York: United Nations, 1985, 25 pp. (UN document A/40/893, 19 November 1985). Also in French.

The *Programme* was established by the General Assembly under its resolution 2099(XX), 20 December 1965, and has been continued under relevant resolutions repeated annually until 1971 and biennially thereafter. The Report of the S-G in 1985 contains information on: international law seminars held annually under the auspices of the ILC [662a] at the UN Office at Geneva; activities of the UN Office of the Special Representative of the S-G for the Law of the Sea; fellowships offered at national institutions; UNITAR activities; administrative and operational aspects of the *Programme*.

—b. *United Nations Institute for Training and Research* (UNITAR). c/o United Nations, United Nations Plaza, New York, NY 10017, USA.

Founded in 1963 as an autonomous training and research body within the UN, UNITAR aims to enhance the effectiveness of the UN objectives in general, and to implement the UN teaching programme [672a] in particular. Until 1985, UNITAR, jointly with the UN Office of Legal Affairs, awarded a limited number of fellowships intended to enable qualified government officials and university teachers of international law to acquire additional knowledge of the subject and of the legal work of the UN and SAs. Findings of UNITAR research, seminars, etc. are published as part of UN publications [660a] (until 1987 in category XV, thereafter in category III/K) or UNITAR document series, e.g. Conference reports (CR), Policy and efficacy studies (PE), Regional studies (RS) and Peaceful settlement series (PS).

League of Nations

673a. *League of Nations Conference on the codification of international law, 1930.* Edited by S. Rosenne. Dobbs Ferry, NY: Oceana, 1975, 4 vols.

Contains the records, including debates and minutes, of the First Conference on the codification of international law convened in 1930 by the League of Nations, as well as the editor's introduction to and notes on the Conference. In reply to the LoN Preparatory Committee's request (1927), 30 governments provided information on PIL, notably nationality, territorial waters and responsibility of states; this information, alongside materials from the *Harvard Research in International Law Program, 1927-1940* [389a], served as a basis for the discussions at the First Conference.

—b. *League of Nations Committee of Experts for the Progressive Codification of International Law (1925-1928).* Edited by S. Rosenne, Dobbs Ferry, NY: Oceana, 1972, 2 vols.

Precursor of the ILC [662a], the Committee held four sessions between 1925 and 1928, the work of which is extensively commented on by the editor. Vol. 1, Minutes; vol. 2, documents examined.

—c. *Répertoire of questions of general international law before the League of Nations, 1920-1940/Répertoire des questions du droit international général posées devant la Société des Nations.* Compiled by W. Schiffer, and published under the direction of A. C. Breycha-Vautier. Geneva: Geneva Research Centre, 1942, 390 pp.

674a. Aufricht, H., *Guide to the League of Nations publications: a bibliographical survey of the work of the League, 1920-1947.* New York: Columbia UP, 1951, 682 pp. Reprinted by AMS Press, New York, 1966.

The *Guide* lists and analyses LoN publications and documents within the context of the League's structure and functions. For a subject analysis of LoN materials *see* Breycha-Vautier, A. C., *Sources of information: a handbook on the publications of the League of Nations.* London: Allen & Unwin, 1939. *See also* Reno, E. A., *LoN documents, 1919-1945: a descriptive guide and key to microfilm collection.* New Haven, CT: Research Publs, 1973-, 1-.

—b. Ghébali, V.-Y. and Ghébali, C., *A répertoire of League of Nations serial documents, 1919-1947.* New York: Oceana, 1973, 2 vols.

675. *The League of Nations in retrospect/La Société des Nations: rétrospective.* Proceedings of the Symposium organized by the United Nations Library [Geneva] and the Graduate Institute of International Studies, Geneva, 1980. Berlin: W. de Gruyter, 1983, 427 pp. (UN Library, Geneva. Serial publications. Series E: Guides and Studies, 3).

The contributions examine: institutional aspects of the LoN; case studies of states and the LoN; financial, economic, social and humanitarian cooperation and the LoN. Reminiscences by V. Sokoline and a name index conclude the commemorative essays.

c. Selected Specialized Agencies

676a. Zarb, A., *Les institutions spécialisées dans le système des Nations Unies.* Paris: Pédone, 1980, 598 pp.

In four parts, Zarb's work traces the genesis, particularities, legal status/competences and membership (admission, participation and sanctions) of SAs in the UN system.

—b. Adam, H.-T., *Les organismes internationaux spécialisés: contribution à la théorie générale des établissements publics internationaux.* Paris: LGDJ, 1965-77, 4 vols in 3. (Bibliothèque de droit international, 80). 1st edn 1957.

Vol. 1 concerns mostly SAs based in or dealing with Europe; the other volumes deal with selected SAs in or relating to Africa, Asia and Latin America.

677. Alexandrowicz, C. H., *The law-making functions of the Specialized Agencies of the United Nations.* Sydney: Angus & Robertson, 1973, 181 pp.

The work examines legislative, quasi-legislative actions, convention-making of SAs (including a list of ILO, UNESCO, FAO and IBRD conventions), and their contribution to the development of customary rules and general principles of PIL. *See also* [617c, 626b].

678a. The series 'Bibliothèque de droit international' [373h] (Paris: LGDJ) contains several studies on SAs, e.g. No. 46 (GATT), No. 56 (ICAO), No. 65 (IBRD), etc.

—b. UNITAR [672b] in its Regional Studies series has published various studies concerning the relations between the UN and regional intergovernmental organizations, notably UNITAR/RS/No. 1, 1975; No. 4, 1975; No. 9, 1983, concerning the EC, OAS and ASEAN respectively. *See also* [616b], especially chapter 1 (on the legal status of SAs) and chapter 4 (legal bibliography relating to SAs).

—c. Advisory Committee for the Co-ordination of Information Systems (ACCIS). 16, ave. Trembley, Pt. Saconnex, Geneva, Switzerland.

Publishes a series, 'Guides' to information sources relative to selected SAs, e.g. FAO [681d] and UNEP [717a]. The 'Guides' in the series (with a UN sales no., i.e. GV.E. year) concern mainly the publications and documents issued by a given SA.

679a. *Unesco's standard setting instruments.* Paris: UNESCO, 1981, 960 pp.

Contains the texts of 19 conventions and 23 recommendations on the protection of cultural property, importation of educational and scientific materials, universal copyright and international library statistics. Arranged in the fields of UNESCO's competence.

—b. *New challenges to international law/Nouveaux défis au droit international.* Paris: UNESCO; London: Holmes & Meier, 1979-, 1-.

Intended to encourage critical reflection on various aspects of international law, the series includes works by M. Bedjaoui [727b], E. McWhinney [648a], etc.

—c. Rubanik, K.P., *Mezhdunarodno-pravovye problemy IUNESKO.* Moskva: Mezhdunarodnye Otnosheniia, 1969, 167 pp.

An analysis of the legal status and juridical acts of UNESCO as an SA.

—d. Hajnal, P.I., *Guide to UNESCO.* Dobbs Ferry, NY: Oceana, 1983, 578 pp.

The *Guide* examines four modes of UNESCO's activities, i.e. programmes, normative action, conferences and information. The section on information (chapter 9) includes a study of UNESCO's publishing, of documentation within the UNISIST context and of the 'New World Information and Communication Order'. A selected, annotated bibliography of some 430 works by and about UNESCO, 14 appendices (including Member States, National Commissions, references to relevant declarations, conventions, and recommendations adopted by UNESCO or under its auspices) and an author, subject and title index conclude the *Guide*.

680a. *International labour conventions and recommendations, 1919-1981.* Geneva: ILO, 1982, 1,167 pp.

Supersedes the *International labour code.* Geneva: ILO, 1952, 2 vols. The 1982 work contains the text of 146 conventions and 102 recommendations arranged by broad topical fields within ILO's competence. *See also The consolidated index to the ILO Legislative Series.* New York: UNIFO, 1975, 264 pp.

—b. Osieke, E., *Constitutional law and practice in the International Labour Organisation.* The Hague: Nijhoff, 1985, 224 pp.

The Nigerian author examines the legal practice of ILO.

681a. *Directory of FAO Statutory Bodies and Panels of Experts.* Rome: FAO, 1980, 154 pp. (FAO document M/N 8300/E.9.80/1/900).

—b. *Criteria for formulating resolutions contained in FAO documents.* Rome:

FAO Resolutions Committee, 1979 (FAO document C 79/12-Rev. 2, appendix D).

—c. *Index: FAO Conference and Council decisions, 1945-1972.* Rome: FAO, 1973, 498 pp.

—d. Advisory Committee for the Co-ordination of Information System (ACCIS). *Guide to United Nations information sources on food and agriculture.* Rome: FAO, 1987, 124 pp. (ACCIS Guides to UN Information Sources, 1).

Arranged by subject fields within FAO's competence, the *Guide* examines FAO and relevant subject materials, including computerized databases. Name, subject and title indexes complete the *Guide*.

682a. *International digest of health legislation.* Geneva: WHO, 1947-, 1-.

Continues the information formerly contained in *Bulletin officiel international d'hygiène publique*, 1909-1946.

—b. *Handbook of resolutions and decisions of the World Health Organization*, 4th edn. Geneva: WHO, 1981.

—c. *Vierheilig, M., *Die rechtliche Einordnung der von der Weltgesundheitsorganisation beschlossener Regulationen.* Heidelberg: Decker, 1984, 208 pp.

See also Voncken in [379a].

683. Szasz, P., *The law and practice of the International Atomic Energy Agency.* Vienna: IAEA, 1970, 1,176 pp. (IAEA legal series, 7).

684a. *Copyright laws and treaties of the world.* Compiled by UNESCO and WIPO with the co-operation of the copyright offices of the United States, Gt Britain/Northern Ireland. Washington, DC: Bureau of National Affairs; Paris: UNESCO, 1956, 3 vols.

Contains English translations of copyright laws (including rules and conventions) in force in some 160 countries.

—b. Boguslavskiĭ, M.M., *Voprosy avtorskogo prava v mezhdunarodnykh otnosheniakh: mezhdunarodnaia okhrana proizvedeniĭ literatury i nauki.* Moskva, 1973.

Regional inter-governmental organizations

685a. *Les organisations régionales internationales.* Strasbourg: Université de Strasbourg, Faculté internationale pour l'enseignement du droit comparé, 1978.

The contributors include J.H. Kaiser, Les sources du droit des organisations régionales, and A.C. Kiss, Les relations extérieures des organisations régionales: principes généraux et droit commun.

—b. *Arab and Islamic international organization directory, and Arab/Islamic participation*

260   SELECTED SUBJECT BIBLIOGRAPHY

in other international organizations. Edited by the Union of International Associations. München: Saur, 1984/5, 483 pp.

Essentially based on information contained in [630a].

686a.   Kouassi, E. Kwam, *Organisations internationales africaines.* Préface de R.-J. Dupuy; avant-propos de M. Virally. Paris: Berger-Levrault, 1987, 485 pp. (Collection: Mondes en devenir. Série: Manuels, B.-L., 9).

The Togolese author discusses the concept of international organization in general and the characteristics of African organizations in particular. Part 1, Les organisations de coopération (with focus on OAU); part 2, Les organisations à vocation d'intégration. Includes bibliographic notes and lists of relevant documents.

—b.   el-Ayouty, Y. and Brooks, H.C., *Africa and international organization.* The Hague: Nijhoff, 1974, 250 pp.

—c.   Sohn, L.B., *Basic documents of African regional organizations.* Dobbs Ferry, NY: Oceana, 1971-2, 4 vols.

Published under the auspices of the Inter-American Institute of International Legal Studies, the work contains texts in English of constitutional, legislative and administrative materials relating to East and West Africa and regional organizations. Vol. 4 contains texts of selected Asian regional organizations.

—d.   Ranjeva, R., *La succession d'organisations internationales en Afrique.* Préface de S. Bastid. Paris: Pédone, 1978, 418 pp. (Publication de la *Revue de droit international public, N.S.,* 29).

687a.   *Basic documents of the OAU.* Addis Ababa, 1973, 2 vols.

Contains texts of resolutions, recommendations and statements adopted in the 1963-73 sessions of the Council of Ministers, Assembly of Heads of State and Governments in the OAU.

—b.   Glélé, M.A., *Introduction à l'Organisation de l'unité africaine et aux organisations régionales africaines.* Paris: LGDJ, 1986, 574 pp. (Bibliothèque africaine et malgache, 40).

—c.   Andemicael, B., *The OAU and the UN: relations between the Organization of African Unity and the United Nations.* New York: Africana Publ. Co., 1976, 331 pp. (UNITAR Regional Studies, 2).

688.   *Anuario jurídico interamericano.* Washington, DC: Organization of American States (OAS)/Organización de los Estados Americanos (OEA), 1948-, 1-, annual.

Published in three parts, the *Anuario* reports (with a lag of 2-3 years) on current judicial activities of the OAS. Resembling in part the *UN juridical yearbook* [616b], the *Anuario* also includes a topical bibliography of materials of interest to OAS members. The *Anuario* supersedes the *Inter-American juridical yearbook.* Washington, DC: Pan-American Union, 1946-7. *See also* [OAS], *Ten years of activities, 1971-1981.* Washington, DC: OAS, 1982, 404 pp. *See also* [481b].

689. *Curso de derecho internacional.* Rio de Janeiro: Inter-American Juridical Committee/Comité Jurídico Interamericano, 1974-, 1-, annual. New series, 1983-, 1-.

In close cooperation with the OAS General Legal Division (part of the OAS Secretariat in Washington, DC) the Inter-American Juridical Committee (Rua Senador Verguero, 81 - andar, Rio de Janeiro) prepares legal studies and reports, and convenes (alternately in Rio and Washington) international law courses, comparable to those of ILC [662a]. *See also *Seminario sobre la ensenanza del derecho internacional. 2nd Bogotá, 1979.* Washington, DC: OAS, 1980, 2 vols.

690a. Welch, T., 1982, The Organization of American States and its documentation dissemination. *Revista interamerican de bibliografía*, **32**(2), pp. 200-206.

See also [349].

—b. Columbus Library. OAS General Secretariat, 17th Street at Constitution Ave., Washington, DC 20006, USA.

Contains over 200,000 volumes, 3,000 periodical titles in the OAS fields of competence; acts as a depository library for materials issued by OAS.

691. Haas, M., *Basic documents of Asian regional organizations.* Dobbs Ferry, NY: Oceana, 1974-85, 9 vols.

Contains texts in English of constitutional, legislative, etc. documents of Asian regional organizations. Vol. 8 gives an analytical study of the history, structure and functions of these organizations.

692a. Menzhinskiĭ, V. I. ed., *Mezhdunarodnye organizat͡sii sot͡sialisticheskikh stran: spravochnik.* Moskva: Mezhdunarodnye Otnosheniĭa, 1980, 256 pp.

Examines the activities of socialist intergovernmental organizations, including the Council for Mutual Economic Cooperation (COMECON/SEV) and the Warsaw Pact. *See also* [13]; J. Caillot, *CAEM: aspects juridiques.* Paris: LGDJ, 1971, 413 pp. (Bibliothèque de droit international, 62).

—b. Butler, W. E., *A source book on socialist international organizations of the Communist countries.* Alphen a/R: Sijthoff & Noordhoff, 1978, 1,143 pp.

See also Szawlowski, R., *The system of the international organizations of the Communist countries.* Leiden: Sijthoff, 1976.

—c. Osakwe, C., *The participation of the Soviet Union in universal international organizations: a political and legal analysis of Soviet strategies and aspirations inside ILO, UNESCO and WHO.* Leiden: Sijthoff, 1972, 210 pp.

An interdisciplinary analysis of the politico-legal approach by the USSR to its participation in three SAs. Chapter 1 deals with the contemporary Soviet doctrine on the juridical nature of universal inter-governmental organizations.

ii. HUMAN RIGHTS

693a. Andrews, J. A. and Hines, W. D., *Keyguide to information sources on the international protection of human rights*. London: Mansell, 1987, 169 pp.

Part 1 analyses the theory, structure and function of international and regional protection of human rights; part 2 contains some 660 references to primary and secondary human rights materials published mostly in English since 1945; part 3 includes relevant IGOs and NGOs in the field. An author, subject and title index concludes the work.

—b. Whalen, L., *Human rights: a reference handbook*. Santa Barbara, CA: ABC-Clio Press, 1989, 175 pp.

The guide lists mainly English-language auxiliary resources (directories, bibliographies, glossaries, etc.) in the field.

The following selection of human rights materials published worldwide mostly in the 1980s complements the references contained in [693a,b].

694a *Déclaration islamique universelle des droits de l'homme*. London: Conseil islamique, 1981, 19 leaves.

Original edition published in Arabic.

—b. *Colloques sur le dogme musulman et les droits de l'homme en Islam, 1972-1974*. Beyrouth: Dar-al-Kitab Allubnana, [1975], 258 pp.

—c. *Tabandeh, S., *A Muslim commentary on the Universal Declaration of Human Rights*. London: F. T. Goulding, 1970, 96 pp. 1st (Persian) edn 1966.

695a. Bello, E. G., 1985/V, The African Charter on Human and People's Rights: a legal analysis. *RCADI*, **194**, pp. 9-268.

The appendix contains the draft text of the Charter prepared under the auspices of the OAU.

—b. *Kunig, P. *et al.*, 1985, *Regional protection of human rights by international law: the emerging African system*. Baden-Baden: Nomos, 156 pp. (Verfassung und Recht in Übersee. Beil. Hft 12).

—c. *Seminar on the establishment of regional commissions on human rights with special reference to Africa, Monrovia, 1979*. New York: UN, 1979, 34 pp. (UN document ST/HR/SER.A/4).

696a. Inter-American Court of Human Rights. *Pleadings, oral arguments and documents/Memorias, argumentos orales y documentos*. San José, 1960-, 1-, irregular.

—b. Inter-American Institute of Human Rights/Instituto Interamericano de Derechos Humanos/Instituto Interamericano de Direitos Humanos. Apt. Portal 10081, San José, Costa Rica.

Founded in 1980, following agreement between the Inter-American Court of Human Rights and the Government of Costa Rica, the Institute promotes human rights education and research.

—c. Buergenthal, T., Norris R. and Shelton, D., 1986, *Protecting human rights in the Americas*, 2nd edn. Kehl/Strasbourg: N. P. Engel, 389 pp. 1st edn 1982.

Reviewed in *IJLI*, 1987, **15**, pp. 63–64.

697a. Trindade, A. A. C., 1987/II, Co-existence and co-ordination of mechanisms of international protection of human rights: at global and regional levels. *RCADI*, **202**, pp. 9–435.

Examines the proper interpretation of human rights treaties, the right of petition, communication and the legal basis of reporting obligations, and proposes a 'common core of non-derogable fundamental rights'.

—b. Ermacora, F., *Menschenrechte in der sich wandelnden Welt*. Wien: Verlag Österreichische Akademie der Wissenschaften, 1974–83, 2 vols.

Vol. 1, *Historische Entwicklung;* vol. 2, *Theorie und Praxis*.

—c. *Movchan, A. P., *Prava cheloveka i mezhdunarodnye otnosheniia*. Moskva, 1972.

—d. Velu, J., *Les effets directs des instruments internationaux en matière de droits de l'homme*. Bruxelles: Editions juridiques Swinnen, 1981, 190 pp. (Prolegomena, 2).

See also [297, vol. 8], Dupuy in [210], Alston in [647a].

698a. Bernhardt, R. and Jolowicz, J. A. (eds), *International enforcement of human right. Reports submitted to the Colloquium of the International Association of Legal Sciences, Heidelberg, 28–30 August 1985*. Berlin: Springer, 1987, 265 pp. (Beiträge zum ausländischen öffentlichen Recht und Völkerrecht, 93).

Includes reports on the Soviet concept of human rights, and the Latin American and Afro-Asian aproaches to human rights. The appendix includes texts of selected universal and regional human rights instruments.

—b. *Seminar on the experience of different countries in the implementation of international standards on human rights, Geneva, 1983*. Various pagings (UN document ST/HR/SER.A/15).

699. *Amicorum discipulorumque liber, René Cassin*. Paris: Pédone, 1969–72, 4 vols.

The contributions examine the evolution, problems and methodology of the protection of human rights.

700. Lillich, R. B. and Newman, F. C., *International human rights: problems of law and policy*. Boston, MA: Little, Brown & Co. 1979, 1,030 pp.

A human rights coursebook arranged according to twelve most important human rights issues, rules, complete with comments, bibliographic notes. Includes a documentary appendix. *See also* the human rights textbook by K. Vasak (item 423 in the Andrews and Hines *Keyguide* [693]).

> 701. *Derechos humanos/Human rights/Droits de l'homme: legal social and administrative terms*. Geneva: UN Office at Geneva, Languages Service, Terminology and Documentation Section, 1981, 282 pp. (UNOG publication TERM/32).

Title and text in English, French and Spanish.

> 702a. The refugee problem on universal, regional and national levels. *Thesaurus acroasium*, 1987, vol. 13.

The contributors include K. Obradovic, protection of refugees in armed conflict; N. Singh, activities of the Office of the UN High Commissioner for Refugees; G. Coles, the function of refugee law; and T. Veiter, concepts of refugee law.

> —b. *Refugee abstracts*. Geneva: Office of the UN High Commissioner for Refugees. International Refugee Integration Resources Centre, 1982-, 1-, quarterly.

Contains summaries of official (national, international) documents, publications and periodical articles on treaties, assistance programmes and conferences relating to refugees (including asylum and resettlement).

> —c. Mutharika, A. P., *The regulation of statelessness under international and national law: texts and documents*. Dobbs Ferry, NY: Oceana, 1977, 2 loose-leaf binders.

The constitutional and statutory texts deal not only with stateless persons, but also with nationality and immigration matters.

> —d. *A select bibliography on territorial asylum*. Geneva: UNOG Library, 1977, 82 pp. (UN document ST/Geneva/LIB/SER.B/Ref.9).

iii. INTERNATIONAL CRIMINAL LAW

> 703a. Bassiouni, C., *International crimes: digest/index of international instruments, 1815-1985*. Dobbs Ferry, NY: Oceana, 1985, 2 vols.

In part supersedes the same author's *International criminal law: a draft international criminal code*. Alphen a/R: Sijthoff & Noordhoff, 1980, 249 pp. Systematically arranged, the 1985 work summarizes some 300 official (international, national) and other instruments. Vol. 1 deals with aggression, war crimes, unlawful use of weapons and slavery; vol. 2 deals with torture, aircraft hijacking and drug offences. The instruments listed include historical/scope/bibliographic notes, as well as entry into force/ratifications/reservations.

—b.   Glaser, S., *Droit international pénal conventionnel.* Bruxelles: Bruylant, 1970–8, 2 vols.

Examines international conventions, draft rules, etc. concerning terrorism, apartheid, genocide, drug abuse, etc. having entered into force since 1970.

704a.   Ferencz, B. B., *An International Criminal Court: a step toward world peace. A documentary history and analysis.* Dobbs Ferry, NY: Oceana, 1980, 2 vols.

Traces the history of international criminal law and the endeavours towards establishing an international criminal tribunal. *See also* [705a].

—b.   *Foundation for the Establishment of an International Criminal Court.* 2315 Alcyone Drive, Los Angeles, CA 90068, USA.

Created in 1970, the Foundation seeks to establish uniformity of criminal codes, and to this end furthers the establishment of a relevant international court.

705a.   Bassiouni, C. and Nanda, V. P., *A treatise on international criminal law.* Springfield, IL: C. C. Thomas, 1973, 2 vols.

Vol. 1, *Crimes and punishment* (i.e. penal aspects of PIL); vol. 2, *Jurisdiction and co-operation* (i.e. international aspects of municipal criminal law). The contributions by H. Jeschek, A. Lee, J. W. F. Sundberg, D. Bindschedler, W. E. Butler (on the Soviet concept of aggression) and B. V. A. Rölling among others examine international criminal law in terms of individual and collective responsibility, crimes against peace, humanitarian law of armed conflicts and common crimes against mankind (including terrorism). Vol. 1 also deals with the prosecution of international crimes, including the post-1945 Nuremberg and Tokyo trials, as well as the creation of an international criminal tribunal. Vol. 2 includes studies on extradition and asylum law and practice.

—b.   Lombois, C., *Droit pénal international.* Paris: Dalloz, 1971, 601 pp. (Précis Dalloz).

A French treatise on international criminal law.

706a.   *Vogler, T. and Hermann, J. (eds), *H. Jeschek zum 70. Geburtstag.* 1985, 2 vols.

—b.   *Le droit pénal international: recueil d'études en hommage à Jacob Maarten van Bemmelen.* Leiden: Brill, 1965, 257 pp.

707a.   *Revue international de droit pénal.* Paris: Association française de droit pénal, 1924–, 1–, quarterly.

—b.   *International journal of comparative and applied criminal justice.* Wichita, KS: Wichita State Univ., 1977–, 1–, semi-annual.

708a.   de Schutter, B. and Eliaerts, C., *Bibliographie* [sic] *on international criminal law.* Foreword by H.-H. Jeschek. Leiden: Sijthoff, 1972, 423 pp.

Produced under the auspices of the Centrum voor internationaal Strafrecht,

Brussel, Vrije Universiteit. The bibliography includes some 5,000 references to monographs and periodical articles on international conventional and customary criminal law, including UN activities in the field, as well as war crimes, extraterritorial justice, etc.

—b. Gendrel, M., *Elements d'une bibliographie mondiale du droit pénal militaire des crimes et délits contre la sûreté de l'état et du droit pénal international*. Paris: LGDJ, 1965, 216 pp.

709. *Max-Planck Institut für ausländisches und internationales Strafrecht*. Günterstalstr. 72, Freiburg i/Br, FRG.

Founded in 1938, the Institute conducts research in international criminal law; its library contains some 60,000 volumes in the field.

710a. International Military Tribunal, Nuremberg. *Trial of the major war criminals before the IMT, Nuremberg, 14 November 1945 to 1 October 1948*. Nuremberg, 1947-9. 42 vols.

Contains full official texts of the trial proceedings, as well as various evidentiary materials.

—b. United Nations War Crimes Commission. *Law reports of trials of war criminals*. London: HMSO, 1947, 20 vols.

Contains the summaries of 122 cases before the International Military Tribunals.

—c. International Military Tribunal, Tokyo, *Record of proceedings*. Tokyo, 1946-8, 148 vols.

See also Dull, P. and Umemura, M.T. (eds), *The Tokyo trial: a functional index to the Proceedings of the IMT for the Far East*. Ann Arbor, MI: University of Michigan Press, 1964, 94 pp.

—d. Appleman, J.A., *Military tribunals and international crimes*. Westport, CT: Greenwood Press, 1971, 421 pp.

—e. Graven, J., 1950/I, Les crimes contre l'humanité. *RCADI*, 76, pp. 427-605.

—f. Lachs, M., *War crimes: an attempt to define the issues*. London: Stevens, 1945, 108 pp.

—g. Lewis, J.R. (comp.), *Uncertain judgement: a bibliography of war crime trials*. Santa Barbara, CA: ABC-Clio, 1979, 251 pp. (War/Peace Bibliography series, 8).

711a. Stanbrook, I and Stanbrook, C., *The law and practice of extradition*. Chichester and London: Barry Rose, 1980, 202 pp.

Examines extradition as a method suitable for the enforcement of criminal law, by way of agreements for judicial assistance, extra-territorial prosecution of crimes, etc.

—b. Bassiouni, C., *International extradition and world public order*, 2nd edn. Dobbs Ferry, NY: Oceana, 1983, 2 vols, loose-leaf. 1st edn 1974.

Originally a PhD thesis at George Washington University, the work examines the process of extradition in international law and practice and the extradition practice of the USA in a comparative, multidisciplinary (policy-oriented) context. Includes chapters on asylum/extradition and theories of jurisdiction applicable to extradition in special circumstances (territorial, personal). A subject index, table of cases and index to extradition treaties cited conclude the work.

712a. Friedlander, R.A., *Terrorism: documents of international and local control*. Dobbs Ferry, NY: Oceana, 1979-89, 5 vols.

Traces the history, outlines a typology and examines political and legal aspects of criminal acts throughout the world. The focus is on the US role in combating international terrorism. The appendix includes *Threat of international terrorism*. Proceedings of the Dacor Bacon House Seminar, 1986.

—b. Lakos, A., *International terrorism: a bibliography*. London: Mansell, 1988, 480 pp.

Contains references to primary and secondary materials, including domestic and international legal aspects of terrorism.

—c. Evans, A.E. (ed.), *Legal aspects of international terrorism*. London: Thames & Hudson, 1978, 240 pp. (Studies in International Order).

—d. *Colloque: réflexions sur la définition et la répression du terrorisme, Bruxelles, 1973*. Bruxelles: Editions de l'Université de Bruxelles, 1974, 292 pp.

iv. INTERNATIONAL LAW OF THE ENVIRONMENT

713a. Ruster, B. and Simma, B. (eds), *International protection of the environment: treaties and related documents*. Dobbs Ferry, NY: Oceana, 1975-83, 30 vols + index. 1988-, 1-, loose-leaf.

The collection contains full, English texts (complete with comments and notes) of over 1,000 treaties, some 1,000 acts of international organizations and over 200 municipal laws and decisions relating to the protection of the environment (including pollution control and waste management) from 1945 on.

—b. *Register of international treaties and other agreements in the field of environment*. Nairobi: UN Environmental Programme, 1984, 205 pp. (UNEP document GC/Inform.5, 11).

Regularly updated, the *Register* is a digest of environmental treaty texts.

714a. *L'Avenir du droit international de l'environment/The future of the international law of the environment*. The Hague Academy International Law Workshop, 1984. Edited by R.-J. Dupuy. Dordrecht: Nijhoff, 1985, 515 pp.

—b. *La protection de l'environnement et le droit international/The protection of the environment and international law.* The Hague Academy International Law Workshop, 1973. Edited by A.-C. Kiss. Leiden: Sijthoff, 1975, 650 pp.

The contributors include L. F. E. Goldie, A general view of international environmental law: a survey of capabilities, trends and limits; P. H. Sand, Environmental law in the UN Environment Programme (UNEP); J. G. Lammers, Balancing the equities in international environmental law; A. K. Biswas, Environment and law: a perspective for developing countries; A. C. Kiss, Le droit international de l'environnement: un aspect du droit international de l'avenir, and there are several articles on air, river and sea pollution.

—c. Kiss, A.-C., 1982, La notion de patrimoine commun de l'humanité. *RCADI*/II, **175**, pp. 103-256.

See also Kiss in [200, 714b]; Olmstead, C. J., in [379a] on environmental conservation under international law.

—d. Kolbasov, O. S., *Mezhdunarodno-pravovaīa okhrana okruzhaīushcheĭ sredy.* Moskva: Mezhdunarodnye Otnosheniīa. 1982, 237 pp.

—e. Schneider, J., *World public order of the environment: towards an international ecological law and organization.* Toronto: University of Toronto Press, 1979, 319 pp.

—f. Theutenberg, B. J., *International environmental law: a study of the interrelationship between general international law and treaty law in the field of environmental management.* Malmö: Liber, 1976, 226 pp.

715a. *The international protection of the environment on a regional level. Thesaurus acroasium*, 1982, vol. 11.

Includes articles on the NIEO (B. V. A. Röling and W. D. Verwey).

—b. Barros, J. and Johnston, D. M., *The international law of pollution.* New York: Free Press/Macmillan, 1974, 476 pp.

Part 1 is an interdisciplinary approach to pollution problems; part 2 deals with responsibility for environmental damage, especially in rivers, oceans and the Antarctic region.

—c. *Le droit international de l'environnement humain/The international law of the human environment.* Actes du 23e Congrès de l'AAA de l'Académie de droit international de La Haye, Rabat, 1971. The Hague: Nijhoff, 1971, 153 pp. (*Annuaire de l'AAA*, 1971, vol. 41).

716a. *Columbia journal of environmental law.* New York: Columbia University School of Law, 1973-, 1-, semi-annual.

—b. *Revue juridique de l'environnement.* Lyon: Société française de l'environnement, 1976-, 1-, quarterly.

—c. *International environmental reporter*. Washington, DC: Bureau of National Affairs, 1974–, 1–, monthly.

Part 1, Current reports (issued monthly); part 2, Reference file (collection cumulating texts in English of national and international environmental treaties and legislation).

717a. Advisory Committee for the Co-ordination of Information Systems (ACCIS). *Guide to United Nations information sources on the environment*. New York: UN, 1988, 145 pp. (UN sales publication GV.E.87.0.6).

—b. Hammond, K. A. (ed.), *Sourcebook on the environment: a guide to the literature*. Chicago, IL: Chicago UP, 1978, 613 pp.

v. INTERNATIONAL DEVELOPMENT

718a. Jackson, J. H., *Legal problems of international economic relations*. St Paul, MN, 1986, 1,269 pp.

—b. Kohona, P. T. B., *The regulation of international economic relations through law*. Dordrecht: Nijhoff, 1985, 315 pp.

A legal analysis of multilateral economic agreements and the resultant international economic régimes.

—c. *Le droit des relations économiques internationales. Etudes offertes à B. Goldman*. Paris: Librarie technique, 1982, 429 pp.

—d. Hübner, U., *Die methodische Entwicklung des internationalen Wirtschaftsrechts*. Konstanz: Universitätsverlag, 1980, 37 pp. (Konstanzer Universitätsreden, 96).

Examines the impact of emerging international economic law on traditional sources, subjects of PIL and the role of international organizations in this process.

719a. Perroux, F., *A new concept of development: basic tenets*. London: Croom Helm; Paris: UNESCO, 1983, 212 pp.

A theoretical formulation of a set of concepts, indicators away from the traditional market economic model.

—b. Thompson, C. L., Anderberg, M. M. and Antell, J. B. (eds), *The current history encyclopedia of developing countries*. New York: McGraw-Hill, 1982, 395 pp.

—c. Tuzmukhamedov, R. A., *Razvivaiushchie strany v mirovoi politike. Mezhdunarodnye mezhpravitel'stvennye organizatsii razvivaiushchikhsia stran*. Moskva: Mezhdunarodnye Otnosheniia, 1977.

Includes analysis of the legal effects of resolutions by IGOs relative to developing countries.

720a. Mutharika, A.P., *The international law of development: basic documents*. Dobbs Ferry, NY: Oceana, 1978–85, 6 vols.

Contains texts of agreements on the creation of development banks: legal aspects of technology transfer, etc.

—b. Sauvant, K.P. and Muller, J.W. (comps), *The collected documents of the Group of 77*. Dobbs Ferry, NY: Oceana, 1981–9, 7 vols (Third World without Superpowers, 2nd series).

Formed at the first session of UNCTAD [740a], the Group of 77 has since articulated the collective economic interest of the Third World. The *Collected documents* reflect the Group's position contained in proceedings of international conferences, resolutions, reports, etc. *See also* Sauvant, K.P., *The Group of 77: evolution, structure, organization*. Dobbs Ferry, NY: Oceana, 1981, 259 pp.

—c. United Nations Conference on Trade and Development (UNCTAD). *The Least Developed Countries (LDC). Report*. 1984–, 1– (UNCTAD document TB/B/1059 + add. 1, 1985, UN sales publication: E.year.II.D).

—d. Castañeda, J., La Charte des droits et des devoirs économique des états: note sur le processus d'élaboration; Virally, M., La Charte des droits et des devoirs économiques des états. *AFDI*, 1974, **20**, pp. 31–56 and 57–77 respectively.

721a. Advisory Committee for the Co-ordination of Information Systems (ACCIS), *Register of development activities of the United Nations system*. New York: UN, 1988–, 1–, annual. (UN sales publ. GV.E.year.04).

The *Register* provides summaries of broadly defined development activities of 33 organizations in the UN system from 1987 onward.

—b. United Nations Development Programme (UNDP). c/o United Nations, New York.

Established in 1965, UNDP assists in the socio-economic development, especially of Third World countries, information about which is contained in the annually issued *Report of the [UNDP] Administrator*.

—c. World Institute for Development Economics Research. c/o University of Helsinki, Finland.

Established in 1984 under the auspices of the UN University (Tokyo), the Institute carries out socio-economic development studies at the global and regional levels.

—d. Organisation for Economic Co-operation and Development. *Directory of development research and training institutes in Arab countries*. Paris: OECD, 1988.

Along with the *Register of development research projects in Arab countries* (OECD, 1988), the *Directory* provides information on development research and training in 20 Arab countries.

a. International law of economic development

722a. *Le droit au développement au plan international/The right to development at the international level.* The Hague Academy of International Law Workshop, 1979. Edited by R.-Y. Dupuy. Alphen a/R: Sijthoff & Noordhoff, 1980, 446 pp.

See also UN document E/CN/1984/13 prepared by the Working Group of Governmental Experts on the Right to Development and containing proposals towards a draft declaration on the right to development.

—b. *Droit international et développement. Actes du Colloque international, Alger, 11-14 octobre, 1976.* Hydra (Alger): Office des publications universitaires, [1978], 492 pp.

—c. *Aspects du droit international économique: élaboration, contrôle, sanction: Colloque d'Orléans, 1971.* Paris: Pédone, 1972, 221 pp. (Actes du [1.] Colloque de la Société française pour le droit international).

See also [482].

723a. Garcia-Amador, F.V., *The international law of development: new directions in international law.* Dobbs Ferry, NY: Oceana, 1989, 300 pp.

The topics examined include NIEO, the right to and cooperation for development, the claims of the developing world to sovereignty over natural resources, and the impact of these trends on the development of PIL.

—b. Seidl-Hohenveldren, I., 1986/III, International economic law. *RCADI*, **198,** pp. 9-264.

Complements and supersedes his: International economic 'soft law'. *RCADI*, 1979/II, **163,** pp. 165-246.

—c. Bulajić, M., *Principles of international development law.* Dordrecht: Nijhoff, 1986, 403 pp.

—d. Feuer, G. and Cassan, H., *Droit international du développement.* Paris: Dalloz, 1985, 644 pp. (Précis Dalloz).

The treatise examines the history of (economic) international relations; sovereignty, equality and solidarity as principles of international economic law within the PIL context; legal aspects of developmental institutions (mainly in the UN system); economic sovereignty, technical assistance and technology transfer as developmental actions. *See also* Feuer in [186]; Bennouna in [185].

—e. Benchikh, M., *Droit international du sous-développement: nouvel ordre dans la dépendance.* Paris: Berger-Levrault, 1983, 331 pp. (Mondes en devenir. Série: Manuels, BL, 2).

A Marxist analysis of Western/bourgeois models of development/underdevelopment; part 2 proposes new legal instruments to govern the emerging division of labour between developed and developing nations. *See also* Benchikh in [186].

—f. Marchaha, M., *Contribution à la notion de droit international public du développement*. [Nice], 1976, 491 pp.

An outcome of his PhD thesis, the work examines the socio-economic disparities in the contemporary international community and proposes legal principles for implementing the right to and potential for development of given underdeveloped areas.

—g. Schwarzenberger, G., 1966/I, The principles and standards of international economic law. *RCADI*, **117**, pp. 5-96.

The study delimits the area of international economic law to include the legal aspects of ownership and exploitation of natural resources; production and distribution of goods; international economic and financial transactions; status and organization of persons and institutions engaged in economic activities.

724a. *Les Nations Unies et le droit international economique: Colloque de Lyon, 1985*. Paris: Pédone, 1986, 383 pp. (Actes du 19. Colloque de la Société française pour le droit international).

—b. *Les résolutions dans la formation du droit international du développement. Colloque, Genève, 1970*. Genève, 1971, 189 pp. (Institut universitaire de hautes études internationales. Etudes et travaux, 113).

725a. International Development Law Institute. Via Paolo Frisi 23, 00197 Rome, Italy.

Founded in 1983, the Institute promotes the deployment of legal resources towards solving problems of development and provides training for legal specialists from developing countries.

—b. Institut du droit de la paix et du développement. Université de Nice, 34, ave. E. Henriot, 06000 Nice, France.

Founded in 1968 and directed by R.-J. Dupuy, the Institute promotes training and research especially in the field of international law of economic development.

b. New International Economic Order

726a. Moss, A.G. and Winton, H.N.M., *A New International Economic Order: selected documents, 1945-1975*. New York: UN, 1976, 2 vols (UNITAR Document series, 1).

Contains texts in English of declarations, resolutions, final acts and programmes of action emanating from international bodies, especially UNCTAD, as well as the Group of 77 [720b].

—b. Training materials: basic documents relating to New International

Economic Order. New York: UN, 1983, 67 pp. (UNITAR document TM/83/1). Also in French.

727a. van Themaat, P.V., *The changing structure of international economic law: a contribution to legal history, of comparative law and of general legal theory to the debate on a New International Economic Order*. The Hague: Nijhoff, 1981, 420 pp.

Published under the auspices of the T.M.C. Asser Institute.

—b. Bedjaoui, M., *Towards a New International Economic Order*. Paris: UNESCO; London: Holmes & Meier, 1979, 287 pp. (New Challenges to International Law, 1). French edition *Pour un nouvel ordre économique international*, 1979, 295 pp.

Part 1, International order of poverty and poverty of international order (includes 'international law of indifference'); part 2, international development law and the development of international law (includes normative, institutional actions relative to NIEO).

728a. Franck, T.M., *The New International Economic Order: international law in the making*. New York: UN, 1982, 20 pp. (UNITAR document PE/6; UN sales publication 1982.XV.PE/6).

A succinct historical and analytical study of NIEO between 'congealed politics and legislation', especially with reference to the 'normative' position of Third World countries on the subject.

—b. *Progressive development of the principles and norms of international law relating to the new international order: the compendium*. New York: UN, 1981, 172 pp. (UNITAR document DS/4, English only).

The compendium, to be read in conjunction with the likewise titled report of the UN S-G (UN document A/36/143; 1981, 25 pp.), is complemented by *Analytical papers and analysis of texts of relevant instruments* (UNITAR document DS/5, 15 August 1982, 508 pp.), and *The principle of participatory equality of developing countries in international economic relations . . . amendments to analytical compilation of texts or relevant instruments* (UNITAR document DS/6/Add. 1, 25 September 1984, 54 pp.)

729a. *The New International Economic Order: a selective bibliography*. New York: UN, DHL, 1980, 128 pp. (UN document ST/LIB/SER.B/30; UN sales publication E/F.80.1.15).

—b. Nawaz, T., *The NIEO: a bibliography*. London: Frances Pinter, 1980, 163 pp.

730. Borgese, E.M., *NIEO register: a register of institutions and organisations active in areas related to the NIEO*. Rotterdam: Foundation Reshaping the International Order, 1978, 113 pp.

731a. Rosenberg, D., *Le principe de souveraineté des Etats sur leurs ressources naturelles*. Préface de J.-P. Colin. Avant-propos de M. Bedjaoui. Paris: LGDJ, 1983, 395 pp. (Bibliothèque de droit international, 93).

Part 1, classical PIL ('droit du pillage des ressources naturelles'); part 2, creation of positive PIL rules (including analysis of the UN resolution 1803 (XVII), 1962 on state sovereignty over resources); part 3, sovereignty over resources as a principle of international law of development (including case study of Algeria).

—b. Bennouna, M., 1982/IV, Le droit international relatif aux matières premières. *RCADI*, **177**, pp. 103-191.

—c. Brownlie, I., 1979/I, Legal status of natural resources in international law. *RCADI*, **162**, pp. 245-317.

—d. *Le règlement des différends sur les nouvelles ressources naturelles/The settlement of disputes on the new natural resources.* The Hague Academy of International Law Workshop, 1982. Edited by R.-J. Dupuy. The Hague: Nijhoff, 1983, 487 pp.

—e. Bartels, M. et al., *Bibliography on transnational law of natural resources.* Deventer (Netherlands): Kluwer, 1981, 227 pp.

See also Settlement of disputes within the framework of specialized agencies, UNCTAD, GATT, systems of economic integration and in the field of commodity agreements: a bibliography. The Hague: Peace Palace Library, 1976, 20 pp.

vi. INTERNATIONAL TRADE LAW

732a. *Register of texts of conventions and other instruments concerning international trade law.* New York: UN, 1971-3, 2 vols (UN sales publication 71.V.3; 73.V.3).

—b. *United Nations Commission on International Trade Law Yearbook.* New York: UN, 1968-, 1-, annual (UN document A/CN.9/SER.A/year; UN sales publication: E.year.V.number).

Part 1, report by UNCITRAL on its activities (including those of its Working Group on NIEO) in the given year; part 2, texts of documents examined during UNCITRAL's annual session; part 3, recommendations concerning arbitration and conciliation, a checklist of UNCITRAL documents and a bibliography relating to UNCITRAL and to international trade law (mainly emanating from relevant international organizations).

—c. Szász, I., *The CMEA uniform law for international sales.* Dordrecht: Nijhoff; Budapest: Akadémiai Kiadó, 1984, 284 pp.

Analyses the 'general condition of delivery of goods' (1979 edition) in terms of a uniform trade law between countries of the Council for Mutual Economic Aid (CMEA). *See also* Vincze, I., *The international payments and monetary system in the integration of the Socialist Countries.* Dordrecht: Nijhoff; Budapest: Akadémiai Kiadó, 1984, 186 pp. This work includes an analysis of the structure and functions of CMEA.

733a. Rauh, K., *Die Schieds- und Schlichtungsordnungen der UNCITRAL.* Köln: Heymanns, 1983, 215 pp. (Internationales Wirtschaftsrecht, 2).

—b. Schmitthoff, C. M., *International commercial arbitration*. Dobbs Ferry, NY: Oceana, 1978-, 1-, loose-leaf.

The contributors include: G. Gaja, The New York Convention (3 binders); W. E. Butler, Soviet commercial and maritime arbitration (2 binders): and L. Craig, W. W. Park and J. Paulson, International Chamber of Commerce arbitration (1 binder).

734a. *Hague–Zagreb essays on the law of international trade.* 1971-, 1-, irregular. Edited by C. C. A. Voskuil *et al.*

Contains discussions and reports relating to colloquia or round tables under the joint auspices of the T. M. C Asser Institute, The Hague [406], and the Institute for International Law and International Relations, Zagreb [396], held in Yugoslavia in 1971, 1974 and 1978 and in the Netherlands in 1976, 1981 and 1985. The contributions by scholars from Eastern and Western Europe deal with international sales, standard international trade forms, international commercial arbitration, etc.

—b. *Law and international trade/Recht und internationaler Handel. Festschrift für Clive M. Schmitthof zum 70. Geburtstag.* Edited by F. Fabritius. Frankfurt: Athenäum, 1973, 423 pp.

The contributors include: J. Jakubowski, The autonomy of the international trade and its influence on the interpretation and application of its rules, and A. Farnsworth, UNCITRAL and the progressive development of international trade. Note that Schmitthof prepared a study which formed the basis of the UN document A/6396, Progressive development of the law of international trade.

—c. Schmitthof, C. M. and Simmonds, K. R. (eds), *International economic and trade law: universal and regional integration.* Leiden: Sijthoff, 1976, 252 pp.

Contains the revised papers presented at the Oxford International Symposium on Universalism and Regionalism in International Economic and Trade Law, Christ Church, Oxford, 1973. *See also* contributions in [379a] on restrictive trade legislation and monetary and investment laws.

735a. *Journal of world trade law.* Twickenham, UK, 1967-, 1-, bimonthly.

—b. *Recht der internationalen Wirtschaft.* Heidelberg: Recht und Wissenschaft, 1954-, 1-, monthly.

736a. Advisory Committee for the Co-ordination of Information Systems (ACCIS). *Guide to United Nations information sources on trade and development finance.* New York, 1990 (UN sales publication GV.E.90.02).

—b. Kudej, B., *International trade law: a bibliography.* Dobbs Ferry, NY: Oceana, 1984, 57 pp. (Collection of Bibliography and Research Resources).

737a. *Tax treaties: international tax agreements.* New York: UN, 1948-, 1-, loose-leaf (UN document ST/ECA/SER.C/1-; UN sales publication E. year.XVI.no.).

Includes the text and status of international taxation agreements on income and capital; commercial, agricultural, maritime and transport enterprises.

—b. Diamond, D. and Diamond, W., *International tax treaties of all nations*. Dobbs Ferry, NY: Oceana, 1973-.

Series A, Treaties published by the United Nations (13 vols in 1989); Series B, Treaties not published by the United Nations (23 vols + cumulative index, in 1989).

—c. *Tax treaties between developed and developing countries*. New York: UN, 1970-, 1- (UN document ST/ECA/no.; UN sales publication E.year.XVI.no.) Last report 8th, 1980.

See also UN model tax convention between developed and developing countries [comments]. *Bulletin of international fiscal documentation* (Amsterdam), 1981, 35 (7), pp. 309-313.

738a. *Investment laws of the world*. Dobbs Ferry, NY: Oceana, 1973-, 1-, loose-leaf.

Compiled by, and published for, the International Centre for Settlement of Investment Disputes (ICSID) (created in 1965 within the context of the IBRD), the collection contains texts of some 90 national investment laws and treaties chiefly relating to investment in developing countries.

—b. Fischer, P. (ed.), *A collection of international concessions and related instruments*. Dobbs Ferry, NY: Oceana, 1976-83. 12 vols; 1981-5, 6 vols.

The collection contains annotated texts of concessions (by the state of rights and functions to private persons for carrying out given economic activities) from the Middle Ages to 1976.

—c. Laviec, J.-P., *Protection et promotion des investissements. Etude de droit international économique*. Paris: Presses universitaires de France, 1985, 331 pp.

An outcome of the author's PhD thesis (Paris, 1984), the work includes the definition of the legal aspects of investments and the rights and duties of the investor and country of investment.

—d. Khan-Kabir-ur, *The law and organization of international commodity agreements*. The Hague: Nijhoff, 1982, 416 pp.

Analyses commodity agreements negotiated within the UN system, in terms of their regulatory mechanisms (contracts and treaties) and reciprocity principles. *See also* Johnston, C.R., *Law and policy of intergovernmental primary commodity agreements*. Dobbs Ferry, NY: Oceana, 1976-, 3 binders.

—e. *Les investissements et le développement économique des pays du Tiers Monde: Colloque, Paris, 1967*. Paris: Pédone, 1968, 443 pp.

739a. Simmonds, K.R., *Multinational corporations law*. Dobbs Ferry, NY: Oceana, 1979-, 1-, loose-leaf.

Includes Browndorf, E. and Reimer, S., *Bibliography of multinational corporations and foreign direct investment* (1979–).

—b. *Robinson, P., *The question of a reference to international law in the United Nations Code of Conduct on Transnational Corporations*. New York, 1986.

—c. United Nations Centre on Transnational Corporations. c/o United Nations, United Nations Plaza, New York, NY 10027, USA.

Serves as the Secretariat of the Commission on Transnational Corporations founded in 1974 as a subsidiary body of the UN Economic and Social Council. For the Centre's activities *see also IJLI*, 1987, **15**(5/6), pp. 264–267.

740a. United Nations Conference on Trade and Development. c/o UN Office at Geneva, Palais des Nations, Geneva, Switzerland.

The history of UNCTAD, 1964–1984. New York: UN, 1985, 294 pp. (UNCTAD document PSG/286; UN sales publication E.85.II.D.6). UNCTAD publishes *Trade and development: an UNCTAD review*. 1979–, 1– (reports on trade policies and inter-governmental negotiations); *Trade and development report*. 1981–, 1– (reviews current and long-term trade developments). For a list of publications by, and relating to, UNCTAD *see UNCTAD, 1963–1983: bibliography/CNUCED, 1963–1983: bibliographie*. Geneva: UNOG Library, 1983, 81 pp. *See also Index to resolutions and other decisions of the UNCTAD and the Trade Development Board, 1964–1972*. New York: UN, DHL, 1973, 57 pp.

—b. Weiss, T.G., *Multilateral development diplomacy in UNCTAD: the lessons of group negotiations, 1964–1968*. London: Macmillan, 1986, 187 pp.

A critical analysis of the group negotiating process within the context of UNCTAD.

—c. Simmonds, K.R. and Hill, B.H.W., *Law and practice under the GATT and other trading arrangements*. Dobbs Ferry, NY: Oceana, 1987–, 1–, loose-leaf.

Based on primary and secondary sources, including documents from the Tokyo and Uruguay Rounds. *See also* Hyder, K., *Equality of treatment and trade discrimination in international law*. The Hague: Nijhoff, 1968, 216 pp., which examines continued trade discrimination against the principle of economic equality promoted by GATT.

—d. Broches, A., 1959/III, International legal aspects of the World Bank. *RCADI*, **98**, pp. 301–409.

vii. INTERNATIONAL TRANSPORT LAW

741a. Evans, M. and Stanford, M., *Transport laws of the world*. Dobbs Ferry, NY: Oceana, 1978–, loose-leaf.

278 SELECTED SUBJECT BIBLIOGRAPHY

—b. Jackson, D.C., *World shipping laws*. Dobbs Ferry, NY: Oceana, 1979-, loose-leaf.

—c. *Bergner, M. and Teuchert W. (eds), *Internationales Verkehrsrecht*, 2nd edn. Berlin: Staatsverlag der DDR, 1986, 345 pp.

—d. *Aspects actuels du droit international des transports: Colloque de Mans, 1980.* Paris: Pédone, 1981, 411 pp. (Actes du 14.e Colloque de la Société française pour le droit international).

—e. Cheng, B., *The law of international air transport*. London: Stevens, 1962, 726 pp.

viii. INTERNATIONAL LAW OF COMMUNICATION, INFORMATION

742a. Ploman, E.W. (comp.), *International law governing communications and information: a collection of basic documents*. Westport, CT: International Institute of Communications, 1982, 367 pp.

Includes UN, UNESCO and WIPO documents, mostly on freedom of information, protection of privacy, etc.

—b. *La circulation des informations et le droit international: Colloque de Strasbourg, 1977.* Paris: Pédone, 1978, 365 pp. (Actes du 11. Colloque de la Société française pour le droit international).

—c. McWhinney, E., *The international law of communications*. Dobbs Ferry, NY: Oceana, 1971, 172 pp.

—d. de Visscher, C., *Le droit international des communications. Cours professé à l'Institut des hautes études internationales de Paris, 1921 et 1923.* Gand: A. Buyens, 1924, 152 pp.

—e. The New World Information and Communication Order: a selective bibliography. New York: UN Dag Hammarskjöld Library, 1984, 152 pp. (UN document ST/LIB/SER.B/35; UN sales publication E/F.84.I.15).

743a. *Encyclopedia of international telecommunications law*. Austin, TX: Butterworth Legal Publishers, 1987, 2 vols.

—b. *International telecommunications agreements*. Edited by G.D. Wallenstein and R.V. Brandt. Dobbs Ferry, NY: Oceana, 1977, 3 vols.

Contains annotated texts of agreements concluded mainly under the auspices of the International Telecommunications Union (Geneva).

ix. PIL AND SCIENCE/TECHNOLOGY

744a. *Lleonart, A. J., *Investigación científica y derecho internacional*. Madrid: Consejo Superior de Investigaciones Científicas, 1982, 269 pp.

—b. Gotlieb, A. E., 1981/I, Impact of technology on the development of international law. *RCADI*, **170**, pp. 115-330.

—c. Ziman, J., Sieghart, P. and Humphrey, J., *The world of science and the rule of law: a study of the observance and violations of the human rights of scientists in the participating states of the Helsinki Accords*. Oxford: Oxford UP, 1986, 342 pp.

See also [582b].

Index-Thesaurus

The Index-Thesaurus represents a single alphabetical (word-by-word) sequence of author (individual, corporate), geographical, subject and title entries. Only selected distinctive titles (italicized) are listed. At best summary, neither the (sometimes inverted) subject entries nor their (often reference-oriented) subdivisions adequately reflect topical/geographical/organizational distinctions concerning: PIL concepts, practice *proper to* a given country or IGO, as opposed to PIL works *published in/by* that country or IGO, and/or perceptions about such works *outside* that country/region or IGO. The entries beginning English-language, French-language, Russian language, etc. mainly contain PIL references to secondary resources/reference aids (manuals, dictionaries, etc.), but also include mention of translations of PIL works into or from such languages.

The index entries refer mostly to item numbers in Part II, as well as to page and occasionally footnote numbers in Part I. A requisite number of *see, see also* cross-references, solely reflecting the contents of this *Guide*, should facilitate its use.

AALL newsletter, 415b
abbreviations
   legal, 369–70, 501a
   periodical titles, 216b, 370a
   UN system, 637
Abendrot, W., 177
Abi-Saab, G., 320b, 532c, 627a
Abi-Saab, R., 601c
abstracting services
   conference papers, p. 35
   directories, p. 126
   political science, 450c
   see also indexing services
Academic Council on the United Nations System (ACUNS), 629c
academic degrees, international law
   comparability, 499h
   directories, 377, 380a

Académie de droit international de La Haye, 380a
Académie diplomatique internationale, 542b, 573c
Académie internationale de droit comparé, 432a, 433a
Access to the sea for developing land-locked states, 551
Accioly, H. P. P., 95
accreditation, *see* academic degrees
acquired rights, 531a,e
acquisitions, *see* law libraries
acronyms, *see* abbreviations
Acta juridica, 352
Acta scandinavica juris gentium, 274
acts
 juridical, 510a, 519d
 unilateral, 510b
 see also facts versus legal norms
el-Adah, F., 451d
Adam, H. T., 676b
Adede, A. O., 470a
Adeniran, B., 656b
Adjangba, M. A., 545
adjudication, international, 297 (vol. 2), 667b; *see also* tribunals: international
administrative tribunals, international, 194, 209, 619c
 judicial chronology, 284
 UN, 619b
Advisory Committee for the Co-ordination of Information Systems (ACCIS), 678c
 Specialized Agencies of the UN, guides to information sources, 681d, 717a, 721a, 736a
 UN, directories of databases, serials, 632a,b
Africa
 and Europe, 484a, 516b
 boundaries, 534c
 constitutions, 64a
 human rights, 647c, 695, 698a
 international organizations, 686-7
 international relations, 301b
 law of the sea, 553, 556c
 legal associations, 383-4
 legal systems, 429
 libraries, directory, 416d
 PIL approaches, 325, 457c,d, 474e, 484

 history, 457a,c,d
 study and teaching, 499a
African law digest, 224b
aggression, 213, 579a, 581a, 594, 703a
 bibliography, 594d
 Soviet concept, 705a
Ago, R., 44, 178, 198, 468c
Agrawalo, S. K., 177, 482c
Agreements between the UN and the SAs and the IAEA, 618a
Ahluwalia, K., 617c
air law, 540a, 561d,e
 aircraft hijacking, 703a
 bibliography, 565a
 institutes, 561a, 564
 periodicals, 563a,c,d
 transport aspects, 741e
 treaties, 560b
 see also space law, international
Aitchison, J., p. 111
Aix-en-Provence *colloque*, 482d
Akehurst, M., p. 26(5); 170
Akkerman, R. J., 205
Aktual'nye problemy sovremennogo mezhdunarodnogo prava, 271
Aktual'nye problemy teorii mezhdunarodnogo prava, 504a
Aktuelle Probleme des internationalen Rechts, 380b
Albania, PIL
 dictionaries, 313
 manuals, 110
Alexandrowicz, C. H., 457d, 465e, 468c, 516b, 677
Alexidze, L. A., 515a
Alger *colloque*, 722b
Ali, *see* Sheik R. Ali
Alibert, C., 507c
Állam és jogtudomány, 266
Allen, C. G., p. 111
Allott, A., 534c
Alston, P., 647a
Alvarez, A., 481f, 520f
Amerasinghe, C. F., 109
American Association of Law Libraries, p. 41; 415b
American international law cases, p. 23; 53
American journal of international law, 227
American Society of International Law, 387
 Proceedings, 227, 625a
The American University journal of

international law and policy, 228
Americas
  human rights, 696
  juridical yearbook, 688
  PIL, 467b, 481a
  treaties, 9–11
  see also entries beginning 'Inter-American'; Latin America
Amoun, F., p. 24(3)
analogous reasoning, PIL, 185, 423c, 509f
L'Analyse de texte: méthode générale et application au droit, 498e
analytical conceptualism, 490
analytical tools, p. 27(7)
Anand, R.P., 177, 482a, 485a, 527c, 544
Ancel, M., 422b, 430
Andean economic integration, 190
Andean legal order, 481b
Andemicael, B., 687c
Anderberg, M.M., 719b
Anderson, M., p. 43(1)
Andrassy, J., 131, 178
Andrews, J.A., 693a
Anghelov, S., 479a
Anglo-American approach to law/PIL, 470c
  citators, 369, 370a
  see also common law approach
Anglo-Polish legal colloquia, 324b
Anglo-Soviet PIL symposium, 428a
Anglo-Soviet post-UNCLOS perspectives, 557a
Annales d'études internationales, 449d
Annali di diritto internazionale, 286
Annuaire de droit maritime et aérien, 563c
Annuaire de l'AAA, 380b
Annuaire de l'Association yougoslave de droit international, 20
Annuaire de législation française et étrangère, 72a
Annuaire de l'Institut de droit international, 378
Annuaire diplomatique de l'Empire de Russie, 569
Annuaire du Tiers-Monde, 488a
Annuaire français de droit international, 282
Annuaire suisse de droit international, 292
Annual digest and report of public international law cases, 50
Annual legal bibliography, 338b

Annual register: a review of public events, 452a
Annual review of United Nations affairs, 640c
Antarctica, 183, 187, 534a, 535, 540a
  boundaries, 534a
  documents collection, 535b
Antell, J.B., 719b
anthropocentric approach to PIL, 460; *see also* sociological approaches to PIL
Anuario de derecho internacional, 290
Anuario de derecho internacional público, 245a
Anuario ecuatoriano de derecho internacional, 247
Anuario jurídico interamericano, 688
Anuario uruguayo de derecho internacional, 249
Appleman, J.A., 710d
Arabic countries
  legal systems, 429d
  legislation, 73a
  development, 721d
  see also entries beginning 'Islamic'
Arabic Court of Justice, projected, 523b
Arabic language
  dictionaries, etc., 451d, 636c
  periodicals, 222
    translations, 296
  UN conference terms, 636c
Arangio-Ruiz, G., 458a, 655a
Arbeitsgemeinschaft für juristisches Bibliotheks- und Dokumentationswesen (AJBD), 414d
arbitration, international, 524a–c, 621a
  awards collections, 48c–f
  commercial, 733b, 734a
  dictionary, 524c
  UNCITRAL, 732b, 733a
Archer, C., 627b
archipelagos, 543b
Archiv des Völkerrechts, 280
archives, p. 11(8)
  IGOs, p. 43(5)
Archives diplomatiques, 569
Arctic passages, 543c
Argentina
  legal bibliography, 349
  PIL
    cases, 54, 92
    institute, 390
    manuals, 91, 93
    periodicals, 245
Arguello, A.M., 89

Arias, L., 85
armed conflict
 international, 593c, 596
  codification, 592a, 600d, 601
  dictionary, 612c
  diplomatic conferences, 598-9
  legal regulation, 458b
 non-international, 599b, 601b
 and human rights, 261
arms control
 dictionaries, 584f, 589c
 guides to research, 589d
 periodicals, 588
 PIL aspects, 587a
 see also disarmament; nuclear weapons
Asamoah, O., 653c
Ash, L., 416b
Ashavskiĭ, B.M., 319
Asia
 constitutions, 64b
 Harvard studies in East Asian law, 389b
 human rights, 647c, 698a
 international organizations, 691
 law of the sea, 554-5
 legal association, 383
 PIL aspects, 483, 485
  history, 457a,d
Asian-African Legal Consultative Committee, 383, 483
ASILS international law journal, 228
Asser, T.M.C., 424
 Interuniversitair Instituut (T.M.C. Asser Institute), 406
Association des anciens étudiants de l'IUHEI, 407b
Association H. Capitant, p. 24(6)
Association française pour l'étude du Tiers-Monde, 488a
Association of American Law Schools, 389
Association of Attenders and Alumni of the Academy (AAA), 380b, 529b, 715c
Association of International Libraries, 633c
Association of Student International Law Societies (ASILS), 387b
Associations, 630a
Assumptions and perceptions in disarmament, 587c

asylum, territorial, 705a
 bibliography, 702d
Athens colloquium, 542c
Atherton, A.L., 634c
Atlam, H., 528a
atlases
 PIL, 374a
 Third World, 488c
Attard, D.J., 549b
Aubenas, R., 507c
Auburn, F.M., 659b
Aufricht, H., 674a
Austin, R.H.F., 379a
Australia, PIL
 manual, 40
 yearbook, 261
Austria
 Centre for International Studies, 432c
 PIL
  historiography, 471a
  institutes, 400
  manuals, 139-41
  periodical, 276
  study and teaching, 499e
authentic text (of treaties, etc.), 517d, 636a
authority
 and world order, 400b, 445b
 historiography, USA 197
auto-interpretation, PIL 183, 192
automation, *see under* law libraries
Autorität und internationale Ordnung, 400b
Avakov, M.M., 529c, 580d
Aveney, B., p. 43(10)
aviation treaties, 560b; *see also* air law
Les avis consultatifs et la justice internationale, 670b
Avramov, S., 133
axiological problems, PIL, 648a
el-Ayouty, Y., 686b
Azevedo Soares, 159

Badr, M.G., 527b
Bailey, J.F., 502c
Balázsné Veredy, K., 352
Balladore-Pallieri, G., 155, 180, 619d
Baocun, *see* Pan Baocun
el-Baradei, M., 538d
Baratashvili, D.I., 527d
Barberis, J.A., 481a
Barbulescu, P., 17
Bardonnet, D., 282

Barile, G., 155
Barkun, M., 343
Barros, J., 715b
Barry, D., 455d
Bartels, M., 731e
Bartos, M., 132, 179
Basdevant, J., 312
basic texts, international law/relations
   Bulgarian, 11b
   Czech, 115
   English, 81, 174, 616a, 686c, 687a, 691
   French, 153-4, 494a
   German, 118
   Hungarian, 120
   Polish, 123
   Russian, 130
   Serbo-Croat, 134
   Spanish, 88, 92, 162, 165
   see also case studies, law/PIL; intergovernmental organizations; United Nations
Baskin, IU.IA., 493
Basset, E., 497d
Bassiouni, C., 703a, 705a, 711b
Bastid, S., 185, 193-4, 199, 282, 507c, 512a, 686d
Baxter, R., 511a
bays, 543d
Beaudiquez, M., p. 38(5)
Bedjaoui, M., p. 71; 75, 186, 448c, 474b, 499a, 531d, 727b
behavioural approach to PIL, 436
Beigbeder, Y., 630d
Beiträge zum ausländischen, öffentlichen Recht und Völkerrecht, 402a
Belgium, PIL, 183
   institutes, 401
   libraries, 501a
   manuals, 142-3
   periodicals, 277
belligerents, 602e, 609a
Bello, A., 97
Bello, E.G., 695a
Bemmelen, J.M. van, 706b
Benadava, S., 97
Benchikh, M., 186, 508a, 723e
Benedek, W., 484a
Benevolenskiĭ, V., 448d
Bennett, A.L., 628c
Bennouna, M., 185, 731b
Berber, F., 145

Bergh, A.L. van den, 519b
Bergner, M., 741c
Berlia, G., 181
Bermes, A., 559g
Bernal, M.L., 331b, 417a
Bernhardt, R., 49a, 297, 361, 498a, 499d, 517c, 519c, 576a, 698
Bernstein, H., 427a
Berring, R.C., 331a
Bertrand, M., 647a
Besterman, T., 337a
Bettati, M., 630d
Bevans, C.I., 10b
Bezobrazov, V.P., 378c
Bhattacharya, K.K., 107
Bibliografía jurídica de América Latina, 349
Bibliographic guide to law, 366b
Bibliographie de la Cour Internationale de Justice, 664c
bibliographies
   legal, 349-52, 358-9, 366-8, 432d
   reviews, 371b
   national, p. 38(5)
   Third World, 487b
   PIL, 147, 237, 339-47
      Canada, 348
      French-language, 282
      German-language, 360
      Italy, 286
      Poland, 267
      Scandinavia, 357
      Switzerland, 292
      UK, 294
      USSR, 126, 270, 353-5
   see also indexing services; and under subjects, e.g. humanitarian law, space law, etc.
Bibliotheca internacionalista clásica, 464b
Bibliotheca ius gentium exotica, 457b
Bibliotheca Visseriana, p. 30; 214
Bibliothèque de droit international, 373h, 678a
Bieber, D.M., 370a
Bierzanek, R., 179
Bilancia, P.R., 36b
binding force, PIL, 490
   judicial decisions, p. 24(4); 503a
   UN Security Council resolutions, 656a
Bindschedler, R., 182, 211, 591a
Bing, J., 412a
biographical information
   guides, p. 41(2)

biographical information *contd*
  internationalists, p. 40; 375
  Nobel Prize laureates, 582a
PIL
  bio-bibliographies, 220a, 298, 303, 460, 499c, 573c, 664a
  institutional commemorations, p. 41(3)
Bipoun-Woum, J.M., 484e
Bishop, W.W., p. 29(7); 83
Biswas, A.K., 714b
Black, C.E., 445b
Blankenstein, M. van, 214
Blatova, N.T., 127, 130
Blaustein, A.P., 63a
Bleckmann, A., 492, 499d, 509b
Bledsoe, R.L., 298b
Blenk-Knocke, E., 506e
Blishchenko, I.P., 570e, 587a
Blix, H., 518a
Blondel, A., 193
Bloomfield, B., p. 43(1)
Blue book series, 373a
'Bluebook' citator, 369
Boasard, M.A., 476d
Boasson, C., 580b
Böckstiegel, K.H., 562b, 621a
Boczek, B.A., 298b
Bogaert, E.R.C. van, 143, 183
Bogdanov, O.V., 657c
Boguslavskiĭ, M.M., 684b
Böhm, A., 202
Bokor-Szegö, H., 195, 265, 649a
Bolintineanu, A., 648b
Bolivia, legal bibliography, 349
book reviews
  legal, 371, 414b
  PIL, 283, 364a,b
Bordeaux *colloque*, 478c
Borgese, E.M., 558e, 730
Bos, M., 189, 198, 379a, 468c, 490, 509c, 519b, 621b
Bothe, M., 600b
Boulery, C., 578a
boundaries, 534, 561a; *see also* maritime boundary
bourgeois approaches to PIL, 437a, 474b,d; *see also* Western approaches to law/PIL
Boutros-Ghali, B., 190, 626d
Boven, T. van, p. 26(6); 440
Bowett, D.W., 294, 512c, 543a, 575b, 620a

Bowker American Book Publishing Record Database, 338c
Bowman, M.J., 26
Bozec, *see* Sicart-Bozec, M.
Bozeman, A., 459
Braillard, P., 482b
Brandt, R.V., 743b
Brazil, PIL
  association, 391
  manuals, 94-5
  state practice, 35
Brecht, A., 500d
Breem, W.W.S., p. 24(7)
Brewster, H.R., 647a
Breycha-Vautier, A.C., 673c, 674a
Brierly, J.L., 172
Briggs, H.W., p. 11(1); 663c
British and foreign state papers, 23
British digest of international law, 47a
British Institute of International and Comparative Law, 408
British international law cases, 61
British official publications, 69b
British practice in international law, 47b
British yearbook of international law, 294
Broad terms for UN programmes and activities, 636d
Broches, A., 740d
Broms, B., 136, 191, 594b, 625c
Brooks, H.C., 685b
Browndorf, E., 739a
Brownlie, I., 170, 174, 294, 458a, 499b, 534c, 548b, 592c, 621b, d, 731c
Brunner, G., 520c
Bruns, V., pp. 16, 20(7); 49a, 279
Buddhism and PIL, 475d
Buergenthal, T., 209, 577c, 696c
Bulajić, M., 723c
Bulgaria
  legal bibliography, 351
  PIL, 41, 262
    basic texts, 111b
    manual, 112
    treaties, 14
Bulletin of legal developments, 408
Bulletin officiel internationl d'hygiène publique, 682b
Bulletin on current research in Soviet and East European Law, 273d
Bünzli, K., 520e
Burns, I.R., 534c
Burton, W.C., 412c
Bush, W.M., 535b

Buske, A., 8b
Bustamente y Sirven, A. S. de, 84b
Butler, W. E., 42b, 73b, 220a, 273c,
    345, 354, 428a,b, 455d, 467b,
    472, 473b, 478d, 493, 500f, 502a,
    504b, 543c, 557a, 692b, 733b
Buza, L., 119

Cadwallader, J. L., p. 20(7)
Caflisch, L., 46, 49b, 536a, 546b
Cahier, P., 193, 531b, 570d, 652b
Caicedo Castillo, J. J., 481e
Caillot, J., 692a
A calendar of Soviet treaties, p. 53
California western international law journal, 229
Calogeropoulos-Stratis, S., 593a, 608b
Calvez, J. Y., 473g
Calvo, C., 9, 93, 301a
Camara, S., 301b
Camargo, P. P., 99
Cambridge (England)
    Research Centre for International
        Law, 373e,f
    University, law/PIL catalogue, 340
Cambridge essays in international law, 512c
*Cambridge studies in international and
    comparative law*, 531e
Caminos, H., 540b
Canada
    international relations, 449e, 453
    PIL
        bibliographies, 348
        cases, 52
        institutions, 386, 561a
        periodicals, 225-6
        treaties, 11, 30b
Canadian Council on International Law, 386
Canadian encyclopedic digest, 33b
Canadian treaty calendar, series, 11
Canadian yearbook of international law, 225
Cançado, *see* Trindade, A. A. C.
La capacité de l'ONU de conclure des traités, 650a
*The capacity of international organizations to
    conclude treaties*, 624
Caparros, E., 370c
Capotorti, F., 201
Cardozo, M. H., 500b
Carnegie Endowment for International
    Peace, 320, 381, 515e
Carreau, D., 148

Carrillo Salcedo, J. A., 458c, 526b, 651b
Carroll, B. A., 583c
Carroz, J., 541
Carty, A., 461b
case studies, law/PIL, p. 29(7); 83
    Commonwealth, 51
    see also Anglo-American approach to
        law/PIL; International Court of
        Justice; United Nations
*Case Western Reserve journal of international
    law*, 230
Cases on United Nations law, 651a
Cassan, H., 723d
Cassel, J. G., 78
Cassesse, A., 421c, 458-9, 593
Cassin, R., 699
Castañeda, J., 654a, 720d
Castberg, F., 137, 211, 220a, 494b
Castren, E., 184
Catalog of international law and relations, 338a
Catalog of the Foreign Relations Library, 450b
Catalog of US treaties, 10c
*Catalogue de la Bibliothèque du Palais de la
    Paix*, p. 36; 339a
*Catalogue de sources de documentation juridique
    dans le monde*, 62a
*Catalogue des sources de documentation
    juridique des pays socialistes*, p. 17; 62b
Catalogue of international law, p. 36; 340
catalogues, law libraries
    Cambridge University, 340
    Harvard University, 338a, 345
    Peace Palace, 339
Catholic conceptions of international law,
    464a, 475b
Censo de tratados internacionales, 22a
'Center for the computerization of law
    internationally', p. 38(7)
Center for International Studies, 432c
Center for Oceans Law and Policy, 558b
Centre Charles de Visscher pour le droit
    international, 401a
Centre de droit maritime et aérien, 561a
Centre d'études des problèmes juridiques
    et politiques du Tiers-Monde,
    301b, 488a
Centre d'études des relations
    internationales, 322
Centre for Russian and East European
    Studies, 273d

288   INDEX-THESAURUS

Centre for Studies and Research in International Law and Relations, 380a
Centre for the Study of Socialist Legal Systems, 397c, 428a
Centro de estudios jurídicos hispano-americanos, 481e
Chai, N.Y., 39
Chakhmakchev, A.G., 630c
Champ, *see* Johnson-Champ, D.G.
Change and stability in international law-making, 458a
The changing law of international claims, 528d
The changing law of nations, 462f
The changing structure of international economic law, 727a
Chapman, F.C., 218
Charnay, J.P., 461
Charpentier, J., 623a
Charte des droits et des devoirs économiques des états, 720d
Charte des Nations Unies, 642b
Charvin, R., 185
Chaudhri, M.A., 653d
Chaumont, C., 185, 206, 220a
Chemillier-Gendreau, M., 147, 474c, 510d
Cheng, B., p. 25; 379a, 499b, 507a, 521f, 741e
Cherns, J.J., 67a
Chilaty, D., 585d
Child, J., 454c
Chile
  Instituto de estudios internacionales, 535c
  PIL manuals, 96-7, 481f
Chilecki, E., 355
China, *see* People's Republic of China
Chinese language, PIL
  glossary, English 36b
  translation, 462f
Chinese Society of International Law
  Beijing, 392
  Taipei, 393
Chinese yearbook of international law, 250
Chinese yearbook of international law and affairs, 251
Chiu, H., 12, 36b, 209, 533d, 624d
Chkhikvadze, V.M., 129
Choi, W., 209
Cholganskaia, V.L., 636e

Chopra, S.K., 535a
Christol, C.Q., 507b, 561b
chronologies
  of international relations, 283, 452a
  of United Nations affairs, 640c
Chronology of international treaties and legislative measures, 4
Cichocki, P.F., 400b
La circulation des informations et le droit international, 742b
Cismarescu, M., 125
citations, legal, 370
  uniform system, 369
civil war, 606
civilians
  protection, Geneva Convention IV, 598b
  versus combatants, 602e
Civitas maxima, 455c
claims, international, 528d
Clark, G., 445c
classical international law, *see* contemporary versus classical PIL
Classics of international law, 463a
classification
  bibliography, p. 111
  law, 411a
  PIL, 340, 353b, 361, 497
  state practice, p. 16; 32
Cloşca, I., 306
Clunet, 284
The code of international armed conflicts, 592a
codes
  law, 72b
  PIL, 520g, 592a
La codificación del derecho internacional en América, 520f
codification
  ILC role, 662
  law of the sea, 540b
  LoN conference, 673
  PIL, 178, 188, 194, 520b-g
    customary international law, p. 18; 520a
  private international law, 425
  state responsibility, 528a
  succession of states in respect of treaties, 531c
co-existence
  international law, 480
  international relations, 434b
Coexistence: a review, 428a

Cohen, J.A., 36b, 38
Cohen, M.L., p. 36(4); 331a
Colección de los tratados, convenios y documentos internacionales, 345
Coles, G., 702a
Colin, J.P., 731a
Collected courses of the Hague Academy, *see Recueil des cours de l'Académie de droit international de la Haye*
Collection: Organisation internationale et relations internationales, 623b
Collection of bibliographic and research resources, 337b
Colliard, C.A., 151, 154, 186
Collier, J., 196
Collier, M., p. 38(10)
Collison, R.L., 452b
colloquia, law/PIL
  Anglo-Polish, 324b
  French, 321-2, 461a
  German-Polish, 324a
  German-Soviet, 421b
  Hague/Zagreb essays, 734a
  IGOs, 628b
  see also development; Grotius; human rights; terrorism; etc.
Colombia, PIL manuals, 98-9
Columbia journal of environmental law, 716a
Columbia journal of transnational law, 231
Columbia law review, 231
Columbus Library (OAS), 690b
Combacau, J., p. 24(6); 282, 650b
combatants, status, 609a
Comité international de la Croix-Rouge, 610a; *see also* International Red Cross
commemorative essays
  bibliography, 176
    legal essays, 175
    PIL, 178-213
      institutional commemorations, 379a, 380a, 433c
    see also criminal law, international; humanitarian law; law of the sea; treaties, law of
commentaries, *see* conventions, PIL
Committee of Experts for the Progressive Codification of International Law (LoN), 673b
Committee on the Progressive Development of International Law

and its Codification (ILC), p. 16; 31, 662a
commodity agreements, law of, 738d
common heritage of mankind, 207, 442, 507b
  environment, 714c
  law of the sea, 186-7, 540b, 541, 547a,b, 548a
  natural resources, 731a
common law approach
  periodicals, indexing service, 364a, 365
  PIL historiography, 470a,b
  see also Anglo-American approach to law/PIL
Commonwealth
  international law cases, 51
  legal advisory service, 408
La communauté internationale entre le mythe et l'histoire, 438
communication
  diplomatic, 570c
  new international order, 448b, 742e
  law of, 742a-d
  see also telecommunications
community, international, 99, 185, 438-9, 458
  historiography, 508b
  socialist approach, 128, 190
  see also common heritage of mankind; multicultural aspects of PIL; world order
The community of states, 438
Comparabilité des diplômes en droit international, 499h
Comparative and international law journal of Southern Africa, 224a
Comparative approaches to international law, 428b
comparative law, 187, 422b, 427a, 428-30
  and PIL, 211, 428b, 502a
  bibliography, 432d
  congresses, 432a
  encyclopaedia, 431
  institutions, 382, 433
  periodicals, 432b,c
Comparative law yearbook, 432c
competence, international legal
  ICJ, 670c
  IGOs, 626a
  states, within PCIJ context 49b
Comprehensive dissertation index, 215

computerized (legal) information
    retrieval, p. 39(7); 412a, 417
  periodicals, indexing services, 365,
    366a
  treaties, 29-30
  UN system, 631a
*Conception soviétique de droit international
    public*, 473f
conceptual models, law/PIL
  analytical conceptualism, 490
  community, international, 438, 508b
  customary international law, 519f,
    520a
  international organization, 627a
  jus cogens, 515e
concessions, international, 738b
conciliation, international, 212
A concise history of the law of nations, 455b
Conference of teachers of international law, 381
conferences, international
  bibliography of publications, 316
  forthcoming, calendar, 315
  glossaries, 636b,c
  law/PIL, 126, 317-26, 381, 499f, 515e
  methodological aspects, 214
  see also colloquia; symposia; *and under
    names of sponsoring bodies*, e.g.
    Société française pour le droit
    international; *subjects*, e.g.
    disarmament
Conflict and compromise, 444
conflicts, international, 444, 449d
  periodicals, 583c,d
  Westview series, 612b
Conflit idéologique, 444
Confucian doctrine, PIL, 475c
Congrès international de droit comparé, 432a
Congrès international de droit humanitaire,
    604b
Les congrès internationaux de 1681 à 1899,
    315
congresses, *see* conferences, international
Connelly, A. M., 428b, 456b
Conseil canadien de droit international,
    348, 386
Conseil international des archives, 633b
*The consolidated index to ILO Legislative
    Series*, 680a
Consolidated treaty series, p. 12; 6
Consolidating world public order, 469a
Constantopoulos, D. S., 187, 281
Constantopoulos, J., 187

constitutions
  Africa, 64a
  Asia, 64b
  collections of texts, 63
  IGOs, 616a
    ILO, 680b
  PIL aspects, 421c
  socialist countries, 65a-c, 520c
consular relations, 297(vol. 9)
  dictionary, 299
  laws, regulations, 568
  treaties, 567
*Consultation informelle sur l'enseignement et la
    recherche en droit international public*,
    p. 20(10); 499a
contemporary versus classical PIL, p. 28;
    203, 209, 434c, 455b, 458a, 462e,
    474d, 476a-c, 507, 648a
continental shelf, 550
continuity versus change, *see*
    contemporary versus classical PIL
control, international, 434b, 523a
  IGOs, 623
  UN, 648b
  see also sanctions, international
*Controversial subjects of contemporary
    international law*, 525a
controversies, PIL, 507b(sect.4)
conventions, PIL (including
    commentaries)
  cultural property protection, 679a
  diplomatic relations, 566a,b
  humanitarian law, 598b
  labour, 680a
  law of the sea, 537a,b
  law of treaties, 1
co-operation, international, 297(vol. 9)
copyright, 679
  laws and treaties of the world, 684a
Corbett, P. E., 503a
Corbu, A. C., 510a
Cornell international law journal, 232
corporations, international, 196
Corpus constitutionnel, 63c
Cot, J. P., 589a, 642b
Council for Mutual Economic Assistance
    (CMEA), 692, 732c
  norm-creating, 428a
Council of Europe, p. 16; 32, 416
Council on Foreign Relations, 449b,
    450b
Coursier, H., 602d

courts, *see* tribunals
Coussirat-Coustère, V., 665b
coûtume sauvage, contestataire, 519f
Craig, L., 733b
Crawford, J.R., 261, 529a
crimes, international, 528a, 710d,e
criminal law, international, 301a(vols. 5, 6), 615, 703b, 705a,b
  bibliographies, 708
  digest, 703a
  ILC concept, 528a
  Max-Planck Institute, 709
  periodicals, 613b, 707a,b
  tribunal, proposed, 379, 704a,b
  see also military criminal law, bibliography
crisis, PIL, 206, 461
Croke, M., 656b
Cros, G., 652a
Crow, B., 488c
Cuba, PIL
  manual, 84
  periodical, 246
cultural aspects, *see* multicultural aspects of PIL
cultural property, protection, 679a
Current bibliographic information, 368b
Current law index, 365
Current legal bibliography, 338b
Current problems of international law, 593b
current/retrospective documentary aspects
  bibliographies, p. 38(1)
  treaty collections, p. 15(13)
customary international law, p. 15; 519c,f
  and treaties, 511a
  codification, 520
  continental shelf, 550b,c
  coûtume sauvage, 519f
  digests, 33–47
  evidence, 31, 189
  instant custom, 499b
  UNCLOS III, 548d
Cybichowski, Z., 304
Czechoslovakia, PIL
  basic texts, 115
  dictionary, 300
  manuals, 113–14
  periodicals, 263

Dacor Bacon House seminar, 712a
Dag Hammarskjöld Library, 419

Index to UNCTAD resolutions, 740a
official gazettes in, list of, 66
PIL
  bibliographies, 336a
  guides, 330
Daillier, A., 147
Dalman, *see* Olivart, Ramon de Dalman
D'Amato, A.A., 81, 507c, 519e
Damrosch, L.F., 667a
Danube, international régime, 536a
dar-al-Islam, 476b
data processing
  humanities, social sciences, p. 39(8)
  law/PIL, p. 21(14)
  UN databases, directory, 632a
  see also computerized (legal) information retrieval
Dau, H., 175c
Daudet, Y., 646
Daoudi, R., 570b
David, E., 501a
David, R., 429a
De conflictu legum, 422b
De jure belli ac pacis, bibliography, 465c
Deak, F., 53, 194, 590
debt, state succession to, 530c
The decay of international law, 461b
Decisions of international institutions before international courts, 622
declarations, PIL
  definition, UN, 643a
  on friendly relations, 655a
  human rights, Islamic, 694a
  outer space, 560c
  teaching PIL, 647c
Declarations on principles, 205
declaratory law/soft law, 519e
default, law/PIL, 670a
defence, legitimate, 593e
Degan, V.D., 212, 498e, 521e
Dégradation du droit des gens, 461a
Dehousse, F., 188
Delivanis, J., 593e
Delupis, I., 342
Demokratiĩa i pravo razvitogo sotsĩalisticheskogo obshchestva, 496b
Denmark, PIL
  institute, 398
  manual, 135
  periodical, 274
Denver journal of international law and policy, 233

Denza, E., 566b
depository functions of the UN
    Secretary-General, 3
depository libraries, UN system, p.
    43(7); 419b
Derecho de la comunidad internacional, 439
*Derecho internacional en el sistema
    interamericano*, 481e
Derecho internacional en un mundo en cambio,
    458c
Derrett, J. D. M., 429b
D'Estefano-Pisani, M. A., 84
détente, law of, 585e
Deutsch, K., 192
Deutsche Juristen aus fünf Jahrhunderten,
    471a
*Deutsche Rechtsprechung in völkerrechtlichen
    Fragen*, 58
Deux frontières invisibles, 561a
developing countries
    economic co-operation, 447b
    encyclopaedia, 719b
    environmental law, 714b
    guide to information sources, 487d
    IGOs, 719c
    investments, 738e
    least developed countries (LDC), 720c
    legal documentation, 415a
    PIL, 194, 459, 482
        codification, 520d
        teaching, 499a
    tax treaties, 737c
    see also development; Third World
development
    and disarmament, 445c, 584c
    PIL, 177, 185-6, 723a
        basic documents, 720a
        colloquia, 722
    research activities, institutes, 721, 725
    UN role, 724, 740b
    see also developing countries; economic
        law, international;
        underdevelopment, law of
Developments in international law, 373d
*Developments on the frontiers of international
    law*, 615
Dexter, B., 449b
Di Qual, L., 654b
Diaconu, I., 515c
dialectics, international law/relations,
    185, 437a
    materialist, 437a, 493

Diamond, D., 737b
Diamond, W., 737b
dictionaries
    bibliography, p. 111
    PIL
        English, 298-9
        Czech, 300
        French, 301a
        German, 302-3
        multilingual, 310-13
        Polish, 304
        Portuguese, 305
        Romanian, 306
        Serbo-Croat, 308
        Spanish, 309
    see also encyclopaedias; glossaries;
        vocabularies; terminology; *and
        under subjects*, e.g. armed conflict;
        international relations; etc.
Diederiks-Verschoor, I. H. P., 562b
Diermanse, P. J. J., 465d
Diez, E., 182
Diez de Velasco Valleja, M., 163
digests, PIL, 34a, 43-7a
    copyright law, 684a
    criminal law, 703a
    diplomatic correspondence, p. 17; 569
    IGOs, p. 19; 619a
    PCIJ decisions, 49a
    surveys, 31
        classificatory, 32
    UN affairs, 641a, 644a
    see also law reports
*Les dimensions internationales du droit
    humanitaire*, 602a
Dimitrijević, V., 460
Dimitrov, T., 450a, 631c, 634a
Dinh, *see* Nguyen Quoc Dinh
Dipla, H., 543a
*Diplomatic Conference on the Reaffirmation
    and Development of International
    Humanitarian Law*, 599a
Diplomatic law, 566b
diplomatic law/relations, 570, 630b
    Calvo doctrine, 93
    conferences, 572a
    dictionaries, 299, 573
    digest of diplomatic correspondence,
        569
    diplomatic courier, 662b
    handbooks, 570c, 572
    laws, regulations, 568

privileges, immunities, 389b, 566a,b
Vienna Convention, 566a
directories
  African libraries, 416d
  bibliographies, p. 41(1,2)
  development research, Arab countries, 721d
  disarmament, 589a
  law, USA
    libraries, 416b
    schools, 389a
  peace research, 583
  periodicals, 216a
  PIL
    opportunities in, 387c
    study and teaching, 377
  UN system, publications, 632a,b
  FAO statutory bodies, 681a
disarmament, 195, 585a,d
  agreements, multilateral, 584a,b
  conference, 584c
  and development, 445c
  guides
    to information sources, 589d
    to research, 589a
  images (American, Soviet), 587c
  terminology, 589b,c
  UN role, 584d,e, 585b
dispute settlement, 297(vol. 1), 574b, 575-6
  centre, 738a
  natural resources, 731d,e
  Specialized Agencies of the UN, 731e
  see also arbitration, international; law of the sea; peaceful settlement of disputes; space law
Dissenting and separate opinions at the World Court, 671b
dissertations, 215
  PIL series, 214
Djalili, M.R., 482b
Djonovic, D.J., 643b, 644b
doctrinal positions, PIL, pp. 10, 26, 27(2-4), 29(1-4); see also historiography, PIL
Doctrinas internacionales y autonomía Latino-Americana, 467a
document versus publication, p. 21(15)
  UN definition, p. 21(20)
documentation, IGOs, 631
Documentation et méthodologie juridiques, 501b

Documentation Office for Eastern European Law, 397a
Documents juridiques internationaux, 219b
Documents of international organizations, 634a
Documents pour servir à l'histoire du droit des gens, 455e
Documents to the people, 632c
Dokhalia, R.P., 520d
Dolbert, J.P., 541
Dolman, A.J., 442
Dolzer, R., 460
Dominican Republic, PIL manual, 85
Dominicé, C., 46, 182, 621a
Dorsch, E., 472f
Dowdy, W.L., 547a
Downen, R., 533c
draft articles on succession of states, 530c
draft code of offences against the peace and security of mankind, 662b
draft convention on diplomatic privileges and immunities, 566a
draft international passport for the accreditation of qualifications in international law, 499h
draft rules of the International Tribunal of the Law of the Sea, 546c
Draper, G.I.A.D., 598e
Drewry, G., 454a
Dreyfus, S., 152, 500h
Drobnig, L., 436a
Droit au développement, 722a
Droit de la mer, 538a,b
Droit déclaratoire et droit programmatoire, 519e
Droit des relations internationales, 152
Droit et libertés à la fin du XXe siècle, 186
Droit et relations internationales, 153
Droit et société, 508c
Droit extra-atmosphérique, 561a
Droit international à l'heure de sa codification, 178
Droit international demain, 529b
Droit international des communications, 742c
Droit international et droit interne, 49b
Droit international nouveau dans ses rapports avec la vie des peuples, 481f
Droit public interne et international, 181
Drummond, F.S., 364
dualism/monism in PIL, 198, 211
Duffar, J., 617b
Duffy, J., 487c
Dufour, A., 465c

Duguit, L., 508c
Dull, P., 710c
DUNDIS, pp. 38, 42; 632a
Dupuy, P.M., 149, 630d
Dupuy, R.J., 186, 196, 203, 210, 220a, 380a, 438, 459, 499g,h, 519f, 540b, 548a, 625b, 714a, 722a, 725b, 731d
Durante, F., 557b
Durdenevskiĭ, V.N., 65a, 353a,b
Dutch East Indies, PIL historiography, 471c
Dutch literature in the field of PIL, 288
Dutoit, B., 46, 432a
dynamic approaches to PIL, 445b
Dynamics of international law, 495a

Earth-oriented space activities and their legal implications, 562a
Eastern European states and the development of the law of the sea, 557b
Eastern journal of international law, 254
Eaton, M., 600b
ECDC handbook, 447b
economic law, international, 198, 458b, 621a, 718a-c, 723b,g
    Chinese concept, 440
    CMEA uniform law, 732c
    codification, 178
    conferences, colloquia, 386, 722b,c
    dispute settlement, 574b
    economic rights, Charter, 720d
    methodology, 718d
    series, Asser, 406
    universalism/regionalism, 734c
    see also development: PIL; New International Economic Order
economic zone, exclusive, 549
Ecuador, PIL yearbook, 247
editorial manual, UN, 660b
education and PIL, 459
Edwards, R.W., p. 21(14)
The effect of independence on treaties, 379
The effectiveness of international decisions, 625a
Les effectivités du droit international public, 503a
Les effets directs des instruments internationaux en matière de droits de l'homme, 697d
Les effets juridiques de la sentence internationale, 523a
Egypt, PIL periodical, 222

Ehrlich, L., 122
Eighteen-Nation Conference on Disarmament (ENCD), 584c
Eisenmann, C., 499g
Eisenmann, P.M., 282, 665b
El Salvador, PIL treatise, 90
Eliaerts, C., 708a
Elias, T.O., p. 71; 195, 199, 462c, 484b, 499b, 621b, 667c
Elkind, J.B., 670a
Ellinger, W.B., 497e
Elliot, J.M., 589c
Emory journal of international dispute resolution, 577c
encyclopaedias
    Africa, legal, 301b
    comparative law, 431
    Islam, 301c
    legislation
        Arab, 73a
        USSR, 73b
    PIL
        p. 32; 297, 301a, 304
        Projet d'encyclopédie, p. 33(1)
    telecommunications, 743a
    UN, 658
    see also dictionaries
Enforcing international law, 581a
Engel, S., 194a
Englefield, D., 69b, 454a
English-language constitutions, 63-4, 65b,c
English-language law
    bibliographies, legal
        China, 350
        foreign and comparative law, 432d
    books in print, 372
    commemorative essays, 175b
    indexing service, 364a
    periodicals, guide, 217
    East European legal research, 273
English-language PIL
    dictionaries, 298-9, 310, 313
    encyclopaedias, 297
    glossaries, 171
    periodicals, 223-5, 227-45, 252-4, 259, 261, 289, 294-6
English-language translations, summaries of
    from Arabic, 222
    from Chinese, 36b
    from French, 503a

from Hungarian, 265a, 649a, 602b
from Korean, 257
from Russian, 73b, 128, 271, 307, 448d, 449c, 462d, 474a, 504b, 536d
from Scandinavian languages, 135, 275
from Serbo-Croat, 132
from Spanish, 481b
Entin, M. L., 575e
environment, international law of, 714–15
  digest, 713b
  equity, 714b
  guides to information sources, 717
  treaties, 713a, 716c
  world order, 445b(vol. 4)
Epochen der Völkerrechtsgeschichte, 455b
equality of states, 527c, 625c, 626d
L'Equité et le droit international, 521e
Erades, L., 189, 427b
el-Erian, A., 76, 188, 194
Erickson, R. J., 473e
Erim, I. I., 468c
Ermacora, F., 697b
essays, *see* commemorative essays
Essen, A. van, 540b
Essen, J. L. F. van, 339b
ethnocentric approaches to PIL, 474a; *see also* Eurocentrism, PIL; socialist countries: PIL; Third World: PIL; Western approaches to law/PIL
Eurocentrism, PIL, 168, 459–60, 484d, 531d, 648a; *see also* Western approaches to law/PIL
Europe, Eastern
  constitutions, 520c
  law of the sea, 557a
  legal documentation, guide, 62b
  official publications, 70
  PIL, 472, 499c
    manuals, 110–34
    periodicals, 262–73
Europe, Northern, *see* Scandinavian countries, law/PIL
Europe, Western
  law libraries, guide, 416a
  legal documentation, guide, 62a
  institutes on East European legal research, 397a–c
  PIL
    manuals, 139–74
    periodicals, 276–95
  see also Western approaches to law/PIL
European–African confrontation, 516b
European law libraries guide, 416a
Evans, A. E., 712c
Evans, M., 741a
Evensen, J., 538b
evidence, PIL, p. 10; 509e; *see also* sources, PIL
Evintov, V. I., 517d
extradition, 572b, 705a, 711a,b
Extra-territorial application of laws, 379

Fabritius, F., 734b
facts versus legal/PIL norms, 198; *see also* acts: juridical
Fahl, G., 602c
Falk, R. A., 81, 423b, 445a–c, 469b, 478d, 500c, 606b, 612b
Farnsworth, A., 734b
Fawcett, J. E., 437a, 621d
Federal information sources and systems, 71
Fedoseev, P. M., 453
Feldbrugge, F. J. M., 65c, 273b
Fel'dman, D. I., 128, 353a, 493, 496c, 525b, 653b
Feller, A. H., 568
Ferencz, B. B., 581a, 704a
Ferrari-Bravo, L., p. 20(9); 210, 519a
Ferreira, P. S., 556c
Ferreira de Mello, R., 305
Festschriften, *see* commemorative essays
Feuer, G., 186, 531a, 723d
Feuerstein, P., 196
fiction, law/PIL, 201, 561a; *see also* is/ought
Fiedler, W., 434c
Field, N. S., 368a
Fikentscher, W. p. 153
Filimonova, M. V., 514b
Filosofski ananliz na suvremenoto mezhdunarodnoto pravo, 505a
Finan, J. J., 454c
finance, international, guide (ACCIS), 736a
Finkel, G., 670b
Finland
  legal bibliography, 358
  PIL manual, 136
Finley, B., 653a

fiscal law, international
  documentation bulletin, 737c
  encyclopaedia, French, 301(vols. 5-6)
Fischer, P., 212, 738b
fisheries/INFOFISH, 541
Fitzmaurice, G., 47a, 206, 213, 220a,
  378a,b, 525a, 669a
Flanz, G.H., 63a
Flores, A.A., 72a
Florio, F., 570c
Flory, M., 459
Foda, E., 523b
Fontes juris gentium, pp. 16, 23; 49a, 58
Food and Agriculture Organization
  guide to information sources, 681d
  resolutions, formulating, 681b
  statutory bodies, directory, 681d
force versus law, 437a, 438; *see also*
  power/justice/law; use of force
Foreign affairs, 449b
Foreign law: current sources of codes and basic legislation in jurisdiction of the world, 72b
Forsythe, D.P., 610
Fouilloux, G., 194a
foundations, law/PIL
  for establishment of an International Criminal Court, 704b
  Grotiana, 465a
  Latsis International, 593a
  Reshaping the International Order (RIO), 442, 730
  Vollenhoven, C. van, 406
  World Peace, 638e
Frahm, *see* Oellers-Frahm, K.
France
  Académie internationale de droit comparé, 433a
  PIL
    dissertations, 282, 500h
    institutes, 403-4
    manuals, 147-54
    periodicals, 282-4
    state practice, 43, 301a
    study and teaching, 500g,h
Franceskakis, P., 301a
Francioni, F., 535a
Franck, T.M., 195, 648b, 728a
François, J.P.A., 158, 289
Frangulis, A.F., 573c
freedom of information, 742a
freedom of the sea, 547b

French-language constitutions, 63c
French-language encyclopaedias, 301b,c
French-language PIL
  dictionaries, 310, 312-13
  encyclopaedia, 301a
  periodicals, 225, 277, 282-4
  translations, summaries of
    from Arabic, 222
    from Bulgarian, 262
    from English, 458b
    from Russian, 462, 504b, 561e
Frenzke, D., 110, 121, 355, 472c,e,
  473c
Freymond, J., 610c
Fried, J.H., 192
Friedlander, R., 712a
Friedman, L., 596b
Friedmann, W., 190, 194, 220a, 231
La frontière, 534b
Frontiers of international law, 495a
Las fuentes del derecho internacional americano, 481c
Fujita, H., 499f
functionalism, international law/relations,
  435, 469b, 503c
  IGOs, 206, 670a
fundamental principles of international
  law, 171
Fundamentals of legal research, 501c
Fundamentals of public international law, 339b
Fundamentos del derecho internacional público contemporáneo, 84
Fundstellennachweis. B. Völkerrechtliche Vereinbarungen, 21
Furukawa, I., 204
The future of international law in a multicultural world, 459
The future of the international law of the environment, 714a
The future of the international legal order, 445b

Gaber, M.H.M., 476e
Gaja, G., 515a, 733b
Galtung, J., 443b
Galvez, S.G., 507b
Gamboa, M.J., 299, 573b
García-Amador, F.V., 190, 481b, 528d, 723a
Gascard, J.R., 360
Gavin, C., 538d

Gaviria Lievano, E., 98
gazettes, *see* official gazettes
Geamanu, G., 124
Gebrehana, T., 524b
Gelberg, L., 121
Gendreau, *see* Chemillier-Gendreau, M.
Gendrel, M., 370c, 708b
General Agreement on Tariffs and Trade (GATT)
   dispute settlement, 731e
   guide to information sources, 678a
   law and practice, 740c
general principles of law, p. 25; 200, 211, 458a, 521
   ICJ jurisprudence, 193, 662a
   transformation into PIL norms, 179
Geneva
   colloquia, 586b, 647d, 724b
   diplomatic conferences, 584c, 598a
   institutes, 407a, 586b
   International Geneva yearbook, 630a
   Rencontres internationales, 438
   symposia, 647a, 675
Geneva Conventions, Red Cross, 579a, 598f, 610b
Gengsheng, *see* Zhou Gengsheng
Genov, I., 438
Genovski, M., 112
geographical aspects of PIL, 297(vol. 12)
geographical information, 374a,b
George Washington journal of international law and economics, 238
George Washington University
   Jacob Burns Law Library, 381
   National Law Center, 238
Georgi Dimitrov i niakoĭ problemi na mezhdunarodnoto pravo, 111a
Georgia journal of international law and comparative law, 234
Gerbet, P., 657a
Gerichte, juristische Bibliotheken und juristische Information, p. 143
German Democratic Republic
   PIL
      bibliography, 362
      manuals, 116-18
      periodical, 264
   status, 533c
German-language legal commemorative essays, 175c
German-language legal series, 373j

German-language PIL
   classics, 463b
   dictionaries, 302-3, 311-12, 451b
   law of the sea, 537a, 559d
   periodicals, 264, 276, 278-81
   translations
      from Japanese, 108
      from Russian, 355, 540e
German-Polish colloquium, 324a
German-Soviet colloquium, 421b
German yearbook of international law, 278
Germany, Federal Republic
   disarmament, glossary, 589b
   law, East European research, 273e,f, 397b
   PIL
      bibliography, 361
      dissertations, 280
      historiographies of East European PIL works, 472b-f, 473c
      institutes, 402a,b
      manuals, 144-6
      periodicals, 278-81
   status, 533c
Ghébali, V.Y., 657a, 674b
Gheorghe, G., 17
el-Ghunaimini, M.T., 476c
Gilbertson, G., 311
Ginsburgs, G., p. 53; 41b, 455d
Ginther, K., 196, 484a, 532a
GIPRI, 586b
Girardot, *see* Gutierrez Girardot, R.
Giraud, C., 434d
Glaser, S., 703b
Glassner, M.I., 551b, 559b
Glélé, M.A., 685b
Global problems and world order, 443a
Global problems of mankind and the state, 453
glossaries, law/PIL, 36b, 171, 311; *see also* terminology; *and see under subjects*, e.g. law of the sea; United Nations conferences; etc.
Gödan, J.C., 371b, 402b
Godenhielm, B., 191
Goedehuis, D., 379a
Gold, E., 554
Goldblatt, J., 584b
Goldie, L.F.E., 714b
Goldman, B., 718c
Gomez Robledo, A., 515a
Gonidec, P.F., 185, 301b

Gonzales Campos, J., 162
Goodrich, L. M., 642a
Goralczyk, W., 121
Gordenker, L., 500d
Gorman, G. E., 487b
Gotlieb, A. E., 744b
Gottlieb, G., 445b
Gould, W. L., p. 11(2); 343-4
Goulet, J., 370c
Gounelle, M., 519d
Government gazettes, 66
Government publications review, p. 42; 68c
Government reference books, 71
Grabar, V. E., 353b
Graduate Institute of International Studies, p. 42; 407a
Graefrath, B., 116
Grahl-Madsen, A., 460
Les grands systèmes de droit international, 429a
Grant, J. P., 298
Graven, J., 710e
Graveson, R. H., 430
Great Britain, *see* United Kingdom
Greece, PIL
  periodical, 285
  institute, 405
  Thesaurus Acroasium, 405
Green, L. C., p. 11(12); 33b
Gregory, W., 315
Grenville, J. A. S., 8a
Grewe, W., 202, 455b
Groening, I., 457b
Grolier, E. de, 416d
Gromyko, A. A., 573a
Groom, A. J. R., 435
Gros, A., 8d, 199
Gros Espiell, H., 448b
Gross, L., 31, 192
Grotiana, 221
Grotiana Foundation, 465e
Grotius, H.
  bibliographies, 465c
  classic reprints, 373e,f
  colloquia, 465a,b
  just war doctrine, 595b
Grotius: annuaire international, 418
Grotius Publications, 410
Grotius reader, 465d
Group of 77, 720b, 726a
Gruber, A., 531a
Gründling, L., 549d

Grundnorm, PIL, 211
Grzybowski, K., 473c
Guelff, R., 596c
Guerres, révolutions, Croix-Rouge, 610c
guerrilla warfare, 607a,b
guerrillas, status, 206
Guggenheim, P., p. 23; 46, 49b, 167, 179, 193, 211, 423a
guides to information sources
  Commonwealth law reports, 51
  environment, 717a
  intergovernmental organizations, 631d
  FAO, 681d
  UNEP, 717a
  UNESCO, 679d
  PIL, 327-35
  UN, 660d
  archives, p. 43(5); 633b
Gutierrez Girardot, R., 177
Guyomar, G., 666b

Haas, M., 634d, 691
Hacker, J., 472b
Hackworth, G. H., 34b
Haentsch, G., 451c
Haggemacher, P., 49b, 465b, 595b
The Hague Academy of International Law, 380a
  Recueil, 220a
  study and teaching, 499g
  workshops, 220b
The Hague Conference on Private International Law, 424
The Hague Conventions, 48d, 596b,c, 579a, 585d, 598d, 600c
The Hague Court reports, 48d
Hague-Zagreb essays on the law of international trade, 734a
Hajdú, Gy., 119
Hajnal, P., 631b, 660d, 679d
Halajczuk, B. T., 93
Haller, W., 603b
Halmosy, D., 15
Hambro, E., 49d, 187-8, 642a
Hameray, *see* Rouyer-Hameray, B.
Hamidullah, M., 476d
Hamilton, G., p. 43(1)
Hammond, K. A., 717a
Handbuch der diplomatischen Korrespondenz der europäischen Staaten, 569
Hänisch, W., 451b
Harászti, Gy., 119, 265a, 514d

Harrap's German and English glossary of terms in international law, p. 32; 311
Harris, D.J., 26, 174
Harvard international law journal, 235
Harvard University Law School, 389b
   International Legal Studies Program, 389b
     Library, 417b
       international law/relations catalogue, 338a
     periodical, 235
     Research in international law, 227, 389a
     Studies in East Asian law, 389b
Hasbi, A., 532c
Hassan, F., 429d
Hatschek, J., 303
Hazard, J.N., 42b, 455d
health legislation, international digest, 682a
Heere, W.P., 562b, 565a
Heidelberg colloquium, 698a
Heidtmann, F., p. 36(1)
Hellenic Institute of International and Foreign Law, 285
Helsinki rules/international rivers, 379
Henkin, L., p. 29(7); 83
Henry-Dunant Institute, 611a
Hentsch, T., 607b
Herczeg, Gy., 119, 265a, 602b
Hermann, J., 706a
Hernes, H.M., 508b
Hernon, P., 68b
Hersch Lauterpacht Memorial Lecture Series, 373f, 410
Heydte, F.A., 211
Higgins, R., 197, 470b, 499b, 621d, 650d
Hill, B.H.W., 740c
Hinduism and PIL, 475e
Hines, W.D., 693a
Hingorani, R.C., 106, 647c
Hispano-American law/PIL, 385, 481
historical approaches to PIL, 157, 182, 202, 455, 457; *see also* contemporary versus classical PIL
historical PIL models, 214, 428b, 456a–c
historiography, PIL, pp. 28–9; 347, 466–7, 468d, 507b; *see also* Eurocentrism, PIL; ideology and PIL
Hjersonsson, K., 556b
Ho, P., 350

Hobza, A., 300
Hoffman, S., 192
Holk, L.E. van, 465b
Holler, F.L., 454b
HOLLIS, 417b
Holmes (J.W.) Memorial Lectures, 629c
Hoof, G.J.H. van, 509a, 547a
Hoogstraten, M.H. van, 425b
Hopkins, C., 23, 51
Hord, H.A., 412a
hornbooks, p. 29(7)
host country
   international responsibility, 571
   UN Committee, 641b
Hovet, E., 640c
Hovet, T., 640c
How nations behave, p. 29(7)
How to find the law, 331a
Hrabar, *see* Grabar, V.E.
Hübner, U., 718d
Hudson, M.O., 5, 49e, 83, 389b, 568
Hüfner, K., 634b
human rights, p. 26(6); 297(vol. 8), 697–700
   African Charter, 695a
   Afro-Asian attitudes, 647c
   armed conflict, 261
   conferences, 261, 386, 694b, 698a
   dictionary, 701
   guides to information sources, 693a,b
   humanitarian law, 449d, 608a,b
   Inter-American, 696, 698a
   Islamic Declaration, 694b
   scientists, 744c
   UNESCO competence, 199
   universality, 210, 647a
   world order, 440
humanitarian law, 265a, 602–3, 613
   bibliographies, 614
   conferences, 598f, 599a, 604
   definition, 600a
   Geneva conventions/protocols, 579a, 598, 599b
   guerrilla warfare, 607b
   human rights, 449d, 608a,b
   institutes, 611
   study and teaching, directory, 612a
   see also armed conflict; civilians; war
Humanitarian politics, 610c
humanity
   and sovereignty, 460(sect. 7)
   crimes against, 710e

humanity *contd*
  law of, 438
  see also common heritage of mankind; human rights
Hummerhielm, R., 357
Humphrey, J., 744c
Hune, S., 448a
Hungary
  law
    bibliography, 352
    history of Budapest University Law Faculty, p. 41(3)
  PIL
    basic texts, 120
    historiography, 472c
    periodicals, 265-6
    treaties, 15
Hungdah, *see* Chiu, H.
Huong, *see* Huynh, H. T.
Hur, P., 665b
Hussain, I., 671b
Huynh, H.T., 614a
Hyder, K., 740c

I͡Anovskiĭ, M.V., 653b
IAPSUN reports, 629b
Ibler, V., 179, 308, 356
idealism versus realism, PIL, 202-3, 492, 507b
identity of international law, 499b
ideology and PIL, 436, 444, 458a, 474a,d, 478d; *see also* idealism versus realism, PIL; regionalism in PIL; socialist countries: PIL; Third World: PIL; Western approaches to law/PIL
Ignatenko, G.V., 500e
immunity
  diplomatic, 566a, 570e
  of states, 527a,b, 621a, 662b
  see also privileges and immunities, international
Imperativnye normy v sisteme sovremennogo mezhdunarodnogo prava, 515b
independence
  and interdependence, 460(sect. 6)
  effect on treaties, 379
Index to foreign legal periodicals, p. 37; 364b
Index to legal periodicals, p. 37; 364a
Index translationum, p. 33(6)
indexes
  of Geneva conventions, 598d
  of humanitarian law, 600c, 612a
  of IGO decisions, 681c, 643a, 740a
  of treaties, 26-8
indexing services
  directory, p. 128
  legal, 364-7
  PIL, 283, 361-3
  UN libraries, 368a,b
India, PIL, 37
  institution, 394
  periodicals, 252-4
Indian journal of international law, 253
The Indian Ocean, 547a
Indian Society of International Law, 394
Indian yearbook of international law, 252
Inductive approach to international law, 495b
Inequality and a new maritime order, 545
INFOFISH, 541
information, new international order, 448b
  bibliography, 742e
  law of, 742a-d
information retrieval, legal, p. 39(9); 411b; *see also* computerized (legal) information retrieval
Inman, S.G., 320e
L'Inspection générale, 623b
instant custom, 499b
Instituciones de derecho internacional público, 163
Institut de droit international, Bruxelles, 401b
Institut de droit international, Genève, 378
Institut de hautes études internationales, 404
Institut du droit de la paix et du développement, 725b
Institut for international Ret og Europaret, 398
Institut für internationales Recht, 278
Institut für Ostrecht, 397b
Institut für Völkerrecht und ausländisches öffentliches Recht, 400b
Institut für Völkerrecht und internationale Beziehungen, 400a
Institut Henry-Dunant, 611a
Institut juridique international, p. 24(8)
Institut Nauchnoĭ Informatsii po Obshchestvennym Naukam, 364c
Institut suisse de droit comparé, 433b

Institut universitaire de hautes études internationales, 407a
Institut za Međunarodno Pravo i Međunarodne Odnose, 396b
Institut za Međunarodnu Politiku i Privredu, 396a
Institute for Palestine Studies, 296
Institute for the Study of International Organisation, 638c
Institute of Advanced Legal Studies, 409
Institute of International Law, 378
Institute of International Public Law and International Relations, 405
institutions, law/PIL, directories, p. 40; 376-7
Institutions des relations internationales, 151
Institutions spécialisées dans le système des Nations Unies, 676a
Instituto de derecho internacional, 390
Instituto Hispano-Luso-Americano de derecho internacional, 385
Insurrection under international law, 609b
integration, law of, 201; *see also* Andean economic integration; economic law, international
intellectual property, *see* copyright
Inter-African affairs, encyclopaedia, 301b
Inter-American conferences, 320c,e, 326a, 481c
Inter-American Court of Human Rights, 696a
Inter-American Institute of Human Rights, 696b
Inter-American Institute of International Legal Studies, 686c
Inter-American Juridical Committee, 689
Inter-American juridical yearbook, 688
Inter-American law review, 244
Inter-American PIL, 481
Inter-American treaties and conventions, 9
Interconcept report, p. 111
L'Interdiction de l'emploi de force en droit international, 592b
interdisciplinary approaches to PIL, p. 11(2); 421-49, 456a, 612b, 629b, 692c
intergovernmental organizations (IGO), p. 18; 182, 195, 199, 228, 297(vol. 5), 621, 626-8

abbreviations, 637
archives, 633b
basic documents, 616
bibliographies, 634d
Collection: organisation internationale, 623b
competences, 626
directories, 630
dispute settlement, 577b
functional aspect, 206
guides to information sources, 67b, 454a, 631-2, 634c
 legal/PIL materials, 329
Institute for the Study of International Organisation, 638c
international practice, 210, 623, 627c, 640b
 broad terms of programmes, 636d
 digest of legal activities, 619a
libraries, 633a
Permanent Missions to, 657a
PIL aspects of, 620, 624b
privileges and immunities, 617a
resolutions, 428a, 519e, 625a
study and teaching, 638
succession, 626c, 686d
terminology, 310, 636b,c,e
theories of, 301a, 625c, 626c,d, 627
treaty-making, interpretation, 201, 541, 624a,c,d
USA, USSR roles in, 34c, 692c
see also non-governmental organizations; Specialized Agencies (UN system)
Interim protection: a functional approach, 670a
Internacionalistas españoles del siglo XVII, 464b
International adjudication, 49f
International affairs, London, 449a
International affairs, Moscow, 449c
International African Law Association, 384
International and comparative law quarterly, 295
International Association of Law Libraries, pp. 19, 41; 415a
International Association of Legal Sciences, 382, 430, 698a
International Association of Political Scientists for the UN (IAPSUN), 629b

International Atomic Energy Agency, 618a, 683
International Bank for Reconstruction and Development (IBRD), 678a, 740d
International bibliography: publications of intergovernmental organizations, 632c
International books in print, p. 6(10); 372
International Centre for Settlement of Investment Disputes, 738a
International Chamber of Commerce, 733b
International Civil Aviation Organization, 678
international civil servants, 641b; *see also* administrative tribunals
International Committee for Social Science Documentation, 62a, 216b
International Committee of Comparative Law, 62a, 423a
International Committee of the Red Cross, 610a,c
International congress calendar, 315
International Court of Justice, 199, 201, 426b, 440, 449b, 665a, 667
 basic documents, 664a,b, 665
 bibliography, 664c
 case law, digests, 49–50
 competence, 670c
 consultative opinion, 670b
 jurisdiction, 667b, 670c
 justices, opinions, p. 24(3); 509f, 671
 PIL development, ICJ role, 522, 668
 procedural law of ICJ, 200, 669
 rules of ICJ, 666
 settlement of disputes, 576a, 577a
 writing style, 209
International crimes: digest/index, 703a
international criminal court (proposed), 704b
International custom and the continental shelf, 550c
International customary law and codification, 520a
International Development Law Institute, 725a
International digest of health legislation, 682a
International dispute settlement, 575a
International documentation, 631a
International documents for the 80s, 631c
International documents round-up, 632c
International economic and trade law, 734c

International encyclopedia of comparative law, p. 32; 431
International enforcement of human rights, 698a
Internatioanl environmental reporter, 716c
International information: documents, publications, and information systems of international governmental organizations, 631b
International Information Centre for Terminology, 636f
International Institute for the Unification of Private Law (UNIDROIT), 425a
International Institute of Humanitarian Law, 611b
International Institute of Space Law, 564
International institutional law, 620b
International journal, 449e
International journal of comparative and applied criminal justice, 707b
International journal of law libraries, 414a
International journal of legal information, p. 42; 414a
International Labour Organisation, 680b
 code/conventions, 680a
 USSR participation, 692c
international law, *see* private international law; public international law
International law: a classification for libraries, 497d
International law: a contemporary perspective, 445a
International law: process and prospect, 81
International law: selected sources of information, 331c
International law: teaching and practice, 499b
International law and diplomacy, 281
International law and national behavior, 436
International law and order, 495a
International law and organization, 334
International law and policy of human welfare, 507b
International law and world order, 81
International law and world revolution, 444
International law and the developing countries, 482a
International law and the Grotian heritage, 465a
International law and the international system, 428a
International law and the new African states, 484c

International law and the revolutionary state, 473c
International law and the social sciences, 343
International law and the use of force by states, 592c
International law as applied by international courts, p. 23; 49c
International law as legal order, 402a
International Law Association, 379
  centenary, 379a
International Law Commission, p. 18; 188, 630b, 662a, 663
  Committee on the Progressive Development of International Law, 31, 662a
  seminars, 672a
  yearbook, 662b
International law in a contemporary perspective, 428b
International law in a divided world, 458b
International law in contemporary perspective: the public order, 80
International law in historical perspective, 157
International law in the twentieth century, 192
International Law Moot Court Competition, 228, 387b, 500d
International law opinions, 47c
International law perspective, 236
International law reporter, 55
International law reports, p. 23; 50
International law review, 449f
International law studies, p. 39; 373a
International Law Symposium, p. 34(4)
International lawyer, 237
International legal education newsletter, 389a
International legal materials, p. 13, 31; 219
International legal perspectives, 413
International Legal Studies Program (Harvard), 389b
International legislation, 5
international military tribunals, p. 23; 710a,c,d
International Ocean Institute, 558e
international order, *see* world order
International organization, 638e
International organization: law in movement, 621d
International organization and integration, 616a
international organizations, *see* intergovernmental organizations; non-governmental organizations
International organizations: a guide, 634c

International peace directory, 583a
International political science abstracts, 450c
International Political Science Association, 453
International Progress Organization, 448b
International quarterly, 295
International Red Cross, 613a
  Committee, 610a,c
  conventions, 579a, 596a, 598b-e, 610b
  resolutions, 597
  statutes, 610b
International Refugee Integration Resources Centre, 702b
international relations, 297(vol. 9), 434-9, 449d, 452a, 521d
  and human rights, 686b
  and non-alignment, 447-8
  and PIL, 151-3, 181, 185, 187, 211
  bibliographies, 338, 450
  concepts, 451e,f
  conferences, role of, 317-20
  dictionaries, 451a,d
  guides to information sources, 454
  Islamic, 476d,e
  periodicals, 216a(vol. 2), 450a
  world order studies, 440-6
  see also consular relations; diplomatic law/relations; politics, international
international settlements, 533c
International social science journal, 216, 627a
International society as a legal community, 439
International Society for Military Law and the Law of War, 604a
International Symposium on the Documentation of the United Nations and other Intergovernmental Organizations, 631d
International Telecommunications Union, 743b
International Tribunal of the Law of the Sea, proposed, 546a,c
International uniform law in practice, 425b
International who's who, p. 40; 375
International yearbook and statemen's who's who, 452c
Internationales Recht und Diplomatie, 281
internationalists, biographies, 375
Internoscia, J., 520g
Inter-Organization Board for Information Systems, 632a,b

interpretation, PIL, 197, 436, 498; *see also* analogous reasoning; auto-interpretation; ideology and PIL; treaties, law of
investments, international, 738c
  laws, 738a,b
  Third World, 738e
Ionascu, I., 17
Iriye, K., 475c
is/ought, pp. 20(4), 29(3); 204, 474c, 520g
Isaia, H., 671c
Islam
  encyclopaedia, 301c
  human rights, 694
  international organizations, directory, 685b
  legal systems, 429a,b,d
  PIL approaches, 474e, 476a,c,e
  state conduct, *siyar*, 476d
islands, 543a
Israel, F. L., 581b
Israeli-Palestine conflict, 296
Israelian, V. L., 585b
Istituto Internazionale di Diritto Umanitario, 611b
Italian yearbook of international law, 286
Italy, PIL
  bibliography, 286
  historiography, 471b
  manuals, 155-6
  periodicals, 286-7
  state practice, 44, 59
ius, see entries beginning jus

Jackson, D. C., 741b
Jackson, J. H., 718a
Jacob Burns Law Library, 381
Jacobini, H. B., 467b
Jacobstein, J. M., 364a, 372, 501c
Jacqué, J. P., 510a
Jacubowski, J., 734b
Jagota, S. P., 552
Jahn, E., 383
Jahrbuch des Völkerrechts, 278
Jahrbuch Dritte Welt, 488b
Jahrbuch für internationales Recht, 278
Jahrbuch für Ostrecht, 273e
Janković, B. M., 132
Jankowitsch, O., 447a
Japan
  Institute of Comparative Law, 433c
  PIL, 474e

  periodical, 256
  state practice, 38, 56
  study and teaching, 499f
Jaschek, S., 36c
Jasentuliyana, N., 561c
Jauffert-Spinosi, C., 429a
Jayakumar, S., 57
Jayatilleke, K. N., 475d
Jenisch, U., 559d
Jenks, C. W., 203, 474e
Jennings, R. Y., 169, 190, 509c
Jéquier, N., 628b
Jeschek, A., 706a, 708a
Jessup, P. C., 190, 194, 231, 590
Jessup International Law Moot Court Competition, 228, 387b, 500d
Jewish legal systems, 429a,b
Jewish PIL approach, 474e
jihad, 476b
Jiménez de Arechaga, E., 101, 195, 220a
Jiménez Piernas, C. B., 543b
Johansson, E., 69a
John Bassett Moore Society of International Law, 387c
Johnson, B. T., *see* Theutenberg, B. J.
Johnson, J. T., 595a
Johnson-Champ, D. G., 500a
Johnston, C., 738d
Johnston, D. M., 12, 503c, 507b, 554, 715
Joint Inspection Unit (UN), 623b
Jolowicz, J. A., 698a
Journal du droit international, 284
Journal of African law, 224b
Journal of conflict resolution, 582c
Journal of international law, 257
Journal of international law and diplomacy, 256
Journal of international law and economics, 238
Journal of international studies, 449g
Journal of legal education, 389
Journal of Palestine studies, 296
Journal of space law, 563b
Journal officiel, 22a, 282
Joyner, C. C., 535a
judge-made PIL rules, p. 24(6)
judicial decisions, p. 22
  international tribunals, 522-4, 616b
  digests, 48-50
  IGOs and PIL, 624a-c
  national tribunals, 51-61
  settlement of disputes, 575e, 576a

judicial systems, directory, 376a
Les juges du Tiers-Monde à la Cour internationale de justice, 671a
Jugoslovenska revija zy međunarodno pravo, 272
juridical acts, 510a, 519d
Juris-classeur de droit international, 301a
jus ad bellum, 592, 598f
jus cogens, 508a, 515
Jus et societas, 190
Jus humanitatis, 211
jus in bello, 596a, 598f
   bibliography, 614b
just war doctrine, 595a,b
justice and PIL, 190, 441, 445a,b, 507a,c, see also power/justice/law

Kabir-ur, see Khan-Kabir-ur
el-Kadiri, A., 516a
Khan-Freund, O., 426b
Kaiser, J.H., 685a
Kaliadin, A.N., 587b, 627c
Kalshoven, F., 200, 585a
Kamenov, E., 111a
Kaminski, G., 36c
Kamptz, K.A., 347
Kaplan, M., 500c
Kapoor, S.K., 105
Kapteyn, P.J.G., 616a
Karlsruher juristische Bibliographie, p. 37; 367
Kartashkin, V., 477a
Kasme, B., 333, 650a
Kastner, F., 370b
Katalog iuridicheskikh dokumentatsionnykh istochniokov sotsialisticheskikh stran, 62b
Kavass, I.I., p. 24(7); 10a,d, 273a, 412a
Kehoe, P.E., 411b
Kelsen, H., 192, 194a, 471a, 503b, 505b, 508c, 509e, 526c
Kennedy, D., 509e
Kenny, J.T., 389b
Kenya, diplomacy training programme, 407a
Kewening, W.A., 207
Key concepts in international relations, 451e
Keyguide to information sources on the international protection of human rights, 693a
Khadduri, M., 476b
Khairallah, D.L., 609b
Khan-Kabir-ur, 738d

Khrabskov, V.G., 426c
Kiel Institut für internationales Recht, 278, 421b
Kim, G.F., 532b
Kim, S.S., 445a, 612b
Kime's international law directory, 376b
Kimminich, O., 497e
Kirchner, H., 370b
Kiss, A.C., 43, 186, 200, 547a, 685a, 714b
Klafkowski, A., 122, 304
Klassiker des Völkerrechts, 463b
Klecatsky, H., 471a
Kleckner, S.M., p. 19; 330, 578b, 659a
Klein, E., 533c
Klein, R.A., 527c
Kleinheyer, G., 471a
Klimenko, B.M., 307, 533b
Köchler, H., 448b
Kocot, K., 123
Koh, Kheng-lian, 543c
Kohona, P.T.B., 718b
Kolbasov, O.S., 714d
Kollewijn, R.D., 422b
Kolodkin, A.L., 536d
Kolosov, IU.M., 528c, 561e
Konferenzen und Verträge, 28b
Das Kontinuitätsproblem im Völkerrecht, 434c
Kooijmans, P.H., 475a
Korea, PIL
   periodical, 257
   state practice, 39
   status, 533c
Korean journal of international law, 257
Koretskiĭ, V.M., 378c
el-Kosheri, A.G., 476a
Kouassi, E. Kwam, 686a
el-Kouhene, M., 608a
Kovalev, F., 549e
Kozhevnikov, F.I., 126, 353a
Kramers, J.J., 301c
Kratochwil, F., 445a
Kravchenko syllabus, 500f
Kreća, M., 133
Kreslins, J., 449b
Krieger, T., 497e
Krisafi, K., 110
Krivchikova, E.S., 620e
Kröger, H., 117
Krökel, M., 656a
Kruse, H., 476e
Krylov, S., 477d
Kudej, B., 559c, 736b

Kuehl, E. E., 339a
Kuehl, W. F., 375
Kuhn model, development law, 196
Kuiper, E. J., 465e
Kunig, P., 695b
Kunz, J. L., 462f
Kurdiukov, G. I., 353a, 525b
Kurian, G. T., 487a

labour law, international, 301(vol. 8)
 conventions, 680a
Lachs, M., 195, 200, 203, 212, 317,
 462b, 499c, 561f, 621d, 710f
lacunes en droit international, 509f
La Fontaine, H., 48f
La Pradelle, A. G. de, 48e, 301a, 466b
La Pradelle, P. G. de, 533a, 598f
Lagonisi conference, 515e
Laing, L. H., 52
lakes, international régime, 536a
Lakos, A., 712b
Lamar Society of International Law,
 563b
Lamberti-Zanardi, P., 59
Lammers, J. G., 200, 536e, 714b
Landheer, B., 339b, 506c
land-locked states, 551
Langlois, M., 348b
Language, law and diplomacy, 451f
Language of international law, 502a; *see also
 entries beginning* linguistic aspects;
 multilingualism; translations,
 law/PIL
Lapenna, I., 473f
Larson, A., 474e
Laszlo, E., 582a
Latin America
 Antarctica, 535c
 human rights, 696c, 698a
 law of the sea, 440, 556
 OAS, 690
 PIL, 210, 326a, 474e, 481
  historiography, 467
  institutes, 385, 390-1
 treaties, 9, 97, 431b
Laun, R. von, 281
Lausanne *colloque*, 628b
Lauterpacht, E., 47b, 50, 173b, 624b
Lauterpacht, H., 172-3, 423c, 470c,
 669d
 memorial lectures, 373f
Laviec, J. P., 738c

law
 abbreviations, 370
 text analysis, 498e
 translation problems, 502a
 see also entries beginning legal
Law acquisition national, 366a
Law and force in the international system,
 437a
Law and international law: a bibliography,
 337a
Law and judicial systems of nations, 376a
Law and legal information directory, 376c
Law and power in international relations,
 437a
Law and practice of the ICJ, 665a
law books
 bibliographies, 338b,c
 in print, p. 39; 372
 recommended for libraries, 389a
 reviewed, 371
Law in East and West, 433c
law libraries
 associations, 415
 automation, 411b,c, 412a
 directory, European, 416a
 handbooks, 411a,b
 national, p. 43(1)
  USA, 376c, 417a,b
 periodicals, 414
 see also Peace Palace: Library; public
  international law: library collections;
  United Nations: libraries
Law library journal, p. 42; 414b
*The law-making functions of the Specialized
 Agencies*, 677
The law of international institutions, 620a
The law of nations, 172
law of the sea
 Africa, 557c
 Asia, 554-5
  China, 209
 bibliographies, 559
 conferences, 537a, 542
 conventions, 537b, 538a
 environmental rules, 200
 Europe, Eastern, 557a
 history, 187
 Latin America, 556
 national legislation, 539a,b, 549a, 550a
 North America, 55
 terminology, 558g
 treaties, 539c,d
 tribunal, proposed, 546

UN Office for Ocean Affairs, 539e
USSR, 557a
see also common heritage of mankind; entries beginning ocean
The law of the sea in our time, 546
The law of treaties, 512c
The law of war, 596b
The law of war and peace in Islam, 476b
law reports, p. 22
  PIL, 48-61
  war crime trials, 710
Law/Technology, 388
Lay, S.H., 560b
Lazarev, M.I., 540e
League of Nations (LoN), 675
  codification, PIL, 673a,b
    Committee of Experts, 662a
  indexing service, 368a
  international law questions, 673c
  publications, guides, 674
  treaty series, 4
League of Red Cross Societies, 610b
Leary, V., 445c
The Least Developed Countries, report, 720c
Lee, R.S., 561c
legal abbreviations, 370
legal developments, newsletter, 408
legal information
  journal, 414a
  retrieval, 412a
legal methodology, 501b
legal periodicals
  bibliographies, 217, 338c
  indexing services, 254, 261, 287, 364-5
legal practitioners, directory, 376b
legal publishers, 411b, 420
legal reasoning, 494a
Legal reference services quarterly, 414c
Legal resource index, 365
Legal restraints on the use of force, 593b
legal systems/jurisdictions, 429
  guide, 72b
  index, 366a
Legal thesaurus, 412c
legislation
  international
    guide, 72b
    Society of Comparative Legislation and International Law, 295, 408
    treaties as legislation, 190

national
  Arab countries, 73a
  USSR, 73b
  periodicals, 72a, 277
  see also law of the sea; national legislation and treaties
Legislative series, ILO, 680a
Legislative series, UN, p. 21(19); 645
La légitime défense en droit international public moderne, 593e
Leistner, O., 176, 216
Lekner, M.A., 340
Lengenfelder, H., p. 41(1); 416d
Leurquin de Visser, F., 501b
Lerat, P., 498e
Levie, H.S., 592a, 601a,b, 605a,b, 614b
Levin, D.B., 455d, 504a, 570e, 575d
Levy, J.P., 559g
Lewanski, R.C., 416c
Lewis, J.R., 710g
lex ferenda/lex lata, 204, 458a
Lexikon des Rechts: Völkerrecht, 302
Li, T., p. 35(1)
librarianship, legal, *see* law libraries
Likhachev, V.N., 478b
Lillich, R.B., 700
linguistic aspects
  of humanitarian law, 612d
  of international law/relations, 451f, 502a
  of legal documentation, 502c
Lipstein, K., 196
List of treaty collections, p. 13; 25a
Little, R., 443a
Llanos Mansilla, H., 96
Lleonart, A.J., 744a
Lombois, C., 705b
London, University of
  Centre for the Study of Socialist Systems, 397c
  PIL study and teaching, 428a
London Institute of World Affairs, 449a, 495b, 620a
London Naval Conference, 585d
López Jiménez, R., 90
Lowe, V., 47b
Lowenfeld, A.F., 422a
Luard, E., 548c, 606a
Luk, I., 477c
Lyon *colloques*, 667b, 724a
Lyons, G.M., 638a
Lysen, A., 381

Macalister-Smith, P., 381
McDonald, R. St. J., 33a, 507b
McDougal, M. S., 80, 197, 434e, 445b, 498d
McGowan, Y. H., 51
Mackenzie, N., 52
McKinlay, R. D., 443a
McLure, C. R., 68b
McMahon, J., 621d
McNair, A. D. (Lord), 47c, 173, 213, 512c
McWhinney, E., 196, 198, 199, 203, 444, 462e, 469a, 474a, 504b, 585e, 648a, 667d, 742c
Maggs, P. B., 42b
Mahoney, M., 487b
main/subsidiary PIL sources/resources, p. 10
Maîtres et doctrines du droit des gens, 466b
Makarczyk, J., 195
Makowski, J., 16
Malaya law review, 258
Malaysia, PIL
 periodical, 258
 state practice, 57
Mal'tsev, V. F., 13
Manchester University, Melland Schill monographs, 373g
Mangone, G. J., 534a, 543c
Mangovski, P., 133
Manin, A., 154
Manner, E. J., 184, 191, 379a
Mans *colloque*, 741d
manuals, PIL, p. 28
 reviews, bibliographic, 74, 344
maps, bibliography 374a
Marchaha, M., 723f
Marcic, R., 211, 468a, 471a
Marek, K., 49b, 182
marine resources, 540b, 548a
maritime agreements, 539d
maritime boundary, 209, 552
maritime law, journal, 563c
maritime order, new, 545
Marke, J. J., 411c
Marotta Ranjel, V., 577b
Martens, F., 19b, 418
Martens, G. F., p. 12; 7, 25c, 346, 455e
Martitz, F., 7
Marulli-Koenig, L., 632c
Marxist-Leninist approaches to PIL
 French, 322, 508a, 723e
 Soviet, 128, 477a, 504b
 see also dialectics, international law/relations: materialist; ideology and PIL
Masmoudi, M., 448b
Mateesco-Matte, M., 561, 621b
Mavungu, M.-di-N., 577a
Max-Planck Institutes, 402b
 für ausländisches und internationales Strafrecht, 709
 für ausländisches und öffentliches Recht und Völkerrecht, 402a
Mayall, J., 438
Mayer-Maly, D., 468a
medical law, international, 379a
 WHO decisions, 682b,c
 see also health legislation, international digest
Medina Ortega, M., 627d
Meissner, B., 355
Mekong, international régime, 536a
mélanges, *see* commemorative essays
Melland Schill monographs, 373g
Melville, A., 417a
Mémoires, plaidoiries et documents (CIJ), 48f
memorial lectures, 373f, 406, 629c
Memorias, argumentos orales y documentos, 696a
Mendlovitz, S. H., 445a,b, 478d
Mensah-Brown, A. K., 457c
Menschenrechte in der sich wandelnden Welt, 697b
Menzhinskiĭ, V. I., 593d, 692a
Mériboute, Z., 531c, 586b
Merkl, A. J., 194a, 471a
Merrills, J. G., 341, 575a
Mersky, R. M., p. 43(1); 364a, 501c
Messner, J., 212
Mestral, A. L. C. de, 77
methodology
 comparative law, 428a,b, 430
 documentary aspects, p. 28
 economic law, international, 718d
 legal, 501b-d
 PIL, 322a, 490-6, 501a, 503a, 509b
 see also analogous reasoning, PIL; classification; interpretation, PIL; periodization, PIL
Meulen, J. ter, 418, 465c
Mexico, PIL manuals, 86-8
Meyriat, J., 67b
Mezhdunarodnaia zhizn', 449c

Mezhdunarodnoe pravo: bibliografiia, 353
Mezhdunarodnoe pravo: problemi metodologii, 493
Mezhdunarodnoe pravo i sovremennost', 496c
Mezhdunarodnoe pravo i vnutrigosudarstvennoe pravo, 500e
Mezhdunarodnye organizatsii sotsialisticheskikh stran, 692a
Mezhpravitel'stvennye konferentsii, 319
Miaja de la Muela, A., 164, 198, 464b
Michaels, D. B., 566b
microforms, as evidence, 412b
Middle East, international law/relations, 296
Midgley, E. B. F., 435
Miehsler, H., 211
Miles, E. L., 500d
military criminal law, bibliography, 708b
military tribunals, international, 710a,c,d
Millar, T. B., 8c
Milosavljević, M., 132
Mironov, N. V., 42a
Miskin, C., 327
Misra, K. P., 448b
Misra, S. N., 107
Les missions permanentes auprès des organisations internationales, 657
Mitteilungen der AJBD, 414d
Moca, G., 125
model convention texts, 617a, 737c
Model plan for the classification of documents concerning state practice, 32
modern versus traditional PIL, *see* contemporary versus classical PIL
Modzhorian, L. A., 127, 525b
Mohr, M., 528a
Monaco, R., 156, 620d
Moncayo, G. R., 91
Moneta, C., 535c
monism/dualism in PIL, 198, 503b
Monthly bibliography, I–II (UNOG), p. 42; 368a
Montpellier *colloques*, 542a, 586a
Montreal symposium, 562a
Moody, M., 338a
Moore, J. B., 34b, 49f, 387c
moot court, *see* Jessup International Law Moot Court Competition
moral aspects of international law, *see* values and PIL
Morgenstern, P., 118, 335
Morin, J. Y., 79

Morozov, G., 638b
Morris, G. L., 507b
Morris, M. A., 556c
Morvay, W., 361
Mosler, H., 49a, 198–9, 439, 521a, 576a
Moss, A. G., 726a
Mostecky, V., 28a, 331a, 338b
Les motivations des actes juridiques en droit international, 519d
Les mouvements de libération nationale et le droit international, 532
Movchan, A. P., 428a, 520b, 561e, 697c
Moya-Dominguez, M. T. del R., 93
Moys, E., p. 41, 411a, 416a
Mu, *see* Rui Mu
Mueller, H. P., 411b
Mujerva, N., 76
Müller, J. P., 166
Muller, J. W., 720b
Müllerson, R. A., 426c
multicultural aspects of PIL, p. 32; 265a, 459–60, 621b
multilateral diplomacy, IGOS 628b, 629b, 740b
multilateral treaties, status, 3
Multilateral treaties: index, 26
Multilateral treaties deposited with the Secretary-General, p. 13; 3
treaty-making process, 513-14
multilingualism
IGOs, 636a
treaties, 498a, 517d
Multilingualism in international law and institutions, 636a
Multi-system nations and international law, 533c
Multum non multa, 196
Münch, I. von, 8b, 144, 187, 207, 378e
Munich colloquium, 562b
municipal law
and PIL, 49b, 181–2, 201, 421a,c, 422–3, 428a
library collections, 419a, 433b
Soviet perceptions, 211, 421b, 500e
Murphy, C., 441
Murty, B. G., 76
Muslim PIL, *see* Islam
Mutharika, A. P., 702c, 720a
Myers, D. P., 25b

Nadelmann, K. H., 34d
Nafziger, J. A. R., 209

Nagore, A.P., 591b
Nagy, K., 119
Nagy, L., 62b, 352
Nahlik, S.E., 195, 609a
Names of countries and adjectives of nationality, p. 39; 374b
Nanda, V.P., 705a
Napoletano, V., 287
Nascimento Silva, G.E. do, 95
national behaviour and international law, 436
national conceptions of PIL, 204
National legal bibliography, p. 42; 366a
national legislation and treaties
  continental shelf, 550a
  economic zone, 549a
  law of the sea
    Latin America, 556a
    North America, Asia, Pacific, 555
national liberation movements, 525a, 532
  codification, 528a
  see also guerrilla warfare; guerrillas, status; partisans, legal status
nationality
  adjectives, 374b
  laws of, 702c
Les Nations Unies et la formation du droit, 648a
Les Nations Unies et le droit international économique, 724a
Les Nations Unies face à un monde en mutation, 647d
natural law and PIL
  evolution, 212, 468a
  international relations, 435
  Marxist criticism, 468b
natural resources, 731b-d
  Antarctica, 535b,c
  law of the sea, 548a
  sovereignty of states, 731a
  transnational law, bibliography, 731e
Naumann, J., 634b
Naval War College, USA, 373a
navigation, international
  rivers, 536
  straits, 543c
Nawaz, M.K., 203, 522
Nawaz, T., 729b
negotiations
  disarmament, 585d, 587b
  PIL, 124, 186, 317
  UNCLOS III, 538d
  UNCTAD, 740b

Netherlands
  Documentation Office for Eastern European Law, 397a
  PIL
    historiography, 471c
    institute, 406
    judicial decisions, digest, 61
    manuals, 157-8
    periodicals, 288-9
Netherlands international law review, 289
Netherlands yearbook of international law, 288
Neubauer, R.D., 548d
neutrality, 194, 211, 579a, 591
  bibliography, 614b
  collection of laws, regulations, 590
  ICJ decisions, 49b
  UN context, 213
New approaches to international relations, 500c
New challenges to international law, 679b
New code of international law, 520g
New directions in international law, 177
New directions in the law of the sea, 540f
New Haven Studies in International Law and World Public Order, 197
New horizons in international law, 462c
New horizons of international law and developing countries, 482c
New International Economic Order (NIEO), 388, 648b, 715a, 727-8
  bibliography, 729
  documents, 726
  ILA Committee, 379
  institutions, register, 730
  training materials, 726b
New perspectives and conceptions of international law, 484a
New World Information and Communication Order, 742e
New York convention, 733b
New York University journal of international law and politics, 239
New Zealand, legal index, 261
The newly independent states and international law, 320a
Newman, F.C., 700
Nguyen Quoc Dinh, 147
Niboyet, J.P., 301a
Nicaragua, PIL manual, 89
Nice
  colloque, 652c

Institut du droit de la paix et du développement, 725b
Niciu, M.I., 125
Nicol, D., 656b
Nicoloudis, E.P., 515d
Nigerian annual of international law, 223
Nobel Peace Prize laureates, 582a
Nogueira Porto, L. de A., 374a
non-aligned countries, 448
  bibliographies, 447a, 448c
  documents, 447
  UN role, 648c
Non-appearance before the ICJ, 670a
non-governmental organizations, 619a, 630d
non-international armed conflict, 601b,c, 614
non-legal elements in PIL, 492, 579b
non liquet, PIL, 206
Nordisk folksrättslig litteratur, 357
Nordisk tidskrift for international ret og jus gentium, 274
Nordquist, M.H., 538a, 555
Norman, P., 432d
normative concept of law (NCL), 490
norms, PIL, 211, 458a, 460, 490, 510d, 523a
  conflicts, UN Charter, 652a
  IGOS, 621c
  imperative, 515
    jus cogens, 508a
  treaty interpretation, 517a
  see also facts versus legal/PIL norms
Norris, R., 696c
North Atlantic Treaty Organization (NATO), 585e
Norton, J.J., 440
Norway, PIL
  manual, 137
  periodical, 274
Nouveaux défis au droit international, 679b
Novadounghian, G., 18b
Novaia inostrannaia literatura po obshchestvennym naukam: gosudarstvo i pravo, 364c
Novaia sovetskaia literatura po gosudarstvu i pravu, 364c
nuclear weapons
  and PIL, 184
  dictionary, 585c
  non-proliferation treaty, 586c

see also International Atomic Energy Agency
Numers, S. von, 191
Nuremberg trials, 705a, 710a
Nussbaum, A., 455b

OAS Treaty Series, 9
The OAU and the UN, 687c
obligation in international law, 172, 423a
Obradović, K., 702
observers in the UN system, 657b
Obychnoe oruzhie i mezhdunarodnoe pravo, 587a
ocean development, publications, 558c; *see also The Indian Ocean*
Ocean development and international law, 558a
Ocean policy study series, 558b
Ocean yearbook, 558d
O'Connell, D.P., 531e, 540c
Oda, S., 38, 56, 195, 546c, 558d
Oellers-Frahm, K., 574b
Oeser, E., 117, 575c
Offerhaus, J., 422b
Office of Legal Affairs, *see* United Nations Office of Legal Affairs
official gazettes, p. 18; 66
official publications, 67
  definition, p. 21(15,20)
  guides, 68a, 366a, 411a
  records, UN, p. 21(18,19); 660a
Official publications of the Soviet Union and Eastern Europe, 70
Official publications of Western Europe, 69a
officials
  of IGOs, 641b
  of states, protection, 571
Ökçün, A.R., 18a
Okeke, C.N., 525a
Okoye, F.C., 484c
Ökrös, E., p. 41(3)
Olivart, Ramon de Dalman y Olivart, 345
Oliver, C.T., 34d, 421c, 440, 507b
Olkçuen, A.G., 18a
Olmstead, C.J., 714c
Olton, R., 451a
Ompteda, D.H.L., p. 9; 347
Les ONG et le droit international, 630d
OON kak instrument po podderzhaniiu i ukrepleniiu mira, 580d
opinio juris, p. 15; 519b,f
Oppenheim, L., 173a
order, international, *see* world order

Ordre et désordre, 438
ordre public, 427b
Organisation for Economic Co-operation and Development (OECD), 721d
Les organisations internationales entre l'innovation et la stagnation, 628b
Les organisations régionales internationales, 685a
Les organismes internationaux spécialisés, 676b
Organization of African Unity, 687b,c
  basic documents, 687a
  dispute settlement, 577c
Organization of American States, 688
  Columbus Library, 690b
  documentation, 690a
  study and teaching, 689
  treaty series, 9
Organizatsiia ob"edinënnykh Natsii i razoruzhenie, 585b
Organizatsiia Varshavskogo Dogovora, 13
Organs and instruments of the United Nations, 661b
Orléans *colloque*, 722c
Orosz, A., 352
'orphan, harlot, jailor' PIL theories, 192
Orrego Vicuña, F., 535c, 549c
Osakwe, C., 520c, 692c
Osieke, E., 680b
Osmanczyk, E.J., 658
Ostapenko, D.D., 500e
Österreicher, S., 487c
Österreichische Zeitschrift für öffentliches Recht und Völkerrecht, 276
Österreichisches Handbuch des Völkerrechts, 141
Osteuropa-Recht, 273f
Ostrower, A., 451f
Ottoman Empire, treaties, 18b
Otvetstvennost' v mezhdunarodnom prave, 528c
el-Ouali, A., 523a
outer space
  colloquia, 562c
  guide to information sources, 565b
  law of, 379a, 561b,f, 562d
  terminology, 584f
  UN role, 499b, 560c
  see also space law, international
Outrata, V., 114b, 115
Owada, H., 38
Oxford symposium, 734c

Pae, C., 39
Paenson, I., 310
Palestine question
  periodicals, 296
  UN resolutions, 655b
Palestine yearbook of international law, 296
Pambou Tchivounda, G., 318
Pan-American Union Treaty Series, 9
Pan Baocun, 104
Panebianco, M., 210
Panhuys, H.F. van, 45, 200, 616a
'panorama of the law of nations', 157
Państwo i prawo, 268
Papadakis, N., 559b
Paradisi, B., 455c
Pardo, A., 507b, 547b
Paris *colloques*, 542b, 738e
Paris, Université de, international law/relations institutes, 404, 461, 488a
Park, C., 39, 555
Park, W.W., 733b
Parliament and information, 69c
parliamentary materials
  IGOs, p. 43(4)
  United Kingdom, 69c
Parry, A., 298a
Parry, C., p. 12; 6, 23, 24b, 47a, 51, 61, 76, 196, 298a, 509e
Parsons, K.O., 327
The participation of the Soviet Union in universal international organizations, 692c
partisans, legal status, 179
Partsch, K.J., 600b
Pashukanis syllabus, 500f
Pasicrisie internationale, 48f
Pastuhov, V., 320d
patent law, international institute, 402b
Patna Declaration, 647c
'patrimoine commun de l'humanité', 186
Paulson, J., 733b
payments, international, socialist countries, 732c
Pays en voie de développement et transformation du droit international, 482d
peace, 581–2
  and international law, 580a
  bibliography, 583c
  Draft Code of Offences against Peace, 662b
  encyclopaedia, 582a
  institutes, 388, 586a, 588a, 725b

Islamic concept, 476b,c
Pugwash Conferences, 582b
Peace Palace, 381
  Library, p. 42; 418
  catalogue, 339
peace treaties, 579a, 581b; *see also* The Hague Conventions
peaceful co-existence, 480
peaceful settlement of disputes, 386, 415b, 575d
  bibliographies, 578
  IGOs, role in, 577b
  judicial, 195, 575e, 576a, 577a
  treaty provisions, 574a
  UN role, 648b
  see also arbitration, international; dispute settlement
peacekeeping, UN role, 580c,d, 593a
Peaslee, A.J., 63b, 616a
Pechota, V., 432d
Peggel, W., 117
Pellet, A., 147, 521c, 642b
Pemberton, J.E., 67b, 68a, 69b
People's China and international law, 36b
People's Republic of China
  bibliography, legal 350
  law of treaties, 12b
  periodical, 449g
  PIL, 36, 440, 473d, 474e, 533c
    manuals, 103-4
    maritime boundaries, 209
    yearbook, 250
  status, 533c
  treaties, 12b
  yearbook, 449g
Perassi, T., 471b
perceptions of PIL, *see* ideology and PIL
Perez Gonzales, M., 379b
periodicals, p. 31
  abbreviations, 216, 370a
  Bowker Serials Bibliography Database, 338c
  directories, 216
  see also legal periodicals; United Nations: serials, directory; yearbooks of international relations, bibliography
periodization, PIL, 126, 207, 353b, 455b,d
Permanent Court of Arbitration, 48c
Permanent Court of International Justice, p. 22; 48a,b, 49b,e

permanent missions, 641b, 657a
Perroux, F., 719a
Perruchoud, R., 49b, 597
Peru, PIL
  manual, 100
  periodical, 248
Pescatore, P., 201
Petit manuel de la jurisprudence de la CIJ, 665b
Pharand, D., 535c
Philippine yearbook of international law, 259
philosophy of PIL, *see* theories, PIL
Pictet, J., 598c, 600a, 602a,d, 603
Pimsleur, M.G., 372
Pindić, D.D., 657a
Pinto, R., 22, 152, 284, 606c
piracy laws, 389b
Piradov, A.S., 561e
Pisani, *see* D'Estefano-Pisani, M.A.
Plano, J.C., 451a
Le plateau continental dans le droit positif actuel, 550b
Platzöder, R., 537, 546d
Pleadings, oral arguments and documents
  ICJ, 48b
  Inter-American Court of Human Rights, 696a
Ploman, E.W., 742a
Plötz, Vertrags-, 28b
Poitiers *colloque*, 534b
Poland, PIL
  basic texts, 123
  colloquia, 324a,b
  encyclopaedia, 304
  historiography, 472d, 499c
  manuals, 121-2
  periodicals, 267-8
  treaties, 16
Polish yearbook of international law, 267
politics, international
  abstracts, 450c
  association, 453
  bibliographies, 450
  dictionaries, 451c,d
  guides to information sources, 454
  handbooks, 452b
  periodicals, 216a(vol. 2), 450a
  PIL aspects, 434, 436, 523a
  regional, 478d
  see also international relations; power/justice/law
Politis, N., 48e

pollution
  of international watercourses, 536e
  PIL aspects, 715b
'polysystemic model', 426c
Porto, see Nogueira Porto, L. de A.
Portuguese language
  PIL dictionary, 305
  PIL manuals, 94-5, 159-61
positivism and PIL, 468c, 490
Posta, I., 120
Potocny, M., 113, 620e
Pour un nouvel ordre économique international, 727b
power/justice/law, 507a; *see also* force versus law
practice, international legal, p. 15(6); *see also* intergovernmental organizations: international practice; state practice
Practice and method of international law, 491
Pravo i sila v mezhdunarodnoĭ systeme, 437a
Pravopreemstvo osvobodivshikhsia gosudarstv, 529c
precedent, international law, p. 24(5)
Preiser, W., 202, 456c, 457b
Preparatory Commission for the International Sea-Bed Authority, 546c,d
prescription process, PIL, 197
The present state of international law, 379a
primary/secondary PIL evidence/source, pp. 10, 25
Principles of public international law, 170
prisoners of war
  Geneva Convention III, 598b
  in international conflict, 605
private international law, 422b, 423c, 424-5
  and PIL, 426, 427b
  bibliography, 432d
  codification, 178, 425
  encyclopaedia, French, 301a(vol. 7)
  institutes, 402b, 425a
  periodicals, 237, 284
privileges and immunities, international, 566b
  IGOs, 616b, 617a,b, 621a, 641b
  SAs, 617c
'prize in international law', 409
problem-solving, PIL, 203
The process of change in international law, 320a
'process of law' approach in PIL, 495b

study and teaching, 499b, 500g
progressive development of international law, 31, 662a
progressive development of the law of international trade, 734b
protection
  of the environment, 714b, 715a
  of human rights in the Americas, 696c
  of investments, 738c
  of officials of foreign states, 571
  of war victims, 601a
Protestantism and PIL, 475a
Protocols additional to the Geneva Conventions, 599b
  commentary, 600a,b
  index to Protocol rules, 600c
Przetacznik, F., 571
public access to government information, 68b
public health, legislation, 682a
public international law
  bibliographies, p. 36(4); 147, 151, 336, 361-3, 428b
  concepts, 182, 194, 297(vol. 7), 499b, 507b, 515
    national, 204
  development, 31, 193, 458-62, 615, 648a
    IGO role, 655a
    UN role, 645, 650d, 659b
  evidence, 490, 509e
  facts versus law, 198
  guides to information sources, 327-35
  history, 182, 455-7
  indexing services, 237, 361-3
  library collections, p. 41; 381, 402a, 404, 407a, 414b, 417-19a
  methodologies, 490-5, 501-2
  problem-solving approach, 203
  socio-economic context, 322
  study and teaching, 499-500
  theories, 503-8
  yearbooks, bibliography, 218
  see also classification, PIL; crisis, PIL; developing countries: PIL; historiography, PIL; regionalism in PIL; etc.
Public international law: a current bibliography of articles, p. 37; 361
Public international law and international organization, 330
Public international law and the future world order, 440

publishers
  directory, p. 146
  legal, 411b
  PIL, 420
  see also official publications; scholarly publishing, directory
Pugwash Conferences on Science and World Affairs, 582b
Puig, J.C., 439, 467a, 507c
Puto, A., 110

Questions of international law, 265a
A quiet revolution: the UN Convention on the Law of the Sea, 538c

Radoĭnov, P., 626b
Raistrick, D., 370a
Rajan, M.S., 648c
Raman, V., 197
Randelzhofer, A., 8e
Ranjel, see Marotta Ranjel, V.
Ranjeva, R., 540b, 686d
Rao, K., 203
Rauh, K., 733a
Rauschning, D., 360
Rawls, J., 441, 507c
Razumnyĭ, I.A., 559e
Razvivaiushchie strany i mezhdunarodnoe pravo, 482e
Razvivaiushchie strany v mirovoĭ politike, 719c
Re Qua, E.G., 487d
realism, see idealism versus realism, PIL
Réalités du droit international contemporain, 322b
Reams, B.D., 53
Das Recht der internationalen Organisationen, 620c
recognition of states, 529a, 572b
'recognized manifestation of international law' (MIL), p. 22; 490
recommendations, see declarations, PIL; resolutions
records management, IGOs, p. 43(5)
Recueil des cours de l'Académie de droit international de La Haye (RCADI), 220a
Recueil des traités de la SdN, 4
Recueil des traités et conventions conclus par la Russie, 19b
Recueil des traités et conventions en vigueur auxquels la France est partie, 22
Red Cross, see International Red Cross
reference sources, PIL, 331; see also bibliographies; guides to information sources
reference versus research problems, p. 28(9)
refugees, 702b
regionalism in PIL, 84a, 460, 467, 478–85, 507a; see also ideology and PIL
Register of development activities of the UN system, 721a
A register of legal documentation in the world, p. 17; 62a
Regout, A., 558f
Reibstein, E., 466a
Reimer, S., 739a
Reims rencontres, 322
Reisman, W.M., 80, 197
relativism, impact
  on PIL, 648a
  on treaty validity, 514c
The relevance of international law, 192
Relevé des traités et accords internationaux (ONU), 3b
religious conceptions of PIL, 464a, 475
Remacha, J.R., 165
Rencontres de Reims, 322
Rencontres internationales de Genève, 438
Reno, E.A., 674a
Répertoire de la correspondance des Etats Européens, 569
Répertoire de la pratique française en matière de droit international public, 43
Répertoire de la recherche sur le désarmement, 589a
Répertoire des décisions et des documents de la procédure écrite et orale (CPJI, CIJ), p. 23; 49b
Répertoire des institutions d'enseignement et de recherche en droit internationale, 377
Répertoire of questions of general international law before the LoN, 673c
Répertoire of the practice of the Security Council, p. 19; 644a
Répertoire sur l'enseignement du droit international humanitaire, 612a
Repertory of disarmament research, 589a
Repertory of practice of the United Nations, p. 19; 641a

Reports of international arbitral awards, p. 23; 48c
Reports of judgements, advisory opinions and orders, 48a
representation, *see* consular relations; diplomatic law/relations
reprints, law/PIL, 372(vol. 3), 410
research, law/PIL, pp. 11(1), 28(9)
  directories
    study and teaching, 377
    USA, 376c, 417a
  guides, 331a, 491, 500h, 501a,c
  information retrieval, 415a
  see also methodology; study and teaching, international law/organization
Research Centre for International Law, 410
Research in international law (Harvard), 389b
Research tips in international law, 328
Reshaping the International Order (RIO), Foundation, 730, 442
resistance, armed, 179
resolutions
  economic law, international, 724b
  FAO, 681
  Institute of International Law, 378
  International Red Cross, 597
  technology transfer, 186
  UN, 643a, 653c, 654
  UNCTAD, 740a
  WHO, 682b
resources, *see* sources/resources, PIL
Resources, régimes, world order, 442
responsibility, international, 528b,c
  codification, UN, 528a, 653b
  criminal law, 705a
  host country, 571
  ICJ decisions, context of, 49b
  states, 297(vol. 10), 662b
    bibliography, 528a
  water pollution, 535e
restatements of PIL rules, 379, 662a
Rethinking the sources of international law, 509a
retrospective aspects, *see* current/retrospective documentary aspects
Review of socialist law, 273
reviews, *see* law books: reviewed; manuals, PIL: reviews, bibliographic

revisionist approach to PIL, p. 45; 519f
Revista de derecho internacional, 246
Revista de derecho internacional y ciencias diplomáticas, 245b
Revista peruana de derecho internacional, 248
revolutionary process and PIL, 477b
revolutionary state and PIL, 473e
Revue belge de droit international, 277
Revue de droit international, de sciences diplomatiques et politiques, 449f
Revue de droit international et de législation comparée, 277
Revue de droit pénal et de droit de guerre, 613b
Revue de la recherche juridique du droit prospectif, 194a
Revue égyptienne de droit international, 222
Revue générale de droit international public, 283
Revue héllénique de droit international, 285
Revue interdisciplinaire d'études juridiques, 449h
Revue internationale de droit comparé, 432b
Revue internationale de droit pénal, 707a
Revue internationale de la Croix Rouge, 613a
Revue internationale de la théorie du droit, 508c
Revue juridique de l'environnement, 716b
Revue québécoise de droit international, 226
Revue roumaine d'études internationales, 269
Reynolds, T.H., 72b
Rhode, G.F., 12
Rhyne, C.S., 82, 376a
Rideau, J., 624c
Riedmatten, H. de 475b
Rifaat, A.M., 594a
Riggs, F.W., p. 111
The right to development at the international level, 722a
Rikhye, I.J., 580c
Riphagen, W., 200-1, 422b
Ritter, J.P., 46
Rivero, J., 500g
rivers, international
  Helsinki rules, 379
  status, 536
Rivista di diritto internazionale, 287
Roach, J.A., 600c
Robert, J., 181
Roberts, A., 596c
Roberts, A.D., 24c
Roberts, J.E., 66

Roberts, L.M., 175a
Robinson, J., p. 27(3); 334
Roche, A.G., 541
Rodley, N.G., 481d
Rodrigues, A., 619e
Rodriguez Araya, R., 54b
Rodriguez Iglesias, G.C., 201
Rohn, P., 27, 30a, 500d, 638a
Le rôle du temps dans la formation du droit international, 510d
The role of domestic courts in the international legal order, 423b
Röling, B.V.A., 195, 205, 213
Rollet, H., 22
Rollin, H., 621d
Romania, PIL
  association, 395
  dictionary, 306
  historiography, 472e
  manuals, 124-5
  periodicals, 269
  treaties, 17, 306
Rönnefarth, H., 28b
Ronning, N., 481d
Rosas, A., p. 20(5); 184
Rosenberg, D., 731a
Rosenblad, E., 602e
Rosenne, S., 317b, 491, 507b, 517e, 665a, 666a, 673a,b, 669b
Rosenthal, B., 187
Ross, A., 135
Ross, B.I., 419a
Ross, D., 659b
Rotblat, J., 582b
Rotkirch, H., 184
Rouen *colloque*, 542a
Rousseau, C.E., 149, 204, 220a, 373h, 532c, 593c
Rouyer-Hameray, B., 626a
Rovine, A.W., 34
Royal Institute of International Affairs, 294, 449a
Rozakis, C.L., 542c
Rozkuszka, W., p. 11(8)
Ruda, J.M., 92
Ruddy, F.S., 53
Rui Mu, 440
Ruiz Moreno, I., 54a
'rule of law' approach to PIL, 495b
  study and teaching, 499b, 500g
  see also norms, PIL
Rule of Law Research Center, 638d

Rumpf, H., 579b
Russia
  Archives diplomatiques, 569
  PIL
    bibliographies, 353b
    treaties, 19b
  see also USSR
Russian language
  PIL
    basic texts, 130
    dictionaries, 307, 310, 313
    manuals, 126-9
    periodicals, 270-1, 449c
    translations from/into, 173, 271, 462f, 504b
  UN system, terminology, 636e
Ruster, B., 713a
Ruzié, D., 421c
Ryan, K.W., 40

Saab, *see* Abi-Saab
Saenz de Santa Maria, P.A., 162
Šahović, M., 521d
Saifulin, M., 308
Salacuse, J.W., 429c
sales, international, 734a
  CMEA uniform law, 722c
Salinas Araya, A., 535c
Salmon, J.J.A., 183, 185, 188, 198, 501a, 657a
Salzburg, international law/relations institutes, 400b, 432c
San Francisco, UN Conference, 639
San Remo conferences, 604a,b
Sanchez Rodriguez, L.I., 162
sanctions, international, 510c, 581a
  UN role, 650b
Sand, P.H., 714b
Sandoz, Y., 600a
Sarin, M.L., 483, 648b
Sastry, K.R.R., 475e
Sathiratai, S., 482b
Satow's guide to diplomatic practice, 572a
Sauvant, K.P., 447a, 720b
Sbornik deĭstvuiushchikh dogovorov, 19a
Sbornik dogovorov Rossii, 19b
Sbornik mezhdunarodno-pravovoĭ dokumentatsii, 332
Sbornik mezhdunarodnykh dogovorov, 19a
Scandinavian countries, law/PIL
  bibliography, 357
  manuals, 135-38

Scandinavian countries, law/PIL *contd*
    periodicals, 274–5
Scandinavian studies in law, 275
Scelle, G., 220a, 598f
Schaaf, R.W., p. 11(4); 631a
Schachter, O., 190, 378a, 462a, 650c,d
Schambeck, H., 471a
Schermers, H.G., 199, 620b, 626c
Schiffer, W., 673c
Schill, *see* Melland Schill monographs
Schindler, D., 478a, 596a, 600d, 603b
Schlochauer, H.J., 207, 303, 380a
Schmitthoff, C.M., 733b, 734b,c
Schmittroth, J., p. 126
Schneider, J., 714e
scholarly publishing, directory, p. 146
Schreuer, C.H., 400b, 622
Schröder, J., 471a
Schroers, R., 324a
Schutter, B., 708a
Schwartz, M.D., 562c
Schwarzenberger, G., p. 23; 49c, 171, 211, 220a, 456a, 495, 499b, 507b, 723g
    G. Schwarzenberger Prize in International Law, 409
Schwarzkopf, L.C., 71
Schwebel, S.M., 195, 524a, 594c, 625a
Schweisfurth, T., 473a
Schweizer, M., 529b
Schweizer Jahrbuch für internationales Recht, 292
Schweizer Studien zum internationalen Recht, 373i
Schweizerische Vereinigung für internationales Recht, 373i
Schwerin, K., 344, 373j, 497d
Schwietzke, J., 329
science
    and peace, 582b
    and PIL, 203, 744
    see also technology
Les sciences sociales dans l'enseignement supérieur: droit international, 499g
Scott, G.L., 12b, 48d, 320c, 378, 463a, 464a
Scovazzi, T., 535a
Scupin, H.U., 544
sea, law of, *see* law of the sea
sea-bed
    non-seabed provisions, 548d
    peaceful uses, 647c
    Preparatory Commission, 546c

Seara Vazquez, M., 87
The search for world order, 441
Sebek, V., 557a
secondary/primary PIL evidence/source, pp. 10, 25
Le secrétaire-général des Nations Unies, 657d
Seide, K., 524d
Seidl-Hohenveldern, I., 140, 211, 302, 620c, 621a, 723b
self-determination, 185, 531c
seminars
    human rights, 261, 695c, 698b
    PIL, 460
        study and teaching, 689
        UN role, 647c
    terrorism, 712a
Sen, B., 572b
Senarclens, P. de, 628b, 647a
Sepúlveda, C., 86, 481c
Sereni, A.P., 471b
serials, *see* periodicals
Série législative des Nations Unies, 645
series, p. 39
    international law/relations, 49a, 214, 405, 407a, 612b
    legal, 372(vol. 3), 373a–i
        bibliography, German-language works, 373j
    PIL, 410, 679b
settlement of disputes, *see* dispute settlement
'seven pillars of international law', 171, 456a
Severis, M., 614a
Seydoux, C., 614a
Shaker, M.I., 586c
Shapiro, L., p. 53
Shaw, M., 47b, 168
el-Shaybani, 476b
el-Shaybani Society of International Law, 296
Sheik, R. Ali, 585c
Sheikh, A., 436
Shelton, D., 696c
Shepard's law review citations, 370a
Shestakov, L.N., 515b
Shibaeva, E.A., 620e
Shihata, I.F.I., 670c
shipping laws, international, 741b
Shraga, D., 547a
Shtab-kvartira OON, 657c
Sicart-Bozec, M., 671a

Sieghart, P., 744c
Silva Cunha, 160
Simma, B., 139, 499e, 528a, 713a
Simmonds, K. R., 540f, 734c, 739a, 740c
Simon, D., 624a
Simon, S., 602b
Simons, A. P., 642a
Simons, W. B., 65b
Simpson, A. W. B., p. 29(4)
Sinclair, I., 663a
Singapore, PIL
 periodical, 258
 state practice, 57
Singh, N., 37, 379b, 459, 702a
Singham, A. W., 448a
Sinjela, A. M., 551a
Sinnaswamy, F., 67b
Siorat, L., 509f
Sipkov, I., 41
SIPRI yearbook, 588a
Sistema interamericana a traves de tratados, 481b
The 6th Committee of the General Assembly and international law, 653d
siyar, 476b,d
slip law, treaties (USA) 10a
Slouka, Z., 550c
Slovar' mezhdunarodnogo prava, 307
Slovník verejného prava československo, 300
Slusser, R. M., p. 53
Smouts, M. C., 657d
Snyder, F. E., 482b
Sobakin, V. K., 130
Sobranie traktov i konventsiĭ, 19b
social law, international, Max-Planck Institute, 402b
social sciences
 and PIL, 343, 507b
  bibliography, 343
  study and teaching, 499g
 documentation, 62a, 583b
 periodicals, bibliography, 216b
 reference sources, p. 35(1)
social security, international law of, 301a(vol. 9)
socialist countries
 constitutions, 65, 520c
 economic law, international, 732c
 human rights, 265a
 ICJ justices, 671c
 IGOs, 692a,b
 international relations, 128

legal documentation, 62b, 415a
legal institutes, 397
legal periodicals, 273
PIL, 128, 129, 184, 459, 473c, 477c, 648a
 historiographies, 472
 indexing service, 362
 methodology, 493
 theories, 437a, 505
 see also Marxist-Leninist approaches to PIL
socialist internationalism, 111a, 128, 479
Sociedade brasileira de direito internacional, 391
Società italiana per l'Organizzazione Internazionale, 44
Société belge de droit international, 277
Société de législation comparée, 72a
La Société des Nations: rétrospective, 675
Société française pour le droit international, 403
Société québécoise de droit international, 219b
Société suisse de droit international, 373i
Society of Comparative Legislation and International Law, 295, 408
sociological approaches to PIL, 142a, 205, 434b, 439, 503a, 505b, 506-7a, 526b
'soft law', 189, 509a, 519e, 648a, 723b
Sogawa, T., 56
Sohn, L. B., 209, 445c, 517b, 651a, 686c
Sokoline, V., 675
Solari, Tudela, L., 100
Solf, W. A., 600b,c
Sørensen, M., 76
Sotirova, A. S., 505a
Sotsializm i mezhdunarodnoe pravo, 477c
A source book on socialist international organizations of the Communist countries, 692b
Sourcebook on the environment, 717a
sources, PIL, 198, 213, 499b
 codification, 178
 contemporary/classic, 203
 ICJ decisions, context of, 49b
 Latin American doctrine, 210
 Soviet doctrine, 203, 212
 theories, 509-10
The sources and evidences of international law, 509e
Les sources du droit international, 49b

Sources, organization and utilization of international documentation, 631d
sources/resources, PIL, p. 11(13)
Sourioux, J. L., 498e
South African journal of comparative and international law, 224a
South African yearbook of international law, 224b
sovereign equality of states, 527c
sovereignty, 49c, 213, 456a, 473g, 526
  history, 179
  over natural resources, 548b, 731a
Sovereignty within the law, 474e
Sovetskaia Assotsiatsiia Mezhdunarodnogo Prava, 270, 428a
Sovetskaia literatura po mezhdunarodnomu pravu: bibliografiia, 353a
Sovetskiĭ ezhegodnik mezhdunarodnogo prava, 270
Sovetskoe gosudarstvo i pravo, 271
Sovetskoe zakonodatel'stvo i mezhdunarodnoe pravo, 42a
Soviet law and government, 271
Soviet law and international law: a bibliography, 354
Soviet legal system, 42b
Soviet public international law, 473e
Soviet treaty series, p. 53
Sovremennoe mezhdunarodnoe pravo, 130, 462d
Sowjetunion und Völkerrecht, 355
Sozialistisches Völkerrecht, 473a
space law, international, 297(vol. 11), 540a, 561a,c,e
  bibliographies, 563a, 565a
  colloquia, 562a,c
  dispute settlement, 562b
  periodicals, 563
  UN role, 499b, 569a
  see also air law; disarmament; outer space
Space law perspective, 562c
Spain, PIL
  classics, 464a,b
  institute, 385
  manuals, 162-4
  Marquis de Olivart collection, 345
  treaties, 22a
  yearbook, 290
Spanish language, PIL
  basic texts, 92, 162, 165
  dictionaries, 309-10, 312, 451c
  manuals, 84-93, 96-102
  periodicals, 245-9, 290
  translations from/into, 173, 464a
The Spanish origin of international law, 464a
'spatialisme ou fictionalisme juridique?', 561a
Specialized Agencies (UN system), 676-8
  law-making, 677
  privileges and immunities, 617c
specialized international law, *see* criminal law, international; economic law, international; environment, international, law of; trade law, international; etc.
Speeckaert, G. P., 630a, 634d
Sperdutti, G., 198, 210
Spinedi, M., 528a
The spirit of Uppsala, 460
Sprudzs, A., p. 11(1); 10a, 24a, 413, 415a
Squire Law Library, 340, 497b
Sri Lanka, PIL treatise, 109
Srnska, M., 114a
Staat und Recht, 264
Staatsrecht, Völkerrecht, Europarecht, 207
Stanbrook, I., 711a
Stanford, M., 741a
Stanford journal of international law, 240
Starke, J. G., 169
Starushenko, G. B., 477b
Starzhina, J., 522
Stashevskiĭ, S. G., 561e
state practice, 193
  classification of documents, 32
  digests, p. 16; 33-47
  evidence, substantive/documentary, p. 15
  Islamic, 476
  law of the sea, 539b,e, 549c
  see also customary international law; intergovernmental organizations: international practice
statelessness, 702c
Statement of treaties and international agreements, 3b
states, 297(vol. 10), 504b, 652b
  competences, 49b,c, 423a
  creation of/newly independent, 320b, 529
  handbooks, political, 452b,c
  judicial systems, 376a

names of, UN terminology, 374b
  see also land-locked states; non-aligned countries; succession of states
Statemen's who's who, 452c
Statusverträge im Völkerrecht, 533c
Statutes and rules of procedure of international administrative tribunals, 619c
Steinberger, H., 526a
Steiner, H.J., 468d
Steiner, O., 402a
Steiner, W.A., 340, 364b, 497b
Stepan, J., 218
Stjernquist, N.N., 357
Stockholm Institute for Scandinavian Law, 275
Stockholm International Peace Research Institute (SIPRI), 588a
Stödter, R., 379b
Stone, J., 445b, 468a, 507a
straits, international, 543c
Strasbourg *colloque*, 742b
Strategic Arms Limitations Talks (SALT), 585d
Strategy of world order, 445c
Stratis, *see* Calogeropoulos-Stratis, S.
Strijbosch, A.K.J.M., 471c
Strohl, M.P., 543d
The structure and process of international law, 507b
Strupp, K., p. 29; 303, 344, 455e
Studie z mezinarodniho prava, 263a
Studies and essays in international humanitarian law, 603a
Studies in East Asian law, 389b
Studies in international law, 106, 109
Studies in the administration of international law, 381
Studies in the history of the law of nations, 457d
Studies in transnational legal policy, 373b
Studies in world public order, 197
Studies on a just world order, 373c
Studies on socialist legal systems, 557a
Studii cercetari juridice, 269
study and teaching, international law/organization, 185, 207, 380-1, 499-500, 638
  bibliography, 500a
  directory, 377
  institutions, 380a, 629c, 638c
  OAS programmes, 689
  UN programmes, 672
  see also education and PIL; *and subjects*, e.g. human rights; humanitarian law, etc.; *countries*, e.g. France, USA; etc.
Stuyt, A.M., 48f, 471c
Suarez, F., 464a
subject collections, library directories, 416b,c, 417a; *see also* law libraries
Subject headings for the literature of law and international law, 338b, 340, 364b
subjects of international law, 525a,b
  ICJ decisions, context of, 49b
  see also intergovernmental organizations; states
subsidiary/main PIL sources/resources, p. 10
substantive/documentary PIL typology, p. 10
succession of states, 531, 626c
  bibliographies, 530c
  in respect of matters other than treaties, 530b
  in respect of treaties, 211, 530a
Sucharitkul, S., 541
Les sujets du droit international, 49b
Sukkary, S., 451d
Sullivan, C.D., 565b
Sundberg, H.G., 138
Sur, G., 498b
Surbiguet, M.G., 22
Survey of international arbitrations, 48f
Survey of Malaysian law, 258
Suter, K., 607a
Suy, E., 183, 207, 303, 510b, 515e
Svenska Institutet för internationell Rätt, 399
Sverdlovskiĭ IUridicheskiĭ Institut, 478b
Sweden
  legal bibliography, 359
  PIL
    institute, 399
    manual, 138
    periodical, 275
Sweeney, J.M., 83
Sweet & Maxwell, 420a
Swinarski, C., 600a, 603a
Switzerland
  international law/relations institutes, 407a, 433b, 611a
  PIL
    codification, 520e
    manuals, 166-7

Switzerland *contd*
  PIL *contd*
    periodical, 292
    state practice, digest, 44
    Swiss Federal Council, 598a
    see also Geneva; Lausanne *colloque*
Syatauw, J.J.G., 485b, 529b
Sybesma-Knol, N., 559f, 657b
syllabi on international law
  anthology, USA, 500d
  USSR, English translations, 428a, 500f
Symbolae Verzijl, 213
Symposia
  Antarctic development, 535c
  economic law, international, 734c
  PIL, Anglo-Soviet, 428a
  UN
    documentation, 631c,d
    universality, 647a
  see also colloquia, law/PIL; seminars
systematization, *see* classification
Système informatisé de l'ONU pour les traités (SIONUT), 29
systems analysis, PIL, 456b, 496
  surveys, 469b, 493
Szabö, I., 265a
Szasz, I., 732c
Szasz, P., p. 21(19), 683
Szegö, *see* Bokor-Szegö, M.
Szekely, A., 88, 556a
Szepesi, J., 331c
Szirmay, Zs., 520c
Szladits, C., 432d

Tabandeh, S., 694c
Tabory, M., 2, 612, 636a
Taiwan, PIL
  society, 393
  yearbook, 251
Takács, L., 125
Takano, Y., 108, 499f
Talalaev, A.N., 514b
Tammes, A.J.P., 189
Tandon, M.P., 55, 107
Tandon, R., 55, 107
Tangsubkul, P., 554
Taube, M., 472a
Tavernier, P., 510d, 642b
tax treaties
  collection of texts, 737a,b
    between developed and developing countries, 737c
    UN model tax convention, 737c

Taylor, P., 435
Tchirkovich, S., 20
Tchivounda, *see* Pambou Tchivounda, G.
The teacher in international law, p. 40; 499c
teaching, *see* study and teaching, international law/organization
Teaching about international organizations, 638a
Tearle, B., 175b
technology
  and international relations, 449d
  and natural law, 468a
  transfer and IGOs, 186
  see also science
Teitelbaum, G.W., 369
telecommunications, 621b, 743a,b
temporal aspects of PIL, 510d, 519c, 648a
  documentary context, p. 27(8)
  see also current/retrospective documentary aspects
Teoria y formación de la sociedad internacional, 627d
Teoriia mezhdunarodnogo prava, 504b
terminology
  arms control, outer space 584f
  disarmament, 589b
  Interconcept report, p. 111
  International Information Centre, 636f
  law of the sea, 558g
  PIL, p. 32; 310
  UN, 636b–d
  Terminology bulletin, 661a
territory, 533a,b
  asylum, territorial 702d, 705a
  extra-territorial application of law, 379
  see also boundaries; states: competences
terrorism, 703b, 712a,c,d
  bibliography, 712b
  conference papers, 388
  ILA rules, 379
Teuchert, W., 741c
Texas international law journal, 241
textbooks, *see* manuals, PIL
Thailand, legal journal, 260
Tharp, P.A., 496a
Themaat, P.V. van, 727a
theories, PIL, 192, 503–8
  evolution, 168, 195–6
  history, 466a
  see also dualism/monism in PIL; Eurocentrism, PIL; functionalism,

international law/relations;
Marxist-Leninist approaches to
PIL; etc.
Théories et réalités en droit international public,
503a
The theory and practice of peacekeeping, 580c
thesauri
  bibliography, p. 111
  legal, 412c
  UN programmes, 636d
  UNBIS, 660c
Thesaurus Acroasium, 405
La thèse et le mémoire de doctorat, 500h
theses, *see* dissertations
Thessaloniki, PIL institute, 405
Theutenberg, B.J., 460, 540d, 714f
Thierry, H., 150, 153, 668
Thieya, *see* Wang Thieya
Third United Nations Conference on the
    Law of the Sea (UNCLOS III)
  African states, contributions, 553
  bibliography, 556c
  Latin America, 556a
  official; summary records, 537a
Third World
  bibliographies, national, 487b
  encyclopaedia, 487a
  guides to information sources,
    487c,d
  ICJ justices, 671a
  institutions, 301b, 487a, 489
  international relations, 482b
  investments in, 738e
  New International Economic Order,
    positions on, 728a
  PIL, 482b, 507b
    bibliographies, 428b, 486
    historiography, 468d
    study and teaching, 106, 380a,
      407a, 499a
  UNCLOS III, positions on, 516a
  yearbooks, 488a,b
  see also developing countries; non-
    aligned countries
*The Third World and international law:
  selected bibliography*, 486
The Third World and international relations,
  482b
Third World atlas, 488c
*Third World attitudes toward international
  law*, 482b
Third World Centre for Research and
  Publishing, 448b

The Third World without Superpowers,
  447a, 720b
Thirlway, H.W.A., 520a
Thomas, A.J., 488c
Thompson, C., 719b
Thompson, L., 619e
Thompson, W.R., 446
Tipson, F.S., 469a
Tokyo
  trials, 705a, 710c
  Waseda University, 433c
Toman, J., 114a, 460, 465b, 596a,
  598d
Tomuschat, C., 621a
Toro Jiménez, F., 102
Toronto University, Centre for Russian
    and East European Studies, 273d
Toulouse *colloque*, 509d
Toward a just world order, 445a
Toward world order and human dignity, 197
Towards a new international economic order,
  727b
Towards wider acceptance of UN treaties,
  650a
Toynbee, A., 581b
Trade and development, 740a
trade law, international, 734b
  bibliography, 732b, 736b
  colloquia, 734a
  GATT, 678a, 740c
  UN information sources, guide, 736a
  UNCITRAL, 732b
  UNCTAD, 740a,b
  see also commodity agreements, law of;
    finance, international;
    investments, international; etc.
traditional/modern approaches, *see*
  contemporary versus classical PIL
Les traités dans la vie internationale, 512a
translations law/PIL, p. 33(6); 502,
  636a; *see also* English-language
  translations; French-language PIL:
  translations; etc.
Transnational associations, 638e
transnational law/relations, 194, 443b,
  739a
  periodicals, 231, 242
  UN
    Centre, 739c
    code of conduct, 739b
transport law, international, 741c
  collection of texts, 741a
  colloquium, 741d

transport law, international *contd*
  see also air law: transport aspects;
    shipping laws, international
Trapero-Ballestero, A., 459
treaties, law of, 190, 213, 379, 297(vol. 7), 511–14
  bibliographies, 518b
  centres, information retrieval, 30
  collections of texts, 2, 4–23
    bibliographies, 25
    indexes, 26–8
    LoNTS, 4
    UNTS, 2
  databases, 29–30
  glossaries, 1, 512c
  handbook, 518a
  interpretation, 201, 498d,e, 516–17
  research guides, 24
  status, 3–4, 9, 10d, 21–2
  Vienna Convention, 1, 201
  see also Agreements between the UN . . .; conventions; PIL; *and subjects*, e.g. air law; environment, international law of; peace treaties; etc.
Treaties and other international act series (TIAS), 10a
treatises, p. 28
Treaty profiles, 27
Treaty series, 23
Treaty sources in legal and political research, 24a
Trejos, R., 440
trialist approach to PIL, 507c
tribunals
  international, decisions, 510a, 522–3
  national, PIL decisions, 389b, 423b
  regional, Arab Court of Justice, 523b
  see also administrative tribunals, international; judicial decisions; military tribunals, international; *and subjects*, e.g. criminal law, international; law of the sea; human rights; etc.
Triffin, N., 372a
Trindade, A.A.C., 35, 95, 697a
Triska, J.F., p. 53; 65b
Trood, R.B., 547a
Trotabas, L., 500g
The true worlds: a transnational perspective, 443b
Truyol y Serra, A., 198
Tunkin, G.I., 128, 190, 203, 211–12,
    220a, 353a, 421b, 437, 462d, 474d, 480a, 496b, 499h, 504b
Turkey, treaties, 18a; *see also* Ottoman Empire, treaties
Tuzmukhamedov, R.A., 448d, 719c

Udokang, O., 531b
Uibopuu, H.J., 211, 479b
Ul'ianova, N.N., 514a
Ulrich's international periodicals directory, p. 31; 216
Uncertain judgement: a bibliography of war crime trials, 710g
underdevelopment, law of, 723e
UNESCO
  activities/publications, guide, 679d
  works by/under auspices of UNESCO (mentioned in *Guide*), pp. 6(9), 33(6); 111; 216b, 412b, 416d, 420f, 602a, 719a
  human rights, 199
  information, right to, 742a
  International social science journal, international organization, concept, 627a
  PIL, 679c
    manual, 75
    series, 679b
    study and teaching, 499a,g,h
    study and teaching, directory, 377
  Reports and Papers in the Social Sciences, obligation, international/state interpretation, 423a
  self-determination, 185
  standard-setting instruments, 679a
  USSR participation, 692c
UNIDIR, 589a
UNIDROIT, 425
unification, private law, 425
A uniform system of citation, p. 39; 369
unilateral acts, 510b
Union académique internationale, 63c, 301c, 312
Union of International Associations, p. 33; 629a
United Kingdom
  law/PIL institutes, 397c, 408–10
  official publications, 69b
  PIL
    Anglo-Soviet symposium, 428a
    historiography, 470b,c
    ILA, 379

INDEX-THESAURUS 325

manuals, 168-74
periodicals, 294-5
state practice, 47, 61
treaties, 23
Centre, 30c
United Nations
  acronyms, 637
  activities
    broad terms of programmes, 636c
    development-oriented, register, 721a
    functions and titles, 661c
    organs and instruments, 661b
    reports/reviews/yearbooks, 640
    space activities, resources, 560a
    see also United Nations: international practice; United Nations: conferences; United Nations: publications
  anniversary, 40th, 647a
  archives, guide, 633b
  basic texts, 616-17a, 639, 651
  bibliography of, 634b
  biographical information, 635
  Broad terms for UN programmes and activities, 636c
  case law, 651a
  Charter, 642, 652a,b
    application, colloquium, 652c
    bibliography, 652d
    provisions, practice, 593b, 641a
  codification of PIL, *see* International Law Commission
  commissions, legal
    ILC, 662-3
    Preparatory Commission for the International Sea-Bed Authority, 546c
    UNCITRAL, 732b, 733a, 734a
  committees, legal
    Progressive Development of International Law (ILC), p. 16; 31, 662a
    Relations with the Host Country, 641b
    6th Committee, UN General Assembly, 653d
  conferences
    codificatory, negotiating procedures, 317, 646
    disarmament, 584c
    glossary of conference terms, 636b
    international organization, San Francisco, 639
    law of the sea, UNCLOS III, 537a, 538d
    law of treaties, 1
    succession of states, 530
  control methods, 623b, 648b
  conventions
    consular relations, 567
    diplomatic relations, 566
    law of the sea, UNCLOS III, 537b, 538a
    law of the sea, UNCLOS III, bibliography, 559a
    law of treaties, 1, 618a
    law of treaties, bibliographies, 518b, 618b
    succession of states, 211, 530a,b
    succession of states, bibliography, 530c
    see also United Nations: treaties
  Dag Hammarskjöld Library, 419b
    bibliographies, 518b, 530, 559a, 578b, 618b, 652d, 729a
    government gazettes in, 66
  databases, directory (DUNDIS), 632a
  decisions, UN General Assembly, 653c
  declarations, memorandum, 643a
    friendly relations, 655a
    outer space, 560c
    right to development, draft, 722a
  development activities, register, 721a
  diplomatic privileges, immunities, 566a
  disarmament, 584a,c-f
  documentation, guides, 660a,d,e
    PIL aspects, 659a,b
  documents, index (UNDOC), 660c; *see also* United Nations: publications
  economic law, international, 724
    New International Economic Order, 726-30
  encyclopaedia, p. 32; 638
  fortieth anniversary, symposium, 647a
  glossaries, 635b
  guides to information sources, 660d,e
  headquarters, 657c
  human rights, 695c, 698b, 701
  immunities of states, 527a
  international law-making, 647c, 648a, 651a; *see also* International Law Commission; United Nations Office of Legal Affairs; United Nations: PIL materials, guides

326 INDEX-THESAURUS

United Nations contd
  international organization
    IGO privileges, immunities, 617a
    San Francisco Conference, 639
  international practice, UN organs,
    641a, 644a
  judiciary powers, 212; see also
    International Court of Justice
  law of the sea, 537-9, 546c,d, 549a,
    550a
    bibliography, 559a
  law of treaties, 1, 618a
    bibliographies, 518b, 618b
    see also United Nations: treaties
  libraries, 419
    directory, 633a
    indexing services, 368
  Names of countries and adjectives of
    nationality, 374b
  observers, status, 657b
  Official records, 660a
  Organs and instruments, 661b
  outer space, 560a,c, 562d
  neutrality, 213
  peaceful settlement of disputes, 547a,
    576b, 577c
    bibliography, 578b
  peacekeeping, 580c
  Permanent Missions, 657a
  PIL materials, guides, 329, 631a,
    659a,b
  publications, p. 21(20)
    catalogue, 660a
    clearing house, 489
    guides, 631c, 660d,e
    see also United Nations documents,
      index
  resolutions, 499b, 654, 655b
    UN General Assembly, 643
    UN Security Council, 644
  rivers, international, 536c
  San Francisco Conference, 639
  seminars
    human rights, 695c, 698b
    PIL, 647c, 672a
  serials, directory, 632b
  space activities, resources, 560a
  structures/methods, workshop, 648b
  study and teaching, 672
  succession of states, 530a,b
    bibliography, 530c
  tax treaties, texts, 737a,c

  terminology, 661b,c
    disarmament, 589b
    human rights, 701
    law of the sea, 558g
    Terminology bulletin, 661a
    see also United Nations: glossaries
  Third World Centre, 489
  trade law, texts, 732a
    UNCITRAL, 732b
  Transnational Corporation Centre,
    739c
  treaties
    collections of texts, 539, 560c,
      737a,c
    register, 713b
  UNTIS, 29
  UNTS, 2
  Who's who in the UN, 635
United Nations Administrative Tribunal,
  194, 619b
United Nations Bibliographic
  Information System (UNBIS),
  419b, 660c
United Nations Centre on Transnational
  Corporations, 739c
United Nations Commission on
  International Trade Law
  (UNCITRAL), 732b, 733a
United Nations Commission on Trade
  and Development (UNCTAD),
  740
United Nations Development Program
  (UNDP), 721b
United Nations document series symbols, 660c
United Nations documentation: a brief guide,
  660e
United Nations documentation news, 660a
United Nations documents: current index
  (UNDOC), 660c
United Nations editorial manual, 660b
United Nations Environmental
  Programme (UNEP), 717a
United Nations functions and titles, 661c
United Nations General Assembly,
  653a-c
  declaration of legal principles
    governing . . . outer space, 560c
  disarmament, 584b,e
  non-use of force, 621b
  Proceedings, 643a
  Resolutions, 643a
  6th Committee, 653d

United Nations Institute for
    Disarmament (UNIDIR), 589a
United Nations Institute for Training
    and Research (UNITAR), 672
  regional studies, series, 678b
  seminars, 460, 631d
United Nations Joint Inspection Unit
    (UNJIU), 623b
United Nations juridical yearbook, 616b
United Nations law making, 648a
United Nations legislative series, pp. 18,
    21(19); 645
United Nations Office at Geneva
    (UNOG)
  ACCIS guides, 678c
  Arabic-French-English dictionary,
    451d
  ILC documents, guide, 662a
  Library, p. 42; 419a
    bibliographies, 336b, 368a
    international law, classification, 497d
    official gazettes, analysis, 66
United Nations Office for Ocean Affairs
    and the Law of the Sea, 539e
United Nations Office of Legal Affairs,
    p. 19; 643a, 662b, 672a
  publications, 659a
United Nations Office of the High
    Commissioner for Refugees, 702b
United Nations Office of the Special
    Representative of the Secretary-
    General for the Law of the Sea,
    539b,c, 559a
*United Nations Programme of assistance in
    teaching, study, dissemination and
    wider appreciation of international
    law*, 672a
United Nations Secretary-General,
    648b, 657d
  Special Representative for the Law of
    the Sea, 539b,c
United Nations Security Council, 207,
    656
  international practice, répertoire, 644a
  resolutions, 644
United Nations system
  acronyms, 637
  archives, guide, 633b
  associations, 629
  bibliographies, 634a,b,d
  documentation, 329, 631b, 632, 634c,
    636e

  legal/PIL aspects, 631a
  seminars, 631c,d
  libraries, directory, 633a
*The United Nations system: international
    bibliography*, 634b
United Nations Treaty Information
    System (UNTIS), 29
United Nations Treaty Series (UNTS),
    p. 13; 2
United Nations University, 661d
United Nations War Crimes
    Commission, 710b
*United States contributions to international
    organizations*, 34c
*United States treaties and other international
    agreements (UST)*, 10a
L'universalité est-elle menacée?, 647a
universality
  of economic law, international, 734c
  of human rights, 210, 694a
  of PIL, 460, 474a, 478b-d
  of the UN, 647a
  see also regionalism in PIL
Universelles Völkerrecht, 139
*The university teaching of social sciences:
    international law*, 499g
Uppsala University, international law
    seminar, p. 34; 460
Urkunden zur Geschichte des Völkerrechts,
    455e
Uruguay, PIL
  manual, 101
  yearbook, 249
USA
  Council on Foreign Relations, 449b,
    450b
  government publications, 71
  intergovernmental organizations,
    contributions to, 34c
  law
    bibliographies, 338b,c
    libraries, 381, 417
    schools, 376c, 389a
    World Peace through Law Center,
      388
  PIL
    American international law cases, 53
    historiography, 469, 470c
    historiography of Soviet PIL works,
      473b,e
    manuals, 80-3
    Naval War College series, 373a

USA *contd*
  PIL *contd*
    opportunities, directory, 387c
    periodicals, 219, 227-44
    state practice, digests, p. 16,
      p. 20(7); 34
    study and teaching, 389a, 500
    treaties, 10
    world order studies, 80-1, 197, 244, 373c, 469
Uschakow, A., 355, 472d, 480b
use of force, 579a, 592b,c, 593a,c,d
  prevention, 593b, 612b, 621b
  see also war
Usenko, E.T., 428a
USSR
  arbitration, commercial, 733b
  constitution, 65c
  disarmament, 587b
  human rights, concept, 697c, 698a
  IGOs, 620e, 692c
  international relations, 437a, 448d, 449b
  law of the sea, 557a
    bibliography, 559e
  legal system, 42b
  legislation, 73b
  official publications, guide, 70, 353a
  PIL, 428a, 473e
    bibliographies, 126, 353a, 354
    codification, 520c
    colloquia, 421b, 428a
    dictionary, 307
    historiography, 477
    historiography, non-Soviet, of Soviet PIL works, 473
    and legislation, 42a
    manuals, 126-30
    and municipal law, 421b
    methodology, 493
    periodicals, 270-1
    periodization, 455d
    and private international law, 426c
    states, newly independent, 529c
    study and teaching, 428a, 500e,f
    subjects of PIL, 525b
    treaties, 19a
    see also Russia; Western approaches to PIL

Vademecum, p. 139
Válki, L., 265a, 505b
Vallée, C., 550b
Valticos, N., 621c
values and PIL, 186, 492a
Vambery, J., 2
Vambery, V., 2
Vamvoukos, A., 473d
Vanderbilt journal of transnational law, 242
Vargas, J.A., 556c
Varia juris gentium, 289
Vasak, K., 602a, 700
Vasco, M., 309
Vasilenko, V.A., 510c
Vázques de Menchaca, F., 464b
Vedel, G., 181
Veiter, T., 702a
Vellas, P., 494a
Velu, J., 697d
Venezuela, PIL manual, 102
Verdross, A., 139, 211, 213, 220a, 471a
Veredy, *see* Balázsné Veredy, K.
Vergé, C., 346
Verosta, S., 212
Verri, P., 612c
Verträge der Bundesrepublik Deutschland, 21
Vertrags-Plötz, 28b
Das Vertragsrecht der internationalen Organisationen, 624d
Verwey, W.D., 648b
Verzeichnis und Stand der Verträge, 21
Verzijl, J.H.W., p. 33(1); 157, 213, 497a
Veuthey, M., 607b
Vienna Conventions
  on Consular Relations, 567a
  on Diplomatic Relations, 566
  on Succession of States in Respect of Treaties, 530
  on the Law of Treaties, p. 12; 1, 511-12a, 516a, 517b
  on the Law of Treaties concluded between States and International Organizations and between International Organizations, 201, 618a, 621a
Vienna school of law, 471a
Vierheilig, M., 682c
Vignes, D., 195, 540b
Villalón-Galdames, A., 349
Villiger, M.E., 511
Vincze, I., 732c
Vinogradoff, P., 214
violence/war, 607b
Virally, M., 76, 195, 204, 206, 220a, 657a, 720d

Virginia journal of international law, 243
Virginia University, Center for Oceans Law and Policy, 558b
Visions of world order, 507a
Visscher, C. de, 142a, 194, 214, 220a, 378d, 401a, 498c, 503a, 517f, 669c, 742d
Visscher, P. de, 142b, 220a, 378d
Visseriana, *see Bibliotheca Visseriana*
Vitanyi, N., 521b, 536b
Vitoria, F. de, 464a
vocabularies
  bibliography, p. 111
  international law, 502b
Vogler, T., 706a
Völkerrecht als Rechtsordnung, 199, 402a
Völkerrecht eine Geschichte seiner Ideen, 466a
Völkerrecht, Recht der internationalen Organisationen, Weltwirtschaftsrecht, 621a
Völkerrecht und Friede, 580a
Völkerrecht und internationale Beziehungen, 362
Völkerrecht und rechtliches Weltbild, 211
Völkerrecht und Rechtsphilosophie, 212
Völkerrechtliche Verträge, 8e
Die Völkerrechtsgeschichte, 456c
Völkerrechtswissenschaft und Lehre von den internationalen Beziehungen, 499e
Vollenhoven C. van
  Foundation, 616a
  Memorial lectures, 406
Volova, L. I., 533b
Voncken, J., 379a
Voprosy avtorskogo prava, 684b
Voprosy mezhdunarodnogo prava, 271
Voprosy teorii mezhdunarodnogo prava, 504b
Voprosy universal'nosti i effektivnosti mezhdunarodnogo prava, 478b
Voskuil, C. C. A., 734a
Vukas, B., 134, 514c
Vuyst, B. M., 619c

Waldock, C. H. M., 172
Walker, G., 70
Wallenstein, G. D., 743b
Wang, D. T. C., 36a
Wang Thieya, 507b
war, 579a, 613b
  bibliographies, 583c, 614b
  civil, 606
  concept, 593c, 600d
  Islamic, 476b
  just, 595
  law of, texts, 596
  PCIJ decisions, context, 49b
  see also armed conflict; humanitarian law; use of force
war crimes
  bibliography, 710g
  collection of texts, digest, 703a
  trials, records, 596b, 710a,c
  UN War Crimes Commission, 710b
The war system: an interdisciplinary research, 612b
war victims, Geneva conventions, 598b
Ward, R., 8c
warfare, conduct of, 596a; *see also* guerrilla warfare
Warsaw Pact, documents, 13
Waseda University, Institute of Comparative Law, 433c
Wasserman, S., 376c
Wasserstein, B., 8a
Wasum, S., 546a
waterways, pollution, 379a, 536d; *see also* rivers, international
Watts, A. D., 298a
Ways and means of making the evidence of customary international law more readily available, 31, 192
Wehberg, H., 378
Weiler, J. H. H., 458a
Weill, G., 412b
Weisbaum, E., 421c
Weisflog, W. E., 502a
Weiss, T. G., 740b
Welch, T., 690a
welding approach to PIL, 457c
Wengler, W., 206
Western approaches to law/PIL, p. 20(9); 459, 474a
  bibliography, 428b
  Chinese legal materials, 350
  Islamic countries, 476e
  periodicals, 273
  research centres, 397
  socialist countries, 184
    USSR, 211, 428a, 455d
  see also bourgeois approaches to PIL; Eurocentrism, PIL
Western Europe and the development of the law of the sea, 557a

Western Hemisphere, PIL, 326a, 481d;
    see also Americas; *entries beginning
    Inter-American*; Latin America
Weston, B.H., 81, 197
Wetter, G.J., 524c
Wyer, F., 300
Whalen, L., 693b
Wharton, F., 34b
Whiteman, M.M., p. 16; 34b
Whitlock, R.E., 12
who's who, p. 41(2)
Who's who in the UN and related agencies,
    p. 40; 635
Wiek, K., 478d
Wiener rechtstheoretische Schule, 471a
Wigmore, J.A., 34d
Wiktor, C.L., 11, 348a
Wilberforce, Lord, 379, 621b
Wilkinson, P., 451e
Willemin, G., 610c
Williams, J.W., 74, 328
Williams, S.A., 77
Williams, S.M., 562b
Winch, K.L., 374a
Winton, H.N.M., 726a
Wolfke, K., 123
Wolfrum, R., 421b
Woodhouse, R., 583a
workshops, PIL, p. 34; 220b; 415a,b
World armaments and disarmament, 588a
World Bank, *see* International Bank for
    Reconstruction and Development
World bibliographical series, 452b
World bibliography of bibliographies, 337a
*World bibliography of international
    documentation*, 450a, 634a
world community, *see* community,
    international
*World constitutive process of authoritative
    decision*, 445b
*World Court and the contemporary international
    law-making process*, 667d
World Court reports, 49e
World encyclopedia of peace, 582a
World Federation of UN Associations,
    661e
World Health Organization, 682
    USSR participation, 692c
World Institute for Development
    Economics Research, 721c
World Intellectual Property Organization
    (WIPO), 684a, 742a

World jurist, 388
World of learning, p. 41; 377
World order, 197, 440-3, 517a
    foundation (RIO), 442
    models project (WOMP), 445b
    PIL aspects, 211, 444, 507a
    symposium, 460
    USA, 80-1, 244, 373c
    historiography, 197, 469
    see also community, international;
        information, new international
        order; New International
        Economic Order
World Peace Foundation, 638a
World Peace through Law Center,
    p. 39(7); 388, 445c
World Press Centre, 489
World Treaty index, 27
*Wörterbuch der Aussenpolitik und des
    Volkerrechts*, 451b
Wörterbuch der internationalen Beziehungen,
    451c
Wörterbuch des Völkerrechts, p. 32; 303
wounded and sick, Geneva Convention,
    598b
*Writings on Soviet law and Soviet international
    law*, 354
Wühler, N., 574b
Wypyski, E.M., 217

Yakemtchouk, R., 484d, 506b
Yale journal of international law, 244
Yale studies of world public order, 244
Yambusic, E.S., 517a
Yasseen, K., 516a, 517b
Yearbook of air and space law, 563a
Yearbook of comparative law, 432c
Yearbook of international organizations, p. 41;
    630a
Yearbook of socialist legal systems, 273c
Yearbook of the AAA, 380b
Yearbook of the International Court of Justice,
    664a
*Yearbook of the International Law
    Commission*, p. 18; 662b
Yearbook of the United Nations, 640b
Yearbook of world affairs, 449a
yearbooks of international relations,
    bibliography, 218; *see also entries
    beginning* Annuaire, Anuario,
    Jahrbuch; *United Nations juridical
    yearbook*; UNIDROIT

Yemin, E., 649b
Yoo, J. Y., 582a
Yugoslavia, PIL
  basic texts, 134
  bibliographies, 272, 356
  dissertations, 272
  historiography, 472f
  indexing service, 363
  institutes, 396
  manuals, 131-3
  periodical, 272
  treaties, 20

Zacklin, R., 320a, 636a
Zagayko, F. F., 414b, 497d
Zagreb: Hague-Zagreb colloquia, 734a
Zajtay, I., 430
Zarb, A., 676a
Zbiór umów międzynarodowych Polskiej RL, 16

Zbornik prace z medzinarodneho prava, 263b
Zeitschrift für ausländisches öffentliches Recht und Völkerrecht, 279
Zeitschrift für Luft und Weltraumrecht, 563d
Zeitschrift für Völkerrecht, 279
Zeller, O., 371b
Zeller, W., 371b
Zemanek, K., 211, 528b, 621a, 624d
Zhou Gengsheng, 103
Zhukov, G. P., 468b, 561e
Zidouemba, D., 416d
Ziman, J., 744c
Zimmerman, B., 600a
Zourek, J., 592b
Zuleta, B., 537b
Zürcher Studien zum internationalen Recht, 373i
Zweigert, K., 427a, 431